Integrative Process

Integrative Process

Follettian Thinking from Ontology to Administration

MARGARET STOUT

JEANNINE M. LOVE

PROCESS CENTURY PRESS
ANOKA, MINNESOTA 2015

INTEGRATIVE PROCESS: Follettian Thinking from Ontology to
Administration

© 2015 Process Century Press

Process Century Press
RiverHouse LLC
802 River Lane
Anoka, MN 55303
www.processcenturypress.com

Cover graphic: http://www.deviantart.com/art/Art-Nouveau-Border-
Adrienne-34481608

Toward Ecological Civilization Series
Jeanyne B. Slettom, Series Editor

ISBN 978-1-940447-06-3
Printed in the United States of America

Series Preface: Toward Ecological Civilization

We live in the ending of an age. But the ending of the modern period differs from the ending of previous periods, such as the classical or the medieval. The amazing achievements of modernity make it possible, even likely, that its end will also be the end of civilization, of many species, or even of the human species. At the same time, we are living in an age of new beginnings that give promise of an ecological civilization. Its emergence is marked by a growing sense of urgency and deepening awareness that the changes must go to the roots of what has led to the current threat of catastrophe.

In June 2015, the 10th Whitehead International Conference will be held in Claremont, CA. Called "Seizing an Alternative: Toward an Ecological Civilization," it claims an organic, relational, integrated, nondual, and processive conceptuality is needed, and that Alfred North Whitehead provides this in a remarkably comprehensive and rigorous way. We propose that he can be "the philosopher of ecological civilization." With the help of those who have come to an ecological vision in other ways, the conference will explore this Whiteheadian alternative, showing how it is sufficiently advanced to provide the shared vision so urgently needed.

The judgment underlying this effort is that contemporary research and scholarship is still enthralled by the 17th-century view of nature articulated by Descartes and reinforced by Kant. Without freeing our minds of this objectifying and reductive understanding of the world, we are not likely to direct our actions wisely in response to the crisis to which this tradition has led us. Given the ambitious goal of replacing now dominant patterns of thought with one that would redirect us toward ecological civilization, clearly more is needed than a single conference. Fortunately, a larger platform is developing that includes the conference and looks beyond it. It is named Pando Populus in honor of the world's largest and oldest organism, an aspen grove.

In preparation for the conference, and in support of the larger initiative of Pando Populus <pandopopulus.com>, we are publishing this series, appropriately named "Toward Ecological Civilization."

John B. Cobb, Jr.

Toward Ecological Civilization Series

Other books in this series

An Axiological Process Ethics, Rem B. Edwards
Panentheism and Scientific Naturalism, David Ray Griffin
Theological Reminiscences, John B. Cobb, Jr.
Organic Marxism, Philip Clayton and Justin Heinzekehr

Dedication

This book is dedicated to all those scholars and practitioners who have kept Mary Follett alive in the hearts and minds of business and government administrators, social workers, community developers, and political and management theorists. It is often the rare few who recognize brilliance in unlikely places and who take the time to unearth ideas that are considered unpopular or even dangerous under particular regimes and eras. Of particular note must be: Matthew Shapiro and the members of the Mary Parker Follett Network, biographer Joan Tonn, and authors Benjamin Barber, Warren Bennis, John Child, Angela Dumas, Peter Drucker, Tokihiko Enomoto, Brian Fry, Pauline Graham, Michael Harmon, Rosabeth Moss Kanter, Paul Lawrence, Jane Mansbridge, Kevin Mattson, O. C. McSwite, Henry Metcalf, Henry Mintzberg, Nitin Nohira, Sir Peter Parker, Jos Raadschelders, Camilla Stivers, and Lyndall Urwick.

CONTENTS

Foreword

I am grateful to Margaret Stout, Jeannine Love, and Miroslaw Patalon for introducing me to the work of Mary Follett. She was a colleague of White-head rather than a disciple, since she studied at Radcliffe when the earlier generation of process and pragmatic philosophers such as William James, Charles Peirce, and Josiah Royce were at Harvard.

At the heart of the wider community of process and pragmatic think-ers has long been the idea that the world is made up of processes that are constantly bringing about new syntheses of the past. Follett called this "integrative process" based on "creative experience." Charles Hartshorne wrote at length about "creative synthesis." Henry Nelson Wieman described the human good as generated in a process of "creative transformation." Whitehead regarded the process of many becoming one as "creativity" and he held that every event whatsoever is an instance of this. He provided the most thorough analysis of this process. Together these writers show how different the world looks when seen in terms of the ongoing processes of integration instead of substantial objects in motion.

When Follett was at Harvard it was easy to imagine that the ideas being discussed there would ground future thought over a wide spectrum. However, the research university moved away from this promising begin-ning. It preferred to divide up knowledge into separate disciplines with little regard for relations among them. Ontological questions were set aside. James, Peirce, Royce, and Whitehead were marginalized. Follett was almost forgotten.

We sense some comeback on the part of the men I have mentioned, but the renewal of interest in Follett has been more dramatic. Whereas subsequent developments have been such that the issues important to these men are hardly discussed in departments of philosophy, in the case of the professions of management and administration, the evolution of thought has led back to Follett's concerns. Today she can be seen as anticipating the current needs. For the wider process movement, this growing enthusiasm for her ideas is a beacon of hope.

In any case, the specifically Whiteheadian community can rejoice that her thinking relates insights shared with Whitehead to some of the most important fields of thought and practice. These include politics, international relations, and economics. Of special importance is her contribution to thought about management and governance. Whiteheadians believe that Whitehead's conceptuality is relevant to every field of thought and practice, but showing this and drawing out its implications is still largely a project barely begun. Follett's work moves us forward a long way. We will rejoice to watch as Stout, Love, Patalon, and others continue along the lines she has set.

John B. Cobb, Jr.
Claremont, CA
December 1, 2013

Preface

The impetus behind this book was a paper written for the Normandy Conversations on Mary P. Follett, hosted by the University of Rouen's Research Center in Management Sciences, October 25-26, 2012. Among the suggested conference themes was "Follett's Renewed Vision of Democracy"—a topic both authors have written about in dissertations and previously published work. Therefore, an abstract and a letter of interest in participating was submitted which resulted in an invitation to submit a completed paper for peer review prior to the conference.

During the literature review and content analysis conducted for the paper, it rapidly became evident that a book along the lines of a Follett reader would be most fruitful for our purpose, particularly given page limitations for the conference paper. Thus, both efforts progressed simultaneously—a draft version of this manuscript and the brief excerpt for the conference paper.

The conference paper was presented and the feedback received during both peer review and discussion helped shape the final manuscript. Specifically, we received praise for the comprehensive interpretation of her work and the purpose to position Follett as an important contributor to American pragmatism as well as process philosophy. There was a high level of concurrence that without such a thorough approach, Follett's work is often misinterpreted and misunderstood, especially when considering only her application to management theory or conflict mediation and negotiation. The argument that there is a common ontological mismatch in such attempts was accepted as a valid basis for our approach to Follett's work.

We believe this reorganization of Follett's thought with exemplary quotes from all but one (*The Speaker of the House of Representatives*) of her published papers, lectures, and books will give a comprehensive and coherent representation of her model for understanding democracy as a way of becoming and living. We have endeavored to quote as liberally as possible and to interpret as little as possible to maintain Follett's voice throughout, and we hope that the charm and wit lost from her conversational narrative style will be outweighed by the usefulness of a systematic presentation of her argument for "true democracy" (Follett, 1998, 156).

Subsequently, after attending the Ninth International Whitehead Conference (September 9-12, 2013) in Krakow, Poland, "Society and Process—from Theory to Practice," it became clear that a bridge between Whitehead and Follett needed to be built to fully position her within that philosophical lineage and to support Whiteheadians in the project of application. Thus, we invited Miroslaw Patalon, a Whiteheadian scholar, to join us in fleshing out the linkages previously discussed by Stout and Staton (2011). Professor Patalon applies process philosophy and theology to ministry and social work, thereby providing an applied perspective appropriate to Follett's thinking.

Margaret Stout, Assistant Professor
Department of Public Administration
Rockefeller School of Policy and Politics
West Virginia University
PO Box 6322 / 325 Willey Street
Morgantown WV 26506-6322
304-293-7978
Margaret.Stout@mail.wvu.edu

Jeannine M. Love, Assistant Professor
Department of Political Science and Public Administration
Roosevelt University, Mail Stop 835
430 S. Michigan Ave
Chicago, IL 60605
312-322-7159
jmlove@roosevelt.edu

with

Miroslaw Patalon, Professor
Department of Education and Social Work
Pomeranian University
ul. Boh. Westerplatte 64
76-200 Slupsk, Poland
48 (59) 84 05 924
patalon@apsl.edu.pl

Acknowledgments

The authors would like to acknowledge the important contribution of Carrie Staton, MPA, to the project of situating Follett within process philosophy. Specifically, her recognition of Follett's similarity to Whitehead spurred the initial exploration of their shared ontological assumptions. This investigation resulted in an article entitled, "The Ontology of Process Philosophy in Follett's Governance Theory" published in *Administrative Theory & Praxis* (Stout & Staton, 2011), which is the foundation of chapter 10. We are indebted to her astute intellect and intuition!

The authors would also like to acknowledge institutional support for research that enabled completion of this manuscript. Margaret Stout received support from the West Virginia University Senate Grants for Research and Scholarship 2012 (R-12-026) and 2013 (R-13-049). Jeannine Love received support from Roosevelt University in the form of a Faculty Research Leave in Fall 2012, as well as research assistance from Roselyn Abassah-Manu. The authors would also like to acknowledge the following publishers for permission to use substantive portions of or concepts from previously published articles.

- Chapter 1: SAGE Journals for Stout, Margaret and Love, Jeannine M. 2013. "Relational Ontology: A Grounding for Global Governance." *Administration & Society* doi: 10.1177/0095399713490692.

- Chapter 1: American Society for Public Administration for Stout, Margaret. 2012. "Competing Ontologies: A Primer for Public Administration." *Public Administration Review* 72(3), 388-98.

- Chapter 1: Public Administration Theory Network for Stout, Margaret. 2010. "Revisiting the (Lost) Art of Ideal-Typing in Public Administration." *Administrative Theory & Praxis* 32(4), 491-519.

- Chapter 2: Public Administration Theory Network for Stout, Margaret. 2012. "Toward a Relational Language of Process." *Administrative Theory & Praxis* 34(3) 407-32.

- Chapter 2: Public Administration Theory Network for Stout, Margaret and Staton, Carrie. 2011. "The Ontology of Process Philosophy in Follett's Governance Theory." *Administrative Theory & Praxis* 33(2) 268-92.

- Chapter 8: SAGE Publications for Stout, Margaret. 2010. "Back to the Future: Toward a Political Economy of Love & Abundance." *Administration & Society* 42(1), 3-37.

- Chapter 10: Public Administration Theory Network for Stout, Margaret and Staton, Carrie. 2011. "The Ontology of Process Philosophy in Follett's Governance Theory." *Administrative Theory & Praxis* 33(2), 26-92.

- Chapter 11: Taylor & Francis Group for Stout, Margaret and Love, Jeannine M. 2015 (forthcoming). For Follett, Mary Parker in *Encyclopedia of Public Administration and Public Policy, 3ʳᵈ Edition*.

- Chapter 12: National Center for Public Performance (NCPP) at the School of Public Affairs and Administration (SPAA), Rutgers University-Newark for Stout, Margaret and Love, Jeannine M. 2014. "The Unfortunate Misinterpretation of Miss Follett." *Public Voices* 13 (2), 11-32.

- Chapter 13: Taylor & Francis Group, CRC Press for Stout, Margaret. 2013. *Logics of Legitimacy: Three Traditions of Public Administration Praxis*.

- Chapter 14: SAGE Journals for Stout, Margaret and Holmes, Maja H. 2013. "From Theory to Practice: Utilizing Integrative Seminars as Bookends to the Master of Public Administration Program of Study." *Teaching Public Administration 31*, 186-203.

❧ 1 ❧

Complementing Follett's Work

Mary Follett[1] was a highly esteemed Progressive Era public intellectual, scholar of political theory, social worker, and management consultant to both industry and government in the United States and the United Kingdom until her death in late 1933. Follett's overall emphasis was on governance writ large as opposed to the management of organizations in particular. Regardless of sector, Follett's answer to a well-ordered and just society "lay in democratic governance" (Graham 1995a, 15) as described in her primary published works: *The Speaker of the House of Representatives* (Follett 1896), *The New State: Group Organization the Solution of Popular Government* (Follett 1918), "Community is a Process" (Follett 1919), *Creative Experience* (Follett 1924), *Dynamic Administration* (Metcalf and Urwick 1942), and *Freedom & Co-ordination* (Urwick 1949).

At core, Follett's study was of *modes of association of human beings in groups*, drawing upon every discipline that could help inform that understanding: philosophy, ethics, political theory, law, sociology, psychology, biology, physics, and mathematics. Follett considers these many sources, identifying correspondences, correlation, corollaries, and "cross-fertilizations" (Follett 2013c, xvii) that inform her critiques of both hierarchy and competition and her affirmation of a theory of integration as the proper basis for organization and governance in civil society, government, and industry.[2] In these ideas, Follett gave voice to what would later be called a feminist perspective in administrative theory (Banerjee 2008; Kaag 2008; Mansbridge 1998; McLarney and Rhyno 1999; Morton and Lindquist 1997; Nickel and Eikenberry 2006; Pratt 2011; Stivers 1990; Witt 2007).

But by this we do not mean that Follett was a feminist. While Follett was both a woman in public service in myriad roles from social worker to presidential advisor (Tonn 2003) and a female public intellectual, Follett herself did not claim to be part of the women's movement in her time. Instead, she pursued a non-gendered understanding of human being: "The essence of the woman movement is not that women as women should have the vote, but that women as individuals should have the vote. There is a fundamental distinction here" (Follett 1998, 171). Thus, her thinking gave voice to what is better described as a "culturally 'feminine'" (Stivers 2000; 2002a, 128) rather than a *feminist* philosophical perspective.

Although "she did not attempt to be a 'systematic philosopher'" and may indeed "have considered it intellectual arrogance" (Drucker 1995, 8), when considering her writings as a whole, "what is particularly attractive about Follett's ideas is that they mesh seamlessly with one another. . . . Furthermore, her ideas are comprehensive" (Graham 1995a, 25). Indeed, while not a *philosopher* as such, Follett analyzes and discusses concepts and principles from ontology to administration, with consideration of the practical implications of philosophy and theory at every conceptual layer of social action in between.

Follett's work responded to the social conditions of her time, which were not so unlike our own. Describing her historical context, Follett (2003e) claimed society was in desperate need due to: "(1) . . . exploitation of our natural resources whose day is now nearly over; (2) keener competition; (3) scarcity of labour [*sic*]; (4) a broader conception of the ethics of human relations; (5) the growing idea of business as a public service which carries with it a sense of responsibility for its efficient conduct" (122). Clearly, in our current crisis of social, economic, and environmental sustainability in a globalizing society, the challenges she sought to address have only grown in urgency. This argument is discussed further in Chapter 13.

Another reason for addressing Follett's work now is that there has been a resurgence of interest in her work since the late 1980s in management, business, mediation and conflict resolution, social work, and public administration. This interest is evident in a comprehensive biography (Tonn 2003), recent reprints of her books (Follett 1998, 2013a) and edited volumes (Graham 1995b; Metcalf and Urwick 2003; Urwick 2013), regularly updated reference book chapters (see for example, Fry and Raadschelders 2013; Shafritz, Hyde, and Parkes 2004), and a plethora of references to her work in contemporary literature, as reviewed in Chapter 12. In short, these scholars, editors, and publishers agree that the contemporary context and increasingly participatory practice in both organizations and governance around the world presents a more welcoming milieu for Follett's theory and practice than existed in the past. As management expert Warren Bennis (1995) puts it, her "remarkable body of writing was . . . ahead of her time" (181). Scholars and practitioners alike marvel at her innovative brilliance and "the richness of her perceptions and the completeness of her coverage" (Lawrence 1995, 291), so much so that she was given the moniker "prophet of management" (Drucker 1995, 9).[3]

Indeed, upon her rediscovery in contemporary management theory, renewed interest in her work blossomed. In a content analysis of the Social Science Citation Index, Fry and Thomas (1996) found that between 1969 and 1990 Follett's writings were cited by 129 authors in 96 different journals. The trend has dramatically increased since 1980 due to increased interest in negotiation, mediation, and conflict resolution. However, most references were cursory in nature and her organizational theories were cited much more frequently than her political ideas. As has been noted before, Tonn's (2003) extensive and detailed biography of Follett's life and work "does a good job of summarizing Follett's writings but mostly refrains from interpretation" (Stivers 2006, 473). Unfortunately, many of scholars attempting to do so misinterpret her thinking (Stout and Love 2014b), which is explained further in Chapter 11.

Therefore, a clear and comprehensive recapitulation and book-length treatment of Follett's body of work is needed if her full theoretical contribution is to be treated seriously by scholars. This is particularly important to the field of public administration where Follett's two main theoretical strands are woven together: political theory and management theory. However, Follett's recognition that power is inherent in all social action makes both threads important to all types of administrative practice. Following, this book is designed for use by scholars in research and by students in graduate level courses that explore the philosophical, historical, and intellectual foundations of public administration and social work, given the fact that she began as a political theorist and ended as a management theorist, while also practicing social work.[4] However, it is useful to other management and service fields, particularly those that interface with the public in some way. Furthermore, it will be of use to philosophers who wish to move theory into practice.

As applied scholars, we offer a unique perspective from which to assist in this project. Furthermore, we come to Miss Follett's writing from practice in community development, social work, and ministry, discovering in her grounded philosophy something that fits our actual experiences and provides accurate explanations of why things happen the way they do, in accordance with both her critiques and creative affirmations. As theorists, we also see how her thinking so clearly parallels process philosophy and presages many of our most valued contemporary pragmatist and postmodern theorists, as noted in the endnotes to each chapter.[5] Not to consider Follett along the Western process thought lineage from Heraclitus forward is a travesty.[6] This book clarifies her position in that genealogy.

In terms of Follett's personal lineage, since there are both in-depth and brief biographies readily available (see for example, Graham 1995b; Mattson 1998; Metcalf and Urwick 2003; Tonn 2003; Urwick 2013), we will refrain from extensive commentary on Follett's personal and professional profile. However, a brief introduction to her life and work is appropriate to situate her ideas historically. Furthermore, an overview of her intellectual contribution and how it was received both then and now further contextualizes her ideas and why they are still salient, or perhaps even particularly pertinent, to meet the challenges of contemporary governance in a postmodern society. Both are provided in this introduction.

However, the principal purpose of this book is to *recapitulate* and *explain* Follett's thinking in a manner that comprehensively and coherently integrates the many philosophical assumptions that prefigure her unique recommendations for the practice of integrative process. This is necessary because when her prescriptions are taken out of the context of her philosophical assumptions, they are frequently misconstrued by those coming from a different worldview. This issue is explained in Chapter 11.

An even more fundamental barrier to accurate understanding is presented by Follett's unique narrative style that easily leads to misinterpretation. Some note that such errors may be due to reliance on secondhand interpretations: "I would suggest reading the front matter by Barber, Mansbridge and Mattson after completing the book. While these scholars summarize accurately, their reviewing of the cold facts and opinions expressed in the text misses Follett's passion and intensity. Read her words, for one learns through her writing" (Cunningham 2000, 91). We concur—scholars drawing from Follett may *summarize* accurately, but they often do not *interpret* correctly.

However, we argue this stems not only from reliance on secondhand interpretation, but on an incomplete grasp of Follett's philosophical underpinnings. Given the robust nature of Follett's theoretical approach, selecting only bits and pieces of her thought for consideration is an approach that lends itself readily to misinterpretation. In short, one cannot pick up the essays and lectures in *Dynamic Administration* (Metcalf and Urwick 2003) or *Freedom and Co-ordination* (Urwick 2013) and fully grasp their meaning without having read *The New State* (Follett 1998), "Community is a Process" (Follett 1919), and *Creative Experience* (Follett 2013c). It is clear in those later lectures that Follett is assuming her audiences had already read earlier works and were looking for further explanation and application of her concepts to their particular context. Indeed, Follett's administrative theory is the *culmination* of her body of thought; the level of analysis at which both her philosophical concepts (ontological assumptions, psychosocial theory, epistemological principles, and beliefs) and practice-oriented theories (ethics, political theory, and economic theory) all move into action as an integrative whole.

In sum, due to widespread misinterpretation and perhaps the incomprehensibility of her actual meanings to many scholars, "Follett's ideas constitute a difference that public administration has never integrated" (Stivers 2006, 475). This book seeks to remedy this problem by re-presenting Follett's work in a manner that keeps her "relational process ontology" (Stout and Love 2013b)—Follett's message of *integrative process permeating all of social action*—always at the forefront of interpretation.

FOLLETT'S LIFE AND WORK

Mary Follett was born September 3, 1868, to an affluent Quaker family and grew up in Quincy, Massachusetts, a southern suburb of Boston. She attended Thayer Academy in neighboring Braintree—still regarded as one of the nation's leading preparatory schools. While family needs delayed her continuing studies, in 1892 she enrolled in the Society for the Collegiate Instruction of Women in Cambridge, Massachusetts (later Radcliffe College, now integrated within Harvard University), studying economics, government, law, and philosophy. While at Radcliffe she also spent a year at Newnham College in the University of Cambridge. Her research thesis was published in 1896, prior to graduation, as *The Speaker of the House of Representatives*, quickly becoming an esteemed study of political science. She graduated *summa cum laude* in 1898 but, as a woman, was unable to receive a doctorate.

From 1900 to 1908 Follett joined the social work staff of the Roxbury Neighborhood House—a settlement house in one of Boston's ethnically and economically diverse neighborhoods. Continuing with this type of activity, in 1908 Follett became involved in the community centers movement as chair of the Women's Municipal League's Committee on Extended Use of School Buildings. In 1911 the committee successfully opened the East Boston High School Social Center as an experiment. The success of the initiative proved to be a catalyst for the development of other centers. It was through these experiences that Follett became fascinated with the practice of democracy as a way of life, informing her next scholarly works, *The New State: Group Organization the Solution of Popular Government* (Follett 1918) and "Community is a Process" (Follett 1919).

Also bringing her advocacy work into the realm of industrial relations, Follett served as a member of the Massachusetts Minimum Wage Board and in 1917 she became vice-president of the National Community Center Association. She was also involved in *The Inquiry*, a social reform movement founded by the Federal Council of Churches in America. These experiences widened her focus from the public and nonprofit sectors to include business management from the 1920s until her death.

However, her increasing activities as a consultant and advocate did not quell her scholarly inquiry, which culminated in *Creative Experience* (Follett 1924), refining much of the more philosophical thought presented in *The New State* (Follett 1918). In 1926, she moved to England to live and work, including continued studies at Oxford University. From this point forward, Follett became a popular lecturer to both government and industry, exporting her relational process philosophy and experiences in civil society to the other societal spheres. She gave lectures at Harvard University, Syracuse University, the Taylor Society, the Ford Hall Forum in Boston, the Bureau of Personnel Administration in New York, the American Historical Association, the American Philosophical Association, the Rowntree Conference at Oxford University, and the London School of Economics. She also consulted with the League of Nations, the International Labor Organization in Geneva, and United States President Franklin D. Roosevelt.

FOLLETT'S INTELLECTUAL CONTRIBUTION

Follett's work is, quite literally, an homage to Harvard University's illustrious role in the emergence of both American pragmatism and process philosophy.

Follett was actively engaged in Harvard life as a lecturer and developed her thinking in large part through her interpretations of and interactions with Harvard professors, both during and following her studies at Radcliffe. Specifically, she references Harvard's philosophy and psychology professor Edwin Holt, psychology professors William James, Josiah Royce, and Gordon Allport, philosophy professor Alfred North Whitehead, Law School Dean Roscoe Pound, and ethics professor Richard Cabot.

Based on her relational approach to group process, Follett is viewed in the field of public administration as a *process theorist* (Harmon 2006; Harmon and McSwite 2011). The importance of understanding her work in light of Whitehead's process philosophy was introduced by Stout and Staton (2011). Furthermore the value Follett brings to the development of process language—one that differs markedly from Whitehead's employment of hierarchical concepts that carry over from static, atomistic ontology—has also been explored (Stout 2012b). In short, Follett provides coherent linkages from concepts drawn from relational process ontology and language, psychosocial theory, epistemology, and beliefs to ethics and political, economic, and administrative practice—a project with which contemporary Whiteheadians grapple and are encouraged to continue. The Ninth International Whitehead Conference theme was "Society and Process—from Theory to Practice" and the Tenth International Whitehead Conference theme will be "Seizing an Alternative: Toward an Ecological Civilization." These conference themes emphasize the need to move from the abstract to the practical, from ontology *per se* to what it actually *means to life*.

Because of this unique capacity to bring philosophy together with practice, biographer Joan Tonn (2003) shows that during Follett's lifetime, she was highly regarded and respected in philosophical circles in the academy and among management and administrative leaders in both business and government. In fact, *The New State* sold well enough to be reprinted five times in the early 1920s. Similarly, *Creative Experience* "was widely reviewed in the academic and popular press and with one exception was received very favorably" (Tonn 2003, 384). In his review of *Creative Experience*, sociologist Charles A. Ellwood assessed every chapter as "'a vital contribution to social theory,'" calling Follett "'the foremost woman thinker along social and political lines of our time, and perhaps one of the most philosophical thinkers in the field of social theory of all time'" (as quoted in Tonn 2003, 385). Her continued work was published posthumously in two collections of essays, *Dynamic Administration: The Collected Papers of Mary Parker*

Follett (Metcalf and Urwick 1942) and *Freedom & Co-ordination: Lectures in Business Organisation by Mary Parker Follett* (Urwick 1949).

Indeed, the philosophical depth of Follett's associational theories is extraordinary. Management theorist Rosabeth Moss Kanter (1995) believes "Mary Parker Follett was a quintessential utopian and a romantic" (xvii), but in the critical sense described by Yeats as one "who rose against the Age of Enlightenment with its overconfidence in reason and systems" (Parker 1995, 287). Thus, she was Romantic, "but not all starry-eyed" (290). In his review of *The New State* in the *Journal of Philosophy, Psychology and Scientific Methods*, Harry A. Overstreet characterized it as "'a philosophy come back to earth. The One and the Many are there; the Universal and the Particular; Monism and Pluralism; objectivism and subjectivism; real personality; unity of opposites; compenetration, and all the rest; but they do not float in the metaphysical ethers. They are tied to the homely behaviors of men and women in society'" (as quoted in Tonn 2003, 305).[7]

On the other end of the spectrum, in his introduction to *Freedom & Co-ordination*, Lyndall Urwick (2013) warns "if any reader feels disposed to question the validity of Mary Parker Follett's reasoning on the ground that she was not a 'practical man'—she was a woman who never attempted to manage a business in her life—he is urged to turn to David Lilienthal's own account of the brilliantly successful experiment he directed [Tennessee Valley Authority]. He will find there example after example of the application in practice of every one of the principles which she had developed theoretically" (xiv). But this is also evident in the myriad stories of practice in communities and industry woven throughout her writing. In short, Follett succeeds where so many others fail—in his review of *Creative Experience*, sociologist Arthur E. Wood stated that the "'genius of Miss Follett's work lies in her effective synthesis of theory and practice'" (as quoted in Tonn 2003, 385).[8]

Interpretive barriers of message

In her writing and lectures, Follett was unafraid to "offer audacious argument on behalf of deeply held democratic beliefs" (Barber 1998, xvi). For example, "a vivid rhetoric permeates *The New State*, and more than one reviewer would find fault with it" (Tonn 2003, 301).[9] Her "sometimes passionate prose made [political scientists] uneasy" (307), as did her approach of engaging "closely with the world of practice without ever undertaking conventional research" such that her ideas were sometimes received as "idiosyncratic rather than reliably demonstrable" (Child 2013, 86). Furthermore, because she "was writing with the language of her time—a language heavily influenced by Hegelian idealism" (Mansbridge 1998, xxvi), "her declaration that the state is the ultimate group . . . may not have been very popular in an era that saw the rise of totalitarian governments in Europe" (Fry & Raadschelders 2014, 154). O'Connor (2000) reflects, "I think much of her history has to do with her political incorrectness. She was a Hegelian at a time when the power of the state, particularly the German state, was increasingly suspect" (187). Indeed, "from the 1930s until very recently, Follett was 'subversive'" (Drucker 1995, 1). Ideas like constructive conflict leading to integration were "unintelligible" in the 1930s and 1940s (4). As a result of her substantive message, for five or six decades leading into, during, and following World War II, Follett's work was marginalized and discredited as unimportant. By 1950 "she had become a nonperson'" (2), or at best "a cult figure" (Bennis 1995, 177).

However, even for those who have become interested in Follett's message, due to Follett's theoretical complexity, Tonn (2003) argues that many scholars have "a fundamental misunderstanding of Follett's argument" (308). As an example, Tonn (2003) notes that in an attempt to correct misunderstandings of the group process explained in *The New State*, Follett emphasizes the notion of modes of association in the social process, as opposed to the formation of actual groups in her *Philosophical Review* paper, "Community is a Process." Similarly, Lord Haldane's[10] introduction to the September 1920 edition of *The New State* focuses largely on the theory underlying the book, seeking to emphasize and clarify her unique philosophical position as one "principle" or "theory" permeating all of her thinking (Haldane 1920, v, vi):

> It is the exposition of a principle which is not stated for the first time, but which, in the form and connection in which she states it, seems to place many difficulties in a new light, and to lay to rest controversies, some at least of which have arisen out of misinterpretation of what is fundamental. Vagueness about first principles is at once the source of confusion in conception and of waste of valuable energy. Now Miss Follett's book sets itself firmly to avoid this vagueness. (Haldane 1920, v)

We describe this theory as *integrative process*. Haldane (1920) asserts that the ontological debate between monism and pluralism underlies difficulties in the political economy of modern society. He argues that Follett eruditely ends this philosophical argument over first principles—*both of which are grounded in a static ultimate*, whether conceived as the whole group or the whole individual—with her notion of integrative process grounded in empirical evidence from observations in community, government, and industrial contexts. She shows that the ultimate nature of existence is a complex, constantly changing composition of interconnected groups formed by unique contributing individuals. Through integration "individuals and groups stand in no antithesis to one another" (Haldane 1920, x); through process no particular configuration can rightfully claim permanence or sovereignty. Indeed, there "is no passive element in an assemblage" (xiv).

Follett's philosophical conception of the theory of integrative process is informed by interdisciplinary study and her articulation of a cohesive understanding of ontological principles, psychosocial theory, epistemological principles, and beliefs along with the application of these concepts to ethics, political theory, economic theory, and administrative theory. Each conceptual element builds upon the others, with her understanding of relational process ontology expressing itself through all of the other conceptual layers in what she sees as a "self-creating coherence" (Follett 2013c, 61). Thus, when Follett's body of work is analyzed as a whole, "one can come away from it with a sense of satisfaction in her fundamental consistency of thought" (Phillips 2010, 57).

From this conceptually consistent theory of integrative process, Follett critiques frameworks based on both idealism and realism in the form of positivism and behaviorism, while promoting an alternative pragmatist framework. Indeed, Follett never vacillates between any of the dialectical positions, dualisms, or binaries that she critiques. Through her understanding of integration, Follett (1918, 1919, 1924) consistently promotes a "3rd (neither monist nor pluralist) position" (Tonn 2003, 317) that is a true synthesis—paradoxically both and neither idealist/realist, humanist/instrumental, or conservative/liberal. As she puts it, "Idealism and realism meet in the actual" (Follett 1919, 587). She asserts that "the essence of this . . . is as important for ethics as for physiology or psychology; for sociology its value is inestimable" (Follett 2013c, 88). But perhaps more importantly, it should be the basis of all types of social action—in "politics, industry and law" (74-75) as well as "ethics" (295).

Unfortunately, when her recommendations for practice are read without this background knowledge, Follett's message of integrative process permeating all of social action is lost. Indeed, her ideas are often reinterpreted through the very dualistic lenses she is refuting. Those who do not fully comprehend her ontological assumptions, her carefully revised psychosocial theories, her relational and phenomenological epistemological assumptions, and how they intertwine with her Quaker belief system, can easily misread her recommendations for participatory ethics, politics, economics, and administration. In short, misinterpretations are due to a lack of awareness of Follett's underlying relational process ontology. Without actively interpreting Follett's work through this lens, there is a danger of fundamental misinterpretation.

Therefore, we argue that taking Follett's prescriptions for practice out of the philosophical context from which they are formed must be avoided. It is this philosophical perspective that this book seeks to make clear, by presenting her ideas in a more systematic fashion, and more concisely than would be required by reading her full body of work.

Interpretive barriers of style

Beyond misunderstandings of her message, there is a more basic barrier to understanding Follettian thinking, even among sympathetic readers who may experience "a sense of frustration because the diffuseness and circularity of her writings make it so difficult to get a clear picture of" her philosophy (Phillips 2010, 57). As Fry and Raadschelders (2013) kindly describe it, her writing style has "a certain rhythm" (151). Follett's narrative tends toward the conversational, interspersed liberally with stories that illustrate the principles she is explicating. As a result, while some appreciate this "unique trait" of "relating abstract philosophical views in stories of concrete, everyday experience" (O'Connor 2000, 183), many feel reading Follett can be daunting due to her "often difficult prose" (Mattson 1998, xxx). Harold Laski wrote that *The New State* "'suffers from being written in a hideous journalese that deprives it of no small part of its effectiveness'" (Tonn 2003, 306). Some judge this to be "a sometimes opaque social scientist style that characterized much of the political work of the period before and after World War I" (Barber 1998, xv). For example, in *The New State*, "eschewing for the most part citations, explanatory footnotes, references, and even an index, Follett adopts an informal style....To modern readers who are not conversant with Follett's numerous informal, cryptic references to ideas and issues of the day, her book often seems obscure, peculiarly organized, and badly in need of condensation" (Tonn 2003, 267).

Thus, on one hand, "readers are . . . challenged by Follett's erudition: a plethora of academic disciplines (philosophy, political theory, sociology, psychology, and even biology) informs her thought" (Tonn 2003, 267).[11]

Assuming that her audience was similarly well-read and informed, Follett rarely discusses her complete reasoning on discrete concepts, but rather explains pieces of the interconnected whole as they are expressed in various contexts pertinent to the topic at hand. Follett "was never a very systematic writer, she threw out interesting ideas more or less randomly and the thread of consistency is hard to find and harder to follow" (Fox 1968, 521). On the other hand, Follett's use of simple phrases and illustrations obscures the conceptual complexity underneath (Fox 1968). Therefore, while Follett's vision is singular in its thrust, it is highly complex and so "it is hard to examine it in parts, it can only be understood as a whole" (Parker 1995, 290).

In sum, as O'Connor (2000) reflects on Follett's writing, "it is difficult to separate particular strands of her thought, as is required in an expository essay, without ruining their integrity" (177). Nonetheless, we have endeavored to do so herein. Through a systematic analysis of each conceptual layer of her thinking, we recapitulate Follett's message in a style that endeavors to be more organized, while keeping the integrity of her underlying philosophical perspective of integrative process intact.

Follett's intellectual contribution in sum

All in all, Follett was recognized during her lifetime as a brilliant scholar both in terms of her theoretical contributions to pragmatism and process philosophy and her prescriptions for practice in all three sectors of society. Due to the unwelcoming milieu of the post-World War I era that followed, Follett's challenging writing style, and her rather early death at age 60, Harvard ethics professor Richard Cabot sadly admits, "She might have missed the chance to serve her day and generation and to make clearer as she has done the path for many of those who come after her" (Cabot 1934, 82). While the value of her work was rediscovered through the humanistic management movement in the 1980s, many scholars misinterpret her recommendations for practice because they do not understand her philosophical perspective. Her full philosophical framework must be made transparent in order to prevent such misunderstandings. Thus, *making clearer* is the purpose of this book, by actively interpreting Follett's work through the lens of her underlying relational process ontology, organizing her ideas in a more systematic fashion than she does herself, and presenting them more concisely than would be required by reading her full body of work.

A COMPLEMENTARY METHODOLOGY

Follett's interpretive method is quite reminiscent of Weber's (1949) approach to ideal-typing based on conceptual coherence. Specifically, Follett promotes a social science mission of studying and making recommendations for all spheres of human activity.[12] Her aim is "to know how men can interact and coact better" (Follett 2013c, xii) in order to "transform economics and politics, law and ethics" (Follett 1919, 579). However, she recognizes that we cannot do this by simply rearranging behavior at those levels of analysis. Behavior, including that of the institutions of governance, is guided by principles and philosophical assumptions. However, "most people have not decided, have not even thought out what the different principles are. . . . Surely this is a pity. To know what principles may underlie any given activity of ours is to take a conscious attitude toward our experience" (Follett 2013f, 50).

Follett argues that in adopting such a conscious attitude, we will discover that "we cannot departmentalize our thinking. . . . Underneath all our thinking, there are certain fundamental principles to be applied to all our problems" (Follett 2003m, 183).[13] If we attempt to find these principles through individual silos of activity in order to progress in that area, we will likely miss the real drivers of change: "Many think also that it would be well if we could separate politics and business. But far below the surface are the forces which have allied business and politics; far below the surface we must go, therefore, if we would divorce this badly mated couple" (Follett 1998, 216-17). However, Follett does not mean to succeed in this separation—indeed she seeks to help both industry and government operate according to the same democratic principles. By this claim, she means that to change the political economy we must change the shared underlying philosophical commitments that prefigure it, and then seek to replace them with more fruitful principles.[14,15] As she puts it, "I want to show that the basis for understanding the problems of political science is the same as the basis for understanding business administration—it is the understanding of the nature of integrative unities" (Follett 2003m, 190).

Accordingly Follett draws from many disciplinary sources to identify correspondences, correlation, corollaries, and "cross-fertilizations" (Follett 2013c, xvii).[16,17] As she once said, "'I do wish . . . that when a principle is worked out, say in ethics, it didn't have to be discovered all over again in psychology, in economics, in government, in business, in biology, and in sociology. It's such a waste of time!'" (quoted in Cabot 1934, 81). Further-more, she does not limit herself to the sciences and philosophy, or even the academy. Follett was influenced by literally everyone with whom she came in contact—not just those in intellectual circles. Indeed, Lyndall Urwick (2013) sees this as critical to understanding her depth of thought:

> How is it possible that a single woman with no elaborate research technique, no team of assistants could have made a major and original contribution to our knowledge and understanding of administration? The answer is that every individual Mary Follett met—and she made it her business to meet many people—became her willing, if unconscious, research assistant. . . . Whoever she met, and intellectual and social distinction made no difference—it was Lord Haldane of Cloan one minute and a maidservant or a bus conductor the next—she made them talk, from the heart as well as from the head. . . . A profoundly philosophical and scientific mind, she enlisted countless other minds, which were neither, as willing, warm and enthusiastic collaborators. (xvi)

Follett herself notes this practice. For example, in regard to her research on power Follett said, "I am making a list of all the different definitions I come across, by novelists or artists, or whoever, and I find this all helping me in my observation of power in everyday life" (as quoted in Parker 1995, 285). Indeed, she remarks on the fact that "men working quite independently of each other, working in quite different fields, too, are coming to agree on a very fundamental principle" and that this principle of integrative process is "the most interesting thing in the world to me today" (Follett 2013g, 12).

Within her theoretical discussions, Follett draws frequently from select sources, particularly those she engaged in her Cambridge, Massachusetts, intellectual circles, as a means to highlight the connections she is making across the wide ranging areas of study. For instance, she is very complimentary of the organic philosophy of Alfred North Whitehead in the way it explains the unifying process of becoming. To develop her psychosocial theory, Follett relies heavily on Harvard philosophy and psychology professor Edwin Holt's interpretation of Freud, but also draws deeply from pragmatist philosopher (and Harvard psychology professor) William James's understandings of consciousness as well as from the then emerging Gestalt theory of psychology as explained by Harvard psychology professor Gordon Allport. She feels this school of psychological thought "contains the prophecy of the future because it has with keenest insight seized upon the problem of identity, of association, of federalism, as the central problem of politics as it is the central problem of life" (Follett 1998, 317). To consider how these psychological ideas pertain to practical application, Follett refers to her friend and Harvard ethics professor Richard Cabot as an influential source. She also refers often to Roscoe Pound, Dean of the Harvard Law School, and his theory of modern law as an evolving, relational practice.

In her interpretation of these scholars' ideas, Follett is attentive to the importance of language and its meanings: "You will notice that to break up a problem into its various parts involves the *examination of symbols*, involves, that is, the careful scrutiny of the language used to see what it really means" (Follett 2003b, 41). She notes that it is "unavoidable to use symbols; all language is symbolic; but we should be always on our guard as to what is symbolized" (42). In so doing, she often uses unique terminology to make clear her meanings (Stout 2012b). In this sense, Follett presages the Continental scholars of postmodern philosophy who assert the structuring effects of language on identity and knowing. Furthermore her assumption that language and terminology can hold multiple meanings is necessary to develop a coherent ideal-type based on varied theoretical literature.

Even so, Follett insists that this attention to language is not for an esoteric purpose, but rather one that is quite practical: "A serious obstacle to integration which every business man should consider is the language used" (Follett 2003b, 47). Therefore, she urges management theory to change "a good deal of our language" (Follett 2013f, 29). This is even more critical in political and economic theory: "In a book by a recent writer on politics these four words are used in a sentence of three lines: power, purpose, freedom, service. But the author has not told us what these words mean—and we do not know" (Follett 2013c, ix). Her careful attention to such language, and her work identifying unstated principles across spheres, allows Follett to demonstrate that there are multiple interpretations and applications for these terms such as her distinction between *power-over* and *power-with* (Follett 2003j).

Through her careful interpretation of meanings, the basic concept Follett draws from combined theoretical sources is the notion of *integrating* (Follett 2013c, 57). For Follett integrative process is the essential characteristic of the world, both physical and social. She explains that the dynamic ontological process of what she also calls *circular response* can be found in chemistry, engineering, and relativity theory in physics (73-74). She later notes that it is also found in biology, Whiteheadian philosophy, and physiology (Follett 2013h, 80). Follett also notes that the relational and dynamic principle of integration is repeated in conceptual layers that move from physical and metaphysical ontological principles to both the individual psyche and groups of human beings in the social context.

Our methodology

Following from Follett's interdisciplinary method, to organize her thinking in a more logical structure without losing the integrity of her underlying philosophical principles, her conceptual meanings are interpreted using a typology generated to understand patterns of coherency in varying systems of governance (Stout and Love 2013b). Specifically, we use Weber's (1949) ideal-type approach which enables a combination of description, critique, and affirmation. An example of this type of analysis is Hendriks's (2010) model of democracy ideal-types linked to the political and societal cultures underlying each type. Similar applications can be found in *Logics of Legitimacy: Three Traditions of Public Administration Praxis* (Stout 2013b) and a series of articles developing the governance typology employed herein (Love 2008, 2012, 2013; Stout 2012a, 2014; Stout and Love 2013a, 2013b). Similar to these other typologies, the "Follettian governance" (Stout and Staton 2011) ideal-type presented herein can be used to examine both theories and practices to identify their underlying ontological assumptions and to determine whether they fit the ideal-type.

Well-crafted ideal-type models (typologies) consist of two components: generic elements and genetic meanings (Stout 2010c). *Generic elements* are concepts essential to a given phenomenon that are necessary to understand causal relationships—how and why things happen as they do. They are also culturally significant with importance to social actors or theoretical value to inquiry. The generic elements compose the typology as a whole. *Genetic meanings* refer to the particular definitions of the generic elements that create logical coherence within a given ideal-type. Thus, the genetic meanings compose each *ideal-type* within the model.

The generic conceptual elements we consider necessary to formulate a comprehensive theory of governance are: ontology and language, psychosocial theory, epistemology, beliefs, ethics, political theory, economic theory, and administrative theory (Stout and Love 2013b). Taken together, the first four conceptual elements of the ideal-type model (ontology and language, psychosocial theory, epistemology, and beliefs) frame the driving philosophical commitments that prefigure governance forms through what has been called "political ontology"; logically related assumptions about the nature of human being, identity, and social life (Catlaw 2007; Howe 2006).[18] The latter four conceptual elements (ethics, political theory, economic theory, and administrative theory) frame governance forms and practices prefigured by the philosophical grounding. By considering these generic elements as coherent sets, the typology serves exploration of the relationships between various governance practices and the philosophical commitments that prefigure them (Hendriks 2010; White 2000).

To construct the ideal-type, we employed Follett's integrative process to interpret her own work. As recommended by Follett herself in the *practice* of integrative process, we began with the first step: "to break up wholes: to analyze, differentiate and discriminate" (Follett 2013c, 171). Her opaque, roundabout explications were dis-integrated in order to re-integrate them in a more linear and direct pattern of logical argumentation. We disrupted Follett's narrative style; disaggregated conceptual elements from specific situations; used interpretive content analysis to differentiate ideas across categories; and reintegrated her ideas for explication within a cohesive, comprehensive pattern, one conceptual building block at a time. This interpretation relied heavily on logico-meaningful analysis as developed by Sorokin (1957). This approach to categorization identifies "the central principle (the 'reason') which permeates all the components, gives sense and significance to each of them, and in this way makes cosmos of a chaos of unintegrated fragments" (14). Thus, Follett's texts were analyzed in search of a central principle to unite them; a principle that might offer "the appropriate unification of the fragments into a whole according to their logical significance or their logical cobelonging" (14). That principle is *integrative process*, which draws from what we call *relational process ontology* (Stout and Love 2013b).

We offer sufficient interpretation of her work so that her understanding of integrative process is made clear as the thread that weaves itself from ontological assumptions through all other conceptual layers. However, rather than merely paraphrasing her ideas in those chapters and losing the delightful quality and character of her voice and prose, we quote liberally from her published papers, lectures, and books. While this may be somewhat out of the ordinary, we want the manuscript to have the character and length of a collected works, while also providing systematic structure and comprehensive coverage of her ideas, regardless of their source.

The book also includes a robust literature review. In the explication of Follett's thinking, we utilize chapter endnotes to note where her ideas link to contemporary thought, as well as where our interpretation is similar to that of other scholars or where they have noted contextualizing details that we have not. This maintains as much brevity as possible and does not interrupt Follett herself in the core chapters of the book. We intentionally completed our content analysis *prior* to going back through commentaries on her work by others to check for either confirmation or differences in interpretation.[19] Once Follett's work is explicated, other literature is reviewed in the latter chapters to contextualize her thinking in contemporary thought.

THE BOOK'S STRUCTURE

Eight generic conceptual elements are used to analyze, categorize, and interpret Follett's body of work: ontology and language, psychosocial theory, epistemological concepts, beliefs, conception of ethics, political theory, economic theory, and administrative theory.[20] The results are presented in the book's core Chapters, 2 through 9; one chapter for each conceptual element of the typology.

With this explication in hand, Chapter 10 places Follett and White-head in conversation through analysis of the ontological assumptions that clearly position Follett's work within the process thought lineage. The conceptual themes held in common address: (1) the nature of becoming; (2) the role of God in becoming; (3) the nature of difference; and (4) the purpose of becoming. This clear linkage of Follett to process thought establishes a basis for the argument in Chapter 11 for why the recapitulation of her thinking is necessary to correct misunderstandings present in the contemporary literature—misunderstandings that are in large part due to ontological mismatch.

To sum up the book's explication and argument, the Follettian[21] approach to governance is presented in Chapter 12, while Chapter 13 affirms it as a promising approach to governance in the contemporary global context for a sustainable future. Chapter 12 highlights the cross-cutting principles that are evident throughout the conceptual layers discussed in Chapters 2-9: integrative process, the situation, the law of the situation, and the method of integration. Application of these concepts in all forms of group governance is then explained, along with the fruits of integrative process: democracy as a way of life and progress as creative collaboration. The chapter wraps up with a review of contemporary literature applying Follettian thinking to governance, management and administration, negotiation, and social work.

Chapter 13 argues that the contemporary context and its increasing demand for participatory democratic governance around the world presents a more welcoming milieu for Follett's philosophy and practice than existed in the past.

Chapter 14 completes the book with suggestions for how to implement Follettian governance, considering the need to develop the skills of integrative process in daily life as well as through professional education. We end with some reflections on the challenge of affirming Follettian thinking as scholars in an academic milieu that is not so welcoming for such transdisciplinary theory.

CONCLUSIONS

In sum, we are quite pleased that the work of Mary Follett has enjoyed a resurgence of interest that continues today. However, based on substantive misinterpretations of Follett's work—many of which have been noted by other commentators during and since her time—we invite the scholars using her work to reconsider their analysis, or at least present it with clarification of the ontological position from which they are interpreting or critiquing. In support of a clearer understanding of Follett's ontological position, we turn to a systematic recapitulation of Follett's thinking, from ontology to administration.

ENDNOTES

1. We refer to Mary Follett as opposed to the more conventional Mary Parker Follett because this is what she was called before her death (Tonn 2003, xiv).

2. This is how Mesle (2008) describes the project of speculative philosophy seeking a unified understanding; start with a basic principle and imagine it being applied to many fields of thought in order to find an acceptable generalization. As he notes, "the task requires a combination of creative, imaginative, and disciplined thought that few people possess" (Mesle 2008, 16). We argue that this is precisely what Follett does.

3. Follett's moniker, "prophet of management" is often attributed to the edited volume (Graham 1995b), but it was actually George (1972) who noted she was "a prophet in the management wilderness" (139).

4. In the field of public administration, Cunningham (2000) reviewed *The New State* upon its reprinting, bringing it back to the attention of public

administration scholars, while Stivers (2006) reviewed Joan Tonn's biography. A resurgence of attention to Follett in both political and management theory led to her inclusion in *Mastering Public Administration: From Max Weber to Dwight Waldo* (Fry 1989; Fry and Raadschelders 2008), a commonly assigned text in graduate courses, particularly at the masters level. Indeed, Follett has been called "the 'first lady' of public administration" (Morton and Lindquist 1997, 350).

5. O'Connor (2000) suggests that Follett's engagement with philosophy "make[s] her difficult for us to appreciate" (167). Yet she is one of very few scholars to link philosophy to management theory—a discipline that eschewed philosophy for science.

6. Follett herself claims Heraclitus in a footnote in *The New State* (1998, 34).

7. Krupp (1961) similarly notes that while Follett was normative in her theories, which was customary for her day, her theories were informed by both observation and philosophy, and so her results often differ little from subsequent empirical research.

8. Not all agree with this characterization. O'Connor (1996) is somewhat derisive: "Follett situates herself at an abstract, philosophical level in speaking about the compelling but elusive 'law of the situation'; so there is neither a way nor a possibility of grounding her view" (46).

9. O'Connor (1996) criticizes Follett's use of "sweeping, strong claims" and superlatives, suggesting she is "almost obsessed with the concept of unity" (40).

10. Lord Richard Burdon Haldane (1856-1928) was not only a politician, but a Fellow of the British Academy, a cofounder of the London School of Economics, and a Gifford lecturer. He was also an admirer of Whitehead's philosophical work and Einstein's theory of relativity, introducing the two in a reportedly unproductive meeting (Desmet 2007).

11. O'Connor (1996) also notes the breadth of disciplinary sources informing Follett's philosophy, embodying her theme of integration.

12. Barclay (2005) notes Follett's concepts lend themselves to qualitative methodologies that can better help understand dynamic phenomena. Similarly, Child (2013) suggests that Follett's methodology is based in inductive reasoning drawing on empirical observations from "some twenty-five years in of active engagement in community work and other public service, complemented in her later years by frequent interaction with business people and their companies" (86).

13. Mendenhall, Macomber, and Cutright (2000) argue that Follett was "the prophet of chaos and complexity" (203) and that she provides the rationale

for incorporating concepts from the field of nonlinear dynamics (chaos or complexity theory) into the study of social phenomena.

14. Ryan and Rutherford (2000) note that philosophers are required to base their positions on either the individual or the group as the essential unit of humanity, and "each position leads logically to very different ethical and political theory" (Ryan and Rutherford 2000, 216).

15. In this endeavor, Follett uniquely heralds the most recent "ontological turn" (Prozorov 2014a, xxviii) in social theory which recognizes the pre-figuring relationship between ontology and social practices and structures (White 2000).

16. Mendenhall, Macomber, and Cutright (2000) argue that because Follett's concepts were inductively derived from actual social phenomena, there is no danger in applying physical science theories to social science as has been noted in recent decades.

17. Gehani and Gehani (2007) see this interdisciplinary approach as an example of Follett herself being an "integrator looking for synergies across a variety of inter-related disciplines" (391).

18. Morton and Lindquist (1997) similarly note that ontology, epistemology, and ethics are related in an interrelated building-block fashion.

19. Morton and Lindquist (1997) provide a similar philosophical analysis organized around the categories of ontology, epistemology, and ethics. They assert "no one has yet presented a formal philosophical analysis of Follett using contemporary feminism as a framework, particularly as her work relates to public administration" (Morton and Lindquist 1997, 349) and argue that Follett's ideas could help build a coherent theoretical foundation for public administration.

20. For this project, we did not include her book, *The Speaker of the House of Representatives* (Follett 1896) as it is not directly pertinent to our purpose.

21. John Child (1995) uses the term "Follettian" (91).

❧ 2 ❧

Follett's Ontological Assumptions and Language

Ontology is an understanding of existence that informs our assumptions about reality and our worldview or cosmology. *Language* reflects our understanding of ontology and so is discussed within this element of the ideal-type model. Ontological explanations generally consider whether reality is in a static or dynamic state, and whether the source of existence is transcendent or immanent, and singular (One) or plural (Many) in its expression. Discussion of these opposing characteristics traces back to the pre-Socratic Greek philosophers Parmenides and Heraclitus who offer differing conceptualizations of the nature of being and knowing (Graham 2002; Novicevic et al. 2007). Based on Follett's own understanding of dialectical synthesis as integration,[1] we find that her assumptions reflect a synthesis of these opposing pairs that carries through all other conceptual elements of her thinking.

Follett's deepest level of discussion is ontological, often referring to the classical philosophical arguments about existence as the One versus the Many and calling for an integrative alternative to common dualisms that trace to these source assumptions.[2] For Follett, existence is an ever-changing One-becoming-through-Many. "It is the complexity of life which both monists and pluralists seem not to reckon with" (Follett 1919, 579). For this reason, she can be considered both a pragmatist and a process philosopher. Her references to pragmatism are frequent and draw primarily from William James.[3] However, much of her thinking is best reflected in the process philosophy of Alfred North Whitehead, as explained in more detail elsewhere (Stout and Staton 2011).[4]

Whitehead came to Harvard University in 1924, joining the illustrious group of Cambridge intellectuals deeply involved in the American pragmatist movement.[5] He participated in the 1926 Follett-Cabot Seminary, during which Follett discussed the evolving situation and reciprocal relating, emphasizing that "Professor Whitehead, with his conception of an organism as a structure of activities that are continually evolving, had got 'nearer the heart of the truth of this matter than anyone has yet'" (Tonn 2003, 433-34). "In philosophy, our greatest thinkers have given us more than indications of this view of unity. Among living philosophers, I think Professor Whitehead is contributing most to our understanding of this truth" (Follett 2003m, 188). Whitehead's feelings appear to be mutual, suggesting that in the matter of defining justice, "I trust Miss Follett and Plato together" (Tonn 2003, 436). However, it must be noted that Follett's treatise on relational process, *Creative Experience*, was first published in 1924 and many of her ideas were first described in her 1918 publication of *The New State*. Whitehead's *Process and Reality: An Essay in Cosmology* was not published until 1929. While Follett's discussion ran always toward the social level of analysis and Whitehead's remained primarily at the organic level of physical manifestation, the two appear to be contemporaneously mutually influencing in the development of a coherent understanding of reality as a relational process of becoming.

At times Follett is almost dismissive of philosophical debate: "There is no use chasing through the universe for a 'real' you or a 'real' me; it is more useful to study our interactions, these are certainly real" (Follett 2013c, 177). In this sense, her attitude reflects American pragmatism at its core. But her focus on practicalities and actual experience does not deter her from exploration and explication of the profound in the mundane. The following sections detail the multifarious principles that contribute to her ontology: holism, dynamic becoming, relation and relativity, and co-creation. Following her oft-used term of *interweaving*, these ontological principles make up the warp of Follett's philosophy, upon which the wefts of other elements are woven. It is the concept through which all others are reinterpreted to produce Follett's understanding of *integrative process permeating all of social action*, as illustrated in Figure 2.1. The chapter concludes with a discussion of Follett's concerns about language, given its structuring characteristics at the level of ontology (Stout 2012b).[6]

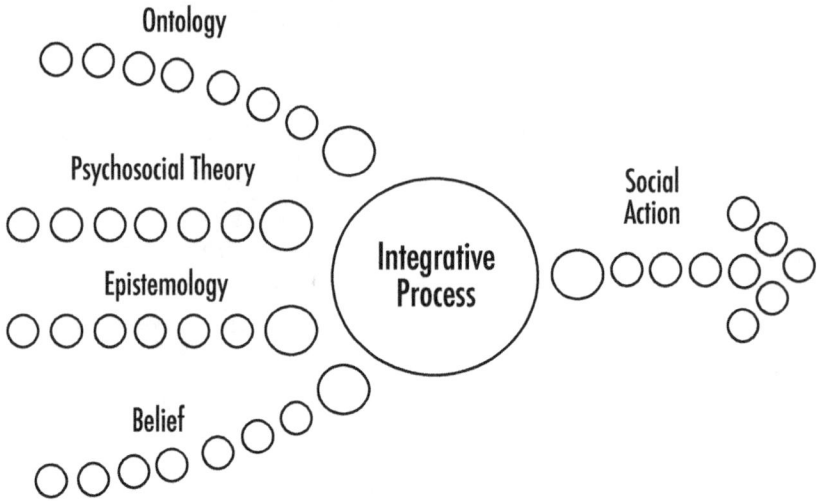

Figure 2.1: Follett's One Permeating Philosophy: Integrative Process

HOLISM

The first ontological principle Follett discusses is the notion of holism: existence is whole and all-inclusive while at the same time accommodating differentiation among its parts.[7] Thus, the terminology Follett uses endeavors to infer wholeness and the ontological impossibility of dualisms and hierarchy. In this way, she seeks to integrate the classical argument over existence as One versus Many into a quality of being that is innately sought: "Wholeness is an irresistible force compelling every member" (Follett 1998, 83) but is never finalized or totalizing. "This is the process of life, always unifying through the interpenetration of the Many—Oneness an infinite goal" (Follett 1998, 284). Follett calls this dynamic wholeness "the total situation," a "happy phrase showing the importance of the outer object of situation as constituent of the behavior process" (Follett 2013c, 55).[8]

Follett notes:

philosophy has long taught us the unity of experience. You can tear it to pieces if you will and find subject and object, stimulus and response, or—you can refuse to; you can claim the right to see it as a relational interplay of forces, as the functioning of a self-creating coherence. Consciousness is the living interplay of self-generating activities. ... The most fundamental idea of philosophy is, I think, the recognition that there is no *Denkform* [thought form] in which as mould [*sic*] all thought is cast, but rather a constant mode of self-generating as thought, a perpetual law of unifying to which the free activity submits itself. (Follett 2013c, 74-75)

This principle carries through to how she understands life: "How can we do away with this artificial separation which is the dry-rot of our life? First we must realize that each has something to give. . . . Let us seek then those bonds which unite us with every other life. Then do we find reality, only in union, never in isolation" (Follett 1998, 191).

Rather than returning to classical thought to develop her thinking, she draws from then contemporary ideas of the Gestalt school of psychology, suggesting that "the *Gestalt* doctrine . . . has long had a place in philosophical thinking" (Follett 2013c, 91). Of contemporary trends, she felt "none is more valuable than the present trend away from atomistic conceptions. Let us therefore look briefly at the *Gestalt* concept which has been called a doctrine of wholes" (91).

Follett clarifies her interpretation of wholeness in some detail in her summary, including a definition of what we would now refer to as *synergy*. "Many writers of the *Gestalt* school say that the whole is 'more' than its constituent parts. I think this word is dangerous; the whole may be *different* from the parts without being *more*. . . . The quarrel over the word *more* is due, I think, to a confusion of thought in regard to a quantitative more and a qualitative more" (Follett 2013c, 98). If we make assumptions that the greater value of the whole is quantitative in nature, "we are making a serious mistake. It would certainly lead us far astray in the social sciences. In politics or economics it would be very dangerous to think of the whole as more or greater than the parts" (98). This is the doorway through which hierarchy enters—One *over* the Many. Furthermore, "those who give a super character to the whole often give it a static character" (99). This is the gateway for giving ontological permanence to the One above the Many. "The dangers of both a super whole and a static whole are seen in a certain treatment of the doctrine of values" (100). If we assume values are quantitative rather than qualitative, the One will always be greater than any of the Many.

Instead of a whole that is separate from and superior to its parts, Follett asserts that the One is *composed* through the ongoing creative experience of the Many in what she describes as "a federalistic growth" (Follett 2013c, 101).[9] Just as "James found that the 'all-form' and the 'each-forms' are not incompatible" (Follett 1998, 265), the parts together are "the whole a-making; this involves a study of whole and parts in their active and *continuous* relation to each other" (Follett 2013c, 102). When considering this as a social process among human beings, and environment is added as a whole a-making, you have "the total situation—also a-making" (Follett 102). Thus, Follett's commonly used term for the One or the whole a-making is *the situation*.

This understanding of the whole a-making does not permit hierarchy because it is a "*self-creating* coherence" (Follett 2013c, 61, emphasis added) as opposed to one that is ordered. Furthermore, the desire to engage in the unifying process "is not a reduction, a simplification, it is the urge to embrace more and more, it is a reaching out, a seeking, it is the furthest possible conception of pluralism, it is pluralism spiritually not materially conceived. Not the 'reduction' to unity but the expansion towards unity is the social process. That is, the expanding process and the unifying process are the same" (Follett 1919, 582).

Indeed, as will be explained in further detail in discussion of her psychosocial theory, Follett insists upon the importance of the individual in its unique qualities. She asserts, "the opposite of all particularity may yet keep its oneness with everything individual, that in fact its authority is derived from nothing else but interweaving *individual* activity" (Follett 2013c, 48).

DYNAMIC BECOMING

It is in the gerundial terminology of *a-making* and *unifying* that Follett's second integrative principle is strung onto the ontological warp—the notion of dynamic becoming as opposed to static being. Follett asserts, "When we have really acquired the dynamic habit of mind which we boast of now, and think always in terms of process, we shall think of both organism and environment, individual and situation, as activities" (Follett 2013c, 129)—"what might be called the *evolving* situation" (55, emphasis added).[10] The hierarchical binary problems of both a static, transcendent One and a static, immanent Many are avoided through acknowledgement that existence is always unfolding in a process of becoming.[11]

The dynamic principle accommodates both potentiality and manifestation within the whole. "The unchangeable and the unchanging are both included in the idea of growth. Stability is neither rigidity nor sterility: it is the perpetual power of bringing forth" (Follett 1998, 100).[12] In other words, the paradox of dynamic becoming is that change itself—potential-ity—is the only thing that is constant. Follett uses James to claim we should accommodate potentiality in social life by always using "the 'trailing and' argument to prove that we can never have a unified state, that there is always something which never gets included. I should use it to prove that we can and must have a unify*ing* state, that this 'and' is the very unifying principle. The 'trailing and' is the deepest truth of psychology . . . The 'trailing and' is man's task for ever and ever—to drag in more spirit, more knowledge, more harmony" (Follett 1998, 302). However, given her understanding of the whole, it is brought in from the enfolded potentiality of the Many, not from an externalized One: "each of these essential parts is the tap from an infinite supply—in every man lives an infinite possibility" (139).[13]

Therefore, Follett assumes that "the process must be emphasized rather than product, that the process is continuous, and that the making of wholes and the breaking of wholes are equally important" (Follett 2013c, 103).[14] Activities of disassembling and assembling are punctuated only by moments of observation, not stasis. Indeed, "there are not, as some systems of phi-losophy imply, two principles of the universe, that of fixity and that of flux, there are—'progressive integrations'" (146).

Accordingly, this is how Follett understands the nature of progressiv-ism—an organic developmental process of disaggregation and aggregation into new wholes that is self-generating as opposed to externally directed or goal-oriented. Indeed, she frequently notes that this reality is reflected in all organic processes and forms: "Unification means sterilization; unifying means a perpetual generating" (Follett 1998, 286). She suggests that "to put the conception of unify*ing* in the place of unity might help to bring monists and pluralists nearer together. Spontaneous unifying is the reality for humanity" (Follett 1919, 582).[15] Follett explains that this process is not aggregative or quantitative in nature, but rather an ongoing qualitative change in the whole through dynamic combinations: "Unifying activity is changing its quality every moment. *La durée* [the long term] does not abandon itself, but rolls itself into the new *durée* endlessly, the qualities interpenetrating so that at every moment the whole is new. Thus unifying activity is changing its quality all the time by bringing other qualities into itself" (581).[16] It is a constantly evolving, One-becoming-through-Many.

In short, "there is no result *of* process but only a moment *in* process" (Follett 2013c, 60). Therefore, "the most important thing to remember about unity is—that there is no such thing. There is only unifying. You cannot get unity and expect it to last a day—for even five minutes" (Follett 2013b, 76). Yet, "a mistake we often tend to make is that the world stands still while we are going through a certain adjustment. And it does not. Facts change, we must keep up with the facts; keeping up with the facts changes the facts. In other words, the process of adjustment changes the things to be adjusted" (Follett 2013h, 85). Indeed, this is the very reason law is based on precedent rather than simple principle: "The legal order today is telling us that precedents are to be interpreted in the light of events always in flux" (Follett 2013c, 31).

This dynamic becoming is juxtaposed to static wholes, to which Follett often refers with the German phrase *ding-an-sich*, or thing-in-itself, referring to the Kantian notion of an objective ontological status of separate things (Many) not mediated by perception or conceptualization. However, she also uses it to differentiate the static from the dynamic: "There is no whole, only an infinite striving for wholeness" (Follett 1998, 249). Therefore, Follett commits herself to the endeavor: "The supreme object of my allegiance is never a thing, a 'made.' It is the very Process itself to which I give my loyalty and every activity of my life" (Follett 1919, 581).

RELATION AND RELATIVITY

Follett's third ontological strand is the principle of relation. Within the dynamic whole, the parts are always in relation and therefore relation itself has ontological status: "The value of every fact depends on its position in the whole world-process, is bound up in its multitudinous relations . . . a fact out of relation is not a fact" (Follett 2013c, 12).[17] Despite the empiricist's urge to do so, Follett insists, "you cannot arbitrarily keep distinct that which is not distinct. Experience is unitary" (Follett 2013c, 146). This means that relation is not something formed *after* becoming—it is *part of* the becoming that all things experience.[18]

Drawing from Holt's (1925) book, *The New Realism*, Follett explains what is happening among seemingly separate parts: "reality is in the relating, in the activity-between" (Follett 2013c, 54). Therefore, "subject and object are equally important and . . . reality is in the relating of these, is in the endless evolving of these relatings" (55). We can only understand life fully through this relating, "for objectivity alone is not reality" (54). "Where then is reality? In the objective situation, or in 'the people'? In neither, but in that relating which frees and integrates and creates" (Follett 2013c, 130).

Follett suggests that the phrase "total relativity" is "rather clumsy," but explains she is "trying to express a total which shall include all the factors in a situation not as an additional total but as a relational total—a total where each part has been permeated by every other part" (Follett 2013h, 79). In other words, the parts "all together constitute a certain situation, but they constitute that situation through their relation to one another. They don't form a total situation merely by existing side by side" (79). That would be simple aggregation or addition with a purely quantitative value. To express how relation fits within the total situation more accurately, she draws upon "the language of the mathematical analogy" (Follett 2013c, 55) that "implies that the variables of this formula *may* be interdependent, either being a function of the other" (56).[19] "Or it would be more accurate to say that all the factors in the situation are going through this process of reciprocal relating" (Follett 2013h, 79). This relational characteristic sets the stage for the fourth and final principle composing Follett's ontological warp; co-creation.

CO-CREATION

Follett alternately refers to *circular response* and various terms for the process of *integration* as co-creative processes. As Follett explains, "the doctrine of circular response involved in the theory of integration gives us creative experience" (Follett 2013c, 116). "But the theory of creative experience given to us by the most profound philosophy throughout the ages, and now so happily strengthened by recent research in several fields, shows that the individual can create without 'transcending.' He expresses, brings into manifestation, powers which are the powers of the universe and thereby those forces which he is himself helping to create, those which exist in and by and through him, are ever more ready to respond, and so Life expands and deepens; fulfils [*sic*] and at the same moment makes possible larger fulfilment [*sic*]" (116).[20]

This concept of creating in the circular response reiterates the assumption that the One is not separate from the Many, but rather co-created by the Many: In a whole a-making, "organism and environment do not 'express' but make wholes" (Follett 2013c, 125). She insists, "every advance in physics, physiology and psychology shows us life as process" (Follett 2013c, 118). "And this is a creating process" (119). However, because of the relational and holistic condition of existence, creating occurs with "reciprocal influence" in the "evolving situation" (57).

In other words, the evolving situation is continually unfolding into "the emergent pattern, the complex emergent whole, [that] is formed by the interacting, the relating, of the constituent factors" (Follett 2003m, 198). The Many are continually interacting and through the unifying process of relating, the One is continually emerging anew. "These three—the interacting, the unifying, and the emerging—are not parts of a process in the sense of steps in a process. There is one simultaneous process, and these three are aspects of that process" (198). Thus, in her later work, Follett sees the co-creating of the total situation reflected in theories of emergence found in biology, psychology, and metaphysics. "'Emerging' is the word which is being used more and more every day by scientists to denote the novelty wherever it appears in evolution" (198).

The synergy described in her understanding of wholeness, the making from potentiality described in her explanations of dynamic becoming, and the variation in quality generated in relation all occur from the process of co-creating. "The relating involves an increment that can be measured only by compound interest. . . . This is the same with all organic growth" (Follett 2013c, 64). Follett argues that "the law of geometrical progression is the law of organic growth, that functional relating has always a plus value. . . . A dynamic psychology gives us instead of equivalents, plusvalents . . . These are the 'novelties' in the psychologist's 'critical' moments of evolution" (73).[21] She links this relational progress to the notion of progressivism writ large: "*Progressive* experience on every level means the creating of plusvalents" (73). It is "the doctrine of circular or integrative behavior" that "gives us hints of that 'mystery moment' which leads from the existing to the new, shows us a *progressive* experience, the way of individual and social development" (xv).

Through this progressive experience, "through circular response we are creating each other all the time" (Follett 2013c, 62). This is a quite complex and comprehensive dynamic process.[22] At core, "the relation between whole and parts is one of circular response" (99). However, the circular response is always a response "to a relating" (73). Thus, co-creation is happening in and among all parts of the whole as well as the products of their relatings. First, there is the relatings *within* the parts in which the individual being is becoming in relation with its environment: "It is I plus the-interweaving-between-you-and-me meeting you plus the-interweaving-between-you-and-me, etc., etc." (Follett 2013c, 63). Then we must add the relation *among* the parts: "I never react to you but to you-plus-me; or to be more accurate, it is I-plus-you reacting to you-plus-me. 'I' can never influence 'you' because you have already influenced me; that is, in the very process of meeting, by the very process of meeting, we both become something different" (62-63). Finally, we must add relatings with the environment to accommodate the total situation engaged in the co-creative process. In sum, relating is simultaneously happening within parts, among parts, and between parts and the environment. Follett notes that if this were to be translated into a mathematical formula, it would be a differential equation or set of differential equations that could only be solved through integration.

Integration is the product of circular response, or more clearly stated, integrating occurs through the process of circular response. Follett assumes that unique parts of the whole differ and that the impulse toward unifying requires the integration of those differences: "This is reality for man: the unifying of differings" (Follett 1919, 585). It is through this integration that new configurations occur and both individual and collective progress occurs. Thus, "integrative experience is always progressive experience" (Follett 2013c, 106). However, this is not a simple forward linear or even upward spiral movement. Because of the constant motion of assemblages within the whole, she does not "ignore the part of disintegration in the creative process . . . disruption may be a real moment in integration . . . yet disruption is only a part of that total life process to which, in its more comprehensive aspect, we may give the name integration" (178).

These moments of integration create a plateau of progressive experience to which the next set of differings respond: "Only integration really stabilizes. But by stabilization I do not mean anything stationary. Nothing ever stays put. I mean only that that particular conflict is settled and the next occurs on a higher level" (Follett 2003b, 35). In other words, that which is co-created through the process of circular response is an integration of differences from which new differings emerge, for which new integratings are co-created, and so forth.[23]

Follett deeply believes in this process and the "inexhaustible resources of life, in the fresh powers constantly springing up. The test of the vitality of any experience is its power to unite into a living, generating activity its self-yielding differences. We seek a richly diversified experience where every difference strengthens and reinforces the other. Through the interpenetrating of spirit and spirit, differences are conserved, accentuated and reconciled in the greater life which is the issue" (Follett 2013c, 302). Ultimately, Follett will translate this ontological process into every aspect of social and political life in her understanding of integrative process permeating all of social action: "The activity of co-creating is the core of democracy, the essence of citizenship, the condition of world-citizenship" (302).

A NOTE ON FOLLETT'S LANGUAGE

Follett insists that linguistic meanings have "nearly always ethical connotations which prejudge, which merely in themselves attribute praise or blame" (Follett 2013c, x). Indeed, such bias and prejudice cannot be avoided because "our very language, overlaid with the ideas and emotions of the race, prevents it" (10). Therefore, she suggests "we should take our language too from the concrete daily happenings" (x)—by which she means the actual processes of creative experience as opposed to the faulty ontological perspective of the status quo. To describe this alternative worldview, language would necessarily be holistic, non-discrete, non-binary, nonhierarchical, and gerundial in character (Stout 2012b).[24, 25]

Western languages do not readily lend themselves to relational process ontology. In fact, much of the English language and its structure connotes separation, dualism, hierarchy, and stasis, as noted by Follett. She argues, "Every day we use many more not-understood symbols, many more whole-words, unanalysed [sic] words, than we ought to" (Follett 2003b, 42). "Whole-words" are problematic because they indicate ontological stasis and atomism—unchanging parts that are considered discrete wholes rather than dynamic and related. "It is the solidity of symbols which make them a danger to us" (Follett 2013c, 170). "Our outlook is narrowed, our chances of success are largely diminished, when our thinking is constrained with the limits of an either-or situation. We should never allow ourselves to be bullied by an either-or" (Follett 2003m, 201).

Alternative symbols are needed that will allow integration, which cannot be achieved if we "let one's thinking stay within the boundaries of two alternatives which are mutually exclusive" (Follett 2003b, 33). Therefore, Follett argues we must "develop the language which will express continuous *qualitative* change" (Follett 1919, 581). By qualitative change, she means that not only are all elements in the universe in a constant dynamic state, but that these changes are meaningful and substantive, not simply different quantities of this or that. The process of becoming changes the quality of expression in every moment because "unifying activity is changing its quality all the time by bringing other qualities into itself" (Follett 1919,

581). Therefore, language should reflect the essence of what potentiality is becoming (e.g., greenness) rather than a superficial, static characteristic (e.g., green).[26]

As noted in the explanation of holism, in addition to inferring false stasis, atomism is the doorway through which hierarchy enters—either the One over the Many or any of the Many over any others of the Many. "Those who speak of hierarchy deal with the quantitative rather than the qualitative: they jump from the making to the thing that is made" (Follett 1919, 581). These hierarchies are exacerbated by language that infers not just separation but dualisms that position one of two opposites as better than the other. Indeed, in her discussions of the state, Follett notes "words often applied to it by the monists: it is 'superior,' it is 'supreme,' it is 'over and above'" (580).[27]

Therefore, Follett insists we need to "discard this quantitative way of thinking and speaking" (Follett 1919, 580) because "there is no above and below. We cannot schematize men as space objects. The study of community as process will bring us, I believe, not to the over-individual mind, but to the inter-individual mind, an entirely different conception" (Follett 1919, 581). She suggests, therefore, "perhaps sometime it may seem advisable to get rid of the words 'over' and 'under'" (Follett 2013a, 35). "I say that executives as well as workers object to being under anyone. I have found among chief executives an objection to being over others and a feeling that these words over and under are unfortunate" (36). However, this would require simultaneously disposing of hierarchies of authority and power, which would mean "we have to change our thinking very radically in this respect" (37).

This is precisely what Follett calls for: "community as process does away with hierarchy, for it makes us dwell in the qualitative rather than in the quantitative" (Follett 1919, 580). To describe this different quality of relating or "*modes of association*" (Follett 1919, 582), she creates new terms: *power-over* describes hierarchy and *power-with* describes its non-hierarchical alternative (Follett 2003j). By inserting the preposition *with* Follett adjusts the mode of association to a relational and participatory one which "connotes functional unity" explaining that "the study of the situation involves the *with* preposition" (Follett 2003c, 62). Similarly, she rejects individualistic authority, replacing it with the nonhierarchical law of the situation (Follett 2013a, b). To describe concepts that replace atomistic understandings of behavior as transaction, she uses words that connote the plural and relation in action, such as *interpenetration, interweaving, interpermeation, integration, harmonization, intermingle, interrelating, co-adaptation, inter-individual,* and *synthesis.*

Follett's language also tends toward the gerundial when possible, noting the related character of ongoing process: "All static expressions should be avoided. . . . We must be careful of the 'eds' because they lead to 'wholes,' the wrong kind of wholes. . . . An 'ed' becomes a stopping place to thought" (Follett 2013c, 58). Similarly, "parts, aspects, factors, elements—all these words are too static; we must differentiate into *activities*" (168). She believes "the value of nouns is chiefly for post mortems" (88). Alternatively, Follett thinks "it better when practicable to keep to verbs" (88). Verbs better reflect her ontology: She seeks to express "the doctrine of 'becoming'" (Follett 1998, 99). "This reciprocal influence, this evolving situation . . . is made clearer if for the words thought, purpose, will in a description of the behavior process, we substitute thinking, purposing, willing" (Follett 2013c, 57). Rather than calling for a unified state, she calls for a unif*ying* state (Follett 1998, 245) and unif*ying* process (Follett 1919, 582). Rather than describing integration or creation, she refers to integrat*ing* and creat*ing* (576, 578).

Follett is also quite fond of "the use of mathematical language" (Follett 2013c, 72) and "the language of the mathematical analogy" (55).[28] She believes "the psychologists who are using the language of calculus have opened up whole reaches of thought for us, for the principles of relation as given by differential calculus help us to a clear understanding of this fundamental principle of life" (64).[29] She feels the language of calculus is most appropriate because "we are brought at once to the heart of every situation: the relating of things that are varying, which makes the relating vary" (67-68). However, in using mathematical language, she cautions, "we must not confuse function as relation and function as quantity . . . function is the activity of relating, it is the operation, not what results. A function is always a functioning" (76).

In order to explicate her relational process ontology, Follett uses and recommends further development of language that is holistic (non-discrete, non-binary, and nonhierarchical) and dynamic in character (gerundial). Such language provides contextualization for less familiar terms such as *integrating* and *circular response.* As she notes, "unless we are thinking wholly in terms of process, the statements I am making will be meaningless" (Follett 2003m, 195). Thus, to properly interpret and apply Follett's process relational ontology, we must disallow meanings that infer a lack of relation, power asymmetries, and stasis of any type. Allowing these kinds of meanings to creep into interpretation will have detrimental effects on the progressive development of both individuals and society due to the structuring nature of language at the most fundamental level of ontology, or as Follett might say, creative experience.

SUMMARY ANALYSIS

Drawing on her metaphor of weaving, Follett's ontology entails a number of principles that compose the warp of her philosophy upon which the wefts of all other conceptual elements are woven: holism, dynamic becoming, relation and relativity, and co-creation. Following her oft-used term of *interweaving*, these ontological principles combine to frame a relational process ontology that she describes with terms like *interpenetration, interweaving, interpermeation, integration, harmonization, intermingle, interrelating, co-adaptation, inter-individual,* and *synthesis*. At all times she infers both dynamism and wholeness, and the ontological impossibility of dualisms and hierarchy. In this way, she seeks to integrate the classical argument over existence as One versus Many into a quality of being that is innately sought: "Wholeness is an irresistible force compelling every member" (Follett 1998, 83). "This is the process of life, always unifying through the interpenetration of the Many—Oneness an infinite goal" (284).

Follett calls this wholeness "the total situation;" a "happy phrase showing the importance of the outer object of situation as constituent of the behavior process" (Follett 2013c, 55). However, she is careful to note that this wholeness is composing rather than encompassing—a "whole a-making; . . . whole and parts in . . . active and *continuous* relation to each other" (102). She explains this co-creative process using "the doctrine of circular response" (116) which describes "reciprocal influence" in the "evolving situation" (57). Taken together, Follett's understanding of dynamic, relational, co-creative, embodied, holism is quite dense; as is the language she uses to explain it. She shares a humorous story about the complexity of her propositions in a parable of a schoolboy frustrated by having to learn and use calculus. The instructor tells the student, "'You will have then to leave this universe; in this one we so often have variations in relation to other variations that we are obliged to learn to think in terms of those conditions'" (70). But for her ultimate purpose of altering governance, these dynamic, relational principles enable a more appealing notion of the state:

I have said that the political pluralists are fighting a misunderstood Hegelianism. Do they adopt the crudely popular conception of the Hegelian state as something "above and beyond" men, as a separate entity virtually independent of men? Such a conception is fundamentally wrong and wholly against the spirit of Hegel. As James found collective experience not independent of distributive experience, as he reconciled the two through the "compounding consciousness," so Hegel's related parts received their meaning only in the conception of total relativity. The soul of Hegelianism is total relativity, but this is the essence of the compounding of consciousness. As for James the related parts and their relations appear simultaneously and with equal reality, so in Hegel's total relativity. (Follett 1998, 266)[30]

Through this relational process understanding, "true Hegelianism finds its actualized form in federalism" (Follett 1998, 267)—Follett's way to describe organic wholes a-making in evolving situations. Because each person is a co-creator, this type of whole is democratically acceptable. Playing the monists against the pluralists, Follett suggests, "our loyalty is neither to imaginary wholes nor to chosen wholes, but is an integral part of that activity which is at the same time creating me" (Follett 1919, 579). Thus, at the level of ontology, Follett establishes her primary, cross-cutting principle: *integrative process*. But to arrive at the fullness of this theory, we must add additional conceptual elements. We turn first to psychosocial theory.

ENDNOTES

1. Indeed, Cabot (1934) suggests Follett's pursuit of integration was informed by Hegel's thesis, antithesis, and synthesis. Similarly, Tonn (2003) notes that Follett's notion of unifying draws in part on the Hegelian method of exposition: thesis, antithesis, and synthesis. We suggest Follett's understanding of integration presages the dialectical synthesis concept of horizon fusion described by Gadamer (1997).

2. Ryan and Rutherford (2000) note that the preference for clear-cut dichotomies is based in the fundamentally contradictory philosophical foundations—their metaphysics. Philosophers are required to base their positions on either the individual or the group as the essential unit of humanity.

3. Banerjee (2008) refers to Follett's "pragmatist ontology of interweaving" (10).

4. Enomoto (1995) also links Follett's thinking to Whitehead.

5. Kaag (2008) provides an important review of the historical relationships among the Cambridge intellectuals, particularly among Follett and Richard and Ella Cabot. He notes that Whitehead and Royce were both professors to Ella Lyman Cabot and the close relationship she had with the younger Follett.

6. Drawing on Maturana and Varela (1992), Shapiro (2003) suggests that the whole is internalized in the individual via languaging.

7. In contemporary physics terms, the universe is an enfolded order (Bohm 1980)—an immanent space to which there is no transcendent other.

8. Tonn (2003) notes that many of the case illustrations of the total situation used in *Creative Experience* are drawn from her colleague Ada Eliot Sheffield (sister of T. S. Eliot), a Boston social worker.

9. This assumption mirrors the Whiteheadian notion of experience as being fundamental from the quantum to universal level of analysis (Mesle 2008). This is likely due to both having drawn from James (1909).

10. In contemporary physics terms, the universe is an unfolding order (Bohm 1980).

11. As Whitehead explains, the world is composed of events and processes (Mesle 2008).

12. Shapiro (2003) links Follett's thinking to emancipatory systems philosophy and general evolutionary thought. "Evolution is defined here as a process of dynamic and internally driven development by which differences unpredictably give rise to new relationships, and relationships unpredictably give rise to new differences, and so on, leading to progressive liberation and capacity for creation" (Shapiro 2003, 586).

13. Here, Follett differs importantly from Whitehead's (1979) notion of eternal objects and God's role in becoming.

14. This is quite similar to the contemporary understanding of assemblages (Deleuze and Guattari 1987) which are in a constant state of reconfiguring, but which are together composing through their myriad connections the whole.

15. Fox (1968) argues that Follett uses unifying, integration, and synthesis interchangeably.

16. Here it would seem that Follett is familiar with Bergson (2001) and his understanding of multiplicity in becoming.

17. As Whitehead explains, relatedness goes "all the way down to the roots of reality" (Mesle 2008, 8).

18. Whitehead (1978) shares this understanding of the principle of relativity and panexperientialism (Griffin 2007).

19. This differentiation between quantitative uniqueness (atomistic) and qualitative uniqueness (relational) is also made by Mesle (2008).

20. This agrees with the Whiteheadian notion that "'creativity' is the universal of all universals characterizing ultimate matter of fact. . . . 'Creativity' is the principle of novelty" (Whitehead 1978, 21). "The universe is thus a creative advance into novelty" (222).

21. Here, Follett seems to refer both to Whitehead's (1979) notion of novelty as a motivation for change as well as the Bergsonian (Bergson and Mitchell 1920) notion of the vital impulse behind evolution.

22. Morton and Lindquist (1997) see in Follett's concept of circular response a foretelling of the contemporary feminist emphasis on a dynamic, relational ontology.

23. This same organic experience is explained by Whitehead (1979) as the manner in which prehensions are momentarily harmonized in actual occasions of concrescence and how becoming is lured toward novelty and increasing complexity.

24. On this point, Whiteheadian language is problematic as it carries forward cultural connotations in the use of static, binary concepts such as hierarchy and dominance. Thus, Follett's attention to language helps to "criticize, improve, and, in some respects, transcend" Whiteheadian thinking (Mesle 2008, 2).

25. This section draws liberally from Stout (2012).

26. Whitehead similarly struggled with the problem of language and the choice between redefining the meaning of existing terms versus creating new ones—both of which can result in confusion (Mesle 2008).

27. Whitehead (1979) does not excise such language from his process philosophy.

28. Tonn (2003) suggests that Follett is influenced by Holt's (1914) use of mathematical concepts and language in *The Concept of Consciousness*.

29. On this point, Follett agrees with Bergson (2007).

30. Follett's knowledge of Hegel came through Anna Boynton Thompson, a student of Josiah Royce's who was Follett's high school history teacher at Thayer Academy (Metcalf and Urwick 1942).

❧ 3 ❧

Follett's Psychosocial Theory

Psychosocial theory refers to our understanding of self and other human beings. These theories tend to focus on the character of *identity* as unitary or decentered and the *social condition* of the individual as embedded or isolated. *Unitary identity* is a static, coherent narrative on a linear teleological path—the Cartesian self. *Decentered identity* is fluid and responsive to changes external to the subject. In terms of the social condition, *embedded* means that the social context is pre-existing and that individuals relate first to the whole and then to one another as individuals. An *isolated condition* means that there is no *a priori* social bond or stable group identity stemming from relation.

The first weft thread Follett weaves onto the warp of her relational process ontology is psychosocial theory. Follett (1998) describes the individual not as a part but as "a whole seen from a special point of view" (66) that is neither particularist nor collectivist.[1] Thus, Follett interprets the psychosocial aspects of *human* being using her ontological principles. The first principle is multidimensional identity, combining her understanding of dynamic holism, or wholes a-making. The second principle is that of relation or circular response, but here as it pertains to people in relation with the total situation. The third principle brought forward is the co-creation of self and group through integration. These principles are fundamental to the rest of her theories, because regardless of what aspect of social action is in question, Follett argues, "we have human problems with psychological, ethical, and economic aspects, and as many more as you like, legal often" (Follett 2003m, 184).

Always with an eye toward practical application, to build her theories about the individual in society, Follett presents her argument in a manner qualitatively different from the standard logic that begins with the individual and then aggregates individuals into groups. Instead, Follett argues that "I am always in relation not to 'society' but to some concrete group" (Follett 1998, 20); thus, "there is only the group and the group-unit" (21). Therefore, "the group *in relation* must be the object of our study if that study is to be fruitful for politics" (10). Indeed, "group organization is to be the new method in politics, the basis of our future industrial system, the foundation of international order" (3).

Consequently, there is only the socially embedded person-in-community, whose identity is neither unitary nor decentered, but rather is formed through both individual and social experience.[2] This reordering of emphasis from individual as a pre-social foundational unit to one created through interrelatings requires that "social psychology . . . concern itself primarily with the interaction of minds . . . the social individual" (Follett 1998, 21). In brief, to understand society, we must understand the group. To understand the group, we must understand the individual in relation. To understand the individual in relation, we must study actual experience and how relational process ontology is expressed in human beings.

Follett supports her line of reasoning with both psychoanalytic and Gestalt theory, arguing that social psychology will likely inform political organization better than prior efforts in political theory and political science. However, as is her habit, Follett also critiques the very theories she uses as the foundation of her ideas. Specifically, she finds fault in how psychoanalytic theory explains integration within the individual, but without considering the experience in a dynamic fashion. Gestalt theory explains how the individual relates to the situation, without considering how the individuals relate to one another or integrated aspects of themselves. Thus, both theories must be amended to include circular response and the resulting process of integration.

To make these adjustments, she draws heavily on William James's understanding of consciousness, Edwin Holt's interpretation of Freudian psychoanalysis, and the Gestalt theory of psychology as explained by Gordon Allport. However, before explicating her alternative theories we must explain the critique she makes to accentuate the differences she sees between what she calls "particularist" individualism (Follett 1998, 125) based on static atomisitic ontology, and what she understands to be "true individualism" (Follett 1998, 74) based on relational process ontology.

CRITIQUE OF SOCIAL THEORY

Follett critiques the received explanations of the individual in society—particularism and collectivism—arguing that these lead only to the *crowd*. Her critiques are based on a combination of observation in community and industry settings, emerging psychoanalytic and psychological theory, and the variety of sources informing her understanding of relational process ontology. Each critique will be discussed in turn.

Particularism

Follett begins her explanation with a critique of individualism as presently understood—particularist individualism—which includes both atomism and pluralism. She says that we first must recognize particularism as a specific *form* of individualism that is distinct from what she terms "true individualism" (Follett 1998, 3). The true "individual we do not yet know, for we have no methods to release the powers of the individual. Our particularism—our *laissez-faire*, our every-man-for-his-own-interests—has little to do with true individualism" (3). Indeed, the era of *laissez-faire* "has not been an individualistic but a particularistic age" (74). She likens the particularist strain of individualism to the passé "'bead' theory of causation which once prevailed in physics" and warns that applying this theory to individuals and their social relations "is equally fatal for sociology" (Follett 2013b, 78). To emphasize this danger, she calls particularism "the tragedy of individualism" (Follett 1998, 3).

To help make her point, Follett takes aim at two fundamental tenets of particularism. First, she roundly roundly strikes down the idea that the individual can exist outside of society in any way, that the individual is a pre-formed, pre-social being "who stands outside and looks at his groups" and about whom "there is something peculiarly sacred" (Follett 1919, 579). In short, Follett asserts "this individual is a myth" (579). Thus, we cannot use this fictional individual as the building block of groups in pluralism or society as a whole, for "society is not a collection of units" (Follett 1998, 75). Secondly, having rejected the possibility of pre-social individuals, she likewise rejects the claim that individuals are solely responsible for their own circumstances: the bootstrap doctrine. Very simply, she says, "there is no such thing as a self-made man" (62).

For Follett particularist individualism is not just mistaken but these basic tenets are profoundly damaging to both individuals and society. The isolated, self-reliant individual is "too fragmentary an existence" (Follett 1998, 314), causing dysfunction in human relations and eroding the social bond. Follett sees this disruption in the way individuals relate to one another, explaining, "particularistic psychology, which gave us ego and alter, gave us sympathy going across from one isolated being to another" (44). Sympathy, from a particularist perspective, Follett defines as an altruistic feeling experienced by ego (self) for alter (other); "sympathy from the outside" rather than "sympathy from the inside" (Follett 2003l, 218). In the former there is a subject-object relationship in which one feels *for*, while the latter is a subject-subject "feeling *with*" (218, emphasis added) as in the concept of empathy.[3] For Follett sympathy from the inside is "the most real, the most vital sympathy" (219), whereas sympathy from the outside reinforces the myth of particularism and allows hierarchical relations to form.

Collectivism

To address the dysfunction created by particularist individualism, Follett argues that we need the "constant recognition that any whole is always the element of a larger whole" (Follett 1998, 306). However, this is not an endorsement of collectivism. She explains that collectivism is a mistaken interpretation of unity as *static*: "when society is given an interest, this tends with some writers to make an entity of the 'social soul,' the 'group mind'" (Follett 2013c, 41). But Follett insists that "there is no static collective will nor 'group mind'" (207). Therefore, "the idea of a collective will as a unifying of wills"—as in homogenization—"must go" (208).

When collectivism focuses on creating static unity rather than active unifying, the door is opened once again to introduce hierarchy and power-over in the form of One-over-Many. A uniform collective will must be achieved through either voluntary imitation or coerced conformity and both present "the danger of thinking that the individual is less important because the collective aspect of life has aroused our ardor and won our devotion" (Follett 1998, 73). "If we find the life of that group consisting chiefly of imitation, we see that it involves no activity of the real self but crushes and smothers it. Imitation condemns the human race" (37).[4] Coerced uniformity is even worse: "Socialization, which people speak of as a supreme virtue, is often a pure crowd idea, the crowd trying to preserve itself as it is" (Follett 2013c, 128).

When social life takes this form, Follett argues that we have only collectivism and the crowd, not true individualism within groups. "We cannot have any genuine collectivism until we have learned how to evolve the collective thought and the collective will" (Follett 1998, 73); and for this we need the group. Thus, the distinction between the crowd and the group is critical for Follett whose social theory begins with the group. Therefore, it is necessary to flesh out her criticism of the crowd and its relationship to the excesses of both particularism and collectivism.

The crowd

For Follett, the types of individualism found in particularism and collectivism both lead to a social grouping she labels the *crowd* and its various derivatives.[5] Reminding us again of the importance of language, she explains, "the words society, crowd, and group are often used interchangeably for a number of people together" (Follett 1998, 85). However, Follett asserts that a crowd is not a group, nor is it society: "we do not find group forces in multitudes: the crowd and the group represent entirely different modes of association" (85).[6] Unfortunately, because particularism and collectivism dominate ideas about human association, Follett laments that "sociology tells us much of the crowd" (Follett 2013c, xi) but nothing of the other modes of association. Therefore, Follett takes on the task of developing a thorough explanation of the distinction between crowds and groups. Crowds are formed either through aggregation or homogenization, while groups are formed through the relating of true individuals engaging in integration.[7]

One method of crowd formation is pluralism, which Follett describes as an outcome of particularism. Pre-social beings aggregate around pre-existing similarities and experience conflict with one another based on pre-existing differences. Pluralistic organizing and competition create what Follett describes as corporate individuals standing side-by-side under one banner, but who are not actually *with* one another because they have not actively made the group together. In other words, the fragmentation of particularism leads to the artificial and temporary connection of contract among competing collectivities, what is typically understood as pluralism. However, for Follett this distinction between being quantitatively *collected* and being qualitatively *with* reflects the problem that "atomism in any form, of groups as well as individuals, means anarchy" (Follett 1998, 305). Thus, she calls this type of side-by-side association the *crowd*.

Particularist crowds may also become a *herd*. In this situation, individuals congregate based on similarities for the purpose of "seeking the 'comfort' of fellowship" (Follett 1998, 89). While Follett recognizes the emotional need for fellowship that can drive the herd, she questions the mode of association through which it is achieved. "Only further study will teach us to distinguish how much herd instinct and how much group conviction contribute to our ideas and feelings at any one time and what the tendencies are when these clash" (90). Of particular concern is the inability of the herd to accommodate the dynamic nature of individual identity.

In contrast, collectivism yields a crowd Follett describes as an "undifferentiated mass" (Follett 1998, 87) of individuals that creates similarity by removing difference through domination or imitation. "There are no 'differences' in the crowd mind. Each person is swept away and does not stop to find out his own difference" (86). This form of crowd is moved by suggestion and "does not distinguish between fervor and wisdom" (86). Thus, the collectivist crowd is a unified mass held together by crowd emotion and a sense of belonging. "It is a crowd emotion if we all shout 'God save the King.' Suggestibility, feeling, impulse—this is usually the order in the crowd mind" (85). This emotional fervor can transform a collectivist crowd into a *mob*, which is "this crowd emotion carried to an extreme" (88).

All expressions of the crowd—crowd, herd, mass, and mob—lead to homogeneity, where "unanimity is largely superficial and is based on the spread of similar ideas, not the unifying of differences" (Follett 1998, 86).[8] Indeed, both pluralist aggregation of particularist individuals and homogenization within collectivism both attempt to ignore or eliminate difference. Therefore, crowd-association limits the possibilities for social progress, because "the essential evil of crowds is that they do not allow choice, and choice is necessary for progress" (87). As a result, the "large accomplishments of men are not made in crowd-association" (Follett 2013c, xi). Indeed the two understandings of the group lead to two problematic assertions: "(1) that social evolution depends upon individual progress with imitation by the crowd, (2) that evolution means struggle and the survival of the fittest" (93). Follett argues that neither assumption leads to the highest level of individual or social progress.

In considering the ongoing problems of crowd-mentality, Follett fears "we have not yet learned how to live together" (Follett 1998, 3) in a way that encourages active and purposeful co-creation. "If experience is to be progressive, another principle of human association must be found" (Follett 2013c, x)—integration. Thus, Follett embarks upon defining her alternative approach to psychosocial theory.

REVISING INDIVIDUAL AND GROUP PSYCHOLOGY

Having fleshed out her critiques of psychosocial theory, Follett revises individual and group psychology to match her relational process ontology.[9] She asserts that we cannot define the individual outside of groups, as in particularism, nor can we define the individual as coterminous with the group, as in collectivism.[10] These psychosocial theories can only help us understand the crowd. Instead we must understand the individual-in-relation; the true individual in the group. Therefore, rather than using sociology based on particularism or collectivism, Follett employs psychological theory to explain and construct an alternative understanding of the group individual. As might be expected, the principles of relational process ontology provide the metrics against which all potential psychological theories are evaluated. "Any individual psychology which has not recognized the unifying nature of experience, any social psychology which has failed to see this, has dealt not with life but with abstractions from life" (Follett 2013c, 113).

In Follett's time, psychology was on the cusp of recognizing circular response and was beginning to reject the static psychological underpinnings of particularism: ego (self) and alter (other). "Now that we know that there is no such thing as a separate ego, that individuals are created by reciprocal interplay, our whole study of psychology is being transformed" (Follett 1998, 19). She demonstrates with an anecdote regarding the debate between agency and social conditioning. Follett's response requires both: "Only recently I was surprised to see the question asked by a psychologist: 'Is behavior internally or externally conditioned?' The factors of intra and extra-organic stimulation are not only equally important but are bound up together. They must be considered simultaneously. We have now a wholly dynamic psychology" (Follett 2013c, 66).

To formulate this dynamic psychology Follett draws upon two primary theories: psychoanalysis and Gestalt psychology. The complimentary pairing of these theories provides the basis for understanding the psychosocial dynamics that produce the true individual and the group: the circular response of wholes a-making and co-creating through integration.[11]

Psychoanalytic theory

Follett first draws from Freudian psychoanalytic theory, considering the interrelationship between emotional motivation and experience. She relies on Holt's interpretation of Freud, who explains that "psychology now gives us 'desire' as the key word of our individual life" (Follett 2013c, xiii). Follett accepts this but with the caveat that a limited view of desire-based motivation can lead back to particularism where the individual is in a subject-object relationship with others and the environment.[12] "We cannot say if we would be exact that the individual acts upon and is acted upon, because that way of expressing it implies that he is a definite, given, finished entity, and would keep him apart merely as an agent of the acting and being acted on. We cannot put the individual on one side and society on the other, we must understand the complete interrelation of the two" (Follett 1998, 61). When psychoanalysis neglects the interpenetration of desires and environment Follett warns "the therapeutics of the psycho-analyst would contradict his theory if he regarded unconscious wishes as unchangeable" (Follett 2013c, 121).

Follett believes Holt avoids this pitfall by expanding on the relation-ship between individual and environment in which desire formation arises. Instead of a subject-object relationship with the environment where desires become static ends, individual desires are constantly being created anew in the relational situation. According to Follett, Holt defines "experience as an interplay of forces, as the activity of relating leading through fresh relatings to a new activity, not from purpose to deed and deed to purpose with a fatal gap between, as if life moved like the jerks of mechanical toys with only an external wire-puller to account for the jerks, or a too mysterious psychic energy" (Follett 2013c, 80-81). In other words, life "is a process" (81); an ongoing interconnected set of experiences driven forward by wishes in their relatings. Thus, psychoanalysis must allow a deeper understanding of rela-tional action in which we "look for purpose within the process itself" (80).

When we focus on the process instead of static ends, "we can see in our own lives that the urge is always the lack; the goal changes as we try one means after another of meeting that lack" (Follett 2013c, 81). This is never a simple scenario of need (stimulus) and fulfillment (response). Indeed, "the need comes as need only when the possible satisfaction of need is already there. There is no gap in the process. The automobile does not satisfy wants only, it creates wants; this is the meaning of our formula for sociology. The automobile was not invented to solve the farmers' problems. The purpose in front will always mislead us. Psychology now gives us end as moment *in* process" (81). By seeing a given end as a mere snapshot in time within an ongoing process, within the total situation, Follett argues we can begin to understand the interrelationship between desire and the total situation.

To this understanding, we must add knowledge of an ongoing integrating of desires both within the individual and among individuals:

> The Freudian psychology, as interpreted and expanded by Holt gives us a clear exposition of the process of integrating in the individual. It shows us that personality is produced through the integrating of "wishes," that is, courses of action which the organism sets itself to carry out. The essence of the Freudian psychology is that two courses of action are not mutually exclusive, that one does not "suppress" the other. It shows plainly that to integrate is not to absorb, melt, fuse, or to reconcile in the so-called Hegelian sense. The creative power of the individual appears not when one "wish" dominates others, but when all "wishes" unite in a working whole. (Follett 1919, 576)

In other words, multifarious desires within the individual are integrated in the process of psychological development, while the multitudinous desires of individuals are integrated in the group process of social development.

To further delineate between desire as static end and ongoing process, Follett employs gerundial language: "I should like, for social psychology, to express it as follows: Thinking (willing, purposing) is *specific* relating of the interdependent variables, individual and situation, each thereby creating itself anew, relating themselves anew, and thus giving us the evolving situation" (Follett 2013c, 89). This reframing of the psychoanalytic dynamic is a reiteration of the ontological circular response applied to both individual and group psychology. At the psychosocial level, circular response helps us to understand "behavior as a function of the interweaving between the activity of organism and the activity of environment, [and] gives us a new approach to the social sciences" (79). Therefore, Follett draws upon Gestalt theory to clarify her thinking about the group individual.

Gestalt theory

Follett uses "the *Gestalt* theory" and its "concept of wholes" (Follett 2013c, 79) to further explicate the relationship between individual and environment. Follett begins with the Gestalt concept of "figure and ground" in which she sees "a rough analogy to individual and situation" (109-110); two wholes that are mutually defining. Thus, the Gestalt school "denies that physical, psychical, or social situations are made up of elements in a plus-plus relation. The whole, they tell us, is determined, not only by its constituents, but by their relation to one another" (Follett 2003m, 185-86).

However, while Gestalt theory brings unifying holism to group and social psychology, Follett (2013c) must attend to two "fatal" (103) mistakes in the theory: (1) the failure to recognize the total situation as a whole, and (2) the tendency to depict wholes as static rather than dynamic and engaged in circular response. These critiques are interrelated and are therefore explicated jointly. We begin with the two wholes of Gestalt, individual and environment, and then explain Follett's amendments to the theory.

Considering the individual itself as a whole, Follett argues that Gestalt has shown the error of the "dissection . . . method of traditional psychology" (Follett 2013c, 115-16), which aims to understand intrapersonal components of personality and experience as an aggregation of their respective parts. But the individual is not merely a collection of traits to be analyzed in isolation and then reassembled to construct the whole. Instead, Gestalt psychology "tells us of the psychical states and processes whose characteristic properties and activities differ from the properties of their so-called parts" (92). For instance, "personality can never be revealed to us by a study of its constituent traits" (95). Likewise, "perceptions have a quality in addition to the sum of the single sensory excitations . . . Split it into its parts and the essence of the experience vanishes" (92). Drawing from psychoanalyst Edward J. Kempf, Follett calls this the "integrative unity, of a functional whole" (Follett 2003m, 185).

Further, just as the whole vanishes when we attempt to dissect and study the parts, those "elements of experience" themselves are not "susceptible of isolation" (Follett 2013c, 110-11) because "no single characteristic of a man has much meaning until it is understood in its relation to his other characteristics" (96). "Thus in all our study, from that of the simplest perceptual experience, or the physiological structures underlying that experience, up to the work in the field of personality, the same thing is found, the necessity of studying wholes because the nature of the whole is different from that of the parts and could not be deduced from the parts" (94).[13] This leads Follett to be highly critical of "personality studies . . . which tends to divorce person and situation," an endeavor she sees as "so common a blunder in the studies of these psychologists that it constitutes a serious weakness in their work" (60). The individual must be understood as a whole that includes "our perceptual experience, our personal experience, our social experience" (113). Neither the whole nor its parts can be understood in isolation because "the personality in action cannot be studied apart from that general setting within which it acts"—its environment (110).

As with figure and ground, the individual "must be set off against a background of some sort else it is nonexistent" (Follett 2013b, 110). Thus, the environment is the second whole of Gestalt. Follett suggests, however, that environment is often misconceived; it is not merely a backdrop against which the figure of the individual is placed. She explains that "in all social research we see that we cannot dismiss 'social environment' with the mere phrase and let it go at that" (107). The environment is not so inconsequential. Neither, however, does the relevant whole of the environment encompass all of existence. "When we say total environment we of course do not mean total 'total environment'" (109). Instead, environment is "that which is in such immediate relation to the individual that its forces can be reckoned with both as cause of and effect of his activity" (109). Thus, the environment and the individual are defined in relation to one another: "These can never be studied separately and then brought together" (109).

To better demonstrate the relationship between whole-individual and whole-environment, Follett recounts the experience of a social worker trying to help a young boy by providing multiple services. In piecing together the various services that are needed the social worker "is concerned not merely with the child's responses to environment; she must understand that child's behavior is not, to speak exactly, a function of social environment, but a function of the continuous relating of child and environment" (Follett 2013c, 106). These ongoing relatings allow the social worker "to find what we are calling here the 'whole' character of that environment" (107). In other words, because the individual and environment are mutually defined and impacting, these wholes become parts of the new whole; the situation. This addition of a third whole, *the situation*, is Follett's first amendment to Gestalt.

For Follett, then, "'the psychological situation' is always a total situation" (Follett 2013c, 102) that contains the individual and the affected/ affecting environment. But, simply adding this third whole is not sufficient. Continuing with her example of the social worker and the child, Follett demonstrates that these relatings are not between static part-wholes, nor is the total situation-whole static. The adjustment of the child is "not to a static environment. The various and varying activities of the child relate themselves to the various and varying activities around him which constitute his social environment" (105). The total situation is a "complex emergent whole, [that] is formed by the interacting, the relating, of the constituent factors" (Follett 2003m, 198). Therefore, Follett insists Gestalt theorists "must explain the relation of whole to parts as well as of parts to one another, but this they cannot do satisfactorily, I think, without including some description of circular behavior" (Follett 2013c, 99). There must be an accounting for the fact that "you cannot alter any feature [of the whole] without producing repercussions which alter the whole" (Follett 2003m, 188).

Again, Follett sees the problem of assumed stasis reflected in language as an opening for hierarchy. "Many writers of the *Gestalt* school say that the whole is 'more' than its constituent parts. I think this word is dangerous" (Follett 2013c, 98). The language of prioritizing the whole over its parts sets Gestalt theorists up to understand wholes as end products, as the epitome: the One-over-Many. Using this language, once a whole is identified, Gestalt theorists are forced to "come to a stopping place, or at any rate a gap, in their exposition" and therefore "with some the whole seems to be a moment of rest between activities" (99). If one rests in this gap, individual and environment are static. Attention becomes "riveted on the product to the neglect somewhat of the process. In drawing attention so constantly to the uniqueness of the whole, the moreness of the whole, they seem rather to discourage interest in the making of the whole" (103). "To no doctrine must we make swifter or more emphatic denial" (99). Therefore, Follett insists upon her second amendment of Gestalt: wholes are not static but relationally dynamic through circular response.

Follett explicitly corrects for this "fatal mistake wherever it exists" (Follett 2013c, 103) through her purposeful repetition of the ontological whole a-making in the psychosocial phrase "the making of the whole" (103). This change in language can help Gestalt theorists illustrate "a fuller understanding of the dynamic nature of their wholes" wherein "the whole is itself as much a part of the entire process, is itself interweaving with the parts at the same time that the parts are interweaving to make the whole" (99). This interweaving of individual, environment, and total situation places all three dynamic wholes in the process of circular response. The whole-environment "too is a whole a-making, and the interknitting of these two wholes a-making [individual and environment] creates the total situation—also a-making" (102). Follett insists "no penetrating psychological study, no penetrating study of social conditions, is possible without a study of these three wholes a-making" (102). We must consider "not merely the totalness [*sic*] of the situation, but the nature of the totalness [*sic*]" (Follett 2003m, 192). In other words, the total situation "is never a total picture; it is a total activity in which the activity of individual and activity of environment constantly interweave" (Follett 2013c, 106).[14]

In sum, there are "three fundamental principles to guide us in our study of social situations: (1) that my response is not to a rigid, static environment, but to a changing environment; (2) to an environment which is changing because of the activity between it and me; (3) that function may be continuously modified by itself" (Follett 2013c, 73). We must consider the "whole situation as it develops, as the factors interknit to make the whole developing situation" (109) and "this interacting is the 'total situation' of recent psychology" (105). "We must remember that we should always mean by that [total situation] not only trying to see every factor that influences the situation, but even more than that, the relation of these factors to one another" (Follett 2003m, 187). The total situation is always in a process of becoming co-created by the individuals and the environment in the total situation interpenetrating through circular response at all levels of analysis. The individual, environment, and total situation are always assembling the whole and are being assembled by the whole through circular response, if not also through conscious efforts toward integration. Thus, we turn to Follett's explication of both of these psychosocial dynamics.

Psychosocial circular response

Psychosocial, as opposed to ontological, circular response is explained by psychoanalytic theory as the process of forming and integrating desires at the individual level of analysis. However, following Follett's amended Gestalt theory circular response permeates all aspects of individual and group identity formation and is "the psychological term for the deepest truth of life" (Follett 2013c, 116).[15] "Through circular response we are creating each other all the time" (62).[16] This means that "the individual is not adjusted to society; there is a creating relation between them. . . . We are making our environment anew all the time, but that new environment is at the same time recreating us" (128).[17] Each adjustment changes the individual and the group, resulting in further adjustments that again change both individual and group, in an ongoing process.[18] Always attentive to accurately reflecting process in language, Follett advises "henceforth we should use the word adjustment in social situations only if we understand it as an aspect of circular behavior" (129).

In her explication of such circular behavior, Follett relies on the concept of circular reflex found in S. T. Bok's article, "The Reflex-Circle," published in 1917 in Amsterdam, along with Holt's unpublished lectures that explain "the reflex circle and the functional theory of causation" (Follett 2013c, 78).[19] Combining the work of both scholars, Follett first dismisses the traditional "reflex arc" in which a sensory experience from the environment produces a mental trigger followed by an action or response. She argues the reflex arc perpetuates a particularist subject-object relationship in which the subject is constantly responding to external stimuli "as passively as the woodshed accepts the wood" (54). Follett dismisses this idea: "the subject is no more 'a mere reflex arc' than it is an evangelical soul" (55).[20] However even in its stasis, the reflex arc is useful as a starting point as it "will throw much light on the interdependent variables of the formula [of circular response] when we come to use that formula for social psychology" (59), beginning with the subject-object relationship of stimulus-response.

Follett argues that the subject-object relationship within the reflex arc reinforces the separation of subject and environment, even dividing academic disciplines of study. "In the arts, especially painting, the swing of the pendulum between 'subjectivity' and 'objectivity' is most interestingly apparent. In psychology we have the introspectionists and the behaviorists" (Follett 2013c, 54). But both disciplines assume discrete, static subjects of study: internal mental states as separate from external expression. Although behaviorists *seem* to study activity or process, "the neuro-muscular mechanisms of the behaviorists tend in the hands of some writers (only in some) to become as static as the old 'mental states.' Behavior 'pattern' is a figure of speech and not altogether a good one. We shall have, if we are not careful, as much trouble with the 'patterns' of the behaviorists as the behaviorists have felt they had with the 'minds' of the older psychologists" (66).

Thus, Follett's focus on relational activity in process is not "not a wholesale endorsement of what has been called behaviorism" (Follett 2013c, 90). So long as we continue to conceive of subject and object as isolated entities, Follett worries "I do not see how we can run fast enough from one to the other to keep ourselves within the region of truth" (54). She sees the work of both Holt and Bok as "taking a step beyond this" (54) because circular reflex "implies the possible reciprocal influence of subject and object" (55). This insight shows us that the activity of the individual is only in a certain sense caused by the stimulus of the situation because that activity is itself helping to produce the situation which causes the activity of the individual.

In other words behavior is a relating not of 'subject' and 'object' as such, but of two activities" (Follett 2013c, 60). This means "in every situation our own activity is part of the cause of our activity. We respond to stimuli which we have helped to make" (Follett 2003m, 194). Therefore, "what physiology and psychology now teach us is that part of the *nature* of response is the change it makes in the activity which caused so-to-speak the response, that is, we shall never catch the stimulus stimulating or the response responding. The importance of this cannot be overestimated. Stimulus is not cause and response the effect" (Follett 2013c, 60). Rather than a reflex arc "there is *circular* as well as *linear* response, and the exposition of that is the most interesting contribution of contemporary psychology to the social sciences" (Follett 2003b, 44).

The continued acceptance of the reflex arc and the strong hold static, particularist ontology has within psychosocial theory is problematic for Follett. "Circular response seems a simple matter, quite obvious, something we must all accept. Yet every day we try to evade it, every day we act and hope to avoid the inescapable response. . . . I have to put it this way: that response is always to a relation. I respond, not only to you, but to the relation between you and me" (Follett 2003b, 45). "The ignoring of this [condition] is why we find in some psychoanalysts an over-simplification" (Follett 2013c, 120). It is only with the incorporation of circular response in psychosocial theory that we find a synthesis position that eliminates the pendulum swing between agency and conditioning; the individual is both reacting to the environment and changing the environment simultaneously. "To sum up this point: the most fundamental thought about all this is that reaction is always reaction to a relating. Bok finds it in the neuro-muscular system. Integrative psychology shows us organism reacting to environment plus organism" (62).

Thus, it is not enough to consider circular response as merely an ongoing reciprocal relating between subject and environment. "On physiological, psychological and social levels the law holds good: response is always to a relating" (Follett 2013c, 63). As she often does, Follett uses a simple example to illustrate: "A good example of circular response is a game of tennis. A serves. The way B returns the ball depends partly on the way it was served to him. A's next play will depend on his own original serve plus the return of B, and so on and so on. We see this in discussion. We see this in most activity between one and another" (Follett 2003b, 44). Each response is not simply to the action of the other individual but to the ongoing relatings between the individuals within the total situation.

In sum, we can consider "the circular reflex as a law which observation shows us as operating on infra-personal, personal and social levels" (Follett 2013c, 59). At the ontological level of analysis, an individual is physiologically in circular response with the environment. At the psychological level of analysis, the multifarious dimensions of the human being are in circular response creating identity. At the social level of analysis, the multitudinous desires of all involved in the total situation are in circular response, creating the potential for both difference and integration. Thus, "the social bond is a psychic relation" (Follett 1998, 76) where "psychical self-unitings" are "freed from the limitations of time and space" (77). It is this consideration of circular response at the social level of analysis that leads Follett to her next psychosocial principle: *integration*.

Psychosocial integration

Bringing together her revised psychoanalysis and Gestalt theories, Follett formulates an understanding of the psychosocial condition in which individuals are wholes engaged in circular response with the environment, together interweaving the total situation a-making. "What we may now call circular response or circular behavior we see every day as we observe and analyze human relations, social situations" (Follett 2013c, 61). It is through circular response that the total situation a-making, and the whole-parts a-making, are constantly emerging. "Every social process has three aspects: the interacting, the unifying, and the emerging. . . . These three . . . are not parts of a process in the sense of steps in a process. There is one simultaneous process, and these three are aspects of that process" (Follett 2003m, 198). This is an ongoing organic process; an ontological and psychosocial inevitability.

Recognizing circular response is not enough, however, to avoid the pathologies of the crowd and its various manifestations, *purposeful* action is required—circular *behavior*. Through integrative behavior circular response is elevated to conscious activity because "integrative behavior means circular behavior which implies the continuity of experience—an important psychological conception" (Follett 2013c, 107). In other words, integration is "circular behavior"; or "circular response" (129) as applied to social interaction. As such, "circular behaviour [*sic*] is the basis of integration" (Follett 2003j, 105) and integration requires intentionality: "To sum up. The conception of circular response, of integrative behavior, cuts under the meaning of adjustment in ordinary use and gives us adjustment as a creating relation" (Follett 2013c, 129). As Cabot (1934) explains integration, it is composed of mutual evocation, understanding, and uniting of perspectives: "The process is circular or spiral. The evoking is the uniting.

The understanding is the evoking. The uniting is the understanding. As each element plays into all the rest and receives them all, we grow in knowledge and in character" (82). Thus, Follett describes integration as "the basic law of life" (Follett 2003c, 65).[21]

By this Follett does not mean we are to engage simply in "social activities" as this term "does not give us the process described here" (Follett 2013c, 255). Indeed, Follett suggests steering clear of the term "social" altogether: "To most people the word social does not connote that *functional unity* which I think the most valuable conception of contemporary thinking" (256). Instead of the "abstract word social," Follett insists "we must substitute the wholly concrete word integrating" (256). Integration is not just a collection of generic social activities and not just passive circular response. "The heart of the truth about integration is the connection between the relating of two activities, their interactive influence, and the values thereby created" (53). Thus, integration depicts the intentional process of creating "*functional unity*" (256) continually emerging from a conscious effort, the co-creative process of true individuals actively engaging in circular behavior.

Integrative behavior is therefore part of a "social process [that] is a process of coöperating experience" (Follett 2013c, 30) that "cannot be imposed by an outside body. It is essentially, basically, by its very nature, a process of auto-controlled activity" (Follett 2013h, 82). Cooperative experience in integration allows us to avoid the collectivist impulse "to adapt ourselves to a situation—we are all more necessary to the world than that" as well as the particularist impulse "to mould [*sic*] a situation to *our* liking—we are all, or rather each, of too little importance to the world for that" (Follett 2003b, 49). Instead, integration allows us "to take account of that reciprocal adjustment, that interactive behaviour [*sic*] between the situation and ourselves which means a change in both the situation and ourselves" (49). For this to occur, integration requires "a responsible attitude toward our experience—a conscious and responsible attitude" (Follett 2003c, 50). This "*conscious* attitude toward experience means that we note the change which the developing situation makes in ourselves; the situation does not change without changing us" (65). Therefore, integration synthesizes agency and social construction: "Adjusting in the sense of integrating is the perfect union of submission and mastery" (Follett 2013c, 129).

As will be further discussed in reference to her ethics, Follett is insistent that "there *is* a technique for integration" (Follett 2013b, 68) and the development of the normative rationale for active participation in integration resurfaces as an important component of Follett's political, economic, and administrative theories. While ontological circular response and integration are always occurring, it is only when they are brought into the psychosocial domain that there can be conscious integration of the multidimensional self along with intentional integration with others and the environment. From this psychosocial process, we find true individuals forming groups in what Follett refers to as "the new individualism" (Follett 1998, 73).

THE NEW INDIVIDUALISM

With these critiques and revised psychological theories in hand, Follett is prepared to explicate what integration produces at the psychosocial level of analysis: the true individual and the group. Each will be discussed in turn, noting that the order in which they are discussed does not have any substantive meaning. For Follett, the individual and the group are integral to one another and cannot be understood alone.

The true individual

Reviewing her amended psychoanalysis and Gestalt theories, Follett explains that for the individual whole a-making "experience is not a matter of instincts or sensations or reflexes—or of anything else atomistic" (Follett 2013c, 98) so we must "no longer think of personality as a static entity, but as 'so far integrated behavior'" (207). Identity is both relational and dynamic, constantly created anew through the relatings of its internal traits and the relatings with the external environment and total situation.[22] Beginning with the individual whole, Follett envisions humans as an ensemble of biological, emotional, intellectual, psychological, and spiritual aspects interweaving with the environment. The multidimensional, relational individual exists through "collaboration with all the powers of the universe. Man lives on several planes and his development depends on the uniting of them" (145-46). Follett describes the individual as a multifaceted being where a complex set of identities, personalities and experiences are integrated into a dynamic whole a-making that is the true individual.[23] Following James, she explains "since man is a complex of experiences there are many selves in each one" (Follett 1998, 20). The very nature of the individual is "manifold being" (291).

Follett claims, "The state will never get the whole of man by his trying to divide himself into parts. A man is not a father at home, a citizen at the polls, an artisan at work, a business man in his office, a follower of Christ at the church. He is at every moment a Christian, a father, a citizen, a worker, if he is at any time these in a true sense. We want the whole man in politics" (Follett 1998, 291-92). These selves can be at times conflicting but they are all in relation to one another within the whole-self, and none is diminished by the others. "The miracle of spirit is that it can give itself utterly to all these things and yet remain unimpaired, unexhausted, undivided. I am not a serial story to be read only in the different instalments [*sic*]" (318). Indeed, the whole-self is all of these things together and different from any one aspect or simple aggregation of characteristics.

Thus, the dynamic nature of manifold being is not limited to the inter-relatings of *internal* aspects of self. It is also expressed through a complex relational identity which interpenetrates with other multidimensional whole-selves—all of whom are "created by reciprocal interplay" (Follett 1998, 19) in circular response. "The truth is that the self is always in flux weaving itself out of its relations" (Follett 1919, 577). When this is recognized "the fallacy of self-and-others fades away and there is only self-in-and-through-others" (Follett 1998, 8). In other words "there is no way of separating individuals" (60) because "what we think we possess as individuals is what is stored up from society. . . . We soak up and soak up and soak up our environment all the time" (62).[24] As multidimensional selves, individuals are engaged in the ongoing process of integrating both internal traits and external interrelatings, both of which are formulated through circular response. Thus, "the individual is not a unit but a centre [*sic*] of forces (both centripetal and centrifugal)" (75), a "centre [*sic*] of consciousness" (Follett 1919, 580), "a point in the social process rather than a unit in that process" (Follett 1998, 60).

But, the relatings within and between whole-selves in this social process always exist in relation to the total situation: "We, persons, have relations with each other, but we should find them in and through the whole situation" (Follett 2013f, 24). At the social level of analysis, the total situation is often called society—the social ground against which the individual is figured. For the true individualism, "the relation of the individual to society is not action and reaction, but infinite interactions by which both individual and society are forever a-making" (Follett 1998, 61). In other words the individual does not exist outside the whole of society, instead "we *find* the individual through the group, we *use* him always as the true individual—the undivided one—who, living link of living group, is yet never embedded in the meshes but is forever free for every new possibility of a forever unfolding life" (Follett 1998, 295).[25]

To isolate the individual from these varying relationships is to sever this link. "We cannot have any sound relations with each other as long as we take them out of the setting which gave them their meaning and value. The divorcing of persons and situation does a great deal of harm" (Follett 2013f, 24). The co-creation of identity that happens in integration is the core of Follett's psychosocial theory: "the ceaseless interplay of the One and the Many by which both are constantly making each other" (Follett 1919, 580). The result of this dynamic and situated nature of human being is that "our definition of individuality must now be 'finding my place in the whole' . . . But my place is a matter of infinite relation, and of infinitely changing relation" (Follett 1998, 65). Through active integration the individual consciously contributes and responds to his relatings and through these relatings the individual, in turn, is continually co-created anew. Thus, throughout the act of integrating, co-creative action and experience are what sustain the true individual "because his sustenance is relation and he seeks forever new relations" (Follett 1919, 580). As a result, the various facets of identity are in constant evolution. "For just as the organism is responding to many stimuli at the same moment (through sight, hearing, touch, etc.), so man is responding to many people, many duties, many demands, many aspects of the life around him. The integrating of the former responses makes the normal physiological life; the integrating of the latter, the 'balanced' individual" (Follett 2013c, 123).

Taken together, the multidimensional, complex, relational, dynamic self is co-created through circular response with the environment, integration within the self, and integration of the self with others in a variety of groups out to the societal level of analysis. This relatedness produces a sense of belonging or a "consciousness of oneness" (Follett 1998, 45) that is fostered and developed through the ongoing integrative process of life: "Community is a process . . . community is a *creative* process. It is creative because it is a process of integrating" (Follett 1919, 576). "Community is that intermingling which evokes creative power. What is created? Personality, purpose, will, loyalty" (577). From this community comes "true individualism, that is, with the individual as consciously responsible for the life from which he draws his breath and to which he contributes his all" (Follett 1998, 3). Therefore, we turn to her explication of how groups, as opposed to crowds, are co-created by true individuals engaged in the ongoing process of integrating.

The group

Follett argues that if there is to be social progress we must learn to associate in groups rather than crowds, which requires fully understanding their differences. She reminds us that "suggestion is the law of the crowd, interpenetration of the group" (Follett 1998, 86) and that "a crowd is an undifferentiated mass; a group is an articulated whole" (Follett 1998, 87). Therefore, "in crowds we have unison, in groups harmony" (86). This means that groups are not aggregations around a single issue or similarity and they are not unified masses; they are made of articulated parts that interpenetrate to create an integrated whole. This is a qualitative, not quantitative difference—"not one of degree but of kind" (87).[26]

Follett's group synthesizes the fragmented parts of particularism with the unified whole of collectivism and creates a third alternative for social action; the integrated group. She seeks "not only a psychology which looks at us as we are, but a psychology which points the way to that which we may become. . . . Conscious evolution means giving less and less place to herd instinct and more to the group imperative" (Follett 1998, 91). To move from the crowd, herd, mass, or mob to the group requires integration of difference through cooperation as opposed to imitation.[27] Follett recognizes that the idea of cooperation is not new. In fact "many forms of cooperation are being tried" but she insists that "some one [sic] must analyze the psychological process of the generation of cooperative activity" (91).

Follett obliges, explaining that, in contrast to the crowd, when the group is formed through integration "the process of making these decisions by the interpenetrating of thought, desire, etc., transfers the centre [sic] of consciousness from the single I to the group I. The resulting decision is that of the two-self. It is the same with a three-self, a several-self, perhaps a village-self" (Follett 1919, 578). This group-self is not part of an aggregated crowd or the uniform mass acting and speaking in emotional unison. Just as the individual does not merely adapt to the situation, the individual also does not forgo her uniqueness for the group. Follett is staunch about this common misconception: "Before I leave this point, let me call particularly to your attention that this reciprocal relating, co-ordinating, unifying, is a process which does not require sacrifice on the part of the individual. The fallacy that the individual must give up his individuality for the sake of the whole is one of the most pervasive, the most insidious, fallacies I know" (Follett 2013h, 81). "On the contrary, obedience and self-expression, or even self-direction, are reciprocally involved" (Follett 2003n, 275). Individuals are not homogenized; they form groups through a process of harmonization and integration through interpenetration. Differences are integrated in a manner that is unique to each context in ever broadening circles of society.

Therefore, while Follett places emphasis on the group and the development of the group-self through integration, she is careful to stress that the individual does not succumb to the majority. "It is sometimes said . . . 'The individual must yield his right to judge for himself; let the majority judge.' But the individual is not for a moment to yield his right to judge for himself; he can judge better for himself if he joins with others in evolving a synthesized judgment. Our individual conscience is not absorbed into a national conscience; our individual conscience must be incorporated in a national conscience as one of its constituent members" (Follett 1998, 55-56). Additionally, when individual conscience and group conscience are linked through integration, self-interest and collective-interest are inextricably linked within the total situation. Therefore Follett does "not look on self-interest as a bad word . . . But what [she is] urging is that we should be as interested, as self-interested, as possible, but only as members of the highest unity with which we are capable of identifying ourselves" (Follett 2003l, 218).

In this way integration in the group is simply another perspective from which to view the self-adjustment that occurs through integration at the individual level of analysis. To demonstrate the similarity, Follett provides an example from management in which department heads are working toward unifying around goals for the organization:

> Take four heads of departments. You cannot envisage accurately what happens between them by thinking of A as adjusting himself to B and to C and to D. A adjusts himself to B and also to a B influenced by C and to a B influenced by D and to a B influenced by A himself. Again he adjusts himself to C and also to a C influenced by B and to a C influenced by D and to a C influenced by A himself—and so on. Once could work it out mathematically. This sort of reciprocal relating, this interpenetration of every part by every other part and again by every other part as it has been permeated by all, should be the goal of all attempts at co-ordination, a goal, of course, never wholly reached. (Follett 2013h, 78-79)

Here we see that the integrating of individuals within the group is simply the integration that forms the true individual through circular response. The true individual and group are always co-creating one another.

For Follett, then, the integrating of group-self is reflective of the integrating of multiplicity within each individual demonstrated by psychoanalysis and Gestalt: "We know that every individual has many warring tendencies inside himself. We know that the effectiveness of an individual, his success in life, depends largely on these various tendencies, impulses, desires, being adjusted to one another, being made into one harmonious whole. Yet no one can issue a fiat by which I am adjusted, I can only be helped to adjust myself. It is the same with a group . . . Here too the process is one of self-adjustment" (Follett 2013h, 82). This ongoing process of integration results in another whole within the total situation: the group a-making.

Integration that forms the group a-making stems from Follett's first principle of organization; "co-ordination as the reciprocal relating of all the factors in a situation . . . the nature of unity" (Follett 2013h, 78). Groups are co-created in a reciprocal relationship with true individuals. One does not exist without the other and taken together they are always in a process of unifying. "Unity, not uniformity, must be our aim. We attain unity only through variety. Differences must be integrated, not annihilated, nor absorbed" (Follett 1998, 39).[28]

To emphasize this point, whereas difference is problematic in the crowd, difference is essential for the group because "the essence of society is difference, related difference" (Follett 1998, 33); "individual variation is the coefficient of social life" (Follett 2013c, 128). Thus, "individuality is difference springing into view as relating itself with other differences" (Follett 1998, 63). Furthermore, "differences develop within the social process and are united through the social process" (63)—the process of integration. Therefore, individual differences are neither sacrificed nor homogenized in the group: "The word should never be sacrifice, it should always be contribution. We want every possible contribution to the whole" (Follett 2013h, 82). Perhaps more importantly, "every difference that is swept up into a bigger conception feeds and enriches society; every difference which is ignored feeds *on* society and eventually corrupts it" (Follett 1998, 40). Thus it is essential for every individual to actively contribute to the whole through the integration of difference.

The requirement for the individual to consciously participate in integration is given new meaning in light of group formation. "No member of a group which is to create can be passive. All must be active and constructively active" (Follett 1998, 28). It is only through meaningful participation that the consciousness of oneness or what Follett calls "the group-spirit" (Follett 1998, 43) can be generated. This group-spirit is not one that develops through contract (particularism), imitation (collectivism), agitation (emotion), or aggregation (pluralism), but rather through "a slow and gradual creating of unity" (85).

This ontological perspective provides the fuel for catalyzing synthesis. Collectivist static unity that is "is the outcome of agreement based on concurrence of emotion rather than of thought" (Follett 1998, 85) and particularist unity around "a concurrence produced by becoming aware of similarities" (85) are synthesized into *unifying*. Collective will, both homogenous and aggregate, is transformed into a will-forming activity. Furthermore, the relational quality of Follett's ontology carries forward throughout the process of determining will and executing will: "collective will produces collective activity" (Follett 2013c, 206). But this is "continuing activity; at any one moment the function which that activity is of the situation is the collective will. Thus its nature is wholly dynamic. We must think no more in terms of social institutions but of social activities" (207).

Follett believes this sort of dynamic social bond is more productive for both the individual and society and that "conscious group creation is to be the social and political force of the future. Our aim must be to live consciously in more and more group relations and to make each group a means of creating" (Follett 1998, 101). She is optimistic about our potential to move in this direction: "We are emerging from our gregarious condition and are now to enter on the rational way of living by scanning our relations to one another, instead of bluntly feeling them, and so adjusting them that unimpeded progress on this higher plane is secured" (91).

In sum, the group is formed through the active, intentional process of integrating difference among true individuals relating with the total situation. Thus, society is the unifying, intertwining of interpenetrating groups that is a whole a-making. This process has the effect of generating a sense of group identity and group-spirit that fosters a consciousness of oneness stemming from direct experience rather than impositions from external sources. As these groups interpermeate one another in dynamic configurations, society as a whole is co-created. It is the combination of the true individual in actual groups that establishes the foundation for all other aspects of Follett's applied theories.

SUMMARY ANALYSIS

The first weft thread Follett weaves onto the warp of her relational process ontology is her understanding of *human* being in particular; addressing what she argues are fundamental misunderstandings of the individual and the group. Drawing from psychoanalytic and Gestalt theory, Follett argues that true individuals are connected at an ontological level through circular response; however, conscious, active integration is necessary to foster a social bond. Follett's dynamic versions of psychoanalysis and Gestalt underlie true individuals with identities that are the integrative result of both internal and external forces. True individuals are both self-determining and responsive to their environment: "man is at the same time a social factor and a social product" (Follett 1998, 60). True individuals and groups are relating to one another and to their parts within the total situation. Therefore, individuals themselves as well as groups of all sizes and types are wholes a-making, engaged in circular response as part of the situation a-making. Follett argues, "This pregnant truth . . . is the basic truth for all the social sciences" (Follett 2013c, 63).

ENDNOTES

1. Shapiro (2003) describes Follett's perspective as "omnicentric" (589). In this way, Follett's understanding of the individual in circular response with society offers a precursor to the idea of autopoiesis advanced by Maturana and Varela (1992).

2. Child (2013) refers to "the dynamic aspect of relationship," likening Follett to Giddens in his theory of structuration.

3. Empathy refers to the understanding and sharing of a specific emotional experience with another person. Sympathy, however, does not require the sharing of the same emotional experience. Instead, sympathy is a concern for the well-being of another (Lishner, Batson, and Huss 2011).

4. Tonn (2003) notes Follett draws from French sociologist Gabriel Tarde (1843-1904) for imitation theory and from Columbia University sociologist Franklin Giddings (1855-1931) for similarity of kind.

5. Tonn (2003) notes that crowd psychology is a term coined by the French social theorist Gustave Le Bon (1841-1931) as a critique of democracy.

6. This differentiation mirrors Whitehead's (1979) differentiation of types of societies. See also in this context Whitehead's (1967) understanding of values.

7. The crowd is like a Whiteheadian non-social or chaotic society called a nexus. The group is like a Whiteheadian social nexus called a structured society (Mesle 2008).

8. This point would be echoed by Arendt (1998) when she suggests that mass hysteria can lead to a proliferation of singular perspectives wherein "the same experience is multiplied innumerable times" (58).

9. Tonn (2003) notes that the discipline of psychology at the time was embattled between behaviorism led by John B. Watson (1878-1958) and the structuralism promoted by Edward B. Titchener (1867-1927). The Gestalt theory of Max Wertheimer (1880-1943) and the psychoanalysis of Sigmund Freud (1856-1939) were just entering the fray.

10. This is aligned with what is now understood in radical immanence: "You are, in part, a composite of the roles in which you participate, even though you overflow that composite" (Connolly 2013, 182).

11. Tonn (2003) frames Follett's psychological principles as three: circular response, integrative behavior, and the total situation. Here, the total situation is assumed by both circular response and integrative behavior.

12. Tonn (2003) notes that Follett wishes to replace psychoanalyst Edward J. Kempf's definition of behavior as "'wishes opposed by the resistance of the environment'" with "'confronting the activity of the environment'" (373).

13. Here, Follett provides a definition of what we now understand as synergy (Fuller 1975).

14. The total situation thus defined presages the concept of horizons described by Gadamer: "We define the concept of 'situation' by saying that it represents a standpoint that limits the possibility of vision. Hence essential to the concept of situation is the concept of 'horizon.' The horizon is the range of vision that includes everything that can be seen from a particular vantage point" (Gadamer 1997, 302).

15. Fox (1968) observes that Follett uses the terms *functional relation* and *activity-between* as synonyms for circular response.

16. Here, as Child (1995) notes, Follett anticipates Giddens's (1984) theory of structuration.

17. Weinberg (1996) suggests Follett's psychosocial theories are a precursor to Bowenian family systems theory and its understanding of how interpersonal dynamics fuel behavior.

18. Here, Follett's thinking mirrors the Whiteheadian notion of identity as a flow of experience that continually arises from a combination of continuity and novelty in the process of concrescence and its various prehensions

(Mesle 2008). This combination may be explained by the example of an electron: "The individualisation of the charge arises by a conjunction of two characters, in the first place by the continued identity of its mode of functioning as a key for the determination of a diffusion of pattern; and, in the second place, by the unity and continuity of its life history" (Whitehead 1948, 155).

19. Tonn (2003) notes that in addition to Holt, Follett references Oxford physiologist Charles S. Sherrington in regard to the reflex arc.

20. Follett's critique of the reflex arc is similar to John Dewey's (1896) understanding in "The Reflex Arc Concept in Psychology."

21. This is similar to the Whiteheadian notion that "novelty is the root of life" (Mesle 2008, 48), as opposed to the notion of a static, enduring identity. See also Cobb's (1975) application of this principle to man's responsibility for co-creating history through active multiplication of an individual experience.

22. Here again, we see that Follett "anticipates Giddens's concept of structuration" (Child 1995, 91).

23. Morton and Lindquist (1997) align Follett's understanding of the individual as dynamic and relational, both autonomous yet formed through reciprocal relatings with other unique individuals, with contemporary feminist understandings of the individual.

24. Tonn (2003) notes that others at the time were objecting to the dualisms of self and other, individual and society, including Charles Horton Cooley, George Herbert Mead, and John Dewey. Perhaps for this reason Boje and Rosile (2001) and O'Connor (2000) misinterpret Follett's work as drawing from Dewey. But in terms of publication dates, this is innacurate and according to Follett herself, "'In the first place he is not original (I have never got a single idea from Dewey)'" (as quoted in Tonn 2003, 377).

25. This understanding of identity formation is a portent of assemblage (Deleuze and Guattari 1987).

26. Again, this differentiation is like Whitehead's differentiation of types of societies (Mesle 2008).

27. Fox (1968) notes that large portions of *The New State* are devoted to explaining healthy group process as integration, which is then clarified in *Creative Experience.*

28. As interpreted by Mattson, "the unity achieved by interpenetration derived from, and did not discard, pluralism and difference" (1998, xliii).

ஃ 4 ஃ

Follett's Epistemological Concepts

Epistemology describes how we know about the world in terms of how knowledge is structured and how truths are justified. *Foundationalism* assumes that a set of static truths exists upon which all knowledge is built; we can know truth through either formal logic (rationalism) that is justified internally or systematic observation (empiricism) that is justified externally. Alternatively, an understanding of existence in a dynamic state denies the possibility of foundational truths and instead looks for *coherence* among sets of beliefs. This leads to the assumption that either we can only know through belief (internal justification) or through temporary snapshots that are artificially fixed (external justification). For Follett, knowledge is produced through a co-creative process that evolves among all within the situation.[1]

Much of Follett's epistemological explication is contained in *Creative Experience*.[2] For Follett knowledge is relational and continually unfolding in response to the dynamic situation. While she appreciates expertise, she is critical of relying solely on experts for knowledge, preferring instead calls for all "to base our life on actual experience, of my own plus that of others" (Follett 2013c, 29). In doing so we employ what she refers to as a "scientific attitude of mind" (29).[3] We also open ourselves to the integrating of multiple perspectives, creating knowledge by "watching varying activities in their relatings to other varying activities" (68) within the total situation.[4]

Follett's epistemology, therefore, reflects her relational process ontology and her understanding of the psychosocial condition. As such, knowledge is constantly being created and recreated anew through active experimentation and integration. This approach is in stark contrast to knowledge accumulation based on static, objective truths verified through the scientific method by experts. Thus, Follett begins her affirmation with a critique of the scientific method in order to clearly differentiate her approach to knowledge production.

CRITIQUE OF MAINSTREAM EPISTEMOLOGIES

In building an argument for her epistemological approach and social science method, Follett critiques rationalism, idealism, empiricism, and even some aspects of pragmatism.[5,6] In particular, she is concerned with the status of static, objective facts as the foundation for knowledge, the scientific method of validation and verification, and the role of experts as the gatekeepers to accepted knowledge. Each component of her argument will be discussed in turn.

Static objective facts

Follett is first concerned by what she terms "fact-worship"—the belief that there is "an inherent nature in a 'fact' to be revealed to the devout" (Follett 2013c, 153) through objective scientific inquiry. She argues that the empiricist's pursuit of objectivity and neutral facts is misguided, advising that "the kind of objectivity which some of the fact-worshippers are endlessly seeking will be endlessly hidden from them" (11).

The elusive nature of objectivity lies in the assumption that there is a static set of facts that can be neutrally observed. She explains that this misconception is "a mistake we often tend to make" because we think "that the world stands still . . . And it does not" (Follett 2013h, 85).[7] This means we cannot simply gather facts as unbiased data: "A fact is not a preëxisting thing to which a conception may conform, but an eventual thing" (Follett 2013c, 139). Therefore, facts are influenced by our conceptions as part of the very process of observation. "Facts become such for us when we attend to them. Our attending to them is bound up in the situation" (11). Specifically, in "the perception of facts, our 'attention,' is determined by our needs or desires" (10). Because what we choose to consider is guided by preconceived ideas, "the gathering is in itself an interpreting. Interpreting is part of the vision, not something done with the vision" (27).[8]

Just as facts cannot be objectively gathered, once in hand they cannot be neutrally analyzed: "fact analysis is to some extent fact interpretation" (Follett 2013c, 27). Follett explains that due to circular response in the process of observation and analysis, "My behavior in that experience is as much a part of my interpretation as my reflection upon it afterwards; my intellectual, post-facto, reflective interpretation is only part of the story" (Follett 2013c, 140). Thus, as with the collection of facts, "the interpretation of facts depends on needs" (10). Unfortunately, "advocates of fact-finding have not seen the significance of the Freudian 'wish' in its relation to the interpretation of facts" (11).

By this, Follett does not mean that interpretation is merely a matter of individual psychological projection, however. "The value of every fact depends on its position in the whole world-process, is bound up in its multitudinous relations" (Follett 2013c, 12). When considering a situation we must consider "not all the factors one by one, but also their relation to one another. This means, among other things, that when a factor is added to or subtracted from a situation, you have not that situation minus or plus that factor, for all the rest will be changed" (Follett 2003m, 192). Because fact observation and interpretation are subjective, the observer is part of the situation and included in the relatings. In short, facts are defined by their dynamic relationships with one another and the observer within the total situation. Thus, "facts must be understood as the whole situation with whatever sentiments, beliefs, ideals enter into it" (Follett 2013c, 13).

Although her criticism of objectivity is sharp, Follett insists that she should not be interpreted as "showing any skepticism in regard to the value of facts" (Follett 2013c, 24). She understands fact-finding efforts to be useful steps toward "accurate information" (25), but she re-envisions the ontological nature of facts and the role they play in knowledge production. For Follett, socially situated facts become the "scaffolding of a situation" rather than its sole construction (13). She also criticizes how data are gathered, who is involved, and how they are involved: "experts both interpret facts and relate facts.... While information comes to the expert as fact, it usually leaves him as opinion" (Follett 1926, 255). Given this phenomenon, Follett pointedly asks, "Where indeed can we look for the separation of fact and opinion?" (Follett 2013c, 27). Thus, we turn to her critique of the scientific method and technical expertise.

The scientific method

Follett understands that the scientific method is considered the gold standard for knowledge production and verification even within the social sciences: "Each period has its magic word par excellence. A few years ago when science was the word to conjure with, the idea of verifying appealed to us because we were told it was 'scientific'" (Follett 2013c, 139). Follett argues the social sciences follow this trend, in part, because "we have not always understood the relation between quantitative and qualitative analysis" (xvii). Nor have we realized that the former is not an appropriate method for creating knowledge about the social world. Thus, "the social sciences, while learning everything possible from physical science must develop their own method" (139).

Follett's initial objections to the scientific method reflect the problems found when considering facts: observer objectivity and static ontology. Again she finds that objectivity is impossible. Being bound up in the ongoing process of circular response, humans are always intricately interwoven into the total situation of which they are a part. Likewise, all phenomena we would wish to observe are also interweaving. Thus, even if one could step outside the situation to observe, we would be "watching exceedingly complex reactions to a complex environment" (Follett 2013c, 121). But, because we are also part of the situation, there is no way to step outside and observe. "Life is not a movie for us; you can never watch life because you are always *in* life" (134). Thus, the objective observation demanded by the scientific method is impossible.

Likewise, the facts that we wish to test with the scientific method do not oblige our desire to do so. "Facts change, we must keep up with the facts; keeping up with the facts changes the facts" (Follett 2013h, 85). The slippery nature of facts and the impossibility of objective observation means that "testing in an exact sense is an impossibility; we can live and progress and create, and we must use all the conceptions we can get hold of to help us do this, but life never stops long enough for us to 'test,' or rather we cannot get outside life to view it" (Follett 2013c, 135). Thus, "the relation of observation to preëxisting classification has to be worked out on different lines from that which most of us are pursuing at present. To test and discard, to test and verify? Life is not as simple as that, or as 'scientific' either. Life is an art" (141).[9]

These mistaken assumptions of objectivity and stasis are reflected in the very structure of the scientific method. Follett asserts the scientific method relies on balancing idealism and empiricism: using concepts to develop hypotheses that are then tested through perception.[10] This requires reliance on causal relationships that can be conceptualized and then perceived and verified. But "cause and effect are ways of describing certain moments in the situation when we look at those moments apart from the total process" (Follett 2013c, 61) and "we shall never catch the stimulus stimulating or the response responding" (60). Therefore, "we can never understand the total situation without taking into account the evolving situation" (69) and its complex, dynamic, mutually causal relationships.

Without clear causal relationships, verifying with the scientific method becomes impossible. This brings Follett to the problematic relationship between conception (hypothesis) and perception (testing) within the scientific method; two activities that cannot be separated but are always engaged in circular response. Understanding circular response then "corrects the two fallacies in the notion of verifying so often held: a tendency to divorce for the moment thinking and doing (if you separate thought and activity you can test by the criteria supplied by mind); and an ignoring of the self-evolving nature of the specific-response relation. We do not think, and do, and think again, but the thinking is bound up in the doing" (Follett 2013c, 137). Therefore, the scientific method's wall between idealism and empiricism crumbles.

Although Follett believes pragmatism has the potential for moving beyond the problems inherent in the scientific method, she sees vestiges of the faults of idealism and empiricism in its premises as well.[11] Follett worries that some theorists' emphasis may make pragmatism vulnerable to the same errors of idealism. For instance, she complains that pragmatism "still has bits of intellectualism sticking to it" (Follett 2013c, xi) because it retains too much focus on the conceptual, giving too little attention to perception or the experiential.[12] She warns that "conceptual description is fraught with equal danger for social worker, psychiatrist or political scientist, for every one of us" (154-55).

On the other hand, Follett worries that some pragmatists—including James—go too far in their dismissal of concepts. She notes that "rationalists 'verify' within the realm of reason. Pragmatists 'test' in the concrete world" (Follett 1919, 584). Indeed, "the essence of pragmatism, as commonly understood, is testing" (584). However, when pragmatism rejects conceptualizing in favor of perceiving they may fall into the problems of the old empiricist model because "whenever you 'test' you assume a static idea" (584) that can be perceived and verified.

Overemphasis on either concept or perception is problematic because they are "part of the same activity" (Follett 2013c, 145).[13] "Conceptions do not remain conceptions. They enter into the blood and bone of our activities and then from these, new conceptions arise" (145). Thus, Follett sees a simple answer to the ongoing argument about "the priority of thought or action in the social life. There is no order. The union of thought and will and activity by which the clearer will is generated, the social process, is a perfect unity" (Follett 1998, 50). Therefore, Follett argues that pragmatism must integrate concept and precept in a relational, experiential methodology of testing and validation, pursuing a *synthesis* of the two through ongoing experimentation by all in the situation.[14] This is, indeed, how Follett herself developed, tested, and validated her own theories in community and industrial contexts.[15]

Technical expertise

Given her critiques of objective facts and the scientific method, it is not surprising that Follett is also wary of the role of the expert as esteemed fact-finder.[16] She argues, "What we really wish for is a 'beneficent' despot, but we are ashamed to call him that and so we say scientific investigator, social engineers, etc." (Follett 2013c, 29-30). Therefore, "the present apotheosis of the expert, the ardent advocacy of the 'facts,' needs some analysis" (3). This wariness reflects the recurring concern that when one viewpoint, role, or whole within the situation is given priority we open the door to hierarchy. As currently conceived, experts are the gatekeepers for official knowledge within tightly defined areas, thus giving them power over others and creating a false dichotomy between *expert* and *layman*.

Given the extreme complexity of the social world, it is natural that we might turn to experts to help us attempt to understand and order that world. However, this complexity often results in "too great specialization" (Follett 2013c, 104) of expertise, creating siloes of knowledge and more "experts on more questions" (Follett 1926, 253) whose knowledge is limited to their own sub-specializations. This is problematic because in their attempts to master the minutiae of a given area of knowledge, experts often lose perspective on the world outside that area of specialization and how it is relating in the total situation. Follett illustrates this problem with an anecdote in which an expert looking for celery heart rot at a farm is asked if the disease might be impacted by crop rotation and cultivation. "The specialist replied that he didn't know, that he knew nothing of cultivation, he was a specialist on disease!" (Follett 2013c, 104). As this anecdote makes clear, "one of the difficulties about using experts is often the lack of technique for uniting the knowledge of different experts" (104).

More insidiously, specialization creates an atmosphere in which experts have tight control over knowledge production in certain spheres. Thus expertise and interpretation of "facts have intimate connection with the whole question of power" (Follett 2013c, 14) and how power is exercised. Restrictive control over the selection and interpretation of facts leads to power-over others in the situation.[17, 18] Follett demonstrates this oft-overlooked form of power-over as it exists within the organization, with each expert exerting her power in the process of decision making. Due to the social nature of facts and the impossibility of objectivity, "the separation between advice and decision cannot be a rigid one" and "pure information is seldom given by expert to executive" (Follett 1926, 255). "The various experts too, the staff officials, the planning department—all these give more than mere facts . . . By the time this has all been passed up to the head, this decision is already largely pre-determined" (Follett 2013a, 41). Essentially, in the selection and analysis of facts, "conclusions and judgments are already, to a certain extent, woven into the pattern, and in such a way that it would be impossible to get them out" (Follett 2013g, 6). Thus, "the expert's information not only forms a large part of the executive's decision; it is becoming an integral part of the decision-making machinery" (Follett 1926, 253).

This control over others is not just in how observed facts are interpreted and presented but also in what is disclosed by the expert. Common experience tells us "that the withholding of facts is often used as a means to gain power-over" (Follett 2003j, 106). However, just as control over the interpreting and withholding of facts leads to control over others, collaborative interpretation and sharing of facts generates power-with as "consideration of facts reduces power-over" (106). Thus, Follett argues that "the integrating of facts and power is possible, but it would mean a different code from that by which we are at present living" (Follett 2013c, 15).

This need for integrating facts and power raises the question of whose knowledge is to be integrated; or more pointedly, who is allowed to participate in knowledge creation. Under technical expertise a sharp division develops between expert and layman, leading to a rigid dichotomy between "the rule of that modern beneficent despot, the expert, and a muddled, befogged 'people'" (Follett 2013c, 3). But Follett insists that this contrast between expert and layman is a false choice and merely serves to reinforce power-over and forces our hand in giving our consent to being ruled by the experts.

In contrast to this stark division, Follett argues that both expert and layman are experiencing and affecting the situation through circular response. Thus, we must assume that the knowledge that is most important "is already in the situation which the expert investigates; that the investigation of the expert often changes the situation . . . and that the people help to create and to develop, by their response, the situation to which they are responding" (Follett 2013c, 28). This means that in the production of knowledge "there must be a place for experts *and* administrative officials *and* people" (27). Follett's insistence on a place for all in the process is not only critical for knowledge creation but has profound implications for the remaining elements of her thinking, particularly her political and administrative theories.[19]

The critique in sum

In her critique of the scientific method, Follett challenges social science to develop an alternative approach to epistemology: "Our problem is to find a method by which the opinion of the expert does not coerce and yet enters integrally into the situation. Our problem is to find a way by which the specialist's kind of knowledge and the executive's kind of knowledge can be joined. And the method should, I think, be one I have already advocated, that of integration" (Follett 2013b, 70). Therefore, we refer to Follett's approach as *dynamic relational epistemology*, applying her relational process ontology to knowledge production.

DYNAMIC RELATIONAL EPISTEMOLOGY

To reflect the relational process, Follett's epistemology requires that we develop an alternative methodology that considers the total situation without analyzing it from a rationalist or an empirical perspective, or assessing it from an idealistic perspective. Rather, we must synthesize these methods. Indeed, she insists "the present-day respect for facts, for scientific methods, is the first step in this method of seeking the law of the situation" (Follett 2003j, 104). Thus, Follett does not eliminate the need for facts or expertise but reinterprets them within the total situation. The expert's specialized knowledge and experience become integrated with the experiential knowledge of all those involved in the situation. In other words, the "problem before us is one of discovering a technique for unifying" (Follett 2013c, 104).

This method must: (1) consider facts as dynamic social artifacts produced through the process of integration within the total situation; (2) synthesize the most useful aspects of idealism, rationalism, and empiricism; and (3) do so in a manner that does not routinely privilege any one perspective within the situation. Building upon her critiques of objective facts, scientific method, and technical expertise, Follett affirms a dynamic epistemology. She re-envisions knowledge creation within the total situation: social facts are created within a pragmatist method to formulate collaborative knowledge. We examine each of these aspects of Follett's dynamic relational epistemology in turn.

Dynamic social facts

Follett answers her own critiques of the scientific method by first replacing its building blocks. Rather than objective static facts, Follett understands facts to be created by the dynamic social process. At the individual level of analysis, ideals and beliefs shape what we consider important to observe and how we interpret what we observe. "The ardent search for objectivity, the primary task of the fact worshippers, cannot be the whole task of life, for objectivity alone is not reality. . . . As the subjective idealists have over-emphasized the subject, and the realists, the object" (Follett 2013c, 54). However, she argues that when the "swing of the pendulum between 'subjectivity' and 'objectivity'" (54) is stilled through synthesis, the problematic quest for objectivity is resolved and "the 'objective situation' cannot be overemphasized if we understand it as part of a total process" (153). Indeed, Follett has been quoted as saying, "I am beginning to see the synthesis of idealism and realism so clearly" (Mattson 1998, xliii).[20]

Recalling her ontology and psychosocial theory, the total situation is engaged in the process of circular response. Thus, subjective experiences are in actuality inter-subjective, or relational in nature. As such, "unrelated experience is of little use to us; we can never make wise decisions from isolated bits, only as we see the parts in relation to one another" (Follett 2013h, 86). It is through engaging in "the evolving situation, the 'progressive integrations,' the ceaseless interweaving of new specific respondings" that we find "the whole forward movement of existence" (Follett 2013c, 134).

Thus, facts are social processes emerging from the situation and our first step in understanding the situation is "to get at the facts" (Follett 2003a, 74). But the social nature of these facts means that data collection and interpretation change from objective and neutral to a collaborative activity of intersubjectivity. Follett argues that "by making the investigation a joint affair" (Follett 2013c, 17) "fact-finding can be a joint activity" (Follett 2013c, 16), and integration begins immediately in the shaping of which phenomena are considered important. This does not mean that differences of perception and opinion will be overcome. "Interpretation of facts, the relation of facts, still leave room for legitimate disagreement" (Follett 2003k, 240). She acknowledges "that even if we could have a coöperative gathering of facts we should still interpret them differently, but the initial difficulty would be avoided—we should at any rate be looking at the same facts" (Follett 2013c, 16) and this is often "a big step toward final agreement" (Follett 2003a, 75). Thus, joint "participation in the early stages [of investigation] should begin even with the preliminary fact-finding" (Follett 2003l, 224), indeed "the time is coming, I believe, when the advantage of joint investigation of facts as a basis for public policy will become so clear that the public will insist on it" (225).[21] Follett carries this idea forward in her reformulation of the scientific method and expertise.

For Follett, the "best preparation for integration" (Follett 2003c, 61) or "the process of interpenetration" (Follett 1998, 94) is the understanding of the process through which multiple perspectives form a new shared understanding.[22] "When we are looking at the actual situation we are more likely to follow the process necessary to integration, the breaking up of a whole situation into its component parts and considering these separately. My own experience is that nothing gets rid of sides so quickly as this process" (Follett 2003a, 75). Thus, "the object . . . is not to find the best individual thought, but the collective thought" (Follett 1998, 30). In creating social facts together, "we do not go to our group . . . to be passive and learn, and we do not go to push through something we have already decided we want. Each must discover and contribute . . . that which distinguishes him from others, his difference" (29).

Follett reminds us that, with a little reflection, we recognize this nascent process of intersubjective integration in everyday association. When "a man comes forward with an idea . . . none of us believes that that idea arose spontaneously in his mind independent of all previous association . . . it is the result of the process of interpenetration" (Follett 1998, 94). In other words we can best understand facts as social artifacts that are formed through collective experience: "a collective thought is one evolved by a collective process" (34). It is through this process that truth is *co-created*. Thus, Follett takes a constructivist position, arguing that facts are given meaning not as objective data, but as part of the total situation a-making.[23] She explains, "any fact gains its significance through its relation to all the other facts pertaining to the situation" (Follett 2013h, 79). "The value of every fact depends on its position in the whole world-process, is bound up in its multitudinous relations...a fact out of relation is not a fact" (Follett 2013c, 12). In other words, as social artifacts of collective idea-formation, facts have no meaning if they are not understood within the relational, dynamic situation. "On the social level, self and circumstance, thought and concrete experience, are always interweaving; this, not comparing, is the life-process" (135). Therefore, in our creating of knowledge, we must focus our attention on "the activity-between" (135).

Follett insists that understanding subjective/objective facts emerging from the process of the total situation aligns her epistemology with well-established ideas within physics. After all, "was it not several centuries ago that scientists began to look at objects as processes?" (Follett 2013c, 153). When facts become dynamic, knowledge becomes "a living idea" from which "truth may be created" (Follett 1919, 584). The living ideas and the truths they create have short shelf lives, however. "You cannot bottle up wisdom—it won't keep—but through our associated life it may be distilled afresh at every instant" (Follett 1998, 130). Thus, "we must be constantly understanding anew" (226).

However, the dynamic nature of knowledge does not mean that knowledge is constantly created and discarded in rapid succession. "Concept-making is a long, slow process. It is all life working ceaselessly on itself, building itself up" (Follett 2013c, 144). In Follett's dynamic relational epistemology, "one concept is not discarded and another adopted; integration is the law on every plane, and it is the integrating of percepts and concepts that we must study if we would understand the history of thought" (145). Knowledge creation, then, is reformulated as part of an ongoing process of *knowing* that happens through integration.

Follett calls this integrative process "creative experience" (Follett 2013c); "the place where conceptual and perceptual meet" (144). Through integrative creative experience, "we learn how to connect the conceptual and perceptual planes, how to let every fact contribute to those principles which by use again in the factual world becomes again transformed, and thus man grows—always through his activity" (141). In this sense, creative experience is "progressive experience" which "depends on the relating" (54). Through this creative experience, Follett urges us to "seek the plusvalents of experience" (x) whereby we gain more from the interrelatings than from simple aggregation. The method she seems to find most useful for this integrating work is the pragmatist method, to which we now turn.

The pragmatist method

In her description of dynamic social facts co-created through experience, Follett is decidedly a pragmatist.[24] Her pragmatist leanings are further seen in her tendency to demonstrate theory through practical examples of lived experience. But, most strikingly, her pragmatism shines through in her method of utilizing experience as a means of synthesizing concepts and perception—thereby providing an alternative to the scientific method.[25] To promulgate synthesis, Follett urges modern scholars to "abandon the region of abstract speculation and to study the behavior of men" (Follett 2013c, ix) and argues that social science should produce "methods for watching varying activities in their relatings to other varying activities" (68).

Such a dynamic revision of methodology follows from the redefinition of knowledge as a *creative* social process. "The social process is not, first, scientific investigation, then some method of persuading the people to abandon their own experience and thought, and lastly an acclaiming populace. The social process is a process of cooperating experience" (Follett 2013c, 30). The epistemological purpose is to create knowledge through the integration of experience, not to generate static hypotheses to be verified or discarded. The process is not hypothesize, test, and verify or reject. "The process is analysis, discrimination and integration" (187).

Creating knowledge, then, requires that we understand "when and why and how we get genuine integration" (Follett 2013c, 178), which in turn requires developing "careful studies of the method of integration" (178). Because integration is a relational process, the method must combine aspects of participant observation and phenomenology in order to integrate conceptual and experiential elements in knowledge production. It is this process that "should be the study of the student of social sciences" (68-69). But before Follett can fully explicate the process of integration in this revised method, she must first revise the notions of analysis and discrimination.

Given her thorough denouncement of the scientific method and empirical objectivity, at first blush it seems counterintuitive that Follett begins her explanation of method by proclaiming "the time is ripe for empirical studies of human relations, social situations" (Follett 2013c, xi). However, because Follett hopes for a "uniting of idealism and empiricism" (286), a synthesis of concept and perception, she rejects neither *in toto*; only the prioritization of one or the other. This synthesis can best be achieved through the active knowing that happens in a pragmatist approach to experimentation. To demonstrate how synthesis is achieved, a revisiting of the scientific method is helpful: "You will notice that to break up a problem into its various parts involves the *examination of symbols*, involves, that is, the careful scrutiny of the language used to see what it really means" (Follett 2003b, 41).

The scientific method is rooted in the pendulum swing from concept (hypothesis), to perception (experimentation and observation), and back to concept (accept or reject). But for Follett this swing artificially breaks the process of knowing into discrete parts that are elements of a properly integrated activity. So, while Follett calls for "observation and experiment" (Follett 2013c, xii), she also insists our ideas should evolve with our experiences in "the way in which bacteriologists use classification, changing it readily with every new discovery" (141). This requires a different approach to experimentation which Follett describes as an "experimental attitude toward experience" (Follett 2003c, 50-51).

A pragmatist method of experimentation begins with data collection. But because facts are created collectively, consideration of facts within the total situation cannot mean "merely that we must be sure to get all the factors into our problem" (Follett 2013h, 79; 2003m, 191). Gathering information is important, "but that is by no means enough for us to do, we have to see these factors each one affecting every one of the others" (Follett 2013h, 79). The factors involved in the situation include not only facts relating with one another, but also with those individuals who experience them.

Because facts are dynamic and socially understood, collection of data must be reformulated as an interpretive and collaborative process in which each person *experiencing* the situation is also a participant in *interpreting* that situation. Thus, "we must face the fact that if social research is to be made valuable to us, that it is seldom possible to 'observe' a social situation as one watches a chemical experiment; the presence of the observer usually changes the situation. We need then those who are frankly participant-observers" (Follett 2013c, xi). Observation of the data becomes bound up in the creation of the data, and experimentation is an ongoing experiential activity, not a mediating step between data collection and verification of an idea. This means that thought (hypothesis and analysis) and action (observation) cannot be separated but are continually intertwined in an ongoing process of knowledge production.

Follett explains this integration of concept and perception also impacts the activity of data analysis, where knowledge traditionally emerges. Again, separation is not possible: "The activity of knowing includes the knower and the known" (Follett 2013c, 88) and these cannot be understood in isolation. Thus, this perspective forgoes static knowledge altogether "in favor of know-ing, of an activity, of a process which involves knower and known but which never looks from the windows of either. The knower knows (an active verb) the known; reality is in the knowing" (88). Because knower and known are always interpenetrating then "concepts alone can never be presented to me merely, they must be knitted into the structure of my being, and this can be done only through my own activity" (Follett 2013c, 151).

When experimentation is understood as a fundamental method of integrating concept and perception, of evolving relatings within the situa-tion rather than a method of verification, hypotheses are simply part of the ongoing process of experimentation and they are as dynamic and social as our facts. "We should try experiments and note whether they succeed or fail and, most important of all, why they succeed or fail. This is taking an experimental attitude toward experience" (Follett 2003c, 50-51). In the pragmatist method, then, hypotheses evolve within the universe of living ideas, elements within the "interweaving which is changing both factors and creating constantly new situations" (68). Follett jests, "I know of no dump yards where I can go see the discarded hypotheses" (139). Alterna-tively, while "rationalists 'verify' within the realm of reason. Pragmatists 'test' in the concrete world" (Follett 1919, 584). Whereas empiricists focus on objective observation, "far more than observation, we need experiment" (Follett 2013c, 178). "The step beyond is to learn to *create* in both" (Follett 1919, 584) reasoning and observation. This is done through the creative experience of integration.

Therefore, "we can now think of experience more as a creating than a verifying process. Experience is the power-house where purpose and will, thought and ideals, are being generated" (Follett 2013c, 133).[26] Rebutting criticisms of this view, Follett explains, "We are told by a realist that according to pragmatism truth is 'a harmony between thought and things.' Is it not more 'realistic' to say that thought and things interpenetrate and that this is the creating activity?" (Follett 1919, 584). Just as facts become facts when we attend to them, this method of experimentation *creates* truths by interweaving those ideas, concepts and facts that fit within the social context, while adjusting or jettisoning those which are no longer helpful. In this way hypotheses are not discarded or verified; ideas are tested and molded through experience to create a coherent but ever-changing body of collaborative knowledge.

In sum, within Follett's pragmatist method scientific hypothesis testing through data collection and analysis are transformed into a creative experience of participatory, conscious reflection on the total situation; life as ongoing experimentation within progressive experience. Follett describes this pragmatist approach to knowledge creation as having "three steps: (1) a conscious attitude—realize the principles which it is possible to act on in this matter; (2) a responsible attitude—decide which we will act on; (3) an experimental attitude—try experiments and watch results. We might add a fourth step: pool our results" (Follett 2003c, 50-51). Her addendum of a fourth step here clearly points toward a different type of verification, one that reflects Follett's emphasis on creating truth through the integration of dynamic social facts. "There is a test which we may always make, a legitimate question we may ask: Does this activity fit in? This is the deeper meaning of all our wish to 'verify' . . . We verify through the process of creating: no dualism, no *Dinge an sich*, no static moment" (Follett 2013c, 143).

Therefore Follett urges all to engage in "experiments in making human interplay productive" (Follett 2013c, xi). She explains, "we want participant-observers who will try experiment after experiment and tell us which succeed and which fail. For integrating is the fundamental process of life, either as between organism and environment or between man and man" (178). This method fundamentally alters the previously conceived role of technical expertise in knowledge production.

Collaborative knowledge

Because knowledge is created through the integration of varying relatings within the social process, knowledge is not objective and static, but intersubjective and dynamic. Reflecting the principle of co-creation in her relational process ontology, Follett explains that knowledge "will come not through accepting the wisdom of one man, the judge, or of the legal order, but through the interweaving of many desires and attitudes, emotions and ideas, through much trial and error" (Follett 2013c, 41). Thus, Follett's dynamic relational epistemology revises the roles of scientist and technical expert, envisioning a new participatory mode of association in which knowledge is collaboratively created.

While she eschews hierarchical prioritization of scientific or technical expertise that allows power-over, Follett is not anti-expert. Neither does she accept claims that the only alternative is lack of expertise: "we have not to choose between becoming an expert on every subject ourselves and swallowing whole the reports of experts" (Follett 2013c, 29). Instead, as with the empiricist's observations and the idealist's reasoning, expertise must be reconceived within the collaborative process: "the expert must find his place within the social process; he can never be made a substitute for it" (29). Thus, we must change the way experts and non-experts work together.

While changing this relationship does not require that laymen become experts, it does require education. "The training of the citizen must include both how to form opinion on expert testimony and how to watch one's own experience and draw conclusions from it" (Follett 2013c, 29). Follett explains that "this will not make us professional experts; it will enable us to work with professional experts and to find our place in a society which needs the experience of all" (30). Thus, "the central aim . . . we have, is to train ourselves, to learn how to use the work of experts, to find our will, to educate our will, to integrate our wills" (5).

Integrating knowledge of experts and laymen, however, highlights qualitative differences: "They have different kinds of knowledge and experience" (Follett 1926, 256). "The specialist has one kind of knowledge" while others have other types of knowledge and we must "expect to be able to unite them" (Follett 2013b, 71). When we focus only on scientific or technical expertise we overlook common sense experiential knowledge. As Follett reminds us: "if I give instructions to someone who knows less about a matter than I do, he probably knows more than I about some other matter" (Follett 2013a, 37). For progressive experience to result, we must not allow that knowledge to be lost.

Follett explains that this uniting does not require that every individual will participate in every deliberation. Giving an example of applying collaborative knowledge creation in the workplace, she explains: "Our aim in the so-called democratic organization of industry should be, not to give the workmen a vote on things they know nothing about, but so to organize the plant that the workmen's experience can be added to that of the expert; we must see just where their experience will be a plus matter" (Follett 2013c, 20).[27] Thus, we are not called to look for practical experience where it does not exist or force participation where it is not needed, but we "must plan to have the workmen learn more and more of the industry as a whole" (Follett 2013c, 20) so that they can apply their experience in an increasing number of situations. By combining what we know and taking steps to increase the applicability of experience, we move toward creating collaborative knowledge.

Accordingly, Follett's concern is not about expertise per se, but which mode of association is guiding knowledge production. "The expert's information or opinion should not be allowed automatically to become a decision. On the other hand, full recognition should be given to the part the expert plays in decision making" (Follett 1926, 256). Follett believes that "we need experts, we need accurate information, but the object is not to do away with *difference* but to do away with *muddle* . . . to give legitimate play to difference" (Follett 2013c, 6). These differences are the multiplicity of interpretations of a given situation from all involved. Thus, although "a wise decision depends on just as much scientific information as we can acquire," Follett advises that "after we have obtained the greatest amount possible, there will still be difference, and that dealing with difference is the main part of the social process" (7). In order for co-creation to happen, all in the situation must bring their own experiences and perspectives to bear on decisions.

It is important, however, to remember that integrating multiple interpretations means something different than the mere aggregation of perspectives. "If each of us exhausts his responsibility by bringing his own little piece of pretty colored glass, that would make a mere kaleidoscope of community" (Follett 1919, 580). "Little drops of water, little grains of sand—that is a philosophy we have long outgrown. Count the grains, count the drops, count all men and all their activities, and the sum is not life" (Follett 2003f, 309). The goal is not accumulation of individual truths but the co-creation of collaborative knowledge through "a process of coöperating experience" (Follett 1998, 30). Indeed, "the greatest contribution a citizen can make to the state," according to Follett, "is to learn creative thinking, that is, to learn how to join his thought with that of others so that the issue shall be productive" (Follett 1919, 580).

This means that "technical experience must be made a part of all the available experience. When we see expert and administrative official, legislator and judge, *and* the people, all integral parts of the social process, all learning how to make facts, how to view facts, how to develop criteria by which to judge facts, then only have we a vision of genuine democracy" (Follett 2013c, 29). This is truly democratic because no privileged group or "special caste" (Follett 2013c, 29) is given sole discretion for producing knowledge. Instead, "we can all be over and under at the same time" (Follett 2013a, 37). Follett gives an example of this collaborative process from her observations of businessmen discussing centralization and decentralization:

"There was no academic talk . . . Each one had something to add from his own experience of the relation of branch firms to the central office, and the other problems included in the subject. There I found hope for the future. There men were not theorising [*sic*] or dogmatising [*sic*], they were thinking of what they had actually done and they were willing to try new ways the next morning, so to speak" (Follett 2013f, 32).

Such discussions demonstrate the progressive integrations that are generated through active and purposeful collaborative learning. The integrating of multiple perspectives "involves invention" (Follett 2003b, 33) where we are open to the ideas of others and actively participate in the creation of new ways of thinking. "The clever thing is to recognize this and not to let one's thinking stay within the boundaries of two alternatives which are mutually exclusive" (32). In other words, "we never let ourselves be bullied by an 'either-or.' There is often the possibility of something better than either of two given alternatives" (49). Therefore, being actively engaged and having an open mind ready to see things in a new light is critical to knowledge production. People must "acquire the attitude of learning to make them see that education is for life" (Follett 1998, 370). For this reason Follett insists that "every one of us must first acquire the scientific attitude of mind" (Follett 2013c, 30).

While Follett is emphatic that knowledge comes from integrating all relevant experience, and while she disagrees with her critics who insist integration is "too Utopian a method to be worth trying" (Follett 1926, 256), she also does not pretend that this is a simple process. She advises, "We seek reality in experience . . . Experience may be hard but we claim gifts because they are real, even though our feet bleed on its stones" (Follett 2013c, 302). Yet, she does not leave us despondent in the face of the difficulty of this task. Indeed, she applauds "the possibilities of human effort, of disciplined effort, in truth in its Anglo-Saxon meaning (*tryw*) of faithfulness" (303). We can be happily faithful to the continual building and rebuilding of community and collaborative knowledge through the process of integration. Indeed, she advises that we are already often engaged in "that method without realizing that we are doing so" (Follett 1926, 256).

SUMMARY ANALYSIS

Much of Follett's epistemological explication is contained in *Creative Experience* and reflects her relational process ontology and resulting integrative psychosocial identity and condition. As such, knowledge is constantly being co-created and recreated anew through participatory experimentation and integration. Follett's pragmatist epistemology rejects the foundational approaches of empiricism, rationalism, and idealism, along with any form of static truth they might produce. Instead, she allows for a synthesis of internal and external sources of validation, along with the use of evidence, individual interpretation, and perception in analysis. For Follett truth is not something "out there" to be discovered or verified, but is something that is co-created through the social process, involving the experience of all. She calls for all of us "to base our life on actual experience, of my own plus that of others" (Follett 2013c, 29). In doing so we employ what she refers to as a "scientific attitude of mind" (29). We also open ourselves to the integrating of multiple perspectives, creating knowledge by "watching varying activities in their relatings to other varying activities" (68) within the total situation.

Therefore, Follett's methodology for knowledge production is applicable to any process through which integration is possible. Her relational process approach to epistemology accommodates the assertion that the "only test of probable truth is what works best in the way of leading us, what fits every part of life best and combines with the collectivity of experience's demands, nothing being omitted" (James 1955, 61). However, this requires a willingness to engage in the intentional social construction of truth. If one is consciously or tacitly working from a realist or idealist epistemology, integration may not be successful. To overcome this barrier, a change of attitude may be required, which is discussed in Chapter 6.

ENDNOTES

1. Thus, Follett's understanding of epistemology is aligned with phenomenology (see for example, Husserl 1982).

2. Tonn (2003) notes that *Creative Experience* (1924) was the culmination of a rocky collaboration with sociologist Eduard Lindeman, who simultaneously produced *Social Discovery* (1924), although the original intention was to produce a joint "Manifesto" on the phenomenon and study of social conflict.

3. In this way she reflects American pragmatism (see for example, Dewey 1920; James 1907; Peirce 1877).

4. On the point of experimentation and open-minded observation, Tonn (2003) suggests that Follett resembles the progressive thinkers examined

in James T. Kloppenberg's comparative intellectual history, *Uncertain Victory: Social Democracy and Progressivism in European and American Thought, 1870-1920* (1988).

5. Mattson (1998) argues that this carries forward from her own experiences in practice: "For Follett, the democratic processes in social centers showed philosophers how they might evade the endless debate between idealism and realism by synthesizing the best from both approaches" (xliv).

6. Follett appears to follow the arguments made by Bergson (2007) in his book, *The Creative Mind: An Introduction to Metaphysics*.

7. Here, Follett describes what Whitehead (1997) calls the "fallacy of misplaced concreteness" (51).

8. Here, Follett appears to understand Bergson's (2010) claim that intuition is the holistic, non-dualistic knowledge that produces the most accurate knowledge. He believes images to be an intermediate point between idealism and realism—that they were more than mere representations, but something less than matter itself. Such pure perception cannot produce full knowledge because the image loses something in the process.

9. Tonn (2003) suggests Follett disagrees with the pragmatist understanding of verifying put forth by James and Dewey. In this context Cobb (2004) underlines that a human being, along with the culture he or she creates, is neither separated from nature nor placed above it as God's representative who subdues the earth. Rather, he or she is settled in nature and connected with it; nature and culture are unified. Because of this, the sense and fulfillment of human life is not the exclusive result of analyses of the mind (soul) or experiences of the material body as independently operating spheres of experience but rather comes from dialogically creating new possibilities, which in process theology is compared to the dance of life; the meaningfulness of reality consists of its participants' creative acts.

10. Her discussion appears to group together idealist and rationalist approaches to concept formation under the labels of *idealism* juxtaposed to *empiricism*.

11. It is interesting to note that Stever (1986) describes Follett's philosophy as a hybrid of idealism and pragmatism because while she embraces the importance of collective action, she rejects predetermined transcendental norms that would constrain such collaboration.

12. Maddock and Mcalpine (2006) note that Follett was critical of the tendency of pragmatists to separate thinking from doing.

13. This is similar to Whitehead's claim that sense perception is rooted in the perception of *causal efficacy*—our deep sense of interrelating, mutual

causation and co-creation (Mesle 2008).

14. "Follett believed that experimentation and theoretical understanding should serve the purpose of assisting the moral and social progress of the human community" (Mendenhall, Macomber, and Cutright 2000, 203).

15. McLarney and Rhyno (1999) suggest Follett "may have been one of the first action researchers" (302).

16. Tonn (2003) notes that Follett was partially at odds with her peers in her call for the expert, as Walter Lippmann, Herbert Croly, John Dewey, and others were clamoring for more expertise in the social process. For example, she rejects the democratic elitism expressed in Walter Lippmann's *Public Opinion* (1922) and refuses to accept the judge as the sole guardian of truth.

17. While noted in discussion of Follett's Ontological Concepts and Language, the concepts of *power-over* and *power-with* are fully explicated in Chapter 7.

18. Morton and Lindquist (1997) link Follett's examination of power in who controls knowledge to feminist examinations of "knowledge claims in connection with hierarchy and power" (361).

19. In this way, Follett prophesizes the postmodern feminist critique of knowledge as power (see for example, Sandoval 2000).

20. Such a synthesis is described in Whiteheadian thought as "pan-experientialism" (Mesle 2008, 94).

21. Here, Follett presages the contemporary movement toward participatory policy analysis and public planning.

22. Here, Follett follows Hegel (1977) in his understanding of intersubjectivity. Mattson (1998) similarly argues that Follett's thinking was part of the intellectual revolution emphasizing the notion of intersubjectivity.

23. This classical pragmatist language of "truth" and "facts" should not be mistaken for realism, as the pragmatist relational process meanings of these terms are not the same as the positivist atomistic and static meanings which tend to dominate scientific discourse.

24. Tonn (2003) suggests that Follett's refusal to put forward absolute principles in favor of a tentative approach to investigation follows the pragmatist thinking of T. H. Green, Henry Sidgwick, and William James.

25. Indeed, Follett's approach provides what Ansell (2011) describes as pragmatism's "most important" approach to addressing dualisms, an insistence on a "tight coupling between meaning and action" (10) in which the conceptual and empirical are aligned such that "meaning is discovered through action" (11).

26. Morton and Lindquist (1997) liken this focus on experience to feminist epistemology, arguing that Follett's epistemological concepts presage contemporary feminist theory.

27. This same argument was later made by Schmidt (1993).

৯ 5 ৯

Follett's Beliefs

Belief refers to traditions of faith and scientific beliefs about ontology and psychosocial condition. Thus, belief systems gather together sets of assumptions that frame a particular position or perspective. In such systems we find descriptions of existence as either *static* or *dynamic* in *state*, with *sources of existence* being either metaphysical (*transcendent*) or natural (*immanent*) in character. This is the basis of the dichotomy of the divine and the earthly, the metaphysical and the physical, the sublime and the mundane.

Because Follett does not explicate deeply or dwell upon matters of belief, this discussion is necessarily concise. However, it is important to understand how Follett integrates for herself science and faith as a foundation for her applied theories in ethics, politics, economics, and administration. Follett never declares a system of belief, yet she frequently refers to the metaphysical, the spiritual, and even God. For Follett, a participatory universe is collaborating in co-creating all that is: "God is the moving force of the world, the ever-continuing creating where men are the co-creators" (Follett 1998, 103). This assumption is likely drawn from her Quaker upbringing, in which one's relationship with God is very direct and personal. Furthermore, given her study of philosophy, she argues, "We must know now that we are coworkers with every process of creation, that our function is as important as the power which keeps the stars in their orbits" (100).

These types of statements suggest a transcendent power—the process of creation—guiding or working with humankind, which could be interpreted as either monism or pantheism. As such, these statements could be somewhat at cross-purposes with her ontological formulation of One-becoming-through-Many. However, as she explains, in a whole a-making, "organism and environment do not 'express' but make wholes" (Follett 2013c, 125); "nor are subject and object 'products' of a vital force" (55). As such we are Many parts of the whole or the One. "What is the whole doing? It is not a quiet Beneficence watching benignly over its busy children. It does not live vicariously *in* its 'parts' any more than it lives vicariously *for* its 'parts.' The parts are neither its progenitors nor its offspring" (101). There is only "the whole a-making; this involves a study of whole and parts in their active and *continuous* relation to each other" (102).[1]

These explanations clarify her occasional references to what sounds like a transcendent source of being beyond extant beings (God) that orders the whole. Instead, beings themselves *assemble* the whole in dynamic configurations through integration and the impulse toward unifying of ever greater wholes.[2] She notes that this alternative view of spirituality is a demanding proposition:

> That kind of religion which consists of contemplation of other-worldliness is the easy way, and we take to that when we have not enough vitality deliberately to direct our life and construct our world. It takes more spiritual energy to express the group spirit than the particularist spirit. This is its glory as well as its difficulty. We have to be higher order of beings to do it—we become higher order of beings by doing it. And so the progress goes on forever: it means life forever in the making, and the creative responsibility of every man. (Follett 1998, 103)

This is most richly explained in *Creative Experience*: "The doctrine of circular response involved in the theory of integration gives us creative experience" (Follett 2013c, 116).

> But the theory of creative experiences given to us by the most profound philosophy throughout the ages, and now so happily strengthened by recent research in several fields, shows that the individual can create without "transcending." He expresses, brings into manifestation, powers which are the powers of the universe and thereby those forces which he is himself helping to create, those which exist in and by and through him, are ever more ready to respond, and so Life expands and deepens; fulfils [*sic*] and at the same moment makes possible larger fulfilment [*sic*]. (Follett 2013c, 116)

In this way she links spiritual growth with progressive thought in the developmental sense: "We can often measure our progress by watching the nature of our conflicts. Social progress is in this respect like individual progress; we become spiritually more and more developed as our conflicts rise to higher levels" (Follett 2003b, 35).[3] Follett equates this process to a reinterpreted atonement with God: "The unifying of difference is the eternal process of life—the creative synthesis, the highest act of creation, the at-onement" (Follett 1998, 40). But it is the human being that she considers most responsible: "Our task is to make straight the paths for the coming of the Lord—the true Individual" (291).

Here, Follett's thinking moves toward a humanism that considers human-kind as co-creators of spiritual power, created through conscious awareness of the community between us: "that higher creation which we . . . make when we come together. In that way only will spiritual power be generated" (Follett 1998, 79). She describes the creative energy released from this place between us as the "cosmic force in the womb of humanity" (342). She asserts, "We surely to-day have come to see in the social bond and the Creative Will, a compelling power, a depth and force, as great as that of any religion we have ever known. We are ready for a new revelation of God. It is not coming through any single man, but through the men and men who are banding together with one purpose, in one consecrated service, for a great fulfilment [*sic*]" (359-60). These are the statements that more fully describe a form of panentheism—at least in terms of humanity—all beings are co-creating a sacred whole.

But on this point, Follett's ontological ideas suggest inclusion of the non-human world in the process of co-creation as well. When considering the whole as a social process *plus* the environment in a similar reciprocal state as a whole a-making, you have "the total situation—also a-making" (Follett 2013c, 102). This opens the way further to a panentheistic belief system—the One is co-created by the Many, human and nonhuman alike.[4]

However, on this point Follett does not dwell. Instead, similar to Dewey (1934), she aims toward a public faith or a particular type of humanism that holds sacred the spiritual aspects of the socially embedded self: "We believe in the sacredness of all our life; we believe that Divinity is forever incarnating in humanity, and so we believe in Humanity and the common daily life of all men" (Follett 1998, 244). "Democracy is faith in humanity . . . a great spiritual unity which is supported by the most vital trend in philosophical thought and by the latest biologists and social psychologists" (156). Thus "evil is non-relation" (62) and "non-relation is death" (63).

In the embodied sense of panentheism, Follett (2013) insists "the divorce of our so-called spiritual life from our daily activities is a fatal dualism" (87). Instead, "we need a new faith in humanity, not a sentimental faith or a theological tenet or a philosophical conception, but an active faith in that creative power of men which shall shape government and industry, which shall give form equally to our daily life with our neighbor and to a world league" (Follett 1998, 360). Therefore, "every man sharing in the creative process is democracy; this is our politics and our religion" (103). As such, democracy "is a great spiritual force evolving itself from men, utilizing each, completing his incompleteness by weaving together all in the many-membered community life which is the true Theophany" (161).[5]

Here Follett refers to *theophaneia*, the ancient Greek notion of divine disclosure. Thus, the process of democratic interpenetration is spiritual in her mind. "We want to-day to do it spiritually, to direct the spiritual currents in their flow and interflow so that we have not only the external interpenetration—choosing representatives etc.—but the deeper interpenetration which shows the minds and needs and wants of all men. We can satisfy our wants only by a genuine union and communion of all, only in the friendly outpouring of heart to heart" (Follett 1998, 257).

These revisions of divinity, sacredness, and spirituality enable Follett to simultaneously fiercely defend science and the social sciences, albeit not the kind promoted by "the fact worshippers" (Follett 2013c, 54). She insists that the process of true democracy is not metaphysical or religious in the received sense, but rather a matter of social psychology emerging from actual experience.

> We now see that the problem of the compounding of consciousness, of the One and the Many, need not be left either to an intellectualistic or to an intuitive metaphysics. It is to be solved through a laboratory study of group psychology. When we have that, we shall not have to argue any more about the One and the Many: we shall actually see the Many and the One emerging at the same time; we can then work out the laws of relation of the One (the state) to the Many (the individual), and of the Many (the individual) to the One (the state), not as a metaphysical question but on a scientific basis. . . . There is nothing "metaphysical" or "religious" about this. (Follett 1998, 272-73)

Thus, she finds it possible to use these emergent, experientially derived spiritual principles in public activities like jurisprudence, insisting that critics who argue metaphysics leads to the rejection of science are wrong: "This is not a necessary consequence of the recognition of metaphysical principles. We do not want to give up principles except in so far as they are divorced from experience; the empirical road leads always to principles and these are principles in which we can put our faith" (Follett 2013c, 276).

Taken together, Follett's metaphysical humanism linked to democracy and its public ethic enables her to reinterpret the notion of the state as a spiritual chalice rather than a prison.[6] She claims, "the home of my soul" (Follett 1998, 312) is in the unifying state because it provides the method through which wholeness is pursued—integrative process. As Cabot (1934) explains, "Like other forms of human association the State is for Miss Follett a part of the gymnastics of the soul. Self-development through self-government is the formula alike for each individual and for every national group" (81). The state need not be feared if it is merely a process through which differences are harmonized and spiritual power is thereby generated. She calls this power a "coöperative sovereignty" (Follett 1998, 316).

SUMMARY ANALYSIS

Follett does not explicate deeply or dwell upon matters of belief and her comments tend to be rather inconsistent, sometimes referring to theistic concepts, sometimes referring to humanist concepts, and sometimes referring to concepts more akin to alternative spirituality. Taken together, it can be assumed that in the end, Follett's source of being is neither fully transcendent nor immanent; it is sacred, multidimensional, and inclusive of both human and nonhuman beings in a manner that exceeds the limits of humanism. Like Dewey (1934), Follett aims toward a public faith or a particular type of humanism that holds sacred the spiritual aspects of the socially embedded, co-creating self: "We believe in the sacredness of all our life; we believe that Divinity is forever incarnating in humanity, and so we believe in Humanity and the common daily life of all men" (Follett 1998, 244). Therefore, "democracy is faith in humanity . . . a great spiritual unity which is supported by the most vital trend in philosophical thought and by the latest biologists and social psychologists" (156).

ENDNOTES

1. Johnson (2007) sees the same pattern and suggests that taken in whole, Follett's definitions of religion and God "are closer to the concept of spirituality than to the religious doctrines of churches" (432).

2. "It also is clear that Follett saw relating as the means to achieving spirituality in individuals, the workplace and in other realms of society such as the law, politics, psychology, and sociology, culminating in democracy or the new state" (Johnson 2007, 436).

3. This is similar to the Whiteheadian notion that with increased complexity of experience, the ability to affect and be affected increases: "In short, the higher we go toward more complex organisms, the more the power to be *affected* emerges" (Mesle 2008, 72). As Cobb (1982) argues, "because all that I am and do is taken up into the divine life along with all the consequences of my acts in the lives of others, I cannot escape the seriousness, the importance, of how I use my freedom. I see the truth of the idea that everything I do to my neighbor I do also to God" (79).

4. In this way, Follett sounds more akin to new materialism and posthumanism than humanism (see for example, Braidotti 2013; Coole and Frost 2010a).

5. Spirituality is therefore defined as "a means to provide meaning in one's life, to foster growth and development, and to establish connectedness and community, thereby helping individuals see that they are a part of something bigger than themselves" (Johnson 2007, 427). This speaks to Follett's holism and multidimensionality of the human being, integrated spiritual life, as well as her public ethic and understanding of progress.

6. Johnson (2007) would extend this also to the workplace as chalice for spiritual growth and expression.

৯ 6 ৯

Follett's Conception of Ethics

*E*thics are systems of value that guide action. They may be based on *internal sources* that are described as motivations or *external sources* that are described as criteria. Accordingly, they either emphasize *right* as proper action or *good* as an end value (Kagan 1998). While Follett uses the term *right*, its meaning must be co-determined by all within the situation. It may be something the group accepts as proper, or an end value that is considered to be good—the focus is on the *process* through which these decisions are made.

Carrying forward her understanding of the dynamic, relational individual, Follett asserts, "the essence of this psychology ... is as important for ethics as for physiology or psychology; for sociology its value is inestimable" (Follett 2013c, 88).[1] In her discussions of ethics, Follett refers to her friend and Harvard ethics professor, Richard Cabot, as an influential source and supporter of this view. She also refers often to Roscoe Pound, Dean of the Harvard Law School, and his theory of modern law as an evolving, relational practice.[2]

For Follett, the "ethical unit" is the group, not the individual (Follett 2013c, 112). Furthermore, integrative process is the source of ethics, as opposed to an external source of any type. Thus, it is not the *substance* of the collective will but the *process of creating* that is its "germinating centre" (Follett 1998, 49).[3] Following her philosophical approach, the process of generating an ethic is integrative and relational rather than procedural and formal, although she often presents her explanation in the context of law and jurisprudence as they are the application of ethics. This is likely due

94

to Follett's perception that the modern theory of law "points the way with force and convincingness to a New Society based on the evolving not the static principle of life" (Follett 1998, 130). She claims, "We are evolving now a system of ethics which has three conceptions in regard to right, conscience and duty" (52). Thus, her explication is structured around the ethical concepts of right, purpose, loyalty, and obedience; each component will be discussed in turn.

RIGHT

Right is a characteristic assigned to actions a given society or group believes to be good, proper, and just. Right is often expressed through principles, values, and other criteria for judging decisions or behavior. However, it is also often formulated as interest—either individual or collective. Follett's understanding of right is composed of two interweaving characteristics—it can only be legitimately determined through a process which is relational. Each aspect will be discussed in turn.

Right through process

Follett recognizes that in ethical considerations and conflicts, people often expect "some pronouncement as to what is 'right' and what is 'wrong'" (Follett 2003k, 239). However, she explains that "we do not follow right, we create right" (Follett 1998, 52). "Our ideals are involved in our activities. . . . We do not adapt our activities to . . . principles behind" (Follett 2013c 86).[4] As such, predetermined principles can no longer provide the sole basis for ethics. She explains, "We do not 'discover' legal principles. . . . Our law therefore cannot be based on 'fixed' principles: our law must be intrinsic in the social process" (Follett 1998, 131). Thus, "in so far as we obey old standards without interpenetrating them with the actual world, we are abdicating our creative power" (53). Instead, "our ideals must evolve from day to day, and it is upon those who can fearlessly embrace the doctrine of 'becoming' that the life of the future waits" (99). Thus, "the legal order today is telling us that precedents are to be interpreted in the light of events always in flux" (Follett 2013c, 31).

Right through relation

Follett notes that with acceptance of integrative process as the source of an evolving understanding of right, "part of our political and legal science will have to be rewritten" (Follett 2013c, 83). Specifically, Follett argues that "modern law considers individuals not as isolated beings, but in their relation to the life of the whole community" (Follett 1998, 128). In making her argument, she refers to Roscoe Pound's writing on relation: "All that he says of relation implies that we must seek and bring into use those modes of association which will reveal joint interests: those between employer and employee, landlord and tenant, master and servant. Law, he tells us, must find the essential nature of the relation" (Follett 2013c, 47).

Follett also draws from French administrative law scholar Léon Duguit, although adding that his pragmatism is "one that has not yet rid itself of absolute standards" (Follett 1998, 276): "The *droit* [law or right] evolved by a group is the *droit* of that group ... *le droit* comes from relation and is always in relation" (278). His thinking appears to inform her development of evolving, situated ethical principles: "We want to find the law *of* the situation *in* the situation and yet still be guided by law and not by personal or national whims or a narrow self-interest" (Follett 2013c, 152). In this statement, Follett's synthesis of right and good as well as external criteria with internal motivation is revealed.[5]

As she explains further: "We have not to choose between a moral atomism and general ethical laws; principles are immensely valuable—on the other side of the equation, as part of the stuff of the situation, as part of the warp and woof of our concrete life" (Follett 2013c, 142). But principles "should be thrown into the situation in order that from all the intermingling a new thought may be evolved" (142). Furthermore, she notes this does not mean throwing away rational thinking either: "I have said that ethics cannot be divorced from intelligence, that these two are one" (172). However, she is adamant on the point of whether law is objective or subjective: "it is neither, it is both; we look at the matter quite differently" (Follett 1998, 278).[6]

Follett applies the same type of analysis to the notion of right as interest. Right as *self*-interest does not consider others while right as *social* interest pits the individual against the collective in a zero-sum trade-off. There are two problems with these conceptualizations. First, "the expressions social and socially-minded, which should refer to a consciousness of the whole, are often confused with altruism ... this is involved in the old individualism" (Follett 1998, 80). These are "social values, to be sure, in the sense in which jurists use that term—individual values generalized—but not in the sense in which that term was used when social reformers or the architects or the legislators supporting the measure addressed the voters. These speakers used it with its emotional appeal, with its moralistic appeal of 'sacrificing' your individual interests to the 'general good'" (Follett 2013c, 37). Using the example of competing interests between business and labor, Follett reiterates her belief that "any talk of the sacrifice of interests on the employer's part because of altruistic feeling is pure sentimentality; we do not want either side to sacrifice its interests for we want nothing lost, we want all the interests to be united" (170-71). Thus, it is "an understanding of . . . integrative unity which . . . will keep us not only from a false individualism, but also from a false altruism" (Follett 2003a, 82).

Second, framing right as social interest engenders "the temptation to call what *we* think good 'social'" (Follett 2013c, 46). This is simply a re-labeling of self-interest as social interest by those who have the authority or power to do so. "Reformers, propagandists, many of our 'best' people are willing to coerce others in order to attain an end which *they* think good" (Follett 2003j, 102). "We do all of us want our own way, want the way which seems to us right" (Follett 2003l, 214). However, to be legitimate, social interest must be "understood as a unifying of interests benefiting and developing individuals, benefiting and developing society" (Follett 2013c, 48). This means that the social interest is expansive and inclusive of all in that society: "Social interests are the interests of men in their multitudinous and ever-varying *relations*" (47). Therefore, the process through which the social interest is determined must change. For an alternative, she refers to recent developments in psychology, physiology and physics, urging social science and jurisprudence to follow suit. "There seems to be some reason in the development of recent thinking for substituting the term integrating interests—the integrating of individual interests—for that of social interests" (42).

Follett goes on to quote Roscoe Pound: "'The social interest in the individual, the individual interest in the social' must become coordinate expressions" (Follett 2013c, 47). By this she means a formulation of right as a shared interest in which individual desires are woven together without being suppressed in determining what is good, proper, and just: "Our interests are inextricably interwoven. The question is not what is best for me or for you, but for all of us" (Follett 1998, 81). When developed through this relational process, right becomes democratically legitimate because "no mandate from without has power over us" (53).[7] This form of subordination is not others *over* individual; "it means the subordination of the individual to the whole of which he himself is a part. Such subordination is an act of assertion; it is fraught with active power and force; it affirms and accomplishes" (Follett 1998, 82). As an element of self-governance, "morality is not the refraining from doing certain things—it is a constructive force" (53). "When the ought is not a mandate from without, it is no longer a prohibition but a self-expression" (53).

However, in this active co-production, right also carries responsibility: "I should like to emphasize our responsibility for integration" (Follett 2003b, 48). This means that the question of who will be involved in determining right is still somewhat problematic. We must be active participants in co-creating right to meet this test of legitimacy. Yet, in the process of integration, the capabilities of any participant cannot be exceeded. Follett gives an example in her discussion of moral and spiritual capacity: "If a man should tell you that his chief daily conflict within himself is—Shall I steal or not steal?—You would know what to think of his stage of development" (35).

PURPOSE

Follett continues building her new system of ethics by asserting that, like principles, pre-determined ends or values cannot be the sole basis for ethics as is often the case: "A teleological psychology sees an anticipatory purpose . . . a teleological sociology is founded on anticipatory purposes; a teleological jurisprudence conceives the function of law as comparison of present activity with a preconceived purpose" (Follett 2013c, 33). But Follett argues, "No more fatally disastrous conception has ever dominated us than the conception of static ends" (Follett 1919, 578). Therefore, she hopes that jurists "will soon show us explicitly some of the errors involved in a teleological jurisprudence" (584).

Alternatively, Follett asserts that *purpose* must be formed through a relational process that enables difference to result in constructive conflicts that feed into a creative process of integration. The end result of that process is the *collective will*: "an integrating desire which is continuously interweaving with the separate desires" of each member of the group (Follett 2013c, 112).

Purpose through process

Following her understanding of right as determined through relational process, Follett insists that *purpose* must also be determined through relational process: "What I wish to emphasize is the necessity of creating the collective will" (Follett 1998, 48). There can be no firm teleological objective because all of life is in process.[8] "Social ends are not pre-existing things but eventual things" (Follett 2013c, 42). She goes on to explain that "purpose is never in front of us, it appears at every moment with the appearance of will" (Follett 1998, 277). "Our ideals are involved in our activities. . . . We do not adapt our activities to ends in front" (Follett 2013c, 86). Thus, "the whole philosophy of cause and effect must be re-written" (Follett 1998, 57). "Every teleological view will be given up when we see that purpose is not 'preexistent,' but involved in the unifying act which is the life process. It is man's part to create purpose and to actualize it" (58).

Through her synthesis of idealism and realism, Follett explains, "ends and means truly and literally make each other. A system built around a purpose is dead before it is born" (Follett 1919, 579). Instead, "purpose is always the appearing of the power of unifying, the ranging of multiplicity into that which is both means and ends" (Follett 2013c, 82). Follett insists, "Wherever one turns one sees examples of the evolving purpose . . . rather than a preconceived purpose" (32). Again, she emphasizes that this process is relational: "In the social process the purpose is a part of the integrating activity; it is not something outside, a prefigured object of contemplation toward which we are moving" (Follett 1919, 578). Rather than externally imposed principles, "human relation should serve an anticipatory purpose. Every relation should be a freeing relation with the 'purpose' evolving" (Follett 2013c, 83). Therefore, rather than relying on pre-determined ends, "it now seems clear that we must look for purpose within the process itself. We see experience as an interplay of forces, as the activity of relating leading through fresh relatings to a new activity, not from purpose to deed and deed to purpose with a fatal gap between" (81). Indeed, it is community that "creates purpose, continually creates purpose" (Follett 1919, 578).

However, leaving it at that is insufficient. Follett asks, "But if one accepts the notion of an evolving purpose, the next question is one of valuation: who is to decide between the values of various purposes?" (Follett 2013c, 33). To answer, Follett breaks the process down into a set of integrative activities. At the ontological and at much of the psychosocial levels of analysis, integration is understood as the process of circular response—something that simply happens. In the activity of making a group and formulating ethics and guiding ethical action, integration becomes an intentional process used to co-create not only the group, but also what the group considers to be right as well as a shared purpose and collective will. Indeed, "the basis of all coöperative activity is integrated diversity" (Follett 2013c, 174). "We get progress when we find a way that includes the ideas of both or the several parties to the controversy. But this requires hard thinking, inventiveness, ingenuity. We should never think of integration as a foregone conclusion; it is an achievement" (Follett 2003l, 213).

To become more adept at integrating, Follett recommends developing and learning the *method of integration*: "Those who accept integration rather than compromise or domination as the law of social relations will seek the method" (Follett 2013c, 165). Thus, the method begins with a shift in attitude about difference and conflict as opportunities for creative resolution. Follett says, "It seems to me that the phrase integrating individual interests, as referring to both the possible outcome of conflict and the anticipation of conflict . . . is a more fruitful and more legitimate expression than that of social interests, and one supported by both recent legal and psychological thinking as well as by our most profound philosophy" (49-50). Thus, the method includes two phases or components: (1) the anticipation of constructive conflict; and (2) the creative integration of differences. Each will be explained in turn.

Constructive conflict

Follett recognizes that "dealing with difference is the main part of the social process" (Follett 2013c, 7). She asks us to temporarily release preconceptions about conflict in order to consider it from a pragmatist perspective: "At the outset I should like to ask you to agree for the moment to think of conflict as neither good nor bad; to consider it without ethical pre-judgement [*sic*]; to think of it not as warfare, but as the appearance of difference, difference of opinions, of interests. For that is what conflict means—difference" (Follett 2003b, 30). The pragmatist response is to seek the creative possibilities of that conflict—what Follett terms "constructive conflict" (Follett 2003b).[9] She goes on to explain that "when differing interests meet, they need not oppose but only confront each other. The confronting of interests may result in either one of four things: (1) voluntary submission of one side; (2) struggle and the victory of one side over the other; (3) compromise; or (4) integration" (Follett 2013c, 156). She later provides more accessible categorical labels: "There are three main ways of dealing with conflict: domination, compromise and integration" (Follett 2003b, 31).

Voluntary submission and coerced subjugation are the two primary forms of domination. In describing the differences between debate and deliberation, she notes that in the former, "the different groups would come together each to try to prevail . . . When the desire to prevail is once keenly upon us, we behave very differently than when our object is the seeking of truth" (Follett 1998, 308). She notes, "Enough has been said of domination whether obtained by a show of power or use of power" (Follett 2013c, 156). This option is clearly problematic: "To impose one's will upon other[s]; sounds so crude that there are few people who will confess to wishing to do that, but suppose that I am willing to dominate and to acknowledge it; even so, is it the process most likely to succeed in the long run? I think not, because the fellow executive on whom I impose my will, next time will try to impose his will on me" (Follett 2003l, 214-15). Because coercion is unacceptable in a democratic context; "we must solve the problem of uniting men without crushing them" (Follett 2013c, 165). However, oppression isn't the only problem with domination. From a pragmatist perspective, even voluntary submission forfeits the synergistic value of co-creation. As discussed in her critique of the crowd, she chastises such behavior: "Imitation is for the shirkers, like-mindedness for the comfort lovers, unifying for the creators" (Follett 1998, 38).

Because domination is neither democratic nor productive, "we preach 'compromise' as the apex of ethical life, we laude the 'balance of power' as our political and international faith" (Follett 2013c, ix). However, Follett does not agree that compromise is the best answer to domination because "compromise sacrifices the integrity of the individual. . . . No fairer life for men will ever be the fruit of such doctrine" (x). Follett is adamant on this point: "Compromise, the evil of our present constitution of society, politically, industrially and internationally" (164). Indeed, the sacrifice required in compromise is no more laudable to Follett than explicit domination: "I put domination and sacrifice together as based on the same error. If I dominate you, I get what I want. If I sacrifice myself to you, you get what you want. I do not see why one way is any better than the other. The only gain would be if we could both have what we want" (Follett 2003l, 215).

Furthermore, from the pragmatist perspective "compromise too is temporary and futile. It usually means merely a postponement of the issue" and is therefore a "sham reconciliation" (Follett 2013c, 156). Its temporary nature is due in part to our dynamic ontology and identity: "If the self with its purpose and its will is even for a moment a finished product, then of course the only way to get a common will is through compromise. But the truth is that the self is always in flux, weaving itself and again weaving itself" (Follett 2013c, 164). But more concretely, "when we compromise; something is always lost" (Follett 2003l, 214) while the original desire remains. "We now see the false psychology underlying compromise and concession. Their practical futility has long been evident: whenever any difference is 'settled' by concession, that difference pops up again in some other form" (Follett 1998, 114). Specifically, "Freudian psychology shows us that compromise is a form of suppression. And as the Freudians show us that a 'suppressed' impulse will be our undoing later, so we see again and again that what has been 'suppressed' in the compromises of politics or of labor disputes crops up anew to bring more disastrous results" (Follett 1919, 577). Therefore, "nothing will ever truly settle differences but synthesis" (Follett 1998, 114).

Thus, Follett turns to integration as the appropriate method for responding to conflict and difference. It is through integration that we can achieve gain by synthesizing interests, instead of loss by sacrificing them. "Integration means three things: you and I both get what we want, the whole situation moves forward, and the process often has community value" (Follett 2003l, 215). Therefore, "the legal order is now beginning to see that there may often be found by acute, fair-minded, and inventive judges ways of settling disputes which give to both sides what they really want" (Follett 2013c, 44). Through what we would now call mediation or alternative dispute resolution, Follett observes that "opposed interests are not necessarily incompatible interests" (43). "Our 'opponents' are our co-creators, for they have something to give which we have not" (174). The key to this understanding is to embrace fully the meaning of circular response: "If I am never fighting you but always you plus myself, that is, that 'whole' which the interweaving between you and me has created, is creating, we shall have a very different idea of the way to deal with conflict" (129) in which conflict transformation does not require a method "of self-sacrifice, but one of self-contribution" (Follett 2003l, 215).

Considering each of these aspects of conflict, "we see that while conflict as continued unintegrated difference is pathological, difference itself is not pathological" (Follett 2003b, 35). Through this re-conceptualization we need not fear or avoid conflict. "But conflict there will always be in the sense of a confrontation, a facing, to be followed by an integrating" (Follett 2013c, 173). Always with an eye to the practical, Follett admits, "We cannot always reach such happy conclusions . . . but I think we should succeed much more often than we now think possible" (43).

Integrative ethics

Once we attain a shift in attitude that includes the desire to pursue shared interests rather than oppositional individual or social interests and embrace the notion of conflict as difference, we can then enter into sincere conversation with an openness to change. Follett notes that deliberative discussion, as opposed to debate, is "the only genuine democratic process, that of trying to integrate their ideas and interests" (Follett 1998, 308).[10] In these dialogical interactions, creative ideas can be brought forth, with which those involved in the situation may find agreement.[11] Follett explains this process of intentional integration in some detail.[12]

The method of integration begins with sincerity and honesty in communication: "The first rule, then, for obtaining integration is to put your cards on the table, face the real issue, uncover the conflict, bring the whole thing into the open" (Follett 2003b, 38). This is the start of "genuine discussion" which Follett believes "will always and should always bring out difference, but at the same time it teaches us what to do with difference. The formative process which takes place in discussion is that unceasing reciprocal adjustment which brings out and gives form to truth" (Follett 1998, 212).

One technique for overcoming difficulties is progressive decision making, or what we would now call consensus-building. Follett explains: "One way of breaking up wholes in conference is to split the question up as minutely as possible and take the vote as you go along" (Follett 2013c, 166). The point of this exercise is to get at the genuine desires underneath positions—this is where progress can be made toward identifying common ground. By identifying shared desires, the positions are released and reformulated together so that decisions are taken "which unite the desires of both sides" (161). She explains that "when two desires are *integrated*, that means that a solution has been found in which both desires have found a place, that neither side has had to sacrifice anything" (Follett 2003b, 32). This point is important, reflecting back on her critique of domination and compromise: "This was not a compromise because neither gave up anything" (Follett 2013c, 162). Instead, "a way is found by which neither is absorbed but by which both can contribute to the solution" (162).

The reciprocal dialogue and deliberation process also includes what Follett refers to as "a revaluation of interests" which is "an essential part of any unifying process" (Follett 2013c, 171). She explains, "Revaluation is the flower of comparison. This conception of the revaluation of desire is necessary to keep in the foreground of our thinking in dealing with conflict, for neither side ever 'gives in' really, it is hopeless to expect it, but there often comes a moment when there is a simultaneous revaluation of interests on both sides and unity precipitates itself" (Follett 2003b, 38). Unity is precipitated through an organic change of opinion that comes through dialogue: "Through an interpenetrating of understanding, the quality of one's own thinking is changed" (Follett 2013c, 163). "The course of action decided upon is what we all together want, and I see that it is better than what I had wanted alone. It is what *I* now want" (Follett 1998, 25). However, this is not a purely intellectual process. As noted in her discussion of right through process, Follett employs the pragmatist epistemology to synthesize fact and value:[13] "One of the most important results of analysis and discrimination as the first step in the resolution of conflict, is that we find that our decisions must be based upon intelligence as well as upon morals" (Follett 2013c, 170).

Follett explains this transformational process in further detail. "Consider what influences a change of opinion . . . (1) changes in the situation which make me see my interests differently, (2) changes in myself caused by the situation, (3) other things which may give me a deeper understanding of this situation, (4) values when put together look different from the same values considered separately, for in the act of comparison there is a simultaneous view of all values in the field which register themselves to their relative claims, they acquire perspective. Values depend largely on relation" (Follett 2013c, 171-72).

It is often the case that revaluation and evolving opinion reveal a perspective not considered before. Follett notes, "the best way out is always when someone invents something new" (Follett 2013c, 157). Indeed, she notes that integration can be used "as a way out of the dilemma" (162). "Here is the way of progress" (160). "We want the plus values of the conflict" (xiv). This added value comes from the co-creativity inherent to integration. As in Follett's ontology, the whole situation, including potentiality and past experience are included. Therefore, "we must not make the error of thinking that our search for the new means the abandonment of the old . . . creative activity does not disregard the past . . . I like better the term progressive integration" (160).

Again, Follett notes that this is not an easy proposition: "Not all differences, however, can be integrated. That we must face fully, but it is certain that there are fewer irreconcilable activities than we at present think, although it often takes ingenuity, a 'creative intelligence,' to find the integration" (Follett 2013c, 163). Furthermore, she notes that we must not ignore the probability of disintegration and disruption within the creative process of integration: "This point ought to be much further developed, for it would prevent us from too superficial an optimism . . . yet disruption is only a part of that total life process to which, in its more comprehensive aspect, we may give the name integration" (178).

In sum, Follett describes the process of developing shared purpose through constructive conflict and integration along with its progressive value: "The confronting of diverse desires, the thereby revealing of 'values,' the consequent revaluation of values, a uniting of desires which we welcome above all because it means that the next diversity will emerge on a higher social level—this is progress" (Follett 2013c, xiii). Again, in the pragmatist spirit, she remarks, "Some people tell me that they like what I have written on integration, but say that I am not talking of what ought to be instead of what is. But I am not; I am talking neither of what is, to any great extent, nor of what ought to be merely, but of what perhaps may be. This we can discover only by experiment" (Follett 2003b, 34).

LOYALTY REINTERPRETED

Once we understand right and purpose as coming from a relational process of integration, "the new ethics will never preach alter feelings but whole feelings" (Follett 1998, 47). Yet loyalty is essential.[14] "There *is* no group, there is no genuine conference, unless there is loyalty; it is imbedded in the innermost meaning of all human relations" (Follett 2013c, 239). But loyalty must always be to an *us* most broadly conceived. "Sympathy is a whole feeling; it is a recognition of oneness . . . it cannot be actualized until we can think and feel together" (Follett 1998, 47).[15] Therefore, there will no longer be subject-object assumptions of *us* and *them*. Follett asserts that *loyalty* stems organically from our experiences in active relational process. "The only unity or community is one we have made of ourselves, by ourselves, for ourselves" (59). The experience of oneness leads to a sense of loyalty and love of the whole. "We belong to our community just in so far as we are helping to make that community then loyalty follows, then love follows" (59). "The love of our fellow-men to be effective must be the love evolved from some actual group relation" (193).

However, she does note that "fellowship will be the slowest thing on earth to create" (Follett 1998, 193). It is built up gradually through interlocking networks of association.[16] Because relatings are complex and contiguous through our varied social roles, Follett notes that it does not make sense to talk about being disloyal to one group when one is loyal to another because "they are both *your* groups" (Follett 2013c, 238). "We see this error of hierarchy in ethics as well as in political philosophy. We hear there also much of conflicting loyalties, and while the pluralist is satisfied to let them fight or balance, others tell us, surely an equally repugnant idea, that we are to abandon the narrower for the wider loyalty, that we are to sacrifice the lesser for the larger duty" (Follett 1919, 581). Indeed, "there is nothing necessarily discreditable in the politician 'standing by' his friends. The only ethical question is how much that motive is weighing against others. The unethical thing is to persuade yourself that it is not weighing at all" (Follett 2003b, 39). Instead, we must accept that loyalty is a natural feeling that stems from relating and seek to broaden our awareness of our relations to include all of humanity: "My individuality is where my centre [*sic*] of consciousness is. From that centre [*sic*] of consciousness, wherever it may be, our judgments will always issue, but the wider its circumference the truer will our judgments be" (Follett 1919, 580).

OBEDIENCE REINTERPRETED

The last principle included in Follett's discussion of ethics is *obedience*. Obedience can be guided by both formal law and informal social norms, both of which are informed by cultural values. Follett notes that "our nineteenth-century legal theory (individual rights, contract, 'a man can do what he likes with his own,' etc.) was based on the conception of the separate individual" (Follett 1998, 61). Follett worries that this perspective does not consider the creative role the individual plays in the state. She says, "we should have a different attitude toward the conception of 'obedience' from that taken by the pluralists, who repudiate obedience as a loss of individuality, as an abandonment of moral integrity. What they forget is the dynamic nature of their 'moral individual.' Our main duty toward the state is not the contribution of static self, but of a developing self. Hence obedience takes on new meaning" (Follett 2013c, 221).

To Follett, the only legitimate claim to obedience must be generated from the total situation—from the combined people and environment impacted by the decisions and actions taking place. According to Follett, "there is no private conscience" (Follett 1998, 52) because we are always part of the whole. The individual cannot decide what is right or wrong—that comes from the social process. It is "a related conscience, a conscience that is intimately related to the consciences of other men and to all the spiritual environment of our time" (56). Therefore, "that person is intellectually or morally defective who is not taking part in the give-and-take of life" (Follett 2003e, 133). Without such active participation, we cannot be obedient to the legitimate source of what is good, proper, and just. "Our duty is never to 'others' but to the whole" (Follett 1998, 52). "My duty as a citizen is not exhausted by what I bring to the state; my test as a citizen is how fully the whole can be expressed in or through me" (179).

These sentiments are likely the reason some scholars associate Follett with communitarianism. Indeed, she even goes so far as to suggest that the state is responsible for morality: "Its supreme function is moral ordering" (Follett 1998, 333). However, she does not embrace communitarianism's usual commitment to static, hierarchical morals. Follett uses a business example to illustrate: "While I object to the idea that individual professional men have necessarily a higher code than individual business men, I do think that the professions are ahead of business in the fact that their codes are group codes. The errors of the personal equation are thus often corrected" (Follett 2003e, 135).[17]

From this holistic, relational perspective, Follett redefines morality: "What is morality? The fulfillment of relation by man to man . . . This ordering of relations is morality in its essence and completeness" (Follett 1998, 333). Therefore, "democracy must be conceived as a process, not a goal. We do not want rigid institutions, however good. We need no 'body of truth' of any kind, but the will to will, which means the power to make our own government, our own institutions, our own expanding truth" (99).

Follett reiterates often the necessity of direct creation of the state by all citizens as the source of moral authority which will be discussed more fully in her political theory: "How is the state to gain moral and spiritual authority? Only through its citizens in their growing understanding of the widening promise of relation" (Follett 1998, 333). "The state accumulates moral power only through the spiritual activity of its citizens. There is no state except through me" (334). She compares this to both pragmatist epistemology and the Christian notion that God appears only through our deeds. Thus, "there is an active principle in obedience. Obedience is not a passive thing, for it is a moment in process. There is, as a rule, a very elaborate and complex process going on. At one moment in that process something happens which we call obedience" (Follett 2003n, 275).

This obedience is to the "law of the situation" (Follett 2003c, 58)—to the sense of right and purpose formed by the group through integration. Follett suggests that this understanding is in keeping with modern law as explicated by Roscoe Pound: "(1) that law is the outcome of our community life, (2) that it must serve, not individuals, but the community" (Follett 1998, 122). "Every decision of the future is to be based not on my needs or yours, nor on a compromise between them or an addition of them, but on the recognition of the community between us" (79). Thus, just as self-interest and collective interest are synthesized through shared interest, responsibility is mutual: "We cannot get rid of our joint obligation by finding the fraction of our own therein, because our own part is not a fraction of the whole, it is in a sense the whole. Wherever you have a joint responsibility, it can only be met jointly" (Follett 2013b, 74). As with right and purpose, "collective responsibility is not a matter of adding but of interweaving, a matter of the reciprocal modification brought about by the interweaving. It is not a matter of aggregation but of integration" (75).

A NEW PUBLIC ETHIC

This sense of responsibility based on these revised understandings of loyalty and obedience generates a public ethic that might today be framed as sustainable flourishing: "Our new motto must be, Live in such a manner that the fulness [sic] of life may come to all" (Follett 1998, 353).[18] Through such a public ethic, "(1) I am not dominated by the whole because I *am* the whole; (2) I am not dominated by 'others' because we have the genuine social process only when I do not control others or they me, but all intermingle to produce the collective thought and the collective will" (70).

In Follett's ethics, right and purpose must come from relational process alone; not from any external source, domination, or competitive compromise. To determine what is right and to form collective will, we must employ the group method of integration. This integrative process itself will generate loyalty to that purpose and the group and obedience to its shared responsibilities. All combined, ethics becomes an inherently relational proposition—a *public* ethic. Thus, "'justice' is being replaced by understanding" (Follett 1998, 81).[19] This understanding will strengthen in an ongoing fashion what Follett refers to as the "germinating centre" of true democracy: "*the will to will the common will*" (Follett 1998, 49). In this way, ethics establishes the foundation of Follett's democratic political theory as she herself notes: "This will mean changes in both legal and political thinking" (Follett 2013c, 129).

When we switch from the individual to the group as the ethical unit, we must remember Follett's understanding of the group: "In the field of ethics we are coming to see the ethical unit, or determining wish, as a true whole, that is, it is not the arithmetical sum of desires, nor one which has wiped out 'minor' desires, but an integrating desire which is continuously interweaving with the separate desires" (112). She notes that this is not a simple or easy proposition, but that in the pragmatist spirit, we should move forward with the endeavor. "That is all I am urging, that we try experiments in methods of resolving differences" (Follett 2003b, 34). Follett urges us to "now enter upon models of living commensurate with this thought" (Follett 1998, 8). We can begin immediately "by practising [*sic*] it with the first person we meet; by approaching every man with the consciousness of the complexity of his needs, of the vastness of his powers" (160).

SUMMARY ANALYSIS

Follett carries forward her understanding of the dynamic, relational individual into her ethics, asserting, "the essence of this psychology . . . is as important for ethics as for physiology or psychology" (Follett 2013c, 88). For Follett, however, the ethical unit is the group, not the individual (112), and it is the social process which is the source of ethics, as opposed to an external source of any type. Thus, ethics is not the *substance* of the collective will but has the process of *creating* as its "germinating centre [*sic*]" (Follett 1998, 49).

Following her philosophical approach, the process of generating an ethic is integrative and relational rather than procedural and formal, and she claims, "We are evolving now a system of ethics which has three conceptions in regard to right, conscience and duty" (Follett 1998, 52). Thus, her explication is structured around the ethical concepts of right, purpose, loyalty, and obedience; all reinterpreted from her relational process perspective. In short, none of these concepts can be legitimately determined outside of inclusive group processes of dialogue and integration. Through integration, a public ethic is generated that is mutualistic and in which all share responsibility for demanding and giving obedience through a sense of loyalty that is experientially founded. This basis in subject-subject relations produces a sense of fellowship that transforms justice from a hierarchical structure of sympathy to an egalitarian foundation of empathetic understanding.

ENDNOTES

1. Melé (2007) notes that while Follett did not write on ethics in management or business, her ethical principles can be successfully applied in that context.

2. Tonn (2003) notes that Follett draws from the work of Harvard philosophers Josiah Royce, William James, and Edwin B. Holt in their common efforts to create an integrative ethics.

3. Tonn (2003) asserts that it was likely her stirring rhetoric proclaiming the virtues of creating the collective will that set her up for attack as a communist sympathizer. Apparently her emphasis on the process through which it is created was lost.

4. Tonn (2003) notes that Follett's argument about right as a social good and associated rights runs parallel to that of English philosopher Thomas Hill Green, with the exception of her addition of the group process as its source.

5. Follett's explanation of the law of the situation precedes Bohm's (2004) explanation of *necessity* as the final determinant of the results of dialogue— that which may not be turned aside must guide the resolution of difference in dialogue.

6. Here, Follett follows Hegel (1977) in his understanding of intersubjectivity and pre-dates Habermas in his call for communicative action in *Reason and the Rationalization of Society* (1984) and communicative ethics in *Between Facts and Norms* (1998).

7. This is similar to the Whiteheadian notion that "true good is emergent from deeply mutual relationships" (Loomer 1976, 21). The same understanding is underlined by Wieman (1946).

8. This is an important difference to Whitehead's understanding of *initial aim* (as differentiated from *subjective aim*) as being rooted in God: "The initial aim is the causal force of the past, combined with God's presentation of the relevant possibilities *and* a 'lure' toward some rather than others" (Mesle 2008, 102). Granting this "extra" capacity to God as an actual entity is problematic in secular society—what or who stands-in for God?

9. Drucker asserts, "If Mary Parker Follett is known today at all, it is for her 'Constructive Conflict'" (1995, 4). Indeed, this concept is commonly

found in the negotiation and mediation literatures (see for example, Gehani and Gehani 2007; Kolb 1996) and is sometimes also referred to as "fruitful conflict" (Ansell 2011). Jones-Patulli (2011) applies integration to the context of collective bargaining, generating "integrative bargaining." See Chapter 12 for a summary of this contemporary literature.

10. Here, Follett indicates the important differences among debate, deliberation, and dialogue so widely discussed today in deliberative democracy, participatory practice, and conflict resolution (see for example, Escobar 2011).

11. Morton and Lindquist (1997) liken this dialogic approach to "feminist approaches to the ethical resolution of conflict, which focuses on dialectical communication between participants to reach an integrative solution that attends to the needs of all" (363), again demonstrating how Follett's ideas presage contemporary feminist theory.

12. Tonn (2003) suggests the two key elements of the method of integration are: (1) to break up wholes for analysis and (2) to revalue interests.

13. In this description of the process of integration, Follett again pre-dates Habermas in his call for communicative action in *Reason and the Rationalization of Society* (1984) and communicative ethics in *Between Facts and Norms* (1998).

14. Tonn (2003) notes that Follett differentiates herself from both Josiah Royce in *The Philosophy of Loyalty* (1908) as well as Herbert Croly in *The Promise of American Life* (1909) in her reconceptualization of loyalty.

15. In Follett's definition, she better describes the term *empathy* that had been coined in 1909 by E. B. Titchener in the German term *Einfühlungsvermögen*, or "feeling into", later revised as *Empathie* (Stueber 2008). But in her time, this understanding of sympathy was shared: "the primitive, element is *sympathy*, that is, feeling the feeling *in* another and feeling conformally *with* another" (Whitehead 1979, 162). Tonn (2003) also makes this point in her analysis.

16. Donati (2014) makes this same point about social morphogenesis in his theory of relational sociology.

17. It is worthwhile to note here that process theologian John Cobb (1994) presents an idea of Christian communitarianism in which health, work, education, safety, and other earthly needs are integral parts of the salvation project carried out by religions. In the light of this, religions should be *the vanguard of the new age*, but the regulation of social relationships should be based on neighbor solidarity whose model may be found in the Old Testament community of Israel.

18. In this way, Follett more carefully explicates and presages Connolly's

(2011, 2013) understanding of an ethic of cultivation grounded in care for the world. He argues that responsibility follows a *"presumptive responsiveness* to emergent situations (Connolly 2013, 135), noting that this requires neither a relativistic nor absolutist grounding for practical wisdom. Instead it contributes to a "a positive ethos of pluralist engagement" (Connolly 2013, 139).

19. Barclay (2005) notes that Follett replaces the accepted understanding of justice as a static/universal concept with one that is dynamic and contextual and in which fairness has procedural, outcome, and interpersonal experience aspects.

❧ 7 ❧

Follett's Political Theory

Political theory describes how we structure social institutions. Perspectives tend to differ based on whether institutions employ hierarchy or competition to *establish authority* and the *relative strength* of that structuration. For Follett, neither state-driven nor pluralist solutions are considered appropriate. Instead, she recommends the group process of integration as the manner through which governing authority is established in deeply nesting, broadly inclusive federated networks.

As a political theorist, Follett "was both an activist and an intellectual and scholar" (Mattson 1998, xli), following in the footsteps of public intellectual and settlement house activist Jane Addams, as well as an academic scholar following the likes of James and Hegel. As a political scientist, "Mary Parker Follett stands as a germinal thinker" (lix). Her political theory was developed at the end of the American Progressive Era which ran from 1890 into the 1920s. During her social work career, Follett "became interested in the intellectual justifications for the social centers movement" (xxxviii). Her experiences in the field "made Follett sure that democracy could be more than an abstract ideal. It must, she insisted, become a lived reality, a vigorous daily practice" (liv). In short, "she now had experienced democracy firsthand" (xxxix) and "believed her experience in social centers had something to teach social philosophers" (xli). In so doing, she succeeded in "linking her theory to practice" (liv).

The New State: Group Organization the Solution of Popular Government (1918) is the pinnacle of that work: Part I lays out her fundamental principles, Part II explores how far they are expressed in current political

113

forms, and Part III considers how they can be expressed in a new federalism from neighborhood to world. It has been described as "an extraordinary paean to a stronger more participatory form of American democracy" (Barber 1998, xv). However, these ideas were reiterated in later works, and therefore all of her political commentary is brought together in this chapter. In sum, it serves to "give to those who believe representative institutions are reaching a point of exhaustion new ways to think about citizenship, participation and democracy" (xvi).

Follett is described by Kevin Mattson (1998) as one of America's first communitarian critics of liberalism, but not in terms of a pre-ordained solidarity to shared values because she also criticized state socialism as merely another form of hierarchical coercion. It might be better to avoid contemporary labels altogether, given her unique perspective on both political process and form. Follett's primary concern is *modes of association* in human groups, preferring direct participation to representative forms of group governance at any scale and in any sector of society. She also promotes a deeply nesting, networking, and broadly inclusive federalism that grows out of associations at the neighborhood level to maintain local autonomy, while unifying ever more inclusive groups all the way to the global scope. Such a practice of self-governing is the only source of true democratic legitimacy in her view. Clearly, this formulation of democracy does not fully align with any of the received political theories.

To explicate her political theory, Follett begins with a critique of so-called democratic government, then provides a vision of what she believes to be "true democracy" (Follett 1998, 156) in terms of both process and form. Each component of her argument will be discussed in turn.

CRITIQUE OF REPRESENTATION

While Follett recognizes that representative democracy can be a "first step" for "backward countries" where no form of consent currently exists (Follett 2003l, 211), she notes, "but we are also recognizing to-day that it is only a first step; that not consent but participation is the right basis for all social relations" (211). Unfortunately, she also notes that while "many people are now getting beyond the consent-of-the-governed stage in their thinking . . . there are political scientists who are still advocating it" (211). Therefore, she must make clear her critique in order to frame her alternative.

Political theorist Benjamin Barber (1998) notes in the foreword to the reprinted version of *The New State* that Follett offers new ways to think about citizenship, participation, and democracy to "those who believe representative institutions are reaching a point of exhaustion" (xvi). Follett begins her theoretical development with a critique of representation, asserting "we have not yet tried democracy" (Follett 1998, 3). She insists, "The world has long been fumbling for democracy, but has not yet grasped its essential and basic idea" (Follett 2003a, 94). Instead of processes of actual self-governance and agreement, representative governance provides procedures of domination and compromise through ballot box voting.[1] Therefore, she boldly claims, "'representative government,' party organization, majority rule, with all their excrescenses [*sic*] are dead-wood" (Follett 1998, 4). According to Follett, these negative outgrowths include notions of elitism, contract, pluralism, externalized sovereignty, and the atomistic individualism upon which all such representational concepts rest. Each of her interwoven critiques will be considered in turn.

Individualist contract

Follett often talks about political theory in the context of law because democratic societies are constituted under law. However, these laws are based on philosophical assumptions tied to underlying political theory. She notes "the principles of individual rights and contract which have long dominated our courts" (Follett 1998, 126) are a product of "particularist" (125) individualism. However, to be appropriate for democracy, law must be designed to serve the community as a whole. She suggests that nascent forms of democratic law can be found in the limitations imposed on the use of property, freedom of contract, settlements, and the like. Therefore, she believes that law is moving in the direction of considering individuals in relation to the community rather than as isolated beings in some form of social contract: "It is the legal theory of association based on our growing understanding of group psychology which will finally banish contract" (125). She notices court decisions "giving way to sounder doctrine. . . . Our future law is to serve neither classes nor individuals, but the community" (126).

Follett explains that "the paradox of contract is that while it seems to be based on relation, it is really based on the individual. Contract is a particularistic conception" (Follett 1998, 125). This paradox generates dysfunction because "you can have a contractual relation between two wills or you can have those two wills uniting to form one will. Contract never creates one will" (Follett 1998, 124). In other words, unless a process of unification occurs among the parties, the original differing desires will remain, even if an agreement is made to act otherwise. Such agreements are temporary in nature and are based on a single transaction as opposed to an overall relationship or generalized sense of community.

Unfortunately, the existing political system does not engender unification, but instead establishes social contract through two principal methods: representative elitism and popular or interest group pluralism. Follett critiques both due to their respective reliance on domination and compromise in forging agreement, as opposed to actually unifying wills through a democratic process.

Representative elitism

Follett asserts that the founders of the United States were at core elitist because their form of individualism ensured only negative liberty in the form of rights ensured by the state as opposed to the freedom to participate in self-governance. "The framers of our constitution were individualists and gave to our government an individualistic turn. . . . And yet all this was negative. The individual was given no large positive function. The individual was feared and suspected" creating "a tendency towards aristocracy and a lack of real individualism on every side" (Follett 1998, 164). Thus, the first objective of representative institutions was to limit the active participation of citizens and retain decision making authority with elite leaders. Follett argues that this constitutional foundation and its repetition through law has produced and perpetuated subordination of certain classes: "It is static law and our reverence for legal abstractions which has produced 'privilege'" (132).

She explains this pattern by drawing upon the underlying ontology of representation. Ostensibly, "our legislatures are supposed to enact the will of the people, our courts are supposed to declare the will of the people, our executive to voice the will of the people" (Follett 1998, 218-19). But she argues the representative system is not actually designed to get at the will of the people because it is not a static, pre-existing thing "surrounding men like a nimbus apparently from their births on. . . . there is no will of the people" (218-19). Indeed, Follett claims that in ballot box procedures, "it is the desire of the dominant classes which by the sorcery of consent becomes 'the will of the people'" (Follett 2013c, 209).

Follett notes that past attempts to reform the representative system have been based on either fixing the representatives or the people who elect them: "The next step was the wave of reform that swept over the country. The motive was excellent; the method poor" (Follett 1998, 167). "Their methods were principally three: change in the forms of government (charters, etc.), the nomination of 'good' men to office, and the exhortation to induce 'the people' to elect them" (168). But she insists that such reforms will not repair the problems of representation: "This extraordinary belief in officials, this faith in the panacea of a change of characters, must go" (168). Even so, Follett did not call for the ousting of elite representatives themselves: "Democracy I have said is not antithetical to aristocracy, but includes aristocracy" (175). Instead, elites should become part of a new process of democracy in which they are no more or no less than any other participant in self-governance.

Pluralism

Follett argues that although aristocratic founders feared the tyranny of the masses, they also feared executive power and legislative power. In short, "no institution was trusted" (Follett 1998, 165). "Fear, not faith, suspicion not trust, were the foundation of our early government" (165). Therefore, the notion of separating power in order to balance power emerged, leading to not only divided branches of government, but the eventual birth of party politics and other forms of pluralism and interest group competition.[2]

Therefore, Follett continues with a critique of pluralist measures included in the representative system.[3] While representative elitism tends toward hierarchical approaches to decision making, pluralism uses competitive procedures to establish the public will. Follett believes both common formulations of pluralism are faulty: party organization and direct individual votes for a simple majority or plurality. At their core, each of these pluralist mechanisms serves to divide power and seek balance through competition and majority rule voting procedures—whether for representatives and parties or for policy decisions. Follett notes that pluralist approaches are therefore designed "if not to gain power, at least to produce an equilibrium" (Follett 2013c, 182). In the end, the best that these procedures can produce is a compromise in which all parties lose something. "The outcome of group particularism is the balance of power theory, perhaps the most pernicious part of the pluralists' doctrine" (Follett 1998, 306). Follett explains, "Some political scientists make the mistake of considering co-ordination and balance synonymous. Most of the political pluralists do this. The guild socialists tell us that their co-ordinating congress is an arbitrator, or court of appeal, to keep the balance between co-ordinate autonomies. According to the doctrine I am expressing, 'co-ordinate autonomies' is an impossible expression. You cannot have co-ordinate autonomies because co-ordination is the building up of a functional total" (Follett 2003m, 189).

Pluralist competition is particularist in nature because it is based on the notion of individual interest. Follett notes that while "the word interest is today employed by jurists in its psychological sense, until recently that word has been used by the legal order as well as by economists not in its psychological meaning, but as connoting economic advantage" (Follett 2013c, 35). In other words, individual interest is typically monetized in some fashion to equate desires with some type of material advantage. This interpretation allows the notion of limited material resources to enter into the equation, imagining now a static supply of resources available to fulfill competing individual interests in a zero-sum game—what one party wins, another party loses. Follett argues that no resources related to or subject to the effect of human beings are actually limited because desires, spiritual power, and creativity are all organic and are therefore progressive in value at both individual and collective levels. This pragmatist principle is not accepted by pluralism's static, limited, distributive assumptions: "some of the pluralists ostensibly found their books on pragmatic philosophy and yet in their inability to reconcile the distributive and collective they do not accept the latest teachings of pragmatism, for pragmatism does not end with a distributive pluralism" (Follett 1998, 263).

This notion of static resources also creates stasis in interests. Pluralists "tend to make the state purpose static. And the moment they make the state purpose static, they are back in the block universe they have repudiated" (Follett 2013c, 221). Purposes are static at two levels of analysis. First, interests are static within competing individuals and can thereby be represented by either elected officials or by interest groups. Second, once the competition results in a majority ruling, the majority will becomes the public will which remains static until challenged or opened for reconsideration. This procedure results in the domination of all minorities, which pluralism allegedly abhors. As soon as "balance" is achieved it is lost either because interests change or because the original desire re-emerges because it was never fulfilled by domination or compromise.

Follett also shows that when either domination or compromise are the methods of collective decision making, creativity is squelched: "One trouble with the balance of power theory is that we have no progress here" (Follett 2013c, 182). But what is more damaging to democracy is that because some are being dominated in the decision making process, supposed collective will does not produce collective activity. "Whenever you have balance in your premise, you have anarchy in your conclusion" (Follett 1998, 307). Thus, pluralism is "one of the most harmful of our political fallacies" (Follett 2013c, 206) because "chaos, disorder, destruction, come everywhere from refusing the syntheses of life" (Follett 1998, 93).

Follett believes pluralism is harmful for several other reasons. First, pluralists misunderstand group dynamics and the group process as the source of sovereignty: "their thinking is not based on a scientific study of the group, which weakens the force of their theories of 'objective' rights and sovereignty" (Follett 1998, 264). "The pluralists apotheosize the group but do not study the group. They talk of sovereignty without seeking the source of sovereignty" (269).

Second, "many of the pluralists are professed followers of medieval doctrine" (Follett 1998, 264). Contract and rights theory emerged from Enlightenment interpretations of individualism. Because of particularist individualism, she insists both Kant and Hegel see the state as "the fulfill-ment of the individual" (163), but neither philosophy produces *true* democ-racy. "According to many of the pluralists there is an individual who stands outside and looks at his groups and there is something peculiarly sacred about this individual. This individual is a myth. The fallacy of pluralism is not its pluralism, but that it is based on a non-existent individual" (Follett 1919, 579). In her footnote here, Follett compares this mythical individual to the "outside God of the Old Testament" (579).

Third, the pluralist movement "is in part a reaction to a misunderstood Hegelianism" (Follett 1998, 263-64). Because of a fear of an absorbing whole, pluralists atomize the individual and then force the individual into competing groups. Yet, because of a fear of self-interest controlling competi-tion, state mechanisms are put into place to control both individuals and special interest groups. Thus, "individualism and concentrated authority have been struggling for supremacy with us since the beginning of our government. From the beginning of our government we have been seeking the synthesis of the two. . . . I insist that balance can never be the aim of sound political method" (322).

In sum, like a self-fulfilling prophecy, the fears and mistrust embedded in our founding Constitution and laws have created the self-interest they meant to control. This cannot be reformed through surface measures: "It is the system which must be changed" (Follett 1998, 167). This includes the foundational assumptions stemming from all the prior conceptual elements in the model presented herein—ontology, psychosocial theory, epistemology, beliefs, and ethics.

Direct (ballot box) democracy

The most common pluralist groups during the Progressive Era were political parties. Follett focuses quite a bit on the parties and their corruption: "Theoretically the people have the power, but really the government is the primaries, the conventions, the caucuses. Officials hold from the party" (Follett 1998, 167). She asserts, "The muddy stream of party politics is choked with personal ambition, the desire for personal gain" (216). Therefore, Follett is hopeful about the second wave of government reform then taking place: "Now, however, in the beginning of the twentieth century, we see . . . the constructive period of reform begun" (169). She refers in part to state constitutional conventions which were busy adding mechanisms of direct democracy and new forms of nonpartisan local government that moved political authority closer to the people. However, it is guarded optimism: "Merely giving more power to the people does not automatically reduce the hold of the party; some positive measure must be taken if direct government is not to fail exactly as representative government has failed" (178), meaning capture of elected and party leaders by business and other special interests.

Follett worries that fundamental assumptions and procedures are not changing, but merely moving from elite groups to the masses. "Democracy can never mean the domination of the crowd. The helter-skelter strivings of an endless number of social atoms can never give us a fair and ordered world" (Follett 1998, 154). "Democracy means the will of the whole" (142) but she doubts that ballot box voting procedures can actually generate the public will, suggesting the thought that it can is "our Great Illusion" (220). She asks, "Who are the people? Every individual? The majority? A theoretical average? A compromise group?" (220). She insists "the will of the whole is not necessarily represented by the majority, nor by a two-thirds or three-quarters vote, nor even by a unanimous vote" (142). This is true because "democracy is not a sum in addition. Democracy is not brute numbers" (5). Therefore, not unlike James Madison, Follett questions direct democracy reforms and their potential results: "Shall we give the initiative and referendum to a crowd?" (181). "What is the remedy for a 'ruthless majority'? What is the remedy for an 'arrogant minority'?" (209).

Furthermore, she argues that such voting procedures do not generate authentic power because the choices are still framed by the elite: "We are to consider first the doctrine of the consent of the governed. I do not think it will bear our present tests. Mere consent, bare consent, gives us only the benefit of the ideas of those who put forward the propositions for consent; it does not give us what the others may be capable of contributing" (Follett 2003l, 210). Thus, "some of us, indeed, think that consent is a thoroughly overrated matter . . . even if the employee representatives voted on everything, 'consented' to everything, that would not make them free. The vote is a deceptive business altogether. How often we used to see a tiny child driving with his father made happy by being allowed to hold the end of the reins. The vote makes many people happy in the same way; they think they are driving when they are not" (Follett 2003g, 171).

Therefore Follett, *unlike* Madison, suggests that the solution is genuine discussion. However, she is quick to point out that even if these new direct pluralist processes allow time for deliberation, she is not convinced that this type of discussion leads to actual agreement. Instead, she insists it still leads to domination or compromise: "Do we have discussion in debating societies? Never. Their influence is pernicious and they should be abolished in colleges, schools, settlements, Young Men's Christian Associations, or wherever found" (Follett 1998, 209). "In debating you are always trying to find the ideas and facts which will support your side; you do not look dispassionately at all ideas and all facts, and try to make out just where the truth lies. You do not try to see what ideas of your opponent will enrich your own point of view" (210). "When the attention of each side is riveted on its facts, discussion becomes rather hopeless" (Follett 2013c, 17).

Therefore, Follett is not convinced that ballot-box policy making through direct vote, even with opportunities for debate, is the solution to the problems of elitism and party or interest group pluralism (the crowd). "Mere voting is a gesture of agreement rather than real agreement. We cannot obtain genuine consent by a vote any more than you can 'declare' peace" (Follett 2003l, 211). Thus, she looks further into the progressive reforms, specifically to administrative reform and the trend toward social legislation.

Administrative reform

In her discussion of administrative reform, Follett refers to the Municipal Research Bureaus and their attempts to improve local government through administrative responsibility. She hopes that such efforts are working in concert with direct democracy reforms: "We are at present trying to secure (1) a more efficient government, and (2) a real not a nominal control of government by the people" (Follett 1998, 174).[4] In short, she felt administrative efficiency would be better than political party control and provide a stepping stone toward what she called "our new democracy" (175) in which the choice of what to do remains under popular control, but the ability to get things done employs some degree of empowered administrative expertise. Furthermore, she believes social legislation created by the people will be better than the extremes of *laissez-faire* and authoritative regulation produced by political elites.

True to her pragmatist appreciation of knowledge and the scientific perspective to inquiry, Follett sees expertise as the new formulation of aristocracy and just as she suggests aristocrats should be integrated into genuine democracy, so should expertise: "Administrative responsibility and expert service are as necessary a part of genuine democracy as popular control is a necessary accompaniment of administrative responsibility" (Follett 1998, 175). However, she does not abide by administrators wielding power over others any more than elite representatives or party leaders. This leads to the last element of her critique of representation: the externalization of sovereignty.

Externalized sovereignty

Whether legitimated by law, elected representation, expertise, or majority rule, Follett argues that any form of sovereignty that does not directly engage those affected by a given decision or action is not democratically legitimate. She insists sovereignty emerges from an inclusive, participatory process: "Every living process is subject to its own authority, that is, the authority evolved by, or involved in, the process itself" (Follett 2013c, 206). She considers any other formulation of sovereignty to be, at best, based on the notion of "consent of the governed . . . perhaps the most important conception of political science" (197).

Follett argues that consent approaches put people in a position of acquiescence rather than active participation. "This is not enough, to elect officials and then to listen to their policy and consent. . . . There is no democracy without contribution" (Follett 2013c, 215). She denies that sovereignty can be transferred to the state through laws enacted by elected representatives or majority votes based on the consent of the governed. These efforts are "hardly distinguishable from coercion" (200). "There is no will of the people except through the activity of the people. Will and activity do not dwell in separate spheres. Consent is not the technique of democracy" (205).

Nor can sovereignty be further translated into political authority delegated to administrative experts. "We want information of expert or official, not to turn us into rubber stamps, but as the foundation for the social process. The 'consent of the governed' is intellectualistic doctrine; the will of the people is not to be found on this plane at all, but in the concrete activities of everyday life" (Follett 2013c, 205-06). All must be engaged in the doing—experts, representatives, and citizens—because "we cannot carry out the will of another, for we can use only our own behavior patterns. If we consent to the will of the expert or administrative official, it is still the will of expert or official; the people's will can be found only in their motor mechanisms or habit systems" (198-99). "This means that between expert and people is a chasm which ideas cannot cross. It means too that there is no magic by which consent can be converted into will: if the expert or administrative official wills, it will be forever the will of the expert or administrative official" (205).

Follett concludes, "In short, my argument against acquiescence as the people's part in the political process depends first on the fact, in my opinion basic and all important, that different kinds of accurate information are required, that of the expert and that of the people; secondly on the changing nature of the fact-situation; third on the activities of the people as integral with the changing situation" (Follett 2013c, 28). In this statement, she objects to these externalizations of sovereignty for pragmatic reasons—if the governed are removed from decisions or actions, they cannot contribute their creative experience to the process of either. Thus, for Follett, it is not enough to consider consent as participation. Instead, "participation has to take place further back, in the activity from which the policies emerge" (198).

In this endeavor, Follett sees governance on a developmental path:

> We had, first, government by law, second, government by parties and big business, and all the time some sort of fiction of the "consent of the governed" which we said meant democracy. But we have

never had government by the people. The third step is to be the development of machinery by which the fundamental ideas of the people can be got at and embodied; further, by which we can grow fundamental ideas; further still, by which we can prepare the soil in which fundamental ideas can grow. Direct government will we hope lead to this step, but it cannot alone do this. (Follett 1998, 174)

"If our present mechanical government is to turn into a living, breathing, pulsing life, it must be composed of an entire citizenship educated and responsible" (Follett 1998, 168).

Follett is emphatic that in this proposition she is "not hereby glorifying 'the people.' We no longer declare mystic faith in a native rightness of public opinion; we want nothing from the people but their experience, but emphatically we want that. Reason, wisdom, emerge from our daily activities. It is not the *will* of the people we are interested in but the *life* of the people. Public opinion must be built up from concrete existence, from the perceptual level" (Follett 2013c, 216).

The sovereign state

The corollary to Follett's critique of externalized sovereignty is a refusal of what she calls the Sovereign State. Follett characterizes the pluralist state as a *laissez-faire* state—one in which the government minimizes centralized control, leaving decisions and actions up to pluralist competition to the greatest degree possible. She argues against an understanding of individual and state that can pit one against the other; person-against-state. Follett argues the idea of an individual will against the will of the state is "a myth of the pluralists" (Follett 2013c, 220). This oppositional relationship is impossible because there is no state apart from the people who compose it. "Political philosophers talk of the state but there is no state until we make it. It is pure theory" (Follett 1998, 265). Instead, "the state is being made daily and hourly by the activities of its citizens; and as the activity of citizens changes the state, the state exerts a different stimulus on the citizens so that their activity is different" (Follett 2013c, 219).

Due to the rampant corporate and political corruption at the time, she argues,

Everyone knows that our period of *laissez-faire* is over, but socialists wish to give us in its place state control and they mean by that state coercion—we find again and again in their pamphlets the words force, coerce . . . The period of *laissez-faire* is indeed over, but I do not think we want to put in its place a forcibly controlled society, whether it be controlled by the state of the socialists or the experts of a planning board. The aim and the process of the organisation [*sic*] of government, of industry, of international relations, should be, I think, a control not imposed from without the regular functioning of society, but one which is a co-ordinating of all those functions, that is, a collective self-control. (Follett 2013h, 89)

Thus, we turn to her proposal for the processes and forms that will create this new democracy.

THE PROCESS OF TRUE DEMOCRACY

Given these critiques of representation, pluralism, direct vote, and administrative forms of democracy, all of which serve to externalize sovereignty, Follett poses the question, "What is to be the true and perfect bond of union between the multiple groups of our modern life?" (Follett 1998, 258).[5] Follett is firmly against elite domination, but neither does she want simple majority rule by the crowd—the two poles of concentrated authority and individualism that have been competing with one another since the founding of the United States. With elite leaders, the masses act like sheep, while as a crowd, they become an uninformed majority, as feared by Madison. In short, "we do not want a majority in either case, either as a tyrant or as an inert mass" (145).

However, Follett is not supportive of either state socialism or syndicalism which abolishes the state replacing it with workers' organizations, or even guild socialism where the state owns the means of production while the workers' guilds control operations. "The pregnant question for the social scientist becomes, then . . . whether there is any process possible by which desires may interweave" (Follett 2013c, xiii). It is this process that she calls "true democracy" (Follett 1998, 156). She explains, "many people think that democracy means all taking part. If it means only that, I do not believe in democracy. It is the fruitful relating, the interacting of parts, a co-functioning, that we want" (Follett 2003m, 190). Her explication of this alternative approach to democracy is composed of several familiar conceptual elements fundamentally redefined: (1) politics as a creative process of integration; (2) democratic values of freedom and equality as relational power-with; (3) the People as a dynamic, relational whole; and (4) the state as a facilitator of integration.[6] Each conceptual element will be discussed in turn.

Politics as integration

Follett refers to the old saying about democratic reform but notes, "when people say that the cure for the evils of democracy is more democracy, they usually mean that while we have some 'popular' institutions, we have not enough" (Follett 1998, 159). She refutes this notion entirely: "There is only one way to get democratic control—by people learning how to evolve collective ideas. The essence of democracy is not in institutions, is not even in 'brotherhood'; it is in that organizing of men which makes most sure, most perfect, the bringing forth of the common idea" (159). The only way to get true and lasting cooperation is through genuine participation: "Everyone talks to-day of co-operation, but there is no way of making consent spell co-operation. You have to have participation before you can get co-operation" (Follett 2003g, 171).

Follett challenges existing political processes that differentiate between informal political interactions and formal interactions related to governance. "I believe that the political process consists in connecting the will of the people which is in a situation with the will of the people which passes on a situation. How to do this is the problem of democracy" (Follett 2013c, 202). In other words, there cannot be an informal will of the people *and* a formal will of the people via representatives. There must be simply one will generated among everyone in the situation. "When we have a genuine democracy, we shall not have the defective political machinery of the present, but some method by which people will be able not to accept or reject but to create group or whole ideas, to produce a genuine collective will" (Follett 1998, 152). "This is all that democracy means, that the experience of all is necessary . . . Democracy is not 'idealism' but plain common sense" (Follett 2013c, 19).

Therefore, Follett calls for a new method of governance *by* the people that is beyond both representative and ballot box practices. First, to include all ideas, all must participate: "Every man sharing in the creative process is democracy; this is our politics and our religion" (Follett 1998, 103). Second, "choice is not given up but is put further back in the process" (Follett 2013c, 84). In this way, participatory choice is differentiated from ballot box consent: "One of the fundamental differences between consent and participation is that consent is not part of the process, it comes at the end of or after the process. Participation is not only part of the process; it should begin with the beginning of the process" (Follett 2003l, 223).

Finally, the quality of participation must reach beyond pluralist debate or vote: "If we have got beyond mere consent, so also we have got beyond mere participation" (Follett 2003l, 229).

Thus, for Follett, politics still means a social process that determines how society will be governed. However, it is no longer conducted only in the formal institutions of representative government and it no longer carries the pluralist meaning of competing for power over decisions about "who gets what, when, how" (Lasswell 1950). Indeed, "individual competition must, of course, disappear" (Follett 1998, 364). Rather than competing over differences in interests and values, these desires must be brought together through a developmental process that "acts on the principle of participation, and by a method of settling differences, or a method of dealing with the diverse contributions of men very different in temperament, training, and attainments" (Follett 2003l, 213).

So, Follett's project is to "seek a way by which desires may interweave" (Follett 2013c, xiv). This method begins with viewing politics as a relational, rather than competitive project: "Let us look at some of the things participation is not. I mean participation as we are now defining it, not mere taking part, but functional relating. It is not fighting" (Follett 2003l, 225). Instead, "we have participation when we have related thinking, not merely voting, which only registers opinions already formed" (212). Thus, "the main concern of politics is *modes of association*. We do not want the rule of the many or the few; we must find that method of political procedure by which majority and minority ideas may be so closely interwoven that we are truly ruled by the will of the whole" (Follett 1998, 147).

This mode of association cannot be participation as pluralists conceive of it. "If, however, we say that we believe, not in consent, but in participation, we have then to define participation. Mere participation is not enough . . . participation must involve the interpenetration of the ideas of the parties concerned" (Follett 2003l, 212). "Our contribution is of no value unless it is effectively related to the contributions of all the others concerned" (229). Thus, the role of the citizen must change from a passive participant relying on either elite representatives and their experts or interest group leaders to do the work of citizenship on their behalf. "We need to-day: (1) an active citizenship, (2) a responsible citizenship, (3) a creative citizenship—a citizenship building its own world, creating its own political and social structure, constructing its own life forever. Our faith in democracy rests ultimately on the belief that men have this creative power" (Follett 1998, 222). This attitudinal change is necessary in order for changes in the "machinery" to be effective.

This new technology is that of active participation in what we would now call a consensus-building process: "In many committees, boards and commissions we see now a reluctance to take action until all agree; there is a feeling that somehow, if we keep at it long enough, we can unify our ideas and our wills, and there is also a feeling that such unification of will has value" (Follett 1998, 143). This approach is necessary because "majority rule is democratic when it is approaching not a unanimous but an integrated will" (142). Even a unanimous vote is not necessarily the will of the whole because it likely obscures some form of domination, even if only through passivity and imitation. Indeed, this is the fundamental problem of yes or no voting processes. "If participation means playing one's part in an integrative unity, if we want to get what each one has to contribute, what are some of the rules which we should lay down for our guidance? First, I should say, never, if possible, allow an either-or situation to be created . . . by presenting two alternatives, you by no means exhaust the possibilities of a situation; it means a greatly impoverished thinking, a diminution of your mental resources; it often paralyses thinking or canalizes thinking" (Follett 2003l, 219). "In short, we do not get full participation unless we avoid either-or situations" (221). Instead, we must pursue an integration of wills. Integration occurs not through standard deliberation which tends toward debate, but rather "group discussion . . . interpermeation" (Follett 1998, 209) that includes "a cooperative gathering of facts" (Follett 2013c, 17) and "genuine discussion" that "is truth-seeking" (Follett 1998, 210).

Follett explains that psychology gives us the model for this new political process: "The term we have now gained, that of integration" (Follett 2013c, xiv). Just as integration is shown to progress the individual and society at the psychosocial level, just as it is the process for creating ethics, Follett believes integration will improve both politics and the laws it produces. First, its synergistic effect produces more creative and effective policies because nothing is lost. "The doctrine of integrating interests does away with that of the balance of interests" (45). "The moment you try to integrate loss, you reduce loss; as when you try to integrate gain, you increase gain. This is the whole claim of integration over either domination or compromise, the three ways of dealing with conflict. In either of the latter you rearrange existing material, you make quantitative, not qualitative adjustments, you adjust but do not create. . . . By integrating these interests you get the incre-ment of the unifying" (Follett 2013c, 45-46).

Furthermore, implementation is much more effective due to a much stronger commitment to the policies produced: "The same process which evolves the state evolves the law. Law flows from our life, therefore it cannot be above it. The source of the binding power of law is not in the consent of the community, but in the fact that it has been produced by the com-munity" (Follett 1998, 130).

Democratic values redefined

In order to achieve the participatory mode of association necessary for integration as the method of politics and lawmaking, the meanings of underlying democratic values must also be transformed. Follett redefines these concepts based on her understanding of relational process ontology. Specifically, the democratic values of liberty, equality, and unity are each wrapped up in particular conceptions of sovereignty and power that must be evolved. Furthermore, such definitions must be made clear to transform those conceptions: "Authority, power, control, sovereignty are big words, and much has been written about them by learned people in learned language" (Follett 2003g, 174).

Traditionally in liberalism, liberty is understood in its negative for-mulation—freedom from state coercion and the ability to act and think as one chooses so long as there is no infringement on the freedom of others. Equality is understood to mean all individuals are equal in legal treatment and political voice in established governance procedures. While people are rhetorically identified as the ultimate source of sovereignty, governing authority is given over to the representative and pluralist institutions of governance which then exercise power over those people. This is how we achieve unity—through a voluntary acceptance of some level of coercion in exchange for the benefits of participating in society.

Follett notes that these meanings derive from an antiquated under-standing of the individual: "Democracy has meant to many 'natural' rights, 'liberty' and 'equality'. . . the old idea of natural rights postulated the particularist individual; we know now that no such person exists" (Follett 1998, 137). Furthermore, individualist philosophers assert, "'Man's will for power is his most distinguishing characteristic'" (Follett 2013c, 179-80). As a result, "this fear of losing a purely mythical freedom has over and over again been proved to have no basis in reality" (Follett 2003f, 306).

Based on these individualist assumptions, Follett worries about the focus placed on liberty as a "watchword" (Follett 2013c, 286) in the nineteenth century because it is "often expressed in terms of a restriction on freedom. We should, however, see law not as restricting or regulating freedom, but as increasing our freedom by making wider and wider the area in which that freedom may operate. I have theoretical freedom in the forest; I have actual freedom only with the freedom to do, to do and do, in wider relations, in more significant relations, by extending ever more and more the possibility of fruitful response. Men do not lose their freedom in relation but thereby gain it" (288-89). Indeed, Follett insists, "I can only free you and you me. This is the essence, the meaning, of all relation. . . . This reciprocal freeing, this calling forth of one from the other, this constant evocation, is the . . . life-process" (130).[7]

In its positive formulation, liberty "is not measured by the number of restraints we do not have, but by the number of spontaneous activities we do have" (Follett 1998, 138).[8] Therefore, "a highly organized state does not mean restriction of the individual but his greater liberty. . . . A greater degree of social organization means a more complex, a richer, broader life, means more opportunity for individual effort and individual choice and individual initiative" (139). When one has the authority to express oneself in more social contexts, freedom is expanded because "to express the personality I am creating, to live the authority I am creating, is to be free" (Follett 2013c, 193). "No outside power indeed can make us free" because "freedom is not a static condition" (Follett 1998, 71). "I am free when I am creating" (70).

Thus, Follett reinterprets *freedom* to include its positive aspect without losing freedom from coercion, because "integrating desires synthesizes the conceptions of freedom and non-freedom" (Follett 2013c, 289). Through synthesis, "liberty and restraint are not opposed, because ideally the expression of the social will in restraint is our freedom" (Follett 1998, 141). Restraint is not domination when it is authentically self-generated and self-imposed as an active member of the whole. "I think we should ask ourselves to what we owe obedience. Surely only to a functional unity of which we are a part, to which we are contributing" (Follett 2003c, 64). Follett explains, "A man is ideally free only so far as he is interpermeated by every other human being; he gains his freedom through a perfect and complete relationship because thereby he achieves his whole nature. Hence free-will is not caprice or whim or a partial wish or a momentary desire. On the contrary freedom means exactly the liberation from the tyranny of such particularist impulses. . . . The essence of freedom is not irrelevant spontaneity but the fullness of relation" (Follett 1998, 69). Therefore, Follett (2003f) argues, "Now continuous machinery for working out the principles of relation, whether it be in factory or nation or internationally, is of the very essence of freedom. . . . *Collectively* to discover and follow certain principles of action makes for *individual* freedom. Continuous machinery for this purpose is an essential factor in the only kind of control we can contemplate" (304).

This reinterpretation of freedom requires a similar transformation of the understanding of political *power*. As Follett (2013c) notes, "What is the central problem of social relations? It is the question of power" (xiii).[9] "Whether or not there is an 'instinctive' urge to power or only an urge for the means to satisfy desire, the attempt to gain power is the predominant feature of our life" (179-80). But power has numerous expressions in political theory. "Those political scientists who use the words power, control and authority as synonymous, are confusing our thinking" (Follett 2003j, 111). To clarify, Follett (2013c) asks, "Is power force, influence, leadership, manipulation, managing, is it self-control, self-discipline, is it capacity, is it self-expression?" (180).

If we equate power with authority, it may not be particularly problematic. However, if we equate power or authority with control, then the wrong type of power is likely assumed. In the negative freedom scenario, the type of power and authority at play is coercive in nature, or what Follett calls power-over, as noted in Chapter 6. In this sense it is force, influence, leadership, manipulation, and managing. Follett (2013c) believes such "coercive power is the curse of the universe" (xiii). Her remedy is integrative process. "The psychology of integration gives us hints of a new conception of power" (179). She explains, "the integrating of wants precludes the necessity of gaining power to satisfy desire" (184). In other words, when integration is achieved, there is no longer a need for coercive control over others. All that is needed is self-governance to participate in achieving the shared desire.

In this positive freedom scenario, the type of power and authority at play is over oneself and situations of which one is an integral part—self-control, self-discipline, capacity, and self-expression. In this meaning, "power might be defined as simply the ability to make things happen, to be a causal agent, to initiate change. Perhaps the 'urge to power' is merely the satisfaction of being alive" (Follett 2003j, 99).[10] Most importantly, "this self-generated control does not coerce" (Follett 2013h, 88) because "the more power I have over myself the more capable I am of joining fruitfully with you and with you developing power in the new unity thus formed—our two selves" (Follett 2013c, 189-90). "If both sides obey the law of the situation, no *person* has power over another" (Follett 2003j, 105). In this meaning, "all control means a sense of power" because "all activity brings a sense of power" (Follett 2013c, 180). But this is a shared control. Follett explains, "Genuine power is power-with, pseudo power, power-over" (189).[11, 12] "Genuine power can only be grown . . . for genuine power is not coercive control" (xiii).[13] Follett believes such "coactive power" is "the enrichment and advancement of every human soul" (xiii).[14] As applied to the state, "juridical relations then imply always rights with, not over" (189).

In sum, Follett believes "it is possible to develop the conception of power-with, a jointly developed power, a co-active, not a coercive power" (Follett 2003j, 101).[15] This new understanding of power fundamentally changes representative assumptions about the consent of the governed as the foundation of *sovereignty* of the democratic state. "What does the new psychology teach us of 'consent'? Power is generated within the true group not by one or several assuming authority and others 'consenting,' but solely by the process of intermingling" (Follett 1998, 303). In other words, consent means active engagement and support of outcomes, not acquiescence or selection among choices determined by someone else. The only reason pseudo power has come into play is because of the time and logistics involved in integration: "Power-over is resorted to time without number because people will not wait for the slower process of education" (Follett 2013c, 190).

For political power to be democratic, it is also commonly asserted that power must be distributed from its sovereign source. Follett (2013j) obliges: "Power must be distributed from its source? Very well, but what is the source?" (108). For Follett, power is ontologically derived directly by each person as opposed to circuitously stemming from rights bestowed by the state and its institutions, which were originally constituted by people with natural rights. She insists, "There are many ways in which power develops naturally if there is no hindrance" (109). Follett (1998) explains that "an understanding of the group process teaches us the true nature of sovereignty. . . . The atomistic idea of sovereignty is dead, we all agree, but we may learn to define sovereignty differently" (283). In short, political power or sovereignty is generated through the creative process of successful integration. There is no finite supply that must be doled out through authorized representatives. "The power produced by relationship is a qualitative, not a quantitative thing. If we follow our rule throughout of translating everything into activity, if we look at power as the power to *do* something, we shall understand this" (Follett 2013c, 191). This is a "coöperative sovereignty" (Follett 1998, 316), a term she attributes to British Marxist, Harold Laski.

In this understanding of sovereignty and power, there is an infinite potential supply that can only be brought into being through the dynamic relational process of integration. "Here must be the origin of power . . . how it can be produced . . . Whenever we are talking of actual power, then, we are talking of something which is generated by circular response; no, of what is being generated by circular response" (Follett 2013c, 185). Because this inherent power to create resides only within each person, sovereignty cannot be externalized or delegated to representatives or institutions and remain legitimate. "We can never 'give' power, we should recognize all the power which springs up spontaneously within the state, and seek merely those methods by which that self-generating power shall tend immediately to become part of the strength of the state" (Follett 1998, 323). Nor can we give power to abstractions like the *public interest*: "We talk about the public without thinking that we were the public" (336). Instead, Follett urges, "Let us *be* the state, let us be sovereign—over ourselves. As the problem in the life of each one of us is to find the way to unify the warring elements within us—as only thus do we gain sovereignty over ourselves—so the problem is the same for the state" (281).

As always, drawing from psychology, Follett sees this process beginning with the individual integrating the various elements of her own nature to achieve distributed (individual) sovereignty, moving outward in ever widening associations within groups to achieve collective sovereignty in a genuine whole. "A state is sovereign only as it has the power of creating one in which all are. Sovereignty is the power engendered by a complete interdependence becoming conscious of itself. . . . By the subtle process of interpenetration a collective sovereignty is evolved from a distributed sovereignty" (Follett 1998, 271). When collective sovereignty is placed in "an interpenetrating group" (181), the "interweaving experience produces social ends *and* power . . . Interweaving experience creates legitimate power" (Follett 2013c, 192).

This reformulation of power and sovereignty is also the source of Follett's reinterpretation of *equality*. At core, equality focuses on the question of

"Who is to decide what are the ends of society?" (Follett 2013c, 192). Equal opportunity to be the one to do so has traditionally been the democratic answer. However, relational process ontology demands a different solution. As Follett explains, "The group process shows us that we are equal from two points of view: first, I am equal to every one [*sic*] else as one of the necessary members of the group; second, each of these essential parts is the tap from an infinite supply—in every man lives an infinite possibility" (Follett 1998, 139). Therefore, active participation of *all* is needed in the political process and that participation is of equal worth because all have creative potentiality. In short, opportunity must be replaced with actuality to achieve equality.

Thus, the reformulation of power and sovereignty also redefines *unity* as integration within connecting groups of people comprising a whole in which all actively participate. Follett suggests that individualist philosophy fundamentally changed this ancient understanding of collectivities. "From the Middle Ages the appreciation of the individual has steadily grown. The Reformation in the sixteenth century was an individualistic movement. The apotheosis of the individual, however, soon led us astray, involving as it did an entirely erroneous notion of the relation of the individual to society, and gave us the false political philosophy of the seventeenth and eighteenth centuries. Men thought of individuals as separate and then had to invent fictions to join them, hence the social contract fiction" (Follett 1998, 162). These assumptions, however, lead to the slippery slope of enforced contract—of autocratic regimes as seen then in southern Europe. Follett (2003m) argues, "I believe the cause of that lies in the fact that these nations find that unity is necessary and that they have not yet found out how to get it in a better way, or rather how to get nearer a genuine unity" (189).

Therefore, as understood in the nineteenth century, "many of the political pluralists believe that we cannot have unity without absorption. Naturally averse to absorption, they therefore abandon the idea of unity and hit upon compromise and balance as the law of association. But whoever thinks compromise and balance the secret of cooperation fails, insofar, to understand the social process, as he has failed to gather the fruits of recent psychological research" (Follett 1919, 576). As discussed in relation to constructive conflict in Follett's conception of ethics, "We now see the false psychology underlying compromise and concession. Their practical futility has long been evident: whenever any difference is 'settled' by concession, that difference pops up again in some other form. Nothing will ever truly settle differences but synthesis" (Follett 1998, 114).

However, pluralism isn't the only problematic formulation of unity. Follett notes that this understanding of the individual also led to an absorptive whole propagated by idealist T. H. Green, as well as Kant and Hegel before him. "The state was now not to be subordinate to the individual, but it was to be the fulfilment [*sic*] of the individual" (Follett 1998, 163). In other words, only through their relationship to the state could the individual find identity and self-expression. As explained in Chapter 3, neither individualism nor collectivism produces the true individual within a whole a-making.

In either case the state or society holds some degree of dominion over the individual, which is antithetical to an understanding of unity as an inclusive, egalitarian, dynamic process of *unifying*: "we are speaking of a unity which is not the result of an interweaving, but *is* the interweaving. Unity is always a process, not a product" (Follett 2003m, 195). Furthermore, "the ideal unified state is not all-absorptive; it is all-inclusive—a very different matter . . . which I call the unifying state" (Follett 1998, 311). Follett believes the unifying state generates an authentically shared interest: "when we abandon our power-society, we can perhaps use the expression social interest without ambiguity; it can then mean the interest involved in, evolved by, relation" (Follett 2013c, 49). When unity is understood as an evolving process of unifying through integration, the authentic individual is not lost in the relational process: "I must each moment find my freedom anew by making a whole whose dictates, because they are integratings to which I am contributing, represent my individuality at that moment" (Follett 1919, 578).

Again, through integration, a genuine whole does not exercise power-over but rather power-with. "All majority control is getting power *over*. Genuine control is activity between, not influence over" (Follett 2013c, 186). The next step is "to find out what power is and to create it consciously . . . the only genuine power is that over the self—whatever that self may be . . . we have power over ourselves together" (186). "The group-spirit . . . is the Spirit of democracy. . . . We can never dominate another or be dominated by another; the group-spirit is always our master" (Follett 1998, 43). But clearly, in this integrating, unifying whole, we are all always are own masters as well.

The people a-making

With the democratic values of liberty, equality, and unity redefined along with new conceptions of power and sovereignty, an alternative formulation of the People can be created. Follett observes, "We have had within our memory three ideas of the individual's relation to society: the individual as deserving 'rights' *from* society, next with a duty *to* society, and now the idea of the individual as an activity *of* society. . . . Citizenship is not a right nor a privilege nor a duty, but an activity to be exercised every moment of the time" (Follett 1998, 335). Follett is describing an evolutionary path: (1) individual receiving rights from society, (2) the individual owing a duty to society, and (3) individuals creating society together. In the first iteration, the People is created through absorption by the state. In the second iteration, the People is created by the social contract. In the third iteration, the People is constantly forming and reforming through ongoing activity.

In Follett's view, only the last iteration is democratic. "Democracy is the rule of an interacting, interpermeating whole. . . . Democracy is every one building the single life, not my life and others, not the individual and the state, but my life bound up with others, the individual which is the state, the state which is the individual" (Follett 1998, 156). In short, "there are no 'people.' We have to create a people" (220). But this is accomplished by individuals together—not from an external source: "True individualism" includes "individual value as the basis of democracy, individual affirmation as its process, and individual responsibility as its motor force" (74). Therefore, a democratic community—a democratic People—"is neither the anarchy of particularism nor the rigidity of the German machine" (65).[16] "A democratic community is one in which the common will is being gradually created by the civic activity of its citizens" (51). This is why Follett believes "the essence of democracy is creating" (7). If one is not engaged in the creative process of unifying, one is not actually a part of the People.

This reconfiguration fundamentally changes traditional notions of loyalty to the People, typically understood as patriotism. Follett insists that allegiance to any group, including the state, comes from the fact that one "has made the state" and therefore "must recognize the authority of the state" (Follett 2013c, 220). Allegiance, or loyalty, "is bound up in the interweaving relation between ourselves and the state. That interweaving is the dynamo which produces both power and loyalty" (221).

The service state

From this new understanding of the People as a dynamic and relational composition must come a similar redefinition of the *state* as a social function—what Follett calls "the Service State" (Follett 1998, 294). Today, it might be better to use the contemporary term *governance* to understand what Follett means by the state function, because she believes that the same principles and methods—or mode in her terminology—should be applied to all forms of human association, including neighborhoods, occupational groups, and even families.

Suggesting current configurations of the state reveal that the emperor has no clothes, Follett insists, "We come to see that the vital matter is not methods of representation, as the menders and patchers fondly hope, nor even the division of power, as many of the pluralists tend to think, but *modes of association*" (Follett 1919, 582). She proclaims, "Many of us . . . believe in the possibility of ourselves weaving, from out our own daily experience, the garments of a genuine state" (585). This means "associating under the law of interpenetration as opposed to the law of the crowd" (Follett 1998, 23)—a skill and task that cannot be bestowed from external sources. "No one can give us democracy, we must learn democracy . . . it is to learn to live with other men" (Follett 1998, 22). Only through the process of integration "can the true state be grown" (303).

Thus, Follett (1998) queries, "We must see if it is necessary to abolish the state in order to get the advantage of the group" (9). In answer, she argues for a new role of the state, suggesting that "the opposite of *laissez-faire* is co-ordination" (Follett 2013h, 89). However, considering her writings as a whole, it is fair to say this argument would probably be better made with the statement that if the opposite of *laissez-faire* is control, the synthesis of the two is coordination—and synthesis is the position Follett continuously seeks.

Regardless of how her argument is set up, *coordination* is the role of the "new" state Follett envisions. The responsibility of the state is to create the conditions within which integrative processes can operate. "We have said, 'The people must rule.' We now ask, 'How are they to rule?' It is the technique of democracy which we are seeking" (Follett 1998, 155). While much of her exploration focuses on the problem of form, which will be reviewed in the next section, much of it speaks to the function of the state, which is discussed in Chapter 9.

Suffice it to say here that Follett's reconfigurations of the state focus on dynamic function instead of static power, leading to a new moniker: "The best part of functionalism is that it presents to us the Service State in the place of the old Sovereign State. This has two meanings: (1) that the state is created by the actual services of every man . . . (2) that the state itself is tested by the services it renders, both to its members and to the world-community" (Follett 1998, 294). She insists, "We need not fear the state if we could understand it as the unifying power: it is the state-principle when two or three are gathered together, when any differences are harmonized" (314). The "New State" need not be feared because "Genuine control, power, authority are always a growth. Self-government is a psychological process . . . To free the way for that process is the task of practical politics . . . No state can endure unless the political bond is being forever forged anew. The organization of men in small local groups gives opportunity for this continuous political activity which ceaselessly creates the state" (11). Thus, we turn to this particular pattern of organization.

THE STRUCTURE OF TRUE DEMOCRACY: FEDERALISM

Follett argues that the proper organizing form for the new state is federalism. However, she cautions, that she does not mean "the mistaken interpretation of federalism held by some of the pluralists: a conception which includes the false doctrines of division of power, the idea that the group not the individual should be the unit of the state, the old consent of the governed theory, an almost discarded particularism (group rights), and the worn-out balance theory" (Follett 1998, 297). Federalism has nothing to do with the divided or distributed powers, interest groups, contract theory, and particularistic individualism. Ontologically there cannot be a conferring of power so there cannot be a division of it within the state.

On the contrary, it is about unifying in order to generate power: "Sovereignty, we have seen, is the power generated within the group—dependent on the principle of interpenetration . . . Man joins many groups—in order to express his multiple nature. These two principles give us federalism" (Follett 1998, 296). True federalism is achieved through the sovereignty generated through interpenetration and the participation of every man in many groups, all of which are permeable and connected. Therefore "the true 'federalist' is always seeing the relation of these powers to those of the central government. There are no absolute divisions in a true federal union" (298). "The United States is neither to ignore the states, transcend the states, nor to balance the state, it is to *be* the states in their united capacity" (299). However, the unifying cannot stop there. "The United States is not only to be the *states* in their united capacity, but it is to be all the men and women of the United States in *their* united capacity . . . the individual, not the group, is the unit ... Federalism must live through: (1) the reality of the group, (2) the expanding group, (3) the ascending group or unifying process" (Follett 1998, 301).

Follett suggests we must have a fundamental philosophical shift for the sovereign state to become a unifying state of people generating sovereignty through integration: "the state must be the actual integration of living, local groups" (Follett 1998, 245). Therefore, "the task before us now is to think out the way in which the group method can be a regular part of our political system—its relation to the individual on the one hand and to the state on the other" (294). To contribute to this project, Follett lays out a new formulation of federalism, one which is: (1) philosophically aligned with the group process; (2) deeply nested and networked at all levels of society; (3) broadly inclusive of all groups; and (4) dynamic in its approach to representation.

The state as one-becoming-through-many

Follett notes that "the relation of whole to parts is the core of any of our present political problems" (Follett 2013c, 111). However, she believes that the individual and society can only be related in a federalist manner to be philosophically aligned with the group process. The state as a whole can neither be an absorptive One nor a dominating or compromising Many.[17] Instead, we must "now see that the individual and society are different aspects of the same process, so we see that the citizen and the state are one ... that they are absolutely bound up together" (Follett 1998, 140). This is described herein as a relational process ontology of One-becoming-through-Many.

This philosophical grounding is necessary because "federalism can never be fully understood until we see that it is not a governmental form alone but the most fundamental principle of life ... federalism is the embodiment of the theory of circular response and the *Gestalt* doctrine" (Follett 2013c, 111). In other words, federalism is a theory of the whole that should be based on a relational process ontology as opposed to an atomistic static ontology. "The very essence of any legitimate theory of wholes is a relation of the one and the many which makes it impossible to give to the many the mere rôle of consent" (111). Instead, "democratic thinking, in order to be truly the will of the people, must have the character of integrating wholeness" (112).

In her explanation of federalism, Follett goes deeper into her philosophical discussion of unity:

I have said that the political pluralists are fighting a misunderstood Hegelianism. Do they adopt the crudely popular conception of the Hegelian state as something "above and beyond" men, as a separate entity virtually independent of men? Such a conception is fundamentally wrong and wholly against the spirit of Hegel. As James found collective experience not independent of distributive experience, as he reconciled the two through the "compounding consciousness," so Hegel's related parts received their meaning only in the conception of total relativity. The soul of Hegelianism is total relativity, but this is the essence of the compounding of consciousness. As for James the related parts and their relations appear simultaneously and with equal reality, so in Hegel's total relativity. (Follett 1998, 266)

Perhaps somewhat arrogantly, Follett (1998) asserts, "But there is the real Hegel and the Hegel who misapplied his own doctrine, who preached the absolutism of a Prussian State" (267). In this conceptualization, "nationalization is the Hegelian reconciliation" (300).

Follett offers an alternative interpretation: "Green and Bosanquet in measure more or less full taught the true Hegelian doctrine . . . true Hegelianism finds its actualized form in federalism" (Follett 1998, 267). For Follett, "true federalism is the integration of present psychology. This means a genuine integration of the interests of all the parts" (300). This integration must occur at all levels of analysis within the whole—within the individual, within a given group, and among all groups: "As individual progress depends upon the degree of interpenetration, so the group progress depends upon the interpenetration of group and group" (249). Thus, in her reinterpretation of Hegel, Follett differentiates between the unifi*ed* state as an *object* versus the unify*ing* state as a *process*. "The unified state proceeds from the One to the Many. . . . This is not true of the unifying state which I am trying to indicate. Authority is to proceed from the Many to the One, from the smallest neighborhood group to the city, the state, the nation. This is the process of life, always unifying through the interpenetration of the Many—Oneness an infinite goal" (284). In other words, the unified federalism employs a static top-down authority to demand a whole, while the unifying federalism perpetually generates a whole from the ground-up through self-governance. Federalism is an organizing style as opposed to an organization—an instituting practice as opposed to an institution.

Deeply nesting, networking groups

Follett notes the importance of connecting groups from the smallest to the largest social scope in what could be described as a deeply nesting, networking federalism that begins at the most local level.[18] "Community must be the foundation stone of the New State" (Follett 1998, 359). From that immediate group of direct participation, "representatives from neighborhood groups meet to discuss and thereby correlate the needs of all parts of the city, of all parts of the state" (245). Follett insists that the widening of scope need not stop with the state or nation. While she notes "we have had very little idea yet of a community of nations" (354), Follett sees no problem extending the true federalist principle to the world as a whole, and views associations like the League of Nations as opportunities for building a widely inclusive community of nations. "There must be a world-ideal, a whole-civilization, in which the ideals and the civilization of every nation can find a place" (346).

However, to be true to the group principle, this can only be achieved through an understanding, acceptance, and willing of interdependent integration. "A community of nations needs a constitution, not treaties. Treaties are of the same nature as contract" (Follett 1998, 355). It may be this assertion in particular that caused Follett's political thinking to be banished from consideration for so many decades.

Broadly inclusive groups

Follett argues that "democracy rests on the well-grounded assumption that society is neither a collection of units nor an organism but a network of human relations" (Follett 1998, 7). Furthermore, "the Perfect Society is the complete interrelating of an infinite number of selves knowing themselves as one Self. We see that we are dependent on the whole, while seeing that we are one with it in creating it" (84). This means that through at least one point of connection, every individual is actively engaged in making the whole and being made by the whole. Therefore, "the individual not the group must be the basis of organization" (180). She emphasizes this point when she asserts "the essence of the woman movement is not that women as women should have the vote, but that women as individuals should have the vote. There is a fundamental distinction here" (171). But she does note "the individual is created by many groups" (180). Indeed, for Follett, the individual cannot be disaggregated from societal groups—they are completely reflexive in composition.

Therefore, federalism must be broadly inclusive, including groups from civic, political, and economic activities of life: "Other groups than neighborhood groups must be represented in the state" (Follett 1998, 245). She describes these myriad and complex connections as "an infinite number of filaments" that "cross and recross and connect all my various allegiances" (312). Because the individual's spirit cannot be exhausted or divided, we give our whole to each of these roles and relationships. "If you leave me with my plural selves, you leave me in desolate places, my soul craving its meaning, its home" (312). Therefore, none can be excluded from the process of governance: "The home of my soul is in the state" (312). But "the difficulty is that we have not yet found the way of vitalizing the local unit, of making it the means by which all men shall function, shall participate" (Follett 2013c, 226).

To enable group process, these many connected groups must be of relatively small size—intimate enough to accommodate effective integration. "In the small group then is where we shall find the inner meaning of democracy, its very heart and core" (Follett 2013c, 226). Therefore, "the organization of men in small, local groups must be the next form which democracy takes" (Follett 1998, 142). This requirement necessitates a form of representation, but one which fits within Follett's principles.

Dynamic representation

Follett agrees that representation is necessary for simple feasibility at large scale as well as to prevent the crowd mentality from emerging: "There must be representatives from the smallest units to the larger and larger, up to the federal state" (Follett 1998, 251). However, she identifies four requirements for *true democratic* representation: (1) representatives should maintain the goal of coming to an agreement based on larger understanding, not winning a fight; (2) representatives should "maintain an integrating relation with the representative group as the situation changes" (Follett 2013c, 253); (3) representatives must engage constituents in activity, not just intellectually; and (4) representatives must "study things as they vary in relation to the varyings of other things" (254). This ability to understand the total situation is, in Follett's (2013h) view, a better "requirement of statesmanship" (80). "The statesman organizes social facts into legislation and administration. The greater the statesman, the greater power he shows in just this capacity" (Follett 2003e, 144).

However, when considered in light of the other aspects of Follett's political theory, it is clear that situational needs and capacity should guide selection of representatives by the group participants. This will ensure progress "from contract to community" (Follett 1998, 122) in a dynamic, relational manner.

SUMMARY ANALYSIS

During her social work career, Follett "became interested in the intellectual justifications for the social centers movement" (Mattson 1998, xxxviii). Her experiences in the field "made Follett sure that democracy could be more than an abstract ideal. It must, she insisted, become a lived reality, a vigorous daily practice" (liv). Thus, Follett's primary concern is *modes of association* in human groups, preferring direct participation to representative forms of group governance at any scale and in any sector of society. She also believes in a deeply nesting and broadly inclusive federalism that grows out of associations at the neighborhood level to maintain local autonomy, while unifying ever more inclusive groups all the way to a global scope. Follett (2013h) insists "the aim and the process of the organisation [*sic*] of government, of industry, of international relations, should be, I think, a control not imposed from without the regular functioning of society, but one which is a co-ordinating of all those functions, that is, a collective self-control" (89). In her view, such self-governing is the only source of true democratic legitimacy.

Follett's political theory is unique because it stands firmly on a foundation of co-creation, refusing the notion of representation outside of a fully communicative and responsive approach that is also dynamic and changing according to the total situation. Her understanding of a relational People that can only be created through active participation fits the political theory of social anarchism, while her understanding of leadership as emergent from the situation embodies egalitarian social interaction. Thus, in what she calls "true democracy" (Follett 1998, 156), several familiar conceptual elements are fundamentally redefined: (1) politics is a creative process of integration convened and facilitated by the state; (2) democratic values of freedom and equality are relational power-with; (3) the People is a dynamic, relational whole composed through a deeply nesting, networking, and broadly inclusive federalism; and (4) representation is dynamic and determined by the law of the situation.

ENDNOTES

1. Here, Follett presages Marcuse's (1972) critique of what he calls *"sham-democracy"* (54).

2. Pratt (2011) argues that Follett is one of the few American pragmatists to address the issue of power. He suggests that Follett's response to pluralism represents a critique of systematic oppression in a fashion similar to that of Foucault, but one that is actually more useful than Foucault's in the American context characterized by pluralism.

3. Tonn (2003) suggests that Follett's critique of pluralism is lodged at English pluralist thinkers, including Frederic Maitland, John Neville Figgis, A. R. Orage, Ernest Barker, Harold J. Laski, and G. D. H. Cole. Grady (2002) notes that there was a Progressive aversion to factional politics—particular that of English pluralism. Follett followed but amended English pluralism, yet failed to impress political scientists at the time. *The New State* was panned in the *American Political Science Review* and the *Political Science Quarterly*.

4. Tonn (2003) argues that while Herbert Croly and Walter Lippmann promoted the notion of consent from the people and their representatives to what *experts* put forth, John Dewey sought to empower the average citizen. It is perhaps this similarity to Follett that often links her with Dewey in subsequent literature—both wish to temper expertise with participation.

5. Ryan and Rutherford (2000) explore whether Follett is an individualist or a collectivist, arguing that in the Hegelian sense of dialectic, she is both and neither in her own unique synthesis.

6. To release the creative evolution of democracy toward this end, Shapiro (2003) argues that our assumptions about human nature as atomistic and self-interested must change. Follett's ideas of creative experience, constructive conflict, integration, and egalitarian trust along with her participatory practice offer great promise in so doing.

7. This linkage between co-creative becoming of actual entities and freedom is noted in Whiteheadian thought (Mesle 2008).

8. Tonn (2003) suggests that Follett's understanding of freedom was influenced by her experiences growing up in a restrictive New England context. Further, she was heavily influenced by T. H. Green's understanding of positive liberty and his differentiation from the Hegelian concept of the state.

9. Here Follett presages Foucault's (1978) argument that power is constantly being produced through the process of social relation.

10. This reinterpretation of Nietzsche (1968) is commonly found in contemporary philosophy and political theory (see for example, Braidotti 2013; Connolly 2011; Deleuze 2001).

11. Pratt (2011) notes that Follett's understanding of power is constructed using Freud's idea of desire, James's conception of consciousness, and Royce's understanding of will-acts. Boje and Rosile (2001) argue that Follett's understanding avoids the dualistic trap of "all-or-nothing" understandings of power. Her understanding of power-with has been cogently linked to feminist theory and activism (Banerjee 2008).

12. Kaag (2008) argues that in her description, and affirmation, of power-with, Follett "anticipates the writing of Simone de Beauvoir, Hannah Arendt, and Gloria Anzeldua in suggesting that violence is antithetical to power insofar as violence seeks to destroy relationships" (150).

13. This is similar to the Whiteheadian understanding that relational power has a limitless potential for expansion (Mesle 2008).

14. This is similar to the Whiteheadian differentiation of unilateral versus relational power (Loomer 1976).

15. Eylon (1998) explains that the paradox of "empowerment" as typically understood is that it implies that power is a finite commodity controlled by a sub-set within the group. In other words, it is a power-over concept, not a power-with concept.

16. Grady (2002) notes that there was a Progressive aversion to German-inspired statist and juristic approaches.

17. This is where Follett's thinking presages the radicalized Deleuzian interpretation of assemblage that is self-organizing (Deleuze & Guattari 1987) rather than guided by God, as described by Whitehead (1978). This is specifically why the language used to describe microcosmic societies is so critical when applied to the macrocosmic level of human society

18. In this reconfiguration of federalism, Follett presages Donati's (2014) theory of relational sociology, in which relational citizenship "interweaves citizenship in a state . . . and societal citizenship. . . . The relational State is de/centered and articulated in an associational (or federative) manner, whether upward (for example, the European Union) or downward (local communities and organizations of civil society)" (112).

❧ 8 ❧

Follett's Economic Theory

Economic theory describes how we structure the use, exchange, and distribution of resources. Similar to political theory, economic theory describes the type of economic *regulation* (external or internal) and *intensity* of that regulation (weak or strong). External regulation refers to government intervention in economic activities while internal regulation refers to an economy free of government intervention. For Follett, the economy should be self-regulating in the same manner as government—by those involved in the situation and its coordinating networks.

Follett spent the latter part of her life investigating how her ontological and psychosocial principles of human being and association can be applied to industry. However, as indicated by the brevity of this discussion, she did not write extensively on economics, per se, rather using industrial situations to illustrate her ideas. As noted in a lecture, Follett believes, "Here the ideal and the practical have joined hands" (Follett 1926, 75) and so business is a perfect venue in which to illustrate her pragmatic philosophy. "For Follett, a business was not merely an economic unity but a social agency that was a significant part of society" (Graham 1995a, 19). To her, "business and society are not discrete fields of human activity—they are so inextricably interwoven as to be conceptually and analytically inseparable. Business and society are infinitely interpenetrative, and neither can be usefully understood in isolation of the other" (Parker 1995, 283).

Follett (2013c) sees "the central problem of social relations" (xiii) to be the question of power; including economic power among competitors as well as between consumer and producer, capital and labor, and industry and society. She does not often speak of economic classes directly, but does note important differences: "Much of what is written of the 'consumer' is inaccurate because consumer is used as a whole-word, whereas it is quite obvious that the consumer of large wealth has different desires and motives from the consumer of small means" (Follett 2003b, 42). In confronting such deep economic disparities and challenges, Follett responds, "I say only that we shall get no grip on our economic affairs until we acquire a greater capacity than we seem to have at present for understanding how economic factors affect one another at every point" (Follett 2013h, 81). She observes "when one financial adjustment is made, that means only that we have a fresh financial problem on our hands, the adjustment has made a new situation which means a new problem. We pass from situation to situation. It is a fallacy to think that we can solve problems—in any final sense. The belief that we can do so is a drag upon our thinking. What we need is some process for meeting problems" (86). Thus, she carries forward her critique of existing practices and her affirmation of an alternative participatory mode of association in market functions to match that of reformed political functions.

CRITIQUE OF MARKET CAPITALISM

Running tandem with her critique of representative government, Follett asserts that "our constitutions and laws made possible the development of big business; our courts were not 'bought' by big business, but legal decision and business practice were formed by the same inheritance and tradition" (Follett 1998, 167). Specifically, they are both based on the assumptions of particularist individualism. "Our whole material development was dominated by a false economic philosophy which saw the greatest good of all obtained by each following his own good in his own way. This did not mean the development of individuals but the crushing of individuals—of all but a few. ... The result of our false individualism has been non-conservation of our national resources, exploitation of labor, and political corruption. We see the direct outcome in our slums, our unregulated industries, our 'industrial unrest,' etc." (170-71). Thus, her critique considers problems within industry as well as between industry and society.

Within industry, Follett notes that particularist ideas lead to the bifurcation of production into capital and labor. She uses an example of coal operators and miners to illustrate: "Their interests are not the same, but indissolubly united. It is one situation, not two. Only when it is treated as one situation will the authority of that situation appear" (Follett 2013c, 187). She cautions, "If we do not want to be dominated by the special interests of the capital-power, it is equally evident that we do not want to be dominated by the special interests of the labor-power. The interests of capital and labor must be united" (Follett 1998, 114).[1] This requires applying the principles of group process to production, as well as labor relations. "But much of the language expressing the relation between capital and labour [sic] is that of a fight: 'traditional enemies,' the 'weapon of the union,' etc." (Follett 2003b, 47). In sum, she believes "egotism, materialism, anarchy are not true individualism" (Follett 1998, 171).

Between industry and society, Follett footnotes that *laissez-faire* has its rightful place only when there are great numbers of individual producer/consumers in exchange relationships as opposed to the large-scale economy we now have. In the modern economy, government has to take on a regulatory function as the scale of production and exchange expands. But "the error at the bottom of the 'regulation' idea of government is that people may be allowed to do as they please (*laissez-faire*) until they have built up special rules and privileges for themselves, and then they shall be 'regulated'" (Follett 1998, 182). This pendulum swing from *laissez-faire* to regulation results in the problems of poverty and urban decay noted above. Follett attributes this to greed: "While all captains of industry did not fly the black flag, still in the nineteenth century ruthlessness and success too often went together" (Follett 2003e, 143).[2]

Unfortunately, as the economy changed, the underlying theory and philosophy did not: "The regulation theory was based on the same fallacy as the let-alone theory, namely, that government is something external to the structural life of the people" (Follett 1998, 183). But, Follett (2013c) observes, "I do not find the distinction between individual and social made anywhere in actual life" (40). "Nowhere in actual practice do I find the categories of individual and social interest" (40). Therefore, she concludes, "Government cannot leave us alone, it cannot regulate us, it can only express us. The scope of politics should be our whole social life" (Follett 1998, 183).

As always, Follett (1998) seeks the synthesis: "we are giving up both our let-alone and our regulation policies in favor of constructive policy" (182) in the form of proactive social policy. However, she does not mean some sort of beneficent authoritarian redistribution because "*noblesse oblige* is really egoistic" (83). Instead, "success is now seen to depend on something other than domination" (Follett 2003e, 143). Furthermore, Follett notes that "it is significant that two ideas which so long existed together are disappearing together—namely, business as trading, and managing as manipulating" (Follett 2003e, 144). In other words, a new economy based on the assumption of a relational whole would resolve both aspects of her critique—within industry between capital and labor as well as externally between industry and society. This new economy would have a purpose of creating through cooperative self-governance. Each element of this new economic system will be discussed in turn.

CREATING AS THE FUNDAMENTAL DESIRE

Following psychoanalytic theory, Follett believes that in relation to the problem of economic activity, we must get at what we *really* want: "What is demand a symbol of?" (Follett 2013c, 169). She assumes that what we actually desire has little to do with material self-interest beyond the basic necessities. "What we care about is the productive life . . . nourishment of the individual . . . fruitfully united" (xiii). She insists that creating is what we desire: "Play, as useless idling, does not give us joy. Work, as drudgery, does not give us joy. Only creating gives us joy" (Follett 1998, 101). Bifurcating activity into work and leisure or personal versus community activity are simply false dichotomies in Follett's mind: "There was a notion formerly that a man made money for himself, a purely selfish occupation, in the daytime, and rendered his service to the community by sitting on the school board or some civic committee at night" (Follett 2003d, 133).

Instead, Follett (2003d) believes "our work itself is to be our greatest service to the community" (133). She explains, "When people talk of substituting the service motive for the profit motive, I always want to ask: Why this wish to simplify motive when there is nothing more complex? . . . We work for profit, for service, for our own development, for the love of creating something. At any one moment, indeed, most of us are not working directly or immediately for any of these things, but to put through the job in hand in the best possible manner, which might be thought of, perhaps, as the engineer's motive" (145).

If we think about work and service and play as creative acts, the meaning of both career and calling fundamentally change. Then the true purpose of business (as well as any other societal institution) is to provide vehicles and venues through which individuals can co-create. "I have left to last what seems to me the chief function, the real service, of business: to give an opportunity for individual development through the better organization of human relationships. Several times lately I have seen business defined as production, the production of useful articles. But every activity of man should add to the intangible values of life as well as to the tangible, should aim at other products than merely those which can be" (Follett 2003d, 141). Therefore, "a business man should think of his work as one of the necessary functions of society, aware that other people are also performing necessary functions, and that all together these make a sound, healthy, useful community. 'Function' is the best word because it implies not only that you are responsible for serving your community, but that you are partly responsible for there being any community to serve" (134). Thus, the purpose of the economy is reconceived from mere material production to producing opportunities for creative expression.

COOPERATION AS THE PATH TO CREATING

In her discussions of conflict and cooperation, Follett (2013c) repeatedly uses examples of labor-management disputes to illustrate the artificial division of wholes. "Again, labor and capital can never be reconciled as long as labor persists in thinking that there is a capitalist point of view and capitalists that there is a labor point of view. There is not. These are imaginary wholes which must be broken up before capital and labor can coöperate" (167-68). "Parts, aspects, factors, elements—all these words are too static; we must differentiate into *activities*" (168). However, these activities must take a new turn.

According to Follett (1998), in economics, as in politics, "individual competition must, of course, disappear" (364). It should be replaced with various forms of mutualism because true individualism is relational, not particularist. "This is an exchange, or interchange, of services. When we say 'reciprocal service' it seems to me that we are nearer the facts and also that we are expressing that give-and-take of life which is its noblest as it is its most profound aspect" (Follett 2003d, 133). She asserts hopefully, "'Cut-throat' competition is beginning to go out of fashion. What the world needs to-day is a coöperative mind . . . 'coöperative competition'" (Follett 1998, 113). Therefore, she calls for an alternative economic system based on cooperation. This does not eliminate all competition, but instead moves it into a holistic system in which individuals can be more successful through mutual support than if working toward market domination alone. She describes what would later be referred to as "co-opetition" (Hunt 1937)[3]:

> If I have a shop in a country village and spend my life in the illusion that the shop-keeper across the road is my enemy, and that I shall prosper in proportion as he fails, it may be that neither I nor my village will prosper. But if I see that by uniting forces at different points (provided there is enough trade for two), we can make our joint capital more productive. I shall have made this discovery by breaking up the ideal of "keeping store" into its separate activities; in the case of any of these activities I find that I shall do better by joining with my enemy than by fighting him. (Follett 2013c, 167)

She gives other examples of this approach in nascent form in business, the relations of capital and labor, industrial democracy, management, education, immigration, justice, city planning, and social programs. Within industry, she refers to it as "co-management" (Follett 1998, 118), noting, "the great advantage of company officials and workers acting together on boards or committees . . . employers and employed can thus learn to function together and prepare the way for joint control. . . . Industrial democracy is a process, a growth" (119). Between industry and society, she explains, "When it was found difficult to enforce the Rivers' Pollution Act in some towns in England, the mill-owners, who were the chief offenders, were finally won over not by urging them to sacrifice their individual for the social interest, but by showing them that their interest in the long run was unpolluted rivers" (Follett 2013c, 38).

While Follett does not dwell on issues of sustainability beyond her critique of poor social and environmental outcomes associated with the present economic system, she does note that the cooperative approach takes the long view: "Orderly marketing means orderly financing and avoids peaks and dips in the credit situation . . . the difference between competition and joint effort is a difference between a short and a long view" (Follett 2013c, 39). She also notes that through self-governance, we will be more likely to consider the social interest of which we are a part, suggesting that "if we are looking to the future, social interest may be merely a synonym for the unborn—individuals" (41). For this reason, she thinks it best to "substitute for individual and social interests, the idea of the short and the long view" (37).

SELF-GOVERNANCE OF ECONOMIC COOPERATION

Follett suggests that since the founding of the United States, individualism has competed with concentrated authority, and we have been seeking a synthesis of the two ever since. She insists that this cannot be a matter of balance. Actual synthesis must be achieved through the method of true democracy that she describes. This method must be applied to all forms of human association—including economic ones.[4] For Follett's vision of sectoral harmony, production, exchange, and distribution must all be part of an emergent whole that is neither directed nor regulated by external entities.[5] But, "the socialization of property must not precede the socialization of the will ... socialization of the will is the true socialism" (Follett 1998, 74). Follett believed that the next logical step in industrial development would be for the state to own the means of production while the producers control the conditions of production. This is a form of syndicalism. But "we want a state which shall include industry without on the one hand abdicating to industry or on the other controlling industry bureaucratically" (330). Neither *laissez-faire* nor state control will do.

However, some form of coordination is necessary. "All our functions must be expressed, but somewhere must come that coordination which will give them their real effectiveness" (Follett 1998, 321). Therefore, industry—meaning labor and capital as a whole—must be included in the process of the unifying state. "Let them be integrated openly with the state on the side of their public service, rather than allow a back-stairs connection on the side of their 'interests.' And let them be integrated in such a manner that labor itself is at last included in our political organization" (322).

Like politics, then, the market must be self-governing in order to enable the highest levels of creative self-expression and the most fruitful and sustainable production: "(1) efficient management has to take the place of that exploitation of our natural resources whose day is now nearly over; (2) keener competition; (3) scarcity of labour [*sic*]; (4) a broader conception of the ethics of human relations; (5) the growing idea of business as a public service which carries with it a sense of responsibility for its efficient conduct" (Follett 2003e, 122). Follett believes that this merging of ownership and production will create a type of public as opposed to private happiness: "The egoistic satisfaction of giving things away is going to be replaced by the joy of owning things together" (Follett 1998, 81). Only then can individuals and society progress together.

SUMMARY ANALYSIS

Follett sees "the central problem of social relations" (Follett 2013c, xiii) to be the question of power; including economic power among competitors as well as between consumer and producer, capital and labor, and industry and society. In applying her relational process concepts to economics, Follett imagines a change underway: "it is significant that two ideas which so long existed together are disappearing together—namely, business as trading, and managing as manipulating" (Follett 2003e, 144). She envisions a new economic system that would have a purpose of creative production through cooperative competition and emergent self-governance. While markets would remain, they would be transformed into a functional unity with the same democratic operating principles as government.

ENDNOTES

1. Here Follett is quite reminiscent of public intellectual Henry George (1929).

2. Melé (2007) takes care to note that while Follett used the term "corporate responsibility" she limited this term to interactions *within* an organization. However, he notes that her overall perspective on industry can be used to underscore contemporary understandings of corporate social responsibility.

3. Coopetition is a concept that re-emerged in economic development in recent decades (Henton, Melville, and Walesh 1997).

4. Parker (1995) notes "the phenomenal performance of post-war Japan is a reminder that the foundation of prosperity in any industrial society is in a harmony of purposes in its economic and social life" (285).

5. Tonn (2003) notes that while Follett was quite taken with the work of socialist Graham Wallas of the London Common Council, she did not share his faith in that form of collectivism.

❧ 9 ❧

Follett's Administrative Theory

Administrative theory describes how we administer and manage organizations and societal systems. Indeed, the last three elements of the typology are generally integrated in a given culture, hence the notion of *political economy*. Administrative theory includes a number of generic concepts, including: authority and scope of administrative action; criteria of proper administrative behavior; administrative decision-making approaches; and organizing styles (Stout 2013b). Together, these concepts shape prescriptions for the administrative role in organizations (and in society in the case of public agencies), as well as administrators' actions.

Follett's career began as a political scientist and theorist with her publication of *The Speaker of the House of Representatives* (Follett 1896) and her treatise *The New State* (Follett 1918). In this earlier work, Follett focuses most heavily on administrative authority and decision-making in community and public organizations. Thus, because of her holistic perspective on governance, a good bit of the discussion in the chapter on political theory is pertinent to her administrative theory, particularly her explanation of the process of true democracy in all organizations and the administrative role in the Service State.

As she further developed her ideas of integrative process in "Community is a Process" (Follett 1919) and *Creative Experience* (Follett 1924), she began applying it to organizational management where she saw "a demonstration of the possibility of collective creativeness" (Follett 2003a, 93-94). However, her principal elucidation of administrative thought was made through a series of twenty lectures delivered to the Taylor Society in

1926, the U.S. Bureau of Personnel Administration in 1926 and 1927, and the London School of Economics in 1933, as well as several others in conferences ranging from 1925 through 1933. Most of these papers were published posthumously in the edited volumes entitled *Dynamic Administration* (Metcalf and Urwick 1942) and *Freedom & Co-ordination* (Urwick 1949). These essays collectively capture "the broad purview of business management as a total integrative function" (Graham 1995b, 12), covering issues of: constructive conflict, the giving of orders, integrative unity, power, management as profession, responsibility, employee representation, control, consent and participation, conciliation and arbitration, expertise, leadership, planning, authority, and coordination.[1] Throughout these essays, Follett emphasizes the application of integrative process.

However, it must be noted that even in these management papers, she imagines her concepts being applied to both private and public organizations. Therefore, in her discussions of administration, while Follett often uses business and industry in her examples and terminology, management theorist Peter Drucker (1995) argues that Follett was the first to assert that the management function "is not exclusive to business but the generic function of all organizations, even of government agencies" (6). As Follett puts it, she hopes "to show that the basis for understanding the problems of political science is the same as the basis for understanding business administration—it is the understanding of the nature of integrative unities" (Follett 2003m, 190).

Follett's shift in focus from political institutions to business management is a logical move for this "quintessential pracademic" (Morse 2006, 3).[2] Follett sees all complex organizations as the prime laboratories for praxis: "Academic people may hope that what they are teaching will be followed by their students, but business men can actually themselves put into practice certain fundamental principles" (Follett 2003h, 269).[3] Thus, she urges "there is one thing which I think all executives should remember every hour of every day. . . . The way in which you give every order, the way in which you make every decision, the way in which you meet every committee, in almost every act you perform during the day, you may be contributing to the science of management" (Follett 2003d, 139).

In sum, Follett's development of well-grounded administrative theory is the culmination of her body of thought, where both her philosophical (ontological assumptions, psychosocial theory, epistemological concepts, and beliefs), and practice-oriented theories (ethics, political theory, and economic theory) all move into action as an integrated whole. These other conceptual elements must be kept in mind when examining her administrative theory. In fact, taking her administrative theory out of this context can lead to significant misinterpretation, as explained in Chapter 11.

FROM SCIENTIFIC MANAGEMENT TO COLLABORATIVE ADMINISTRATION

Bringing integrative process to bear on the problem of complex organization, Follett begins with a critique and revision of the leading theories of her time. On the one hand, bureaucracy was the received approach to coordinating organizational activities. As conceptualized by German sociologist Max Weber in *Economy and Society*, bureaucracy is characterized by hierarchical authority and accountability, a functional division of labor with hiring based on merit, and specified rules and procedures based on formal rationality that reduce bias and discretion (Weber 1946). Like many others during the Progressive Era who sought greater effectiveness within this model, Follett's thinking was influenced by American mechanical engineer Frederick Taylor's (1911) theory of scientific management and she was an avid reader of the *Bulletin of the Taylor Society* (Tonn 2003, 397). While Taylorism is commonly understood as a technique to achieve better hierarchical efficiency and control, Follett was invigorated by the prospects of this evolving science of management, particularly the possibilities for interdisciplinary integration of scientific discoveries. She was "interested—more interested than anything else in the world—in these correspondences in thinking between scientists, philosophers, and business managers, because such correspondences seem to me a pretty strong indication that we are on the right track" (Follett 2003m, 199).

Echoing Taylor, Follett argued "the most fundamental ideas in business today, that which is permeating our whole thinking on business organisation [*sic*], is that of function. Every man performs a function or part of a function. Research and scientific study determine function in scientifically managed plants" (Follett 2013g, 1). Therefore, she called for extending "the scientific standard" which Follett insisted "must be applied to the whole of business management" (Follett 2003d, 122). From these types of comments, it is clear that Follett's administrative theory could potentially be misinterpreted as a typical *functionalist* approach.

Perhaps the most recognizable list of these management functions is POSDCORB: Planning, Organizing, Staffing, Directing, Co-Ordinating,

Reporting, and Budgeting. Largely drawn from the work of French industrialist Henri Fayol, the acronym first appeared in a 1937 staff paper by Luther Gulick and Lyndall Urwick written for the Brownlow Committee (1937). While Follett did not directly respond to this list, her knowledge of Fayol, her relationship with Urwick, and her engagements with the Brownlow Committee certainly put it within her sphere of consideration. However, true to her typical approach, Follett used her own terminology to discuss the manner in which most of these management activities can be guided by integrative administration principles.

As a start, Follett (2003d) believes it is problematic when organizational functions are isolated and mechanized.[4] She argues that too often scientific study is "applied to only one part" (122) of organizational functioning—to the "the technical side, as it is usually called" (123). It does not attend to "the personnel side, a knowledge of how to deal fairly and fruitfully with one's fellows. . . . That is, one part of business management rested on science; the other part it was thought, never could" (123). Follett argues (2003c,) that "this divorcing of persons and the situation does a great deal of harm" (60).[5] In her view, while Taylor's "scientific management depersonalizes; the deeper philosophy of scientific management shows us personal relations within the whole setting of that thing of which they are a part" (60). For Follett (2003h), then, "relatedness" is her "key word of organization" (258). Therefore, coordination of both people and functions should be included in the science of management.

To attend to both parts of the whole, Follett brings forward her ideas of authority being dictated by the situation and power being generated by the group and rejects bureaucratic hierarchy to ensure order. She also reinterprets Taylor's static functional unity as the process of group integration in the context of complex organization. This leads her to affirm "unifying" as "a process, not as a product. We have to become process-conscious" (Follett 2003m, 195).

This relational process approach to management leads Follett to develop two key principles of administrative theory: (1) *authority* as a group process where all follow "what the situation demands" (Follett 2013b, 22); and (2) *functional unifying* in which interrelated parts are mutually and dynamically influencing. In essence, these two characteristics fundamentally change the *role* of the manager in pursuit of a new *goal* of management: *coordinating the integrative process of unifying functions*. These changes are cross-cutting in their implications for every aspect of administrative practice.

A self-creating, coherent process of functional relating requires a particular set of practices for exercising authority, ensuring fruitful behavior, determining what needs to be done and how to do it, and keeping subsequent actions organized. Once authority is re-conceptualized as situational power-with and functions are understood as relational and dynamic, notions like permanent positions of authority and division of labor become nonsensical. Indeed, because Follett reinterprets authority and functionalism using integrative process, the other practices of bureaucracy and scientific management must be adjusted as well: unity of command and managerial control are redefined as responsive authority and responsibility that are situation-determined; hierarchical organizing style shifts to federalism and non-hierarchical coordination; functional division of labor becomes an ongoing process of coordinating integrative activities; and planning and decision-making are guided by participatory collaboration rather than managerial direction.

While integrative process makes untangling these concepts a challenge, the following sections summarize the ways in which Follett's thinking transforms both Weber's bureaucratic hierarchy and Taylor's functional unity. The command and control of hierarchy is replaced with the law of the situation, which alters the organizational structure, the giving of orders, and answerability. Following this new approach to creating and exercising authority, the goal of maintaining a functional unity is replaced with the process of functional unifying, which transforms how people and functions interact, as well as how functions are conducted, coordinated, and led. We will consider each of these aspects of collaborative administrative practice in turn, focusing first on matters of authority, second on matters of function.

From command and control to emergent authority

Follett is critical of authority in the form of administrative expertise above other forms of knowledge as well as power-over. These are the assumptions of hierarchical command and control. Instead, she argues that in all organizational contexts, authority emerges from active participation in a group process guided by the needs of the situation, the functions for which it calls, and the abilities of those engaged: "Genuine authority arises spontaneously within the process of building up an integrative unity" (Follett 2003m, 205). But because authority is "a moment in interweaving experience" (Follett 2003i, 151), it is not something that can be created and then stockpiled. It must be continually created anew in accord with the evolving situation: "You have no authority as mere left-over. You cannot take the authority which you won yesterday and apply it to-day [*sic*]. . . . In the ideal organization authority is always fresh, always being distilled anew" (Follett 2003i, 151).

However, Follett is not against the exercise of authority *per se*: "Of course we should exercise authority" (Follett 2013f, 24). In fact, she notes "there is another difficulty at the opposite extreme from this, and that is when not enough orders are given. . . . Instead of an overbearing authority, we find that dangerous *laissez-faire* which comes from a fear of exercising authority" (24). Finally, although "authority is not all at the top" (Follett 2003m, 205), it is also not uniformly distributed throughout an organization. Blindly dispersing authority equally is no better than concentrated hierarchical authority, for "to confer authority where capacity has not been developed is fatal to both government and business" (Follett 2003j, 111). Therefore, she calls for an authority based not "on equality nor on arbitrary authority, but on functional unity" (Follett 2003h, 249). This is why Follett (2003g) argues that "any manager who is looking with far-seeing eyes to the progress of his business wants not so much to locate authority as to increase capacity" (181-82), thereby allowing for the effective sharing of authority. Thus, Follett argues (2003j) that "managers . . . should give the workers a chance to grow capacity or power for themselves" (109).[6]

As such, she believes in the use of authority; "authority—of the right kind" (Follett 2003c, 69). For Follett, this is "always the authority of the situation" (69), co-created by all involved. This shift from pre-determined hierarchical authority to the non-hierarchical authority of the situation reflects Follett's underlying idea of power-with rather than power-over.[7] Indeed, she argues that "we actually get more independent power through joint power" (Follett 2003a, 79) because power is the "combined capacities of a group. We get power through effective relations" (Follett 2003h, 247).[8] She argues that the power generated by everyone performing the function for which they are best suited and for which the situation calls will produce appropriate organizational authority because "legitimate authority is the interweaving of all the experience concerned" (Follett 2003m, 204).[9]

Thus, Follett (1998) argues "We can have function and liberty and authority: authority of the whole through the liberty of all by means of the functions of each. These three are inescapably united. . . . And with this unity will appear a sovereignty spontaneously and joyfully acknowledged" (310). We can relinquish "the old theory of authority" and "the illusion of final authority," which is "unrealistic because it tends to ignore the process by which authority is generated" (Follett 2013a, 41). To illuminate her argument that authority is not only "a process" (41), but specifically "a self-generating process" (46), Follett suggests "we ask ourselves where a decision really comes from" (41).[10] She answers, insisting "authority, genuine authority, is the outcome of our common life. . . . It comes from the intermingling of all, of my work fitting into yours and yours into mine, and from that intermingling of forces a power being created which will control those forces" (46). Follett continues this argument: "If then you accept my definition of control as a self-generating process, as the interweaving experience of all those who are performing a functional part of the activity under consideration, does not that constitute an imperative? . . . we must learn, and practise [*sic*], I am sure, the methods of collective control" (Follett 2013h, 89).

In sum, what Follett (2013a) wants to "make clear is that authority is not something from the top which filters down to those below" (43), that merely "co-ordinates the experiences of men" (Follett 2003i, 150). "Instead then of supreme control, ultimate authority, we might perhaps think of cumulative control, cumulative authority" (Follett 2013g, 7). However, cumulative does not mean static aggregation; it is dynamic and generative integration: "What we are seeking in business organization is the method of obtaining a cumulative authority as the interweaving experience of all those who are performing some functional part of the activity under consideration" (Follett 2003m, 205). As such, "authority goes with function" (205).[11]

Authority thus redefined, Follett (2013g) insists that we "should do away with the idea widely held that the president '*delegates*' authority" (3). Instead, she argues, "If we accept the statement that authority is a process, we find that the phrase delegation of authority is a little misleading . . . The form of organisation [*sic*] decides what authority the general manager shall have. Therefore we do not talk about the delegation of authority, because that would seem to imply that someone had the right to all the authority, but that for purposes of convenience he delegated some of it" (Follett 2013a, 44). This re-conceptualization of authority demands a new way of exercising it; hierarchical commands become situational orders.

Situational orders

With authority reconceived, the managerial principle of command and the practice of directing must follow suit. Follett carefully explains how the giving of orders is transformed once freed from hierarchical command and placed with the law of the situation: "orders come from the work, not work from the orders" (Follett 2013f, 31). Therefore, "Our job is not how to get people to obey orders, but how to devise methods by which we can best *discover* the order integral to a particular situation" (Follett 2003c, 59). Just as authority cannot be permanently delegated but emerges from the function within the situation, "one *person* should not give orders to another *person*, but both should agree to take their orders from the situation. If orders are simply part of the situation, the question of someone giving and someone receiving does not come up. Both accept the orders given by the situation" (59). Therefore, she suggests scientific management "really is a matter of *repersonalizing*" (60)—a clear reversal of bureaucratic depersonalization.[12]

Paradoxically, however, Follett notes that this is really both a *de*-personalization of positional authority and a *re*-personalization of the exercise of authority. "How can we avoid too great bossism in the giving of orders and the inevitable resentment which will follow? I think the solution is exactly the same for the special order as for the general order, namely, to depersonalise [*sic*] the matter, to unite those concerned in a study of the situation, to see what the situation demands, to discover the law of the situation and obey that" (Follett 2013f, 22). She goes on to clarify her meaning: "I think it is really a matter of re-personalising [*sic*] . . . a deeper philosophy shows us personal relations within the whole setting of that thing of which they are a part. Within that setting we find the so-called order" (25). Thus, while she prescribes depersonalizing orders to follow the authority of the situation, we must continually attend to the relating of persons within the situation to foster integration.

Since "authority belongs to the job and stays with the job" (Follett 2003i, 149) and the job is continually defined by the evolving situation instead of the organization chart, no organizational member should "have any more authority than goes with his function" (Follett 2013g, 4): "A man should have just as much, no more and no less, authority as goes with his function or his task. People talk about the limit of authority when it would be better to speak of the definition of task" (1). Therefore, each person within the organization has the ability to give orders, as required by function.

This "diffusion of authority" (Follett 2013g, 7) is most effective. Follett (2013i) notes that "in scientifically managed shops this is more and more recognized" (147); thus, "in the best managed plants today there is a tendency for each man to have the authority which goes with his particular job rather than that inhering in a particular position in a hierarchy" (Follett 2013a, 34). As a result, rather than authority being equated with hierarchical position, "we find authority with the head of a department, with an expert, with the driver of a truck as he decides on the order of deliveries. The despatch [*sic*] clerk has more authority in despatching [*sic*] work than the president" (Follett 2013g, 2). In short, "authority should go with knowledge and experience; that that is where obedience is due, no matter whether it is up the line or down the line" (Follett 2003i, 148).

Situational orders successfully synthesize the objective needs of the situation with the subjective desires of all those individuals within the situation through the principle of circular response. "If you accept my three fundamental statements on this subject: (1) that the order should be the law of the situation; (2) that the situation is always evolving; (3) that orders should involve circular not linear behaviour [*sic*]—then we see that our old conception of orders has somewhat changed, and that there should therefore follow definite changes in business practice" (Follett 2003c, 66). Further, she understands the common sense in enabling this dynamic feedback: "We all know that we get the come-back every day of our life, and we must certainly allow for it, or for what is more elegantly called circular behavior, in the giving of orders" (54).

To determine what orders the situation requires, Follett reflects on Taylorism: "You can get in an expert to do it, or you can, as they have done in some places, get each man to make an analysis of his own job. Out of that analysis, rules for the job, or orders, are formulated. Orders are the outcome of daily activity" (Follett 2003n, 273). To remain consistent with her underlying philosophy, Follett insists "the participation of employees in the planning of orders should take place before the order is given, not afterwards" (Follett 2003c, 69). One way to judge whether or not this is happening is by identifying who was involved in the process and at what point. "I have said that it was an advantage to get agreement to instructions, yet it is a fallacy to think that an order gets its validity from consent. It gets its validity long before that, from the whole process to which both order-giver and order-receiver have contributed" (Follett 2013f, 26).

Non-hierarchical organizing

To enable the identification of situational orders, "you must have an organisation [*sic*] which will permit interweaving all along the line" (Follett

2013g, 10). The organizational structure must balance centralization and decentralization: "The form of the organization should be such as to allow or induce the continuous co-ordination [*sic*] of the experiences of men" (Follett 2003i, 150). Therefore, Follett (2003l) argues that "the chief task of organization is how to relate the parts so that you have a working unit; then you get effective participation" (212).

Bureaucratic agencies organize and coordinate parts through a hierarchical chain of unitary command. "I hear more talk of co-ordination than of anything else. Why then do we not get it? One reason is that the system of organisation [*sic*] in a plant is often so hierarchical, so ascending and descending, that it is almost impossible to provide for cross relations. The notion of horizontal authority has not yet taken the place of vertical authority. We cannot, however, succeed in modern business by always running up and down a ladder of authority" (Follett 2013g, 10). Alternatively, Follett reconceives all organizations as communities: "The study of community as process does away with hierarchy, for it makes us dwell in the qualitative rather than in the quantitative" (Follett 1919, 580). Hierarchy itself is a quantitative concept that distributes specified amounts of authority and functional scope.

A qualitative perspective leads Follett to seek federated forms of non-hierarchy as a mechanism for organizing and coordinating action. She argues that if organizing becomes a process as opposed to a product, the resulting dynamic structure is more effective: "Strand should weave with strand, and then we shall not have the clumsy task of trying to patch together finished webs" (Follett 2013g, 10). In other words, interweaving of functions enables the continuously changing relating between the parts and the whole. Such dynamic interconnections support both centralization and decentralization, both vertical and horizontal authority, depending upon the law of the situation.[13, 14]

Referring back to Follett's explanation of federalism based on small interweaving groups, we can surmise that all organizations would look like dynamic, interconnecting networks of functional teams made up of experts and others affected by the issue at hand. Follett argues that this is feasible because the desire to escape hierarchical structure is common. As she quips, "I know a chief executive who says he does not know whether he is at the head or at the bottom and he wishes there was some way of making out a chart that did not put the president at the top" (Follett 2013g, 2). Indeed, in non-hierarchical federations, function and authority within each team would be emergent based on the needs of the situation, and all participants would take part in the activities of the team, from planning to decision to action to evaluation.

Mutual answerability

Continuing with the building blocks established by emergent authority, the manner in which members of the group are evaluated and answerable to one another must also change; the administrative principle of control and management practice of reporting are transformed. Follett explains that these practices should be replaced with a form of mutual answerability: "Collective responsibility should begin with group responsibility" (Follett 2003a, 81).

Situational orders do not lend themselves to the typical criteria used to assess administrative performance: accountability and responsibility. Accountability assumes hierarchy and responsibility assumes autonomy. Follett (2003c) highlights the problem with these assumptions by asking the question, "How can you expect people merely to obey orders and at the same time to take that degree of responsibility which they should take?" (63). Indeed, using the terms "freedom" and "law" as respective equivalents to responsibility and accountability, she argues, "When we see community as process, at that moment we recognize that freedom and law must appear together" (Follett 1919, 578). Therefore, agency and answerability must both be present; behavior must be judged on the degree to which it is *mutually answerable*.

Follett is careful to point out that shared responsibility does not simply mean delegation of responsibility. Indeed, Follett insists that as with authority, responsibility is not something that can be delegated by managers: "Employers sometimes speak of *dividing* responsibility when they are merely *shirking* responsibility. Many people will avoid a decision in order to avoid being held responsible for the consequences. . . . A responsibility spread out thin may save your face when things go wrong, but will not correct the wrong" (Follett 2003a, 79). Instead, mutual answerability accommodates both situational orders and non-hierarchical organizing, for when "authority and responsibility are derived from function, they have little to do with the hierarchy of position" (Follett 2003i, 147). Responsibility is no longer *to* the manager—instead each worker is responsible *for* his or her function. She uses an example to illustrate: "Everyone seemed to be thinking not so much in terms of to whom he was responsible as for what he was responsible—a much healthier attitude of mind" (Follett 2013a, 40). But this responsibility is not isolated—it must include responsibility *within* the coordinating whole. Follett (2003a) is insistent on this clarification, arguing that there is "a very marked difference between being responsible for a functional whole, what we are here considering, and being responsible for our function in the whole, which has been given far more consideration in the past" (80).

In a context of shared responsibility, "it isn't enough to do my part well and leave the matter there. My obligation by no means stops at that point. I must study how my part fits into every other part and change my work if necessary so that all parts work harmoniously and effectively together" (Follett 2013b, 76). In other words, we must not "forget that our responsibility does not end with doing conscientiously and well our particular piece of the whole, but that we are also responsible for the whole" (Follett 2003a, 80). Indeed, she suggests "the first test of any part of business organization and administration should be, I think: how far does this make for integrative unity?" (84). In other words, one must continually consider "whether you have a business with all its parts so co-ordinated" (71).

Relating back to emergent authority, Follett sees this mutual responsibility as another opportunity for increasing power-with. She advises administrators, "If your business is so organized that you can influence a co-manager while he is influencing you, so organized that a workman has an opportunity of influencing you as you have of influencing him; if there is an interactive influence going on all the time between you, power-with may be built up" (Follett 2003j, 105). This power-with translates into *responsibility-with* which unifies workers in their efforts. Follett (2003a) notes from her observations of organizations that "when there is some feeling in a plant, more or less developed, that that business is a working unit, we find then that the workman is more careful of material, that he saves time in lost motions, in talking over annoyances, that he helps the new hand by explaining things to him, that he helps the fellow working at his side by calling attention to the end of a roll on the machine, etc." (82).

The amount and type of responsibility for any individual will vary because "a man should have just as much, no more and no less, responsibility as goes with his function or his task. He should have just as much, no more and no less, authority as goes with his responsibility. Function, responsibility, and authority should be the three inseparables in business organization" (Follett 2003i, 147). Follett suggests that this balance can be achieved through mutual answerability for one's own actions as well as the outcomes of the whole.[15] She sees this as making "the reconciliation between receiving orders and taking responsibility. . . . through our conception of the law of the situation" (Follett 2003c, 64).

This relational approach to responsibility demands a new understanding of how work is done. Here, Follett turns attention from bureaucratic authority and form to some typical organizational functions and the manner in which they are conducted with consideration to integrative process.

From functional unity to functional unifying

The manner in which authority is conceptualized and exercised leads Follett to an understanding of the bureaucratic division of labor and staffing that differs qualitatively from her contemporaries. Perhaps the one point on which she would agree is hiring based on merit, as she clearly believes, "Where knowledge and experience are located, there . . . you have the key man to the situation" (Follett 2003i, 148). Indeed, it is important to note that Follett's rejection of a static, mechanistic functional unity does not mean that functions are not specified: "We shall all agree on one point, however: there should be no haziness in regard to employee functioning in a managerial capacity; the limits of such functioning should be frankly and sharply defined. . . . To be honest and clear-cut in delimiting function is, I believe, essential to the success of the redistribution of function" (Follett 2003a, 88-89). However, Follett worries that scientific management's excessive focus on breaking down the whole into atomistic functions is problematic. She argues that functional unity emerges as an interweaving of individuals and functions within the organization. It "is not a culminating process" (Follett 2013g, 10).[16]

Therefore, a static, atomistic view hinders the coordination and integration essential to *functional unifying*. As such, Follett clarifies that she is not talking about some form of binary relationship between the part and the whole: "One might think that this is a statement affirming that the whole determines the parts as well as that the parts determine the whole, but that would not be strictly accurate. The same activity determines both parts and whole . . . the reciprocal activity of the parts changes the parts while it is creating the unity" (Follett 2003m, 194). She insists that parts must be re-conceptualized as *functions interrelating within the whole*, "so moving together in their closely knit and adjusting activities, so linking, interlocking, interrelating, that they make a working unit—that is, not a congeries of separate pieces, but what I have called a functional whole or integrative unity" (Follett 2003a, 71).

Thus, for Follett, an unmet task of scientific management is that of attending to *functional relating* as opposed to staffing through a static division of labor. We must consider relation at multiple levels of analysis when studying function within the whole: "Just as the *relation* of jobs is a part of job analysis, just as the *relation* of departments is a part of scientific management, so a study of all these relations just mentioned should be a part of the study of business administration" (Follett 2003a, 93). Without this change in perspective from the particular to the relational, functional unifying cannot occur. Therefore, "it is impossible . . . to work most effectively at co-ordination until you have made up your mind where you stand philosophically in regard to the relation of parts to the whole . . . not to a stationary whole, but to a whole a-making" (91).

So as not to lose sight of these relational process underpinnings, Follett reiterates time and again that she is not simply aggregating independent functions into a static whole: "We never 'put parts together' even when we think we do. We watch parts behaving together, and the way they behave together *is* the whole. I say 'parts,' and people often speak of 'factors' or 'elements' in a total, but when we use any of these words we must remember that we are talking of activities" (Follett 2003m, 196). Indeed, "*Functional relating is the continuing process of self-creating coherence*. Most of my philosophy is contained in that sentence. . . . If you have the right kind of functional relating, you will have a process which will create a unity which will lead to further unities—a self-creating progression" (200-01). Such integrative outcomes are sometimes "called an 'interactive accumulation'" (199), as opposed to a culminating process directed by an executive.

Indeed, functional unifying is a process "neither of subordination nor of domination, but of each man learning to fit his work into that of every other" (Follett 2013b, 76). The relational process of functional unifying requires each part to be simultaneously aware of its own function and that of the whole. Isolated functions, like isolated facts, lose meaning without context, without attention to interrelationship within the whole. To achieve active participation throughout this integrative process, Follett (2003l) explains, "We are trying to work out a system of decentralization combined with a satisfactory system of cross-functioning so that the participation I am speaking of may be a continuous process" (224). She asserts that this system must address three principal issues: "how to educate and train the members of an organization so that each can give the most he is capable of; secondly, how to give to each the fullest opportunity for contribution; thirdly, how to unify the various contributions, that is, the problem of co-ordination" (Follett 2003l, 228). While the problem of coordination is addressed as a unique function of exercising authority, functional unifying requires each group member to be effective not only in her own function, but in her ability to participate cooperatively in the integrative process.

To develop capacity in coordinating and cooperating, Follett suggests that development is critical. "The parts of modern business are so intricately interwoven that the worker, in order to have an intelligent opinion in regard to even his own problems, has not only to know something of processes, of equipment, has not only to consider the effect of the introduction of new machinery and the training of the worker; he should also understand the connection between the production and the commercial side, should know something of the effectiveness of the sales organization" (Follett 2003a, 89). In other words, all parts must have an understanding of the whole to which they contribute.

Follett's essays describe the path to this understanding in a variety of terms. All must share an ability to cooperate, and leadership and coordination can play an important role throughout the integrative process. Functions are unified through direct participation in planning, decision-making, and action—all in an ongoing, iterative, integrative process.

Self-organizing coordination

Follett recognizes that with authority stemming from the situation, orders coming from function, and hierarchy removed, the manager's role of control is replaced with a function of organizing the process of functional unifying—what she calls *coordination*. Therefore, as with situational orders, "legitimate authority flows from co-ordination, not co-ordination from authority" (Follett 2003i, 150). Because coordination is the method through which functional unifying occurs, Follett (2003m) argues that "what we call co-ordination, is certainly the crux of almost every problem the organization engineer or the business manager has to deal with" (92). Indeed, Follett (2003l) deems coordination "the crux of business organization" (228) based on her discussions with organizational leaders in both England and America.[17] Therefore, study of the process of integration in organizations—coordination—is crucial. "When we do understand this more fully, it will be a big step forward for business organization" (Follett 2003m, 196).

While managers describe coordination as the most difficult problem with which they contend, Follett suggests that the reason is not its inherent difficulty, but rather a misunderstanding of its meaning and method: "The chief reason, however, that we are not more successful with this problem is that we do not yet fully comprehend, I think, the essential nature of co-ordination" (Follett 2013g, 11). She explains that when we attempt to coordinate function through authoritative control, we fail to achieve the goal because "we have not found what I call the field of control" (11).[18] Follett argues that we cannot take discrete, static parts and coordinate them because coordination must be part of the process of relating through which those parts themselves are being created. Put in organizational terms, departments cannot operate as if independent from one another and from policy makers, then have their activities aggregated as the whole of the organization. "The various departmental policies are being influenced by general policy *while* they are making general policy. This sounds like a paradox, but it is the truest thing I know. Business unifying must be understood as a process, not as a product" (Follett 2003m, 195).

If we instead coordinate through facilitated "integrated authority, as interweaving controls" (Follett 2013g, 12), we will find success. In other words, "it is not the aggregation but the integration of these parts which constitutes the field of control" (13). Therefore, Follett emphasizes, "Of everything I ever say or write on business management there is always the idea of control as the self-directing power of a unity. A genuine co-ordination or integration gives you control" (14). Thus, coordination is the type of participatory control achieved through integrative process, which includes: (1) direct contact of the responsible people concerned; (2) engagement early in the process; and (3) reciprocal relating of all the factors in a situation (Follett 2003f, 297).

This further distinguishes Follett's coordinated control through facilitation from a hierarchical approach. Emergent authority means that "the interacting *is* the control, it does not set up a control, that fatal expression of some writers on government and also some writers on business administration" (Follett 2003m, 202-03). This means that "if control arises within the unifying process, then the more highly integrated unity you have, the more self-direction you get" (205). Thus, she urges us to give up the notion of hierarchical power-over or control-over, insisting that "one part can never get any lasting power over another, but that you can have self-direction by forming integrative unities" (204).

Yet, Follett also accommodates the need to coordinate coordination, if you will, through a centralized process, insisting "it is the president's responsibility to see that all possible contributions are utilized and made into an organized, significant whole subordinated to a common purpose" (Follett 2003n, 283). Thus, coordination remains an executive function, but one which reflects Follett's understanding of federation. Within this type of non-hierarchical structure, work is coordinated through a participatory process. Follett (2003a) suggests that "a form of departmental organization which includes the workers is the most effective method for unifying a business" (81). Drawing from both community and business practice, Follett puts forth the idea of the "experience meeting" (Follett 2013c, 212) which begins by focusing on how the issue at hand is pertinent to the lived experience of participants, asking them to engage in the conversation. This establishes the context for the method of integration—Follett's particular approach to dialogue and deliberation.

Follett is intent on getting the appropriate parties together to engage in this process: "I do not mean by this that I think workers should be consulted on all questions, only on those on which they are competent to have some opinion" (Follett 2013h, 83). Such meetings aim to provide expert information while also eliciting information from laypersons to determine how expert information aligns with experience (Follett 2013c, 213). By using these types of practices, "business practice has gone ahead of business theory, business practice has gone ahead of business language" (Follett 2013a, 34).

Cooperation

In the context of self-organizing coordination and mutual answerability, functional unifying must also be a largely autopoietic. However, this should not be interpreted as autonomy. Indeed, Follett (2003g) argues that "the process of cooperation is, strictly speaking, very different from the process of bargaining" (168). Cooperation requires the open-mindedness of dynamic, relational epistemology: "By this I mean that cooperation is not, and this I insist on, merely a matter of good intentions, of kindly feeling" (Follett 2003d, 123). Citing industrial interviews, "One of the girls said: 'When I first went to a conference committee, I thought I was going there to give my criticism to the management, but I came to understand that cooperation means also taking criticism from the management, and I am more willing now to take it.' One man said: 'I feel in a conference committee that I'm an agent for both sides'" (Follett 2003a, 76). Yet, while she agrees that cooperation is an attitude—"a spirit of co-operation" (Follett 2013b, 76)—"you cannot have successful cooperation until you have worked out the methods of cooperation" (Follett 2003d, 123). In the process of functional unifying we must formulate "an understanding of the methods of cooperation" (Follett 2013b, 76).

Refuting an essay in the *Bulletin of the Taylor Society* that argued there could be no science of cooperation, Follett (2003d) retorts, "The reason we are here studying human relations in industry is that we believe there can be a science of cooperation" developed through "experiment after experiment, by a comparing of experiments, by a pooling of results" (123). For her own contribution to this endeavor, Follett draws characteristics from the method of integration in the group process to describe how it plays out as cooperation in business and industrial relations.

Cooperation is an essential mindset for achieving coordinated control through facilitated coordination, as opposed to managerial direction. Indeed, it is the participatory process of integration itself that ensures control: "We want to arouse not the attitudes of obedience, but the attitudes of co-operation, and we cannot do that effectively unless we are working for a common purpose understood and defined as such" (Follett 2003h, 262). As she recognizes, "in order to control a certain situation, you have to get the co-operation of those fellow executives who are also concerned in that situation" (262). This means that "the degree of control will depend partly on how far you can successfully unite the ideas of these men and yourself" (Follett 2003m, 202). Thus, coordinated control is a form of group control achieved through cooperation, and "the joint machinery of cooperation begins at the very bottom" (Follett 2003l, 223).

Like any group process, organizational coordination must be a purposeful group activity in which all participate cooperatively. "You do not have a co-ordination by two units existing harmoniously side by side . . . these units have to make a unity before you can say that you have co-ordination" (Follett 2003m, 192). For Follett (2003h), coordination is a cooperative, relational process through which functions are interwoven in reciprocal co-creation of "a common purpose, born of the desires and the activities of the group" (262).

While acknowledging the challenges of achieving cooperation, Follett provides two key requirements to foster the process of coordination. First, "for co-ordination we need understanding and for understanding we need openness and explicitness" (Follett 2003l, 221). For this "we have to find out what we really want, ourselves and others, for you can seldom tell by the general phrases people use" (222). Second, integrative coordination requires active participation by everyone in an organization and "that it must begin at the bottom, not at the top" (Follett 2003l, 222). Coordination is not something that can be orchestrated by managers at the top of the organization delegating tasks to individuals or departments within the whole, but is something to be encouraged through careful facilitation and universal cooperation. For this reason Follett advises, "What we want, then, is co-ordination from the bottom and all along the line. This is successful organization engineering" (223).

Emergent leadership

Despite her anticipation of cooperation and self-organizing coordination, Follett firmly insists there is a place for leadership in administrative practice. This is because the law of the situation requires the leadership of expertise and knowledge, and because coordination is a necessary organizational function that can be interpreted as emergent leadership. However, Follett (2003h) notes "a different kind of leader is developing" (259) and "the time is fast disappearing when we need ask ourselves whether we believe in an 'autocratic' or 'democratic' leadership, for we are developing something that is neither, something that is better than either. . . . It is a system based neither on equality nor on arbitrary authority, but on functional unity" (249). This requires a particular type of leadership—what we might refer to today as facilitative, servant, or shared leadership.

Follett's approach to emergent authority requires rethinking the function of organizational leadership, and she notes progress in recognizing the reciprocal relationships between leaders and followers: "It is significant that the fact that the master has a relation to servant as well as servant to master has now general recognition" (Follett 1919, 583). But she wants this reciprocal understanding to carry into all forms of hierarchical relationship: "The flow goes both ways. They [workers] contribute to general policy and then they must conform to general policy. They follow what they have helped to construct. But this latter part is what we forget when we say that general policy dictates departmental policies. We forget that general policy is not an air plant, but has its roots in all that is going on in the business" (Follett 2013a, 43).

Follett (2003g) notes that such diffuse leadership reflects a substantive "change in our thinking" in which there "is the full recognition that labour [sic] can make constructive contributions to management" (181). She argues that "almost everyone has some managing ability, even if it be very little, and opportunity should be given each man to exercise what he has on his actual job. If all on the managerial force have—as, of course, they have—initiative, creative imagination, organizing and executive ability, there are many workmen who are not entirely lacking in these qualities. We want to make use of what they have" (Follett 2003a, 86).[19] Therefore, everyone involved, executives and workers, must be "asked to co-operate in the forming of rules for the job—all this takes away from arbitrary authority" (Follett 2013a, 40).

Given the significance of this change, Follett (2003n) observes, "I have sometimes wondered whether it would be better to give up the word 'leader,' since to so many it suggests merely the leader-follower relation. But it is far too good a word to abandon; moreover, the leader in one way at least does and should lead in that very sense" (291). Thus, instead of jettisoning the term, Follett expands the notion of leadership to include several types: "a leadership of function as well as the leadership of personality and the leadership of position" (277), noting that "leadership of function is tending to become more important than the leadership of personality" (278).

At the time, applied psychology linked leadership with personality traits such as aggressiveness, pugnacity, and fearlessness that are encapsulated in "that conception which emphasizes the dominating, the masterful man" (Follett 2003h, 269); "the autocratic view of leadership" (248). While Follett (2003n) does not dismiss the importance of personality, she argues that traits must enable a "relation between leaders and led which will give to each the opportunity to make creative contributions to the situation" (290). In this type of relationship, leaders "lead by the force of example" (291).

This understanding of leadership married with the notion of functional unifying leads to particular qualities of merit; "In the complications of modern business everything tends to give the lead to organizing ability rather than to ascendancy traits" (Follett 2003n, 284). For Follett (2003h), this means ability in the "fundamental principles of organization": "evoking, interacting, integrating, and emerging" (267). Linking back to the self-organizing coordination, she argues, "Evoking, releasing, is the foundation of co-ordination" (Follett 2003m, 197-98). Leaders "draw out from each his fullest possibilities" (Follett 2003h, 267). The best leaders "can arouse my latent possibilities, can reveal to me new powers in myself, can quicken and give direction to some force within me. There is energy, passion, unawakened [sic] life in us—those who call it forth are our leaders" (Follett 2003n, 293).

Follett explains that *interacting* and *integrating* are linked in the process of functional unifying. She argues that "the leader is more responsible than anyone else for that integrative unity which is the aim of organization" (Follett 2003h, 267). Therefore, "the great leader is he who is able to integrate the experience of all and use it for a common purpose" (268). Follett (2003n) believes this facilitative, coordinating capacity "is pre-eminently the leadership quality—the ability to organize all the forces there are in an enterprise. Men with this ability create a group power rather than express a personal power" (283). Thus, "the best leader knows how to make his followers actually feel power themselves, not merely acknowledge his power" (290).[20] Indeed, the leader develops capacity among group members for interacting and integrating: "the test of a foreman now is not how good he is at bossing, but how little bossing he has to do because of the training of his men and the organization of their work" (274).

Emerging is the logical goal of leadership "because that is the expression so much used to-day to denote the evolving, the creating of new values, the forward movement" (Follett 2003h, 268). Follett asserts that is it the leader "who understands the creative moment in the progress of business, who sees one situation melting into another and has learned the mastery of that moment" (268), and that this "kind of insight which is also foresight is essential to leadership" (Follett 2003n, 280).[21] In this way, leaders "have a vision of the future" (Follett 2003h, 264).

However, leadership for Follett is not positional; it emerges in response to situational authority and the functional capacities of those involved.[22] In this view "each man is responsible for a given set of duties and where the tendency is to give a man leadership up to his capacity for leadership, there is less and less hierarchical authority, above and below, over and under. One man is over another in some things and under him in others" (Follett 2003n, 286). When capacities are developed throughout the organization, "we find leadership in many places besides these more obvious ones, and this is just because men are learning special techniques and therefore naturally lead in those situations" (Follett 2013d, 50).

While accepting the importance of specialized knowledge, following her critique of expertise, Follett (2003n) argues that "you cannot get any profitable 'following' unless your followers are convinced, and you convince them in only one way—by allowing them to share in your experience" (284). Thus, "the tendency is not to check leadership, but to encourage a multiple leadership" (Follett 2003h, 251). This type of shared leadership benefits the whole organization: "This view of leadership is not lessening the power of the leader; it is vastly increasing it" (Follett 2003h, 259) in the form of *power-with* instead of *power-over*. "Since power is now beginning to be thought of by many not as inhering in one person but as the combined capacities of a group, we are beginning to think of the leader not as the man who is able to assert his individual will and get others to follow him, but as the one who knows how to relate the different wills in a group so that they will have driving force" (Follett 2003n, 282). Thus, Follett (2003h) insists, the leader "must know how to create a group power rather than to express a personal power. He must make the team" (247).

In this emergent leadership, Follett (2013b) also redefines *followership*, giving those led a "a very active part to play" (54) within "that intricate system of human relationships which business has now become" (Follett 2003h, 269). Follett (2003n) explains that in functional unifying, "those led have not merely a passive part, they have not merely to follow and obey, they have to help keep the leader in control of the situation. Let us not think that we are either leaders or—nothing of much importance. As one of those led, we have a part in leadership" (289). Therefore, "we have now to lay somewhat less stress than formerly on this matter of the leader influencing his group because we now think of the leader as also being influenced by his group" (Follett 2003h, 247). "That is, we should think not only of what the leader does to the group, but also of what the group does to the leader" (248).

Participatory planning and decision-making

The fundamental method for "making the team" in functional unifying is through direct participation and the skill development it requires: "For here it is even more obvious that cooperation should be sought in the preliminary study of situations, reasons for policies discussed, the purposes of the company explained, reactions anticipated, and training provided" (Follett 2013f, 31). Indeed, Follett anticipates that to some degree, everyone in an organization will be involved in goal-setting and policy-making. She typically refers to these processes as planning, but the characteristics mirror her conception of how the elements of ethics are collaboratively generated.

Reflecting back on POSDCORB, planning, budgeting, and decision-making are related and nearly ubiquitous administrative practices through which functions are determined.[23] Planning is a process through which purpose and strategies are defined, while decision-making is the process through which purposes and strategies are chosen, often considering financial implications. Thus, the three go hand-in-hand. While Follett does not directly address budgeting, it is the financial aspect of planning and can be assumed within that term's umbrella. Follett (2003h) notes that functional unifying cannot be achieved without these activities because "you cannot integrate the parts of your business successfully unless you have your purpose clearly defined. The chief executive should be able to define the purpose of the plant at any one minute, or rather, the whole of purposes. He should see the relation of the immediate purpose to the larger purpose. He should see the relation of every suggestion, of every separate plan, to the general purpose of the company" (261).

However, planning cannot be limited to an executive function, leaving all others to simply act according to formal rules and procedures handed down from above. The total situation can only be understood through the interweaving of understandings of all the situations throughout the organization. Thus, Follett (2003m) argues that planning poses "two fundamental problems for business management: first, to define the essential nature of the total situation; secondly, how to pass from one total situation to another" (209). She reminds her audience that in defining the total situation "satisfactorily," functional unifying is "not inclusiveness alone, but also relatedness, a functional relating" (209). Thus, in assessing the organizational goals for planning purposes, administrators must always be mindful of the essential relatedness of functions. However, reflecting back on self-organizing coordination, this means everyone in the organization must contribute to forming the shared purpose of the organization's total situation.

Using the example of national planning, Follett (2003f) assures that individual organizations "would not be asked to give up their own points of view for the sake of an imaginary 'whole,' for an air-plane [*sic*] view, *a deracine* view; they would be expected to learn how to interweave their points of view, their various policies" (301). Similarly, within organizations "we can never reconcile planning and individualism until we understand individualism not as an apartness from the whole, but as a contribution to the whole" (301).

This reconciliation demands the other aspect of planning—understanding how organizational parts—other situations—can be integrated with the overall purposes. Shifting from one total situation to another may only require changes in the *relating* of functions within the whole; it does not necessarily require the addition or subtraction of functions, although such changes may occur. Again drawing on example, she explains that when a consultant is called in to a business she may determine the best course of action is "not to change any one thing or any two or three things in that department" but instead to make "certain changes in the relation between the factors or sections of which the department was composed" (Follett 2003m, 193). In other cases, the functions themselves may change. Follett illustrates this with an example provided by the manager of a large business: "If my heads of departments tell me that Department D and Department E are co-ordinated, and then I find that Department D and Department E are exactly the same as they were before, then I know that what I have been told is not true; they are not co-ordinated. If they had been co-ordinated, then the parts will be changed, that is, the practice of Department D will differ in some respects from what it was before co-ordination" (193).

However, Follett (2003m) acknowledges "we have not yet answered" (209) the challenges involved in a planning approach that encompasses a view of the total situation.[24] As more parts become involved, the reciprocal relating of the whole becomes harder to see: "When you put it in terms of yourself and Jones in the next room, it seems easy enough to understand . . . However . . . it is by no means so easy to understand when relations become more complex" (196). But, she insists "the mere fact of stating a problem is a long way toward its solution, and many of us are now trying to state the problem of control" (209) in planning for how situations interrelate in functional unifying.

As planning moves into decision-making, Follett (2003i) emphasizes that rather than a culminating moment, "an executive decision is a moment in [this] process" (146). She explains that "the growth of a decision, the accumulation of responsibility, not the final step, is what we need most to study" (146). Therefore, decisions taken should go only so far as consensus is achieved: "As far as our control and our integration correspond, we have a legitimate situation, a valid process" (Follett 2013c, 185). Shared decision-making requires that administrators use alternative tools such as "the conference method which demands from managers the ability to make of differences a unifying, not a disruptive, factor, to make them constructive rather than destructive, to unite all the different points of view, not only in order to have a more contented personnel, but in order to get incorporated into the service of the company all that everyone has to contribute" (Follett 2003g, 175). The integration of all viewpoints impacted by a decision is essential because "seldom is any side right in that absolute sense" (Follett

2003h, 251). Further, she insists "when differences are integrated instead of each side to a dispute claiming right of way, that is when we have control of the situation" and this challenge "illustrates one of my main theses in regard to business management" (250).

Follett provides a practical example in which a purchasing agent for a manufacturer wants to buy a less expensive material but the production head says the cheaper material cannot produce satisfactory results. She insists this is not a situation where the final decision must be a win-lose ultimatum in which the manager determines the outcome. Instead, together, they can seek to find a less expensive material that will maintain quality of the product, thereby allowing integrative process to guide the decision. Follett (2003m) explains, "we should have here the three results which often follow an integration: both parties would be satisfied; the situation would be improved . . . and there might in time be a still wider, a community, value . . . to the consumer eventually effected" (199).

This example underscores the notion that administrators play a *facilitative* rather than *controlling* role in the decision-making process: "If purchasing agent and production manager bring him different conclusions, his task is not to *decide* between them, but to try to unite the three different kinds of experience involved—that of purchasing agent and production manager *and his own*" (Follett 2003h, 261). To ensure integrative outcomes, there must be "a reluctance to take action until all agree; there is a feeling that somehow, if we keep at it long enough, we can unify our ideas and our wills, and there is also a feeling that such unification of will has value, that our work will be vastly more effective in consequence" (Follett 1998, 143). But even if disagreement remains because integration was not complete, Follett notes that "an advantage of not exacting blind obedience, of discussing your instructions with your subordinates, is that if there is any resentment, any come-back, you get it out into the open, and when it is in the open you can deal with it" (Follett 2013f, 26).

Further, the character of this collaborative decision-making process must be considered: "One of the tests of conference or committee should be: are we developing genuine power or is someone trying unduly to influence the others?" (Follett 2003j, 109). Thus, "we can always test the validity of power by asking whether it is integral to the process or outside the process" (Follett 2013c, 193). Here, Follett reasserts that she is not calling for universal inclusion or equal weighting of all workers in all decisions. "Our aim in the so-called democratic organization of industry should not be, not to give the workmen a vote on things they know nothing about, but so to organize the plant that the workmen's experience can be added to that of the expert" (Follett 2013c, 20). She looks to social movements for nascent examples: "The community centre [*sic*] movements, the workmen's education movement, the cooperative movement, to mention only two or three . . . The central aim of these, the most democratic movements we have, is to train ourselves, to learn how to use the work of experts, to find our will, to educate our will, to integrate our wills" (5).

Reflecting her critique of expertise, this consensus-seeking approach to decision-making can become more difficult with the inclusion of experts. There can be a tendency to revert to top-down approaches in which administrators consult experts and allow their input to outweigh all other perspectives. Follett (2003h) warns that managers must resist the urge to turn to experts in order to impose hierarchical authority: "the executive should give every possible value to the information of the specialist" but simultaneously warns, "*no executive should abdicate thinking on any subject because of the expert.* The expert's information or opinion should not be allowed automatically to become a decision" (256).

Thus, "our problem is to find a method by which the opinion of the expert does not coerce and yet enters integrally into the situation. Our problem is to find a way by which the specialist's kind of knowledge and the executive's kind of knowledge can be joined. And the method should, I think, be one I have already advocated, that of integration" (Follett 2013b, 70). Through this approach, Follett (2013c) insists "the integrating of facts and power is possible" (15) but advises successfully doing so "would mean a different code from that by which we are at present living" (15). Only through participatory planning and decision-making in functional unifying will "real authority and official authority . . . coincide" (Follett 2013a, 46).

THE SERVICE STATE

While Follett insisted that her administrative theory and prescriptions for practice were suited to all types of organizations across all sectors of society, she did emphasize their importance in government. Her explanation of what she calls the Service State paints a very different picture of what was then emerging as the field of public administration. In governance, the administrative role has democratic implications beyond those of private organization that cannot be ignored without risking the legitimacy of government as a whole.

Follett makes clear that her reservations are in regard to the *manner* in which administrative expertise is given authority and discretion in public organizations. Following her concerns about the manner in which administrative expertise impacts policy-making (as noted in Chapter 7), Follett is concerned that it also separates government from the governed: "To divide society on the one side into the expert and the governors basing their governing on his reports, and on the other the people consenting, is, I believe, a disaster-courting procedure" (Follett 2013c, 5). This configuration results in an authoritative "Sovereign State" (Follett 1998, 294) as opposed to a functional Service State in which all citizens take part—whether elected representative, expert, or layperson.

Thus, as an extension of her collaborative approach to administration, the Service State redefines *political* authority as a group process among the governing and the governed, all subject to the law of the situation rather than a sovereign state. It also expands the scope of administration to include all functions of governance, and in actuality, all functions of social life. Thus, in the Service State "the only legitimate boss, sovereignty, is, I believe, the interweaving experience of all those who are performing some functional part of the activity under consideration" (Follett 2003j, 109).

The role of public administration

The role of administration in the Service State mirrors the role of leaders in non-hierarchical coordination. Public administrators are charged with facilitating the conditions within which participatory planning, decision-making, and integrative action can occur. The public sphere must engage citizens as active participants in state functions. "To say, 'We are good men, we are honest officials, we are employing experts . . . you must trust us,' will not do; some way must be devised of connecting the experts and the people . . . then some way of taking the people into the counsels of city administration" (Follett 1998, 234). In short, Follett wishes government to function like a community: "I wish to urge in this paper actual group association—the *practice* of community" (Follett 1919, 584).

In community, Follett (1998) asserts, "we need leaders, not masters or drivers" (229). Public administrators are not to be granted positional authority from which to issue orders to the public. However, neither should the opposite be true: "Underneath all the various current uses of the word 'service,' there is the idea of service as expressing man's altruism, labour [*sic*] performed for another, doing good to others. I think there is a more profound meaning to service than this" (Follett 2003e, 132). Follett (1998) emphasizes "we do not want 'servants' any more than we want bosses; we want genuine leaders" (227). Thus, the public administrator must strive to enhance the capacities of the community to enable the sharing of administrative functions, leading to an "increased sense of collective responsibility" (Follett 2013b, 71).[25]

This requires genuine citizen engagement in the Service State; opportunities to lead must be open to everyone and emergent according to the needs of the situation. Follett (1998) sees this as "the kind of leadership which will serve a true democracy, which will be the expression of a true democracy, and will guide it to democratic ends by democratic methods" (228).

However, it must be noted that Follett is ardent in her support of increased administrative authority and expanded scope of action. She believes that the Progressive Era's trends toward direct government and increased social programs are "bound up with . . . the increase of administrative responsibility" (Follett 1998, 172). However, this responsibility should be focused on "the discovery and formulation of modes of unifying" (Follett 1919, 584). As in organizational applications of leadership, the public administrator must possess the ability to recognize, encourage, and coordinate the capacities of the citizenry in collaborative governance. Thus, while the public administrator of the Service State gives up positional authority as a representative of an authoritative state, her scope is broadened to lead integrative process.

To maintain responsiveness to the unfolding situation, Follett calls for "a plastic state" where cooperatively determined "commands may change to-morrow with our changing needs and changing ideals, and they will change through *our* initiative" (Follett 1998, 314). To this end, the public administrator must facilitate an ongoing planning, decision-making, and integrative action process in which the only requirement is that all accept guidance from "what the situation demands" (Follett 2013f, 22). Furthermore, she must be mindful of the unfolding situation of today and the potentialities yet to occur. "This insight into the future we usually call in business anticipating. But anticipating means more than forecasting or predicting. It means far more than meeting the next situation, it means making the next situation" (Follett 2013b, 53).

SUMMARY ANALYSIS

Bringing integrative process to bear on the problem of complex organization, Follett begins with a critique and revision of the leading theories of her time: bureaucracy and scientific management. Offering an alternative, she affirms a unique approach to collaborative administration that transforms the manner in which authority is understood and executed, along with the manner in which the organizing of functions is approached. Both elements of administrative theory are fundamentally transformed through her lens of integrative process. In essence, relational process fundamentally changes the *role* of the manager in pursuit of a new *goal* of scientific management: *coordinating the integrative process of unifying functions.*

These two concepts are cross-cutting in their implications for every aspect of administrative practice: unitary command and managerial direction are redefined as emergent authority and situational orders; bureaucratic hierarchy is replaced with federated networks; accountability and responsibility are synthesized in mutual answerability; functional division of labor becomes an ongoing process of integrating activities; managerial control is supplanted by self-organizing coordination; and executive planning and decision-making are transformed into participatory practices. All members of organizations are to develop capacities for cooperating and coordinating to enable leadership to emerge in response to the situation.

Regardless of application to private or public organizations, Follett's organizational principles and practices embody the difference between *management* and *administration*. By definition, management controls the means to ends and determines those ends, while administration is the process of facilitating the definition of ends and exercising the means to achieve them. Follett's administrative theory focuses on the processes through which true democracy can be facilitated by administrative leaders engaging and empowering experts along with all other affected group members—whether they are employees or citizens. Thus, in both industry and the public sphere, anyone can be a leader and an expert—and in this sense everyone is an administrator.

In her pursuit of such organizational transformation, Follett is well aware of the challenges facing administrators working to facilitate a *community* or *true democracy* approach to collaborative governance in both public and private spheres: "I hope you do not think that I am taking a rose-coloured [*sic*] view of business. Indeed, I am not. I am perfectly aware that in most plants the attitude is, 'I'm the boss. You do what I say'" (Follett 2003h, 269). Similarly, "This may sound absurdly unlike the world as mainly constituted. Is this the way diplomats meet? Is this the way competing industrial interests adjust their differences? Not yet, but it must be" (Follett 1998, 144). However, her observations of changes occurring in administrative practice gave her reason to be optimistic: "at the same time I see signs of something else, and it is on these signs that I am placing my hopes" (Follett 2003h, 269).

ENDNOTES

1. Boje and Rosile (2001) refer to similar "Follettian aspects" of organizational theory (113). Gehani and Gehani (2007) categorize Follett's administrative ideas into six categories: constructive conflict, tacit experiential knowledge, face-to-face communication and participation, shared power and control, dynamic evolving organizations, and strategic contextual leadership.

2. Tonn (2003) suggests Follett turned to business as her focus based on not only requests from leaders in those fields for her tutelage, but because at that time it was becoming one of the most important arenas of social activity and therefore it was critical for democratic control to carry forward into the workplace. She believed her principles could be readily applied to practice.

3. Morton and Lindquist (1997) note that Follett was "enthralled by the practical and experimental nature of learning in business; she found it vital and action oriented" (352).

4. Phillips (2010) concurs, arguing that while Follett was "committed to scientific *approaches* to management" (57) she was not an adherent of Taylor's scientific management.

5. Here Follett's critique of scientific management foreshadows similar critiques of rationalism such as that of Carol Gilligan (1982).

6. Eylon (1998) uses Follett's ideas to transform our understanding of workplace empowerment as a delegation or sharing of power to enabling each person to function according to the law of the situation.

7. As noted earlier, this is similar to the Whiteheadian differentiation of unilateral versus relational power (Loomer 1976).

8. Based on these sentiments, Follett's concepts undergird workplace democracy. Indeed, Eylon (1998) applies Follett's thinking to the practice of workplace empowerment.

9. Here, Follett provides an explanation of ordering processes that is more coherent with relational process ontology than that conceived by Whitehead in his "dominant characteristics" (Mesle 2008, 49). However, in other instances he clearly recognizes the problems with hierarchical language: "Though there are gradations of importance, and diversities of function, yet in the principles which actuality exemplifies all are on the same level" (Whitehead 1978, 18).

10. Boje and Rosile (2001) note that Follett addresses "the relational and dynamic qualities of empowerment within the context of complex theories of organizational power" (113).

11. Parker (1984) argues that Follett's idea on control and authority is prescient as "it predated behavioral and systems approaches to control in management literature by several decades" (736).

12. This idea presages the then-forming Tavistock Institute and the later work of Trist and Bamforth (1951).

13. Tonn (2003) suggests that Herbert Croly supports Follett's call for both decentralization and centralization when he argues in *The Promise of American Life* (1909) that large corporations and a strong federal government are essential to democracy's aims and ideals.

14. Child (2013) argues that Follett's law of the situation precedes contingency theory that would emerge many decades later.

15. In this way, Follett paves the way for Total Quality Management (Deming 2000) and its systems understanding of organizations.

16. Eylon (1998) notes that while Follett focused on dynamic *processes* in organizations, the more popular Fayol and Taylor focused on static *structural* aspects of organizations.

17. Fox (1968) argues that coordination and cooperation are the terms used to indicate the principle of integration applied to the organizational context.

18. Parker (1984) notes that Follett's ideas on coordination predate open systems theory and Schilling (2000) similarly notes her these "may be seen as a subset of interpenetrating systems theory" (229). In this way Follett's work can be seen as presaging by several decades Bertalanffy's (1975) general systems theory, Parson's (1968) theory of social action, Luhmann's (1995) social systems, and Pfeffer's (1997) open systems theory.

19. McLarney and Rhyno (1999) liken Follett's view of leaders and leadership to Henry Mintzberg and Frances Westley, noting, however, that she differs on fundamental issues such as the emergent, egalitarian character of leadership and the prioritization of the group rather than the individual.

For Follett, there are no heroic leaders, but rather group members who all have the potential for leadership.

20. In this way, Follett lays the foundations for theories of democratic leadership (Lewin 1958, McGregor 1960), shared leadership (Katz and Kahn 1978), facilitative leadership (Wilson, Harnish, and Wright 2003), collaborative leadership (Chrislip 2002), and servant leadership (Greenleaf 1982).

21. Follett's description of organizational emergence is similar to the concept of innovation described by Schumpeter (1943).

22. Again foretelling leadership theories, emergent leadership is now understood in terms of the new scientific understanding of the cosmos (see for example, Wheatley 2006).

23. Dumas (1995) notes that, following Follett, planning and design are "the interweaving of all the knowledges" in the situation that emerges from the group and is not driven by the expert or a pre-determined model (208).

24. This is a problem Herbert Simon (1997) would later describe as *bounded rationality*.

25. In this understanding, Follett provides the foundation for the contemporary practices of public engagement and coproduction (see further discussion in Chapter 12).

❧ 10 ❧

Placing Follett and Whitehead in Conversation

with Miroslaw Patalon

While numerous chapter endnotes have pointed out the similarities and differences between Follettian and Whiteheadian ideas, this chapter places Follett and Whitehead, a founder of contemporary process philosophy and theology, in conversation with one another on key ontological concepts that reflect important similarities. We argue that each has something of value to bring to the other. To Follett's benefit, Whitehead augments her ontological grounding and ensures that it is perceived as having sufficient rigor to undergird an alternative to governance based on the Newtonian/Cartesian understanding of existence. Highlighting the ways in which her thinking embraces and reflects process philosophy proper can help establish this foundation. While this has been achieved to some degree in endnotes throughout the previous chapters, a more systematic treatment of the linkages is made here.

On the other side of the equation, Whitehead's process philosophy focuses detailed explication at the ontological level of conceptualization. Taking these abstractions of organic philosophy into ethical, political, economic, and administrative action is quite another endeavor. Whitehead's organic philosophy has been directly linked to political theory: "While modern liberalism was in Whitehead's day a rather diffuse movement, what its proponents all shared was a common aim to reconcile individuality and sociability through a theory of human nature. . . . Process philosophy, too, is concerned with a proper understanding of individuality and sociability, and this, not only as a feature of human nature, but of reality as a whole" (Morris 1991 9, 11). However, there are many diverse interpretations of the implications of Whitehead's ideas for liberalism. While there are many contemporary authors who apply process philosophy to various practical issues (see for example, Cobb Jr. 2002; Connolly 2011, 2014; Daly and Cobb Jr. 1990; Griffin 1988; Pittenger 1989), we believe Follett offers a unique perspective as a contemporary of Whitehead and a more comprehensive treatment of the application of process philosophy to the individual and society. Indeed, Whitehead himself said that in defining justice, "I trust Miss Follett and Plato together" (Tonn 2003, 436). Therefore, Whiteheadians can benefit from the work Follett has done to craft democratic social practices with concepts drawn from relational process ontology. As John B. Cobb, Jr. notes in the Foreword herein:

> The specifically Whiteheadian community can rejoice that her thinking relates insights shared with Whitehead to some of the most important fields of thought and practice. These include politics, international relations, and economics. Of special importance is her contribution to thought about management and governance. Whiteheadians believe that Whitehead's conceptuality is relevant to every field of thought and practice, but showing this and drawing out its implications is still largely a project barely begun. Follett's work moves us forward a long way.

For historical background, Alfred North Whitehead (1861-1947) was a native of England and began his academic career at Cambridge University and the University of London. He later taught for some time at Harvard University. Although much of his early career was focused on mathematics and logic, he later focused on philosophy. It was during this time that he developed his ontological philosophy of organism, which later became known as process philosophy (Irvine 2010). Much of Whitehead's process thought was written and developed in the 1920s, with the pivotal work, *Process and Reality*, being published in 1929 (Irvine 2010). Process philosophy understands "the flux of things [as] one ultimate generalization around which we must weave our philosophical system" (Whitehead 1978, 208). Thus, while it is foundational, it is dynamic and not specifically substantive.

Expanding this pre-Socratic idea of change as the fundamental principle of existence (i.e., Heraclitus), Whitehead developed an organic philosophy that has long been connected to American pragmatism (Patalon 2009). According to thinkers like Charles Peirce, William James, George Herbert Mead, Charles Horton Cooley, and John Dewey, knowledge should always be oriented toward the real world characterized by diversity and change-ability. Abstract and static models are useless fancy; what matters is everyday life and solutions to real problems (the ethical and political dimensions of philosophy). For pragmatists, reality is a dynamic collection of interactions between beings; it is open (processual) in character and every aspect of the world consists of continual becoming. Therefore, pragmatists criticize dualistic reality and abandon the rigid differentiations between the soul and body, consciousness and being, thinking and acting, organism and environment, and individual and society. Rather, people are in ongoing mutual adjustment with one another and the environment. Unfortunately, process philosophers have missed Follett as a key contributor to these elements of American pragmatism.

While the connection between Follett and Whitehead was identified independently based on recognition of parallel ideas (see Acknowledgements), it is important to note that historically the two came into contact with one another through Follett's friend and academic mentor, Ella Lyman Cabot (1866-1934) who drew from Whitehead's thinking (Kaag 2008). While the three were all engaged in Harvard University as students or faculty, Follett's (1892-98) and Cabot's (1889-1906) studies at Radcliffe do not coincide with Whitehead's teaching post (1924-37). However, Follett makes reference to "Professor Whitehead" and his understanding of organic unity in her later writings (see for example, Follett 2003m, 2013h, g), so it is probably accurate to say that the three attended one another's lectures and participated in the "Cambridge intellectuals" (Kaag 2008, 148), a group that also included Charles Peirce, William James, and Josiah Royce; all of whom clustered around American pragmatist philosophy during the Progressive Era.[1]

According to her biographer, Follett worked with Richard Cabot in 1926 to organize the Follett-Cabot Seminary, a "year-long graduate seminar . . . [that] was an outgrowth of Follett's persistent desire to find corollaries among different academic disciplines" (Tonn 2003, 428). Participants in this seminar represented almost every social science department and included Whitehead. During her own lecture to the seminar, Follett discussed the evolving situation and reciprocal relating, emphasizing that "Professor Whitehead, with his conception of an organism as a structure of activities that are continually evolving, had got 'nearer the heart of the truth of this matter than anyone has yet'" (Tonn 2003, 433-34). Whitehead's feelings appear to be mutual based on his comment (above) about Follett's applications of process philosophy to individuals and society. Some of Follett's published work and lectures predate Whitehead's philosophical works and many were offered contemporaneously in the period between 1918 and 1924. But because so many of Follett's papers and records were destroyed upon her death at her request (Tonn 2003), it is difficult to substantiate the relationship much further than this. Therefore, our focus here is on the similarity of their substantive ideas rather than historical genealogy and speculation about who influenced whom.

In this chapter we discuss the most basic concepts of process philosophy that pertain to individual and social human life in order to compare Follett's process thinking to Whitehead's ontological principles.[2] Specifically, the two scholars both address three key ontological questions in a similar fashion: (1) the nature of becoming; (2) the role of God in becoming; (3) the nature of difference; and (4) the purpose of becoming. On the nature of becoming, Follett describes interweaving as both ontological circular response and intentional integration among humans while Whitehead describes concrescence as an ontological process and how consciousness is involved in the process. On the role of God in becoming, Follett describes an evolving co-creation reaching toward perfection, while Whitehead describes a creative impulse expressed in God in its fullest and most perfect form and only partially in all other actual entities, as well as God's relational lure toward truth, beauty, goodness, and love. On the nature of difference, Follett describes the individual in society while Whitehead describes societies of actual entities in relation. On the purpose of becoming, Follett describes individual and social progress through integrating differences while Whitehead describes enjoyment through novelty and contrast.

THE NATURE OF BECOMING

Follettian circular response and integration

For Follett, individuals and the situation within which they interact are co-created in an ongoing process of relational becoming through unconscious circular response and conscious integration she variously calls "interweaving" (Follett 1919, 576), *integration* (Follett 1919, 1998, 2013c, e), *interpenetration* (Follett 1919, 1998, 2013), *coadaptation* (Follett 1998), *synthesis* (Follett 1998), and *harmonizing* (Follett 1998). All conceptualizations draw on Hegel's (1977) term *intersubjectivity* while differentiating the unifying process from the static unity conceived by Hegel. In sum, Follett envisions the individual-in-society as something constantly being made and remade in "the essential life process" (Follett 1919, 576). The human being is an evolving, relational individual, "always in flux weaving itself out of its relations" (577).

However, relations extend beyond human beings. Throughout her writing, Follett is concerned with the reflexive manner in which individuals and the situations in which they are engaged mutually affect one another in a complex, systemic process of reciprocal influence. By *the situation*, Follett means the actual context in which real people are engaged—the environment and all the factors it holds, including physical, institutional, and human aspects. Follett calls the process the *circular response*; the process through which "we are creating each other all the time . . . in the very process of meeting, by the very process of meeting, we both *become* something different" (Follett 2013c, 62-63, emphasis added). "It is I plus the-interweaving-between-you-and-me, meeting you plus the interweaving-between-you-and-me, etc., etc. . . . out to the nth power" (63). For Follett, the circular response is a more accurate depiction of the ontological condition in which related individuals interact with one another and the environment that surrounds them, shaping all in a formative, generative process.

However, the circular response is not directed in any particular fashion by conscious agency—it simply happens. To utilize the circular response as an opportunity for individual and societal betterment, this naturally occurring process can be engaged more intentionally. This conscious process is *integration*, which Follett (2013c) applies to human beings in all social contexts (57). The group process of integration is the intentional process of creating "*functional unity*" (256) among individuals actively engaging in circular behavior in any sector of society. As she understands it, "the method of integration" (178) is composed of a number of processual elements and techniques that are iterative rather than linear in nature. These elements include a relational disposition, a cooperative style of relating, and a participatory mode of association that support a technique for integrating differences for creative outcomes, as is more fully discussed in Chapter 12.

Whiteheadian concrescence

Process philosophy explicates the ongoing ontological process through which individual experiencing expressions or "final facts" (Whitehead 1978, 18) become concrete as *actual entities* or *actual occasions*. At the microcosmic (unobservable) level, actual entities/occasions are "the final real things of which the world is made up . . . drops of experience, complex and interdependent" (Whitehead 1978, 18). These moments of experience or "*feeling*" (Mesle 2008, 95) are implicated in an ongoing process of *concrescence*— Whitehead's term for the process of "becoming concrete" in space and time (Cobb and Griffin 1976, 15). Each instance of concrescence is both physical in terms of space (as matter or energy) and a moment in terms of time (Mesle 2008, 95). Each "event" (Connolly 2011; Deleuze 1992) of becoming constitutes both space and time; hence the interchangeable use of the terms actual entity/occasion. Thus, "the universe is a vast web or field of microevents" (Mesle 2008, 95).

Whitehead uses the term "prehend" to describe the manner in which both physical and conceptual characteristics that exist beyond space and time are brought into existence during concrescence. In other words, unique combinations of qualities are apprehended or grasped and brought into actuality through the process of becoming in each moment. *Prehensions* are associated with three things: (1) pure potentiality or eternal objects; (2) past experiences as actual entities; and (3) the experience of becoming an actual entity in relation with other actual entities. This means there are prehensions in which potentialities or "eternal objects obtain ingression into actual entities" (Sherburne 1966, 235). There are also prehensions in which "the new occasion [entity] draws the past occasion [entity] into itself" (Cobb 2008, 31). Finally, there are prehensions by which one actual entity becomes objectified in another, thus mutually influencing one another as they "enter into each other's constitutions" (Whitehead 1978, 148-49). For Whitehead, "the process of experiencing is constituted by the reception of objects [entities] into the unity of that complex occasion which is the process itself" (229-30).

While the notions of bringing forward past experiences of an actual entity's becoming and the mutual influences of other actual entities in relational becoming are quite tangible, the prehension of infinite potentiality is a bit more abstract. The former two emphasize the *physical* aspects of becoming, while the latter emphasizes the *conceptual* aspects of becoming.

Whitehead (1978) argues that "Pure Potentials" (22) or "potentials for the process of becoming" (29) are held in *eternal objects* (Shaviro 2009).[3] Eternal objects are unchanging, non-temporal ordered potentialities that provide the patterns for that which is possible to manifest in this particular universe. Thus all of creation is an expression of eternal objects, which are the building blocks of existence and experience, and all eternal objects are related to one another (Root 1953). They are eternal in the sense of not changing, but they are non-temporal and can only be expressed to one degree or another by actual entities that include them in their occasions of becoming. During concrescence "potentiality becomes reality" (Whitehead 1978, 149), yet potentiality "retains its message of alternatives which the actual entity has avoided" (149). In other words, while all eternal objects are *potentially* expressed by an actual entity, that which is chosen in prehension provides a particular character that helps define and differentiate occasions of becoming in terms of the "qualities" and "relations" expressed (191). Yet the potential of that which was *not* expressed continues to exist outside of space and time.

The notion of such choices in prehension infers some level of autonomy. Therefore, like Follett, Whitehead brings the notion of agency into the process of becoming. According to Mesle (2008), Whitehead explains this as *positive* and *negative* prehension—the former refers to that which is prehended and the latter refers to that which was not actualized, yet continues to exist as a potential. This "choice-making" process is explained in experiential terminology that does not require and should not infer consciousness, per se. Indeed, Whitehead argues *"consciousness is the subjective form of an intellectual feeling, which arises, if at all, only in a late phase of a moment of experience"* (Griffin 2007, 51). However, Whitehead does explain this freedom as a function of a *dipolar* experience that has *physical* and *mental* (experiential or conceptual) aspects. But this is not a dualistic proposition—every actual entity integrates both *poles* of experience to one degree of complexity or another. The physical pole is associated with the *efficient causation* of prior events that are physically prehended in concrescence (Griffin 2007). The mental pole is associated with *final causation* which enables creativity in what is positively prehended (Griffin 2007). The mental pole is implicated in self-creativity or aim. For Whitehead, *initial aim* is a combination of the causal forces of the past combined with God's lure toward particular potentialities, which will be discussed in the following section. However, each actual entity also has *subjective aim* which guides the results of positive and negative prehension.

Concrescence ends in the moment the actual occasion is completed. At this point, each *subject* of experience becomes an *object* for subsequent actual entities to prehend. So, "in each enduring individual, accordingly, there is a perpetual oscillation between two modes of existence: subjectivity and objectivity" (Griffin 2001, 115-16). However, Griffin (2007) emphasizes that there is no possibility of prehending an actual occasion during the process of concrescence.

Taken together, the process of becoming (concrescence) occurs as actual entities uniquely express potentiality in the characteristics of the eternal objects instantiated, the experience of prior occasions, and the mutual impact of the other actual entities with which they are interrelated in the process of becoming. In this way, actual entities are not only the product of but also the input to the process of becoming. All of existence can ultimately be broken down into actual entities in the process of concrescence: "Every condition to which the process of becoming conforms in any particular instance, has its reason *either* in the character of some actual entity in the actual world of that concrescence, *or* in the character of the subject [actual entity] which is in process of concrescence" (Whitehead 1978, 24). This means that all objects, including human beings, by virtue of their building block actual entities, are participants in this process of creating the world. Participation is therefore not an option—it simply is. Everything is related in mutual influence with the potentiality of eternal objects and actual entities that precede and surround them in space and time.

Interweaving Follett and Whitehead: becoming as relational process

Follett's cornerstone concept of interweaving matches, for the most part, the foundation of process philosophy: concrescence. Interweaving is a concept that connects Follett's ideas of circular response, integration, and interpenetration—the ways in which individuals mutually affect one another's ongoing development. Concrescence is the complex relational process of becoming that includes the various prehensions described by Whitehead. In essence, the two are describing the nature of existence (for a socially situated self for Follett, versus as an actual entity for Whitehead) as a relational process of becoming that is both physical and conceptual, both externally and internally directed. Follett is drawing on general microcosmic ontological and psychological principles to provide a specific macrocosmic explanation of the becoming of individuals in social groups while Whitehead provides a specific microcosmic explanation of co-creation (becoming concrete) and a macrocosmic explanation of individuation (becoming a unique configuration of qualities).

Specifically, during concrescence, actual entities integrate data from several sources: both the pure potential and patterned character of eternal objects, previous actual entities, and contemporary actual entities. Through this integration, a unique actual entity comes into being, an entity that is completely new and different from any of the constituent elements. Similarly, during Follett's process of circular response, individuals interact and mutually influence one another, thereby creating something new that is more than a simple aggregation of the parts. Thus, in both concrescence and interweaving, entities/societies at all scales (sub-individual, individual, and groups of individuals) mutually influence one another in an ongoing relational process. Just as actual entities become through prehensions of the eternal objects, past actual entities, and current actual entities to which they are connected, so do individual people become through circular response with their own (past) experiences in relation with their contemporaries in a given situation.

However, an important difference between the two emerges on the issue of subjectivity and objectivity. While Follett synthesizes these two aspects of relationality—an individual is always both—Whitehead splits up the process of becoming in a way that demands a division of the two positions based on time. At the beginning of concrescence, an actual entity is a causal subject prehending from a variety of sources. At the end of concrescence, an actual entity is an object of prehension by other actual occasions. Therefore during the process of becoming itself, subjects are not engaging in mutual influence. This contradicts Follett's understanding of the continual flow of relational becoming that is, in essence, never "complete" in the sense understood by Whitehead. In other words, interweaving during the process of becoming is expected by Follett.

THE ROLE OF GOD IN BECOMING

Follettian co-creation

Follett does not explicate matters of belief in depth and her comments tend to be inconsistent, sometimes referring to theistic concepts and sometimes referring to humanist concepts. However, she frequently refers to the metaphysical, the spiritual, and even God. For Follett, a participatory universe is collaborating in co-creating all that is: "God is the moving force of the world, the ever-continuing creating where men are the co-creators" (Follett 1998, 103). Therefore, "we must know now that we are coworkers with every process of creation, that our function is as important as the power which keeps the stars in their orbits" (100). These types of statements suggest a potentially directive, transcendent being ("the power") that works with mankind.

Yet, she also asserts that human beings are Many parts of the One. "What is the whole doing? It is not a quiet Beneficence watching benignly over its busy children. It does not live vicariously *in* its 'parts' any more than it lives vicariously *for* its 'parts.' The parts are neither its progenitors nor its offspring" (Follett 2013c, 101). There is only "the whole a-making; this involves a study of whole and parts in their active and *continuous* relation to each other" (102). This suggests that God is immanent and in relation with all else that is becoming, yet differentiated from all other entities. These explanations clarify her previous references to what sounds like a transcendent source of being beyond extant beings that either orders the whole or subsumes the whole (God). Instead, beings themselves, including God, *assemble* the whole in dynamic configurations through integration and the impulse toward unifying of ever greater wholes. This adjusts Follett's conception of God toward a panentheistic system of belief wherein all are part of the divine.

Taken together, it can be assumed that in the end, Follett's source of being is neither fully transcendent nor immanent; it is sacred and multidimensional. This is most richly explained in *Creative Experience*:

> The doctrine of circular response involved in the theory of integration gives us creative experience. . . . But the theory of creative experience given to us by the most profound philosophy throughout the ages, and now so happily strengthened by recent research in several fields, shows that the individual can create without "transcending." He expresses, brings into manifestation, powers which are the powers of the universe and thereby those forces which he is himself helping to create, those which exist in and by and through him, are ever more ready to respond, and so Life expands and deepens; fulfils [*sic*] and at the same moment makes possible larger fulfilment [*sic*]. (Follett 2013c, 116)

Whiteheadian process theology

Whitehead asserts that God is different from "creative potentiality" as well as all other actual entities, but equivalent to all other actual entities at an ontological level through the process of becoming. These "two ultimates are interrelated. They presuppose each other, rely on each other and complement each other" (Wang 2012, 78). Specifically, pure creative potentiality suggests *nothing* as a source of becoming. To finesse the ontological principle that *nothing can come from nothing* as well as to avoid the problem of a transcendent source of becoming, potentiality—the eternal objects described in the process of concrescence—must be actualized in some entity. Whitehead (1978) calls this actual entity God, who "is not to be treated as an exception to all metaphysical principles, invoked to save their collapse" (343). In this sense, God prehends in the same way all other actual entities do and is therefore constituted by potentiality (eternal objects), past instances of concrescence, and the becoming of interrelated actual entities.

However, God is different in the sense of being "their chief exemplification" (Whitehead 1978, 343). Instead of prehending some potentialities and not others as most actualities do, God prehends *all* potentiality. This characteristic of God is described as his "primordial nature" (Griffin 2001, 175) (similar to the mental pole in prehension). So, on the one hand, all potentiality or all eternal objects reside in God's primordial nature, which other actual entities instantiate in unique but less complete patterns. On the other hand, God prehends all of the actual entities constituting the world and its past occasions through his "*consequent* nature" (195). In this sense, God is in part constituted by all that ever was and all that is becoming at any given moment (similar to the discussion of the physical pole in prehension).

This is why process theology has been closely aligned with panentheism (Keller 2003)—all is in God through both his primordial nature and his consequent nature. Furthermore, all actual entities (including God) *experience* to one degree of complexity or another—the reason Whitehead's organic philosophy is often characterized as "pan-experiential" (Mesle 2008, 94), as opposed to panpsychism which infers consciousness. However, due to the differences in complexity, Griffin (2001) clarifies this as "panexperientialism with organizational duality" (6).

However, some contemporary Whiteheadians refuse to treat eternal objects as *necessary* to the process of becoming and simply point to the principle of creativity as the source of potentiality. Such process philosophers are re-conceptualizing process philosophy without God (Ford 1977; Sherburne 1967). These explorations should be welcome, as Whitehead (1978) himself argues that "the merest hint of certainty as to finality of statement is an exhibition of folly" (xiv). From this perspective, "creativity is the ultimate reality of the universe, presupposed by every instance of actuality" (Wang 2012, 150). In short, the essence of becoming, the creative urge itself, is within and expressed by all actual entities and we need not consider God. Instead, we can focus on *creative potentiality* itself as the ultimate source of becoming and how that process works.

For those process philosophers and theologians who accept Whitehead's explanation of the primordial nature of God, through relational becoming God invites or *lures* all other entities to actualize the potentialities or eternal objects in particular ways relevant and of value to the situation, thereby encouraging truth, beauty, goodness, and love. Indeed, it is God's relation to all other actual entities that allows them to *feel* (prior to conscious perception) such values, norms, and ideals (Griffin 2007). God's encouragement toward them is called *initial aim* (Whitehead 1978, 257), thereby generating the metaphor of God as "poet of the world" (464). However, all actual entities share God's autonomous yet relational nature and so aim is present in them as well and they do not always express what God would prefer. Whitehead refers to this freedom as *subjective aim*, which guides both negative and positive prehension as discussed above.

Interweaving Follett and Whitehead: co-creative experience

Both Follett and Whitehead include a conception of God in their understandings about becoming. However, while both imagine God in a co-creative relation with all else that is becoming, they diverge in a manner that has important implications for applying relational process philosophy to ethics, political theory, economic theory, and administrative theory. Specifically, the directive nature of God in Whitehead's notion of God's primordial nature and initial aim are in direct conflict with Follett's notion of co-creation.[4] A fully participatory and immanent understanding of co-creation is based on relational subjective aim without the need for eternal objects or initial aim from God. When God is inserted into becoming in this manner, the question of who stands in for or speaks for God becomes a necessary question in practical matters. Furthermore, it would appear that Follett and Whitehead might also disagree on the point of unchanging eternal objects enfolding potentiality. This static nature of potentiality limits creativity in a way that Follett would likely reject in her conception of co-creative experience and its role in individual and societal progress (discussed below).

However, the notion that God prehends or expresses the fullness of all actual entities in his consequent nature at any given moment would not conflict with Follett's relational view that humankind is fully collaborating in the forces that constitute the universe itself. Furthermore, looking back at Chapter 6, Whitehead leaves another option for establishing aim and value that would agree with Follett; his explanation of sympathy and emotional force. He sees sympathy as a non-sensory perception of "feeling the feeling *in* another and feeling conformally *with* another" (Whitehead 1979, 162) and recognizes that human beings have the potential to develop morality based on "emotional force" (15). Therefore, he might potentially have agreed with Follett that human beings can "find right" together, even without God's initial aim.

THE NATURE OF DIFFERENCE

Follett's individual in society

Building upon the principles of circular response and integration, Follett offers new definitions of both the individual and society and how the two concepts relate. While Western philosophy typically perceives individuals as separate from one another and conceptualizes society as separate from the individual, Follett asserts that neither can exist without the other as both are in a constant process of co-creating. An individual cannot exist outside of the social process; rather, an individual exists "in the ceaseless interplay of the One and the Many by which both are constantly making each other" (Follett 1919, 582). Through this co-creating process, "the fallacy of self-and-others fades away and there is only self-in-and-through-others" (Follett 1998, 8).

Conversely, society cannot exist without the individual, for it is through the integrative process of unifying that society is co-created by individuals in relation with one another. "The interplay constitutes both society on the one hand and individuality on the other: individuality and society are evolving together from this constant and complex action and reaction" (Follett 1998, 65). Participation in the whole is not a choice, it is a given. However, society is not simply individuals aggregated to create a whole: "Collective responsibility is not a matter of adding but of interweaving, a matter of the reciprocal modification brought about by interweaving" (Follett 2013b, 75). Individuals are not connected simply because we act in proximity to one another; our connection is much more fundamental than that, as everything interweaves in its becoming.

Follett emphasizes that participation in the integrating process of society does not infer homogenization. In fact, individuality can only be perceived in a social context. "My individuality is difference springing into view as relating itself with other differences" (Follett 1998, 63). In human groups, "the essence of society is difference, related difference" (33). Difference is expressed through varying perspectives, preferences, understandings, experiences, and ideas. Follett (2003b) argues that such differences can create conflict and disharmony that make living together difficult if poorly handled, thus lessening social progress. However, through the collaborative process of integration, difference and conflict generate opportunities for personal fulfillment and social progress. Indeed, "this is the reality for man: the unifying of differings" (Follett 1919, 588). It is not uniformity that is achieved, but rather harmonization and integration through interpenetration or ongoing co-adaptation. "The test of our progress is neither our likenesses nor our unlikenesses, but what we are going to do with our unlikenesses. Shall I fight whatever is different from me or find the higher synthesis?" (Follett 1998, 96). Thus, "the urge to unity is not a reduction, a simplification, it is the urge to embrace more and more, it is a reaching out, a seeking" (Follett 1919, 583) of difference.

This creation of societal harmony out of individual difference is an important piece of Follett's administrative theory. In her discussions of what she calls *creative process* (Follett 1919) and *constructive conflict* (Follett 2003b), she argues that wherever possible, synthesis should be used to resolve conflict because "only integration really stabilizes" the situation (35). Synthesis is the reaching of a solution "in which both desires have found a place, that neither side has had to sacrifice anything" (32). Through integrative group process, individuals confront diverse interests and desires, which leads to a re-evaluation of one's own interests and values, and ultimately a new solution is co-created that unifies those diverse interests and desires; a solution that is something greater than the original ideas of the individuals. Integrative process is more effective than domination or compromise, which neither lead to creative solutions nor lasting harmony.

Follett further explores the implications of integrating difference in her discussions of power and authority. The process of integration generates *power-with* under *the law of the situation*: "If there is an interactive influence going on all the time between you, power-with may be built up . . . If both sides obey the law of the situation, no *person* has power over another" (Follett 2003j, 105). Instead, it is the situation that holds authority, allowing each person to play an appropriate role given the context in a "self-generating process" (Follett 2013a, 46). It is a "jointly developing power, the aim, a unifying which, while allowing for infinite differing does away with fighting" (Follett 2003j, 115). Power, then, becomes a generative force created through collaboration, which in turn serves to unify individuals in groups, rather than pitting them against one another.

Whitehead's societies

Actual entities are events that do not endure through time—they are occasions that "arise, become, and reach completion. When the becoming is completed they are then in the past; the present is constituted by a new set of occasions [entities] coming into being" (Cobb and Griffin 1976, 19). "Change is the difference between these events" (Mesle 2008, 96). However, actual entities are *microcosmic* and are not experienced or perceived in day-to-day activity. At the macrocosmic (observable) level, many actual entities are part of "the process in which the universe of many things acquires an individual unity in a determinate relegation of each item of the 'many' to its subordination in the constitution of the novel 'one'" (Whitehead 1978, 211). We understand this use of the term subordination to mean modifying, because in the whole of an individual thing or the whole of creation itself, the One is constituted in an ongoing relational process of individual becoming among the Many. What is actually perceived are "macrocosmic entities of everyday experience" which "are groupings of entities termed *nexūs* (plural of nexus)" (Sherburne 1966, 230).

When these patterns are repeated across time and/or space they form what is called a *society*—a special type of nexus "that enjoys social order—i.e., one that exhibits characteristics in each generation of actual entities that are derived from prehensions of previous generations" (Sherburne 1966, 231). What endures is the particular pattern or order of the society of actual entities that share "defining characteristics" (Whitehead 1979, 89). In this way, actual entities are perceived as individual objects in time and space. This enduring pattern brought forward in time through prehension creates sufficient similarity to the previous moment that we are able to perceive actual entities as material, discrete beings or things, when in reality they are a host of actual entities in a process of concrescence.

These are the particular types of prehensions that bring the past actual entity into the new actual entity in a manner that allows them to be perceived as more or less the same. For example, we do not see aging on a day-to-day basis, or the slow erosion of a rock cliff. This similarity across time in space is created through a process of *transmutation* that creates an "identity of pattern in their ingredient eternal objects" (Sherburne 1966, 247). This pattern enables us to perceive the microcosmic at the macrocosmic level. Through transmutation, we perceive not actual entities of the microcosmic level, but instead societies of actual entities at the macrocosmic level. Transmutation carries forward a particular type of ordering that causes actual entities to combine in a manner similar to other societies, while still being unique. This pattern could be likened to the manner in which DNA orders complex organisms by establishing the pattern by which cells aggregate to make a tree as opposed to a human being as they are continually replaced over time. As a result we perceive a physical world of apparent stasis, in which it is possible to view one whole as existing over time, rather than the innumerable actual entities of which it is composed; entities in a constant process of becoming.

However, societies are more than simply a collection of entities with a common characteristic. "Thus, a society is, for each of its members, an environment with some element of order in it, persisting by reason of the genetic relations between its own members" (Whitehead 1978, 89). The key characteristic of a society is that it is self-ordering; "that it is self-sustaining; in other words, that it is its own reason" (89).

There are several types of societies, each with its own characteristics. An *enduring object* is the simplest kind of society, one that is "a purely temporal society, a mere thread of continuous inheritance containing no two actual entities that are contemporaries" (Sherburne 1966, 220). A more complex kind of society is a *structured society*. This kind of society "consists in the patterned intertwining of various nexūs with markedly diverse defining characteristics . . . This structured society will provide the immediate environment which sustains each of its sub-societies" (Whitehead 1978, 103). Structured societies can vary in their *complexity* and *intensity*, concepts which we will explore later. Finally, a *corpuscular society* is a kind of structured society in which the "subordinate societies constitutive of it are all strands of enduring objects" (Sherburne 1966, 216).

Macrocosmic wholes that are physically perceived as independent things (molecules, cells, trees, human beings, etc.) are therefore the results

of negative and positive prehension discussed above—"the actual entities differ from each other in their realization of potentials" (Whitehead
1978, 149)—as well as the different patterns established by various societies. However, neither the unique expression of pure potentiality at the
microcosmic level, nor the distinctness of perceived experiences at the
macrocosmic level mean that actual entities, societies of actual entities,
or any other grouping are *actually* separate. Indeed, process philosophy
asserts the contrary: "Connectedness is the essence of all things" (Morris
1991, 71). This interdependence is an "ontologically given characteristic"
(Cobb and Griffin 1976, 21). "It is not first something in itself, which only
secondarily enters into relations with others. The relations are primary"
(19). However, these relations operate at a microcosmic level that is not
perceivable by the physical senses.

Interweaving Follett and Whitehead: related, yet unique becomings

Both Follett and Whitehead describe the inherent relatedness of co-creative
becoming in a manner that does not deny individuality and celebrates
difference. For Follett, the ontological principle is that individual human
beings are always in society and engaged in the ongoing process of co-
creation—the making of the "self-in-and-through-others" (Follett 1998,
8). Neither can be disaggregated from the other. However, this relatedness
does not connote sameness or agreement. Indeed, it is through relatedness
that difference becomes evident. Each individual is a unique expression
of the various interweavings experienced in becoming. These distinctions
represent our "related difference" (33) as human beings.

Similarly, in process philosophy, actual entities and the various types
of societies composed by them cannot exist independently or completely
separate from other actual entities; nor can eternal objects exist separate from
the experienced world. Furthermore, these actual entities unify in various
configurations or societies, across time and space which can be perceived
by the senses as particular objects, but which are actually in a process of
relational becoming. Nothing transcends the whole and all within the whole
are connected—"relations are primary" (Cobb and Griffin 1976, 19). However, each actual entity is a unique expression and each society is a unique
composition. Thus, the ontological condition is one of interdependent and
interconnected difference, not sameness.

THE PURPOSE OF BECOMING

Follettian progress through collaboration

All combined, the nature of becoming and the nature of difference lead Follett to identify the purpose of human social life as the desire to co-create: "the ever-continuing creating where men are the co-creators" (Follett 1998, 103). An individual's "sustenance is relation and he seeks forever new relations in the ceaseless interplay of the One and the Many" (Follett 1919, 582). It is only through relation that we are able to meet and confront difference, thereby participating in "creative experience" (Follett 2013c, 377), the unifying process of integration, which is "an irresistible force compelling every member" of a group (Follett 1998, 83). The integration of differences is the generative process of life, for "synthesis is the principal of life, the method of social progress" (97). "What then is the law of community? From biology, from psychology, from our observation of social groups, we see that community is that intermingling which evokes creative power" (Follett 1919, 577). This generative power urges us on, "from the amoeba and its food to man and man, as the release of energy, the evocation or calling forth of new powers one from the other" (Follett 2013c, 303). Through it, we achieve "the progress of individual or race" (173).

It follows that to generate the greatest amount of power or the most creative experience, we must be sure "that full opportunity is given in any conflict, in any coming together of different desires, for the whole field of desire to be viewed" (Follett 2003b, 39). The greater the number of differences brought into integrative process, the higher the level of synthesis that can be achieved, thus generating greater individual and social progress.

Whiteheadian creative advance

For Whitehead, the purpose of concrescence—of life—is the "creative advance of the world" (Mesle 2008, 98). Each "occasion arises as an effect facing its past [object] and ends as a cause facing its future [subject]. In between there lies the teleology of the universe" (Whitehead 1967, 194). Engaging in this process as a subject is desirable to all actual entities because it causes *enjoyment*, for "to be, to actualize oneself, to act upon others, to share in a wider community, is to enjoy being an experiencing subject" (Cobb and Griffin 1976, 16-17). The purpose of an individual actual entity cannot be considered separate from the purpose of other actualities in the world; experience is the "self-enjoyment of being one among many, and of being one arising out of the composition of many" (Whitehead 1978, 145). Thus, in considering the enjoyment of any single actual entity, we must also consider the enjoyment of other entities.

Intensity, which is the ideal result of the process of concrescence, leads to greater enjoyment. Maximized intensity is achieved through the incorporation of *novelty* and the experience of *contrast*. Novelty comes through the prehension of potentiality from eternal objects as well as from new qualities from interrelating actual entities. "The actualization of novel possibilities generally increases the enjoyment of experience; for the variety of possibilities that are actualized in an experience adds richness to the experience, and the element of novelty lends zest and intensity of enjoyment" (Cobb and Griffin 1976, 28). Contrast can be experienced either *within* a society or *among* societies. Within societies, as more contrasting actual entities are drawn together in the process of concrescence the intensity felt by the resulting society increases. "Roughly speaking, more complex actualities enjoy more value than simpler ones" (63-64). Among societies, contrast is experienced through diversity. When a given society confronts difference in another society, new prehensions form from the contrast, thereby generating intensity and enjoyment. Whitehead (1978) notes that "intensity of feeling due to any realized ingression of an eternal object is heightened when that eternal object is one element in a realized contrast between eternal objects" (278).

Novelty and intensity themselves, however, are not enough to create the most enjoyment for an entity. Societies, and the entities of which they are composed, must also find *harmony* that maximizes the enjoyment not only of their own experience but also that of the society of which they are a part; the diverse elements must be properly integrated so that maximum enjoyment is produced. Harmony is achieved by prehensions that draw forward past actual entities into the current actual entity and that enable actual entities to mutually impact one another in a complementary way. "For experience to be enjoyable, it must be basically harmonious; the elements must not clash so strongly that discord outweighs harmony. Also, for great enjoyment there must be adequate intensity of experience. Without intensity there might be harmony, but the value enjoyed will be trivial. Intensity depends upon complexity, since intensity requires that a variety of elements be brought together into a unity of experience" (Cobb and Griffin 1976, 64-65).

Thus, diversity is important to the maximization of enjoyment, but is only positive and enhancing if different entities and societies can be harmonized. Whitehead (1978) uses music to illustrate. Two voices singing different but complementary notes offer to the listener a simple enjoyment without much intensity. As the diversity of voices increases to a three- or four-part harmony, the intensity of the sound also increases; as diversity and complexity increase *in a way that creates harmony*, intensity and enjoyment increase. Consider also the sound a piano makes when a child strikes multiple keys at random. While diverse notes may be sounding together, they are not harmonized, offering a large amount of contrast without much value. Through the harmonizing of diverse entities in the concrescence of a new entity or society, intensity and, ultimately enjoyment, is increased. As the second example shows, however, diversity for diversity's sake is not enough; diverse entities must be integrated so that they produce—through prehension—complex, *harmonized* actual entities. The more diverse and complex the harmonized entities, the more intense and, ultimately enjoyable, the experience. Indeed, for Whitehead, "the criterion for progress is, therefore, richness of experience" (Griffin 2007, 45).

Interweaving Follett and Whitehead: harmonizing difference for progress and advance

Rather than seeing difference as a problem, both Follett and Whitehead see it as the source of individual and human progress and advance. In short, if there were no difference, there would be no purpose for social process, no source of enjoyment, and no means for individual or societal progress and growth. In fact, the greater the difference, the greater the enjoyment may be. The greater the degree of synthesis and harmonization, the greater the individual and societal progress will be.

For Follett, differences in perspectives, preferences, and ideas are inevitable. If we perceive these differences as a source of destructive problems, then individual and societal progress can stagnate because we try to avoid or suppress conflict. However, if we see these differences as an opportunity for integration and synthesis, the process of harmonizing differences or "constructive conflict" (Follett 2003b) creates individual and societal progress— what Follett sees as the power of co-creating. Indeed, as more viewpoints are included in that process, the resulting progress is greater. Thus, difference is good, but it can be a problem if perceived and responded to inappropriately.

In Whitehead's philosophy, difference is necessary for maximum enjoyment by actual entities and, ultimately, for the societies composed of them.

In fact, there must be sufficiently intense difference for enjoyment to be experienced. Difference can be achieved either through novelty of expression or contrast with previous or other expressions. This is why complex societies of actual entities experience greater enjoyment. However, too much contrast can create chaos—just imagine the result of too much novelty across time disrupting the appearance of a thing in unpredicted patterns.

Thus, while both scholars celebrate difference, both also note the importance of unifying or harmonizing difference. Without harmony, progress and enjoyment cannot be attained. Differences, then, must be harmonized in the process of becoming and the social processes of living. Both also see this harmonizing process to produce something beyond a mere sum of the parts—what is now commonly referred to as synergy. Thus, both the individual and the group progress and advance in ways that can only be co-created.

THE VALUE OF LINKING FOLLETT AND WHITEHEAD

Follett notes that pursuing social change only at the level of behavior or action is insufficient because underlying assumptions will work their way into behavior, subverting or reverting it to the original philosophical assumptions. This is now understood as the prefiguring characteristic of philosophical commitments (White 2000). In order to successfully change and sustain new behaviors, the underlying philosophical framework must also change. This must go deeper than theory in order to reach the most fundamental assumptions. This is precisely why Follett explores conceptual elements of ontology, psychosocial theory, epistemology, and belief instead of simply offering recommendations for ethical, political, economic, and administrative practice.

The need for a philosophical foundation for any theory of governance has been duly noted in the public administration literature (see for example, Box 2008; Catlaw 2007; McSwite 1997; Waldo 1984). Ontology is the broadest philosophical foundation for theory in that it describes the nature of existence, thereby framing presuppositions about all aspects of life. As Waldo (1984) argues, "Any political theory rests upon a metaphysic, a concept of the ultimate nature of reality" (21). Political philosophies adopt specific ontological assumptions, offering prescriptions for political forms (White 2000). In fact, the term "political ontology" has been used to describe complex assumptions about the nature of human being, identity, and social life in particular (Catlaw 2007; Howe 2006). The relationship between the two components is reflexive: political form implies specific ontology and ontology implies political form. These political forms become primary venues for social action, thus reproducing that which is assumed. Similarly, ontology suggests the logical possibility of only certain political forms. In this way political ontology depicts both what *is* and what *should* be. Indeed, from a Whiteheadian perspective, metaphysical, ideological, and political positions can be assessed by looking at

> the premises about reality they imply. The concrete actions of our daily lives, what we do when interacting with our kin, with other members of groups to which we belong, with other citizens, imply specific goals, individual and collective, motivating our action. Those various goals imply more general attitudes and practices, primary frameworks of understanding and primary behavioral schemata, constituting the acceptable and intelligible boundary conditions for what we think and do. And these features constitute the common good that explicates our felt sense of truth. (Allan 1993, 284)

In short, ontology shapes how we go about living together and this worldview directly impacts public policy (Christ 2003). While ontology is typically studied in philosophy, religion, and physics, such considerations have recently been extended by contemporary social and political theory which has turned away from unthinking adoption of the positivist philosophical commitments that characterize modern western culture, both critiquing its ontology and offering affirmative modifications or alternatives (White 2000). In this process, social practices of all types are being deconstructed in order to understand the types of entities presupposed and the assumed nature of their being, as well as to question the appropriateness of those philosophical commitments and associated values to desired social outcomes. Following from such critical inquiry, ontologies are beginning to confront one another, even in terms of nuances within the dominant culture (see for example, Brigg 2007; Pesch 2008).

Many scholars are looking for an alternative ontology because the Newtonian/Cartesian universe inhabited by self-interested, atomistic individuals does not logically fit prescriptions for participatory democracy and collaborative practice. Therefore, efforts to institute these approaches eventually fail to produce anticipated outcomes. Unfortunately, many of these proposals attend only to the epistemological or psychosocial levels of analysis, while positivist ontology provides explanation for *all* aspects of reality, not just the human elements. Limiting discussion to explanations of the *human* experience of reality as opposed to an explication of its physical ontological necessity leaves the rationale open to considerable challenge. To simply say, "we have to start at bedrock and *assume* that we are all already connected, just as we have assumed in the past that we were not" (Stivers 2008, 93-94) is insufficient explanation. The dominant supposition of disconnection is undergirded by a fully explicated system of positive science in both its physical and social branches; it is defended by "the verdict of science" (Waldo 1984, 21). To blithely replace that assumption with another without a similarly complete explanation lacks the robustness required to do so convincingly. We must explain not just our understanding of human or social reality, but also how we understand its physical and nonphysical attributes. In other words, to withstand positivist critique more is required.

Thus, the aim of linking Follett to Whitehead is to anchor her collaborative systems of governance into a robust ontological foundation. We agree that we need "an inquiry that would have linked a fundamental conception of reality (ontology) with a specific epistemological position . . . with a distinctive form of the political" (Catlaw 2007, 11). In sum, we agree that "the challenge that commands attention for public administration is to begin conceiving the social relations and subsequently governing structures and practices that are rooted in a different political ontology" (Catlaw 2005, 471). However, this call begs the question: What exactly *is* the alternative ontology that fits a directly democratic, collaborative approach to governance? What ontology would help us "*practice* critical theory" (King and Zanetti 2005, xviii)? "Which view of reality helps us to find meaning in public life?" (Stivers 2008, 93). We argue that Follett and Whitehead together provide the answer.

ENDNOTES

1. In these lectures she also refers to Whitehead's student and coauthor, Bertrand Russell (Follett 2003j, 98).

2. Elements of this analysis were explored in earlier publication, so this chapter draws liberally from Stout and Staton (2011). However, analysis is substantively expanded and more nuanced herein.

3. Many contemporary Whiteheadians refuse the necessity of eternal objects as necessary to the process of becoming. These issues will be discussed in relation to the role of God in becoming.

4. This Whiteheadian perspective is explained by Allan (1993) in his analysis of process ideology and the common good in Morris and Hartshorne.

However, Allan himself disagrees with their interpretations and reads Whitehead as consistent with an atheistic process metaphysics, and aligns this view with a "secular communalist liberalism" (283).

❧ 11 ❧

The Necessity of Recapitulation

A likely question for anyone who is familiar with Follett's work would be: Why is this book necessary? Why not simply read some of her original writings? We encourage the reader to do just that because it is only through reading her original writings that one will find the myriad illustrations and practical examples Follett uses to bring her theory to life. Similarly, why not rely on the contemporary literature's interpretation of her work? We encourage this as well. However, in both endeavors, care must be taken to interpret Follett correctly through her philosophical grounding.

For example, when reading only some of Follett's work or relying on contemporary scholars who do so, errors in judgment are likely to occur. For example, while Boje and Rosile (2001) formulate an interesting complementarity between Follett and Clegg's Foucauldian approach to power, it is, in a sense, superfluous. In fact, in focusing only on her notion of power-with, they miss entirely Follett's explication of integration, arguably the precursor of win-win results they instead attribute to Clegg. In short, one cannot pick up *Dynamic Administration* or *Freedom & Co-ordination* and fully grasp its meaning without having *The New State*, "Community as a Process," and *Creative Experience* under one's belt. Even when reading her body of work in its entirety, it is easy to lose sight of the philosophical assumptions on which her recommendations for practice are based. As noted in Chapter 1, this can happen easily due to her writing and lecture style.

More importantly, as argued elsewhere (see Stout and Love 2014b), Follett's work is frequently misinterpreted in the literature due to a lack of awareness of, or ability to grasp the underlying relational process ontology that uniquely characterizes her interpretation of philosophical principles and their application to practice. As Calas and Smiricich (1996) note, "understanding Follett from within *her own philosophical orientation*," including understanding her "very sophisticated and well-developed processual theoretical framework" (149), is critical to accurately interpreting her cross-cutting ideas. Indeed, Stewart (1996) suggests that the comprehensive nature of Follett's philosophy is a stumbling block for many who are looking for easily packaged slogans and therefore find her ideas "too rich" to fully comprehend (175). Therefore, the real problem is the choice to read only *some* of her original writings or to rely solely on secondary interpretations that do not account for her unique ontological perspective.

While not offering analysis or detailed explanation, Tonn (2003) argues that many scholars have misinterpreted Follett's work from the beginning of her writing career, reflecting "a fundamental misunderstanding of Follett's argument—a misunderstanding that persists to this day" (308). Unfortunately, such "paternalistic" (Child 1995, 88) misinterpretations are not limited to those who would critique Follett's ideas, but extend to some of her most staunch supporters. As a result, one management consultant gives a scathing critique in his review of the commentaries responding to Follett in Graham's (1995b) collected works, stating, "Most of these reveal some or all of the commentators' lack of understanding of the material they deign to remark upon, their breathtaking self-absorption and arrogance as they condescend to express their admiration for her at the same time that they misrepresent her thinking as foreshadowing their own, and their lack of the unprepossessing forward-looking, dynamic instincts with which Follett's work was imbued" (Stroup 2007).[1] Although biting, Stroup's (2007) point is well-taken—even some of her greatest proponents fail to understand her fundamental principles.

To support this claim, this chapter offers a number of examples in which Follett's thinking is misinterpreted in the two main strands of thought she wove together—management theory and political theory. Our goal is not to render a mean-spirited critique, but rather to call for a general clarification of Follett's thinking and an appreciation of the fullness of her contribution to political and administrative theory and the fields of practice they inform. Given the robust nature of Follett's theoretical approach, selecting independent elements of her thought for consideration is a practice that lends itself readily to misinterpretation. This is because, as noted in Chapter 9, Follett's administrative theory is the *culmination* of her body of thought; the level of analysis at which both her philosophical (ontological concepts, psychosocial theory, epistemological concepts, beliefs) and practice-oriented theories (ethics, political theory, and economic theory) all move into action as an integrated whole.

Thus, when Follett's recommendations are taken out of that context, her actual meaning is easily lost—often reinterpreted through the very dualistic lenses she is refuting. As she herself warns, "unless we are thinking wholly in terms of process, the statements I am making will be meaningless" (Follett 2003m, 195). Without carefully and actively interpreting Follett's work through the lens of her relational process ontology, misinterpretation is likely, as the following sections illustrate. We argue that these misconceptions produce the very effect Follett warns of: "Our outlook is narrowed, our chances of success are largely diminished, when our thinking is constrained with the limits of an either-or situation. We should never allow ourselves to be bullied by an either-or" (201).

MISINTERPRETATION IN MANAGEMENT THEORY

Management and organizational theory are applied to both public and private organizations. The theoretical focus is primarily on the internal operations of organizations, with more limited consideration of its interactions with the environment. Such relations are typically considered in regard to the sustainability of the organization as opposed to its impact on the environment, with issues like social responsibility being an exception. Thus, this section will focus on matters of theory pertinent to organizational operations.

Ryan and Rutherford (2000) note that Follett's statements are often misconstrued in management theory when taken individually and when interpreted from the dichotomous subject-object perspective typically held in social science. As an example, Urwick (2013) warns that while "Mary Follett's lectures on business organisation [*sic*] are an essential text-book" for those who want to maintain freedom rather than obtain organization "at the price of liberty and equality," her lectures are also "a text-book likely to be neglected by those with a taste for authoritarianism" (xv). Indeed, Follett did not vacillate between any of the many dialectical positions, dualisms, or binaries that she critiqued. Through her understanding of integration, Follett consistently promoted a "third way" that was a true synthesis— paradoxically both and neither idealist/realist, humanist/instrumental, and conservative/liberal. Since Follett didn't abide dichotomies and hierarchies, her ideas are not typically well-received or understood unless reinterpreted from such a lens.

Follett herself notes this challenge: "A very able political scientist writing of leadership treats it as a tropism and discusses why men obey or do not obey, why they tend to lead or follow, as if leading and following were the essence of leadership. Yet this very man has made valuable studies in leadership and the whole trend of his thinking on this subject seems away from this stereotype, yet at that moment, when talking directly of leadership, he reverts to the old idea and speaks of the leadership situation as one of command and obedience" (Follett 2003n, 289-90). Such internal contradictions often appear in discussions of Follett's work, as scholars tend to revert to traditional ideas of management based on hierarchy, which is grounded in a static ontology.

The most basic example of such misinterpretations are those which suffer from what O'Connor (2000) calls "the philosophy barrier" (168), "a preference for research with numerical basis" (Stewart 1996, 176). For instance, in an earlier article O'Connor (1996) herself suffers from this barrier with her claim that "Follett situates herself at an abstract, philosophical level in speaking about the compelling but elusive 'law of the situation'; so there is neither a way nor a possibility of grounding her view" (46). This reflects Stewart's (1996) concern that Follett's "ideas do not easily lend themselves" to empirical exploration and are often neglected as a result (176). Yet, such critiques clearly miss Follett's careful grounding of the law of the situation as well as her other philosophical concepts in ample empirical examples throughout her various works.

These misinterpretations occur in regard to basic principles as well. For example, in their assertion that "organizational behavior cannot be captured in subject or object alone, but must be seen in the interaction between subject and object, since each is a function of the other" Fry and Raadschelders (2014) simplify circular response so far that it is fundamentally misunderstood as a linear causal relationship between binaries. However, this truncation occurs despite their prior recognition that Follett "deplored the habit of severing object (dependent variable) from subject (independent variable)" (155). Here the authors fall into the trap of reverting to static ontology, forgetting that Follett's point is not only about a complex interaction, but a challenge to the very classifications of subject and object themselves. For Follett, reciprocal influence is based on an actual merging of subjects and environment in a manner that disallows discrete categories of any type in the dynamic process of becoming.

Similarly, despite initially defining the law of the situation correctly as "the intersubjective assessment of the situation" (Fry and Raadschelders 2014, 151) later explain it as "the objective demands of the work situation" (166). But in reverting to the static idea of objectivity, this latter description dismisses Follett's explanation of the situation a-making which is both dynamic and intersubjective. In other instances, the law of the situation is truncated to mean "an analysis of the situation of both management and workers" (Boje and Rosile 2001, 108). While this is certainly an aspect of integration applied to the workplace, it is a severely curtailed understanding that perpetuates a vision of management and workers as static parts acting under a purely objective set of circumstances, rather than relating in dynamic functions.

In such incomplete and incorrect interpretations, Follett's description of the relations within the organization are either confused or mishandled. For instance, Follett's concept of control as a coordinating function is lost when it is asserted that she defines "control as 'power exercised as a means toward a specific end'" where power is "the ability to make things happen" (Fry and Raadschelders 2014, 165). Such careless explication depicts power within the organization as power-over and control as coercive. This coercive interpretation of control has even been applied to Follett herself. O'Connor (1996) accuses Follett of making her own "claim to speak authoritatively" (40) and therefore suggests "we can take Follett's counsel to 'give control . . . to the man with the largest knowledge of the situation' [p. 281] as an appeal to give it to her" (41). Clearly, this misreads Follett's sharing of her ideas and expertise as an argument for control, completely missing her thorough and nuanced critique of such claims to authority based on expertise. Power-with turns control into a participatory coordinating function and co-creative experience.

Such misinterpretations of power-with can also be found in the negotiation and conflict resolution literature. Negotiation is a management specialization that has taken a particularly strong interest in Follett's work. Kolb (1996) demonstrates through a careful analysis of the conflict resolution literature that most in the field apply the concept of integration in a manner based on the assumption of atomistic self-interest in which regard for the other is from an instrumental perspective. For instance, as Cohen (2008) notes, Follett's ideas were influential to some of negotiation's canonical works, including Walton and McKersie's (1965) *A Behavioral Theory of Labor Negotiation* and Fisher and Ury's (1991) much-celebrated *Getting to Yes*. But, their bargaining process portrays the integration of interests as a means to achieving self-interest (Kolb 1996), rather than Follett's social interest.

The impact of these misinterpretations of integration and misunderstandings of power-with has rippled out through the literature even to the *integrative* negotiation approach. For instance, Pruitt and Lewis (1975) seem to suggest that compromise approaches can be considered integration, asserting that it "permits the development of trade-offs in which one party's concessions on one issue are exchanged for the other party's concessions on another issue" (622). Clearly, without an understanding of relational process ontology, integration appears to be some form of compromise—the meeting somewhere between two static positions through a negotiation process or worse, through pure domination. When so-called integrative negotiation is undertaken from this perspective it does not escape the atomistic approach to negotiating. Such non-relational understandings are fundamentally mistaken. Others agree with this assessment, leading some to refer to integrative negotiation as a "trade-off" approach rather than a collaborative one (Sass 2007), which has, fortunately, spurred the creation of the new *collaborative* negotiation literature (Cohen 2008) described in Chapter 12.

These misunderstandings are not new. Indeed, they go back to Follett's contemporaries. Like many during the Progressive Era, Follett was an avid reader of the *Bulletin of the Taylor Society* (Tonn 2003, 397) and the influence of scientific management is apparent in her work. Like Taylor, Follett argues "the most fundamental ideas in business today, that which is permeating our whole thinking on business organisation [*sic*], is that of function. Every man performs a function or part of a function. Research and scientific study determine function in scientifically managed plants" (Follett 2013g, 1). Furthermore, she asserts that "there should be no haziness in regard to employee functioning in a managerial capacity; the limits of such functioning should be frankly and sharply defined" (Follett 2003a, 88-89) and "to be honest and clear-cut in delimiting function is, I believe, essential to the success of the redistribution of function" (89). Therefore, she calls for extending "the scientific standard" which Follett insists "must be applied to the whole of business management" (Follett 2003e, 122).

From these comments, it is clear that Follett's administrative theory could be interpreted as a classical scientific management approach. Indeed, Stivers (2006) suggests Follett's accommodation of hierarchy in organizational contexts was a submission to the law of the situation in order to speak across paradigms and "its effect has been to encourage reading of Follett as a fellow traveler of capitalism or as a member of the human relations movement" (476). But as Child (1995) observes, "when British management writers (including Urwick) looked to synthesize the ideas of the two thinkers [Mayo and Follett] into a common managerial philosophy, they adopted a vision of paternalistic, top-down management that came primarily from Mayo and his colleagues and that was, in fact, intrinsically alien to Follett's basic premises" (88). As Stivers (1996) explains, however, to read Follett as "giving managers tools to keep workers in line" is to "miss the fundamental transformation her vision entails" (164). We agree with this assessment.

Perpetuating the assumption that she was aligned with scientific management, Follett has been misinterpreted by some as suggesting a means of management manipulation of subordinates and as only proposing a management technique (Child 1969) in which she is addressing "a tension between two levels—'managers' and 'workers'" (O'Connor 1996, 42). Similarly, Fry and Raadschelders (2014) assert that Follett considered "training people to become efficient instruments of organizational ends" (153) as an integral part of administration. And, even Ryan and Rutherford (2000) suggest that she was an advocate of hierarchy and strong leaders, fully contradicting their assertion that her underlying philosophy eschews such dualisms. This perspective actually echoes her *critique* of scientific management, as explicated in Chapter 9, and is at cross purposes to her unswerving commitment to the multidimensional and holistic nature of human being. Again, such misinterpretations reveal an underlying atomistic, static ontological perspective.

To correct these misconceptions, while Follett supports the scientific study of administration, she believes that when organizational functions are isolated, scientific study is "applied to only one part" (Follett 2003e, 122), to the "the technical side, as it is usually called" (123). It has not been applied "on the personnel side, a knowledge of how to deal fairly and fruitfully with one's fellows. . . . That is, one part of business management rested on science; the other part it was thought, never could" (123). Furthermore, she warns that "this divorcing of persons and the situation does a great deal of harm" (Follett 2003c, 60). To rectify scientific management, Follett (2003m) argues that interpersonal cooperation and coordination of function are essential to functional unity, which must be sought through "unifying" as "a process, not as a product" (195). In this way, while Taylor's "scientific management depersonalizes; the deeper philosophy of scientific management shows us personal relations within the whole setting of that thing of which they are a part" (Follett 2003c, 60). Here, Follett herself notes that without fundamental reinterpretation from a basis of relational process ontology, the concepts of scientific management are wrongheaded.

Despite her robust thought and wide scope of practical application, some such as Fox (1968) claim that Follett "has nothing useful to tell us about organizational structures or administrative devices" (527). Others dismiss her explanations of managerial functions as overly optimistic or at least containing "more idealistic elements" (Fry and Raadschelders 2014, 154). For example, Child (2013) argues that Follett's "confidence in the good intentions of managers . . . clearly needs to be qualified" in light of managerial irresponsibility found in contemporary organizations (88). Similarly, Schilling (2000) charges Follett with being an "idealist" who does not recognize that integration is sometimes not possible (233).

But dismissals such as these clearly ignore the many ways in which Follett's work continues to have many useful things to tell us—as discussed in Chapter 12. And claims of utopianism overstate Follett's position, failing to acknowledge her predictions that the management failures observed both then and now will continue as long as the paradigms of competition and hierarchy are maintained. Indeed, both Tonn (1996) and Morton and Lindquist (1997) explain that Follett's experience in community work left her well aware that most managers did not seek integration or to follow the law of the situation. But charges that she is overly optimistic about the possibilities for integration completely miss the many instances in which this issue is not only mentioned, but discussed in some detail: "Not all differences, however, can be integrated. That we must face fully, but it is certain that are fewer irreconcilable activities than we at present think, although it often takes ingenuity, a 'creative intelligence,' to find the integration" (Follett 2013c, 163).

Thus Follett repeatedly refers to *possibilities* and then offers examples from practical experience. As Roll and Thomas (2014) suggest, her ideas, if interpreted as utopian at all, should "be seen as a utopian society toward which we should aspire, rather than as a set of likely social outcomes that are just around the corner" (180). Hers is a normative prescription for what *could be* rather than a description of what existed in her time (Morton and Lindquist 1997; Tonn 1996). Follett herself acknowledges that she is describing nascent practices that have the potential to become prevalent *only if we foster them.*

MISINTERPRETATION IN POLITICAL THEORY

Political theorists and scientists and public administration scholars alike draw on Follettian thinking. They share a concern for the relationship between the individual and society, and so this is the theoretical focus discussed in this section. Many issues pertaining to internal organizational operations apply to this relation as well, because while the scale is larger, group processes remain the same in Follettian thinking. Here we focus on the relating of person and group for what Follett (1998) calls the "true individual" (295)—her particular way of understanding "the unity of the individual and society" (Follett 2013c, 50) that removes "the suggestion of atomism in the word individual" and "the suggestion of abstraction in the word social" (51).

Because Follett promotes this particular type of unifying, a common misinterpretation of her political theory is a misreading of her ideological position. For example, Fry and Thomas (1996) argue that her description of the state has authoritarian implications. They miss all of the detailed caveats she provides for how the New State must be configured so as not to manifest such tendencies, including her bold critique of Hegel himself: "But there is the real Hegel and the Hegel who misapplied his own doctrine, who preached the absolutism of a Prussian State" (Follett 1998, 267). Similarly, The assertion that Follett argues that "both the group and the state serve a purpose greater than individual interests" (Fry and Raadschelders 2014, 150) is contradicted by Follett's explanation of the reciprocal process of forming individual and group purpose and the social interest. Follett insists that the group is not in some way *more* than individuals, insisting "to no doctrine must we make swifter or more emphatic denial" (Follett 2013c, 99).

This misinterpretation of the relationship between the individual and the group is likewise applied at the psychosocial level of analysis. It is incorrect to assert that because "individuals are created by reciprocal activity" within the group that "'individuality' is not uniqueness, but the capacity for union or the ability to find one's place in the whole" where "determinism is an inevitability" (Fry and Raadschelders 2014, 158-59). Such misinterpretations suggest a commitment to dualisms on the part of the reader, not an underlying contradiction in Follett's theory.

Indeed, for Follett, the fundamental problem of social relations is the question of power. Her differentiation of power-over from power-with shapes her thinking about both social action and structure. Although they have a clear understanding of Follett's application of power-with to the workplace in her later writings (e.g., *Dynamic Administration*), Boje and Rosile (2001) miss the systemic manner in which she addresses power-with at the societal level of analysis in her earlier work. She is not simply focused on "the day-to-day mundane work spaces" (107). Follett explores how power plays out in political, legal, and economic systems and situations as well. Nor should her admission that power-with is *most difficult* in industry be interpreted to mean that power-over may never be eliminated in society. Yet these assertions abound (see, for example, Boje and Rosile 2001; Child 2013; Eylon 1998; Nohria 1995; Pratt 2011). Nohria (1995) articulates this common concern well: "I fear that's what inevitably happens to efforts to introduce a more egalitarian and participative system of authority and explains the short half-life of earlier attempts to create organizations that presented an alternative to hierarchy. . . . someone must make a tough decision, a decision that inevitably will be contested by those who lose out" (161-62).

Some reduce the applicability of principles like power-with and integration to small group process. Roll and Thomas (2014) claim that "collective action problem solving may only work in small, discrete groups" (174). Likewise Child (2013) argues that "while 'power-with' may be attainable in small groups or community associations where the members may not have basically divergent interests, 'power-over' is likely to prevail in larger social systems such as employment relations and in the governance of societies as a whole" (87). These assertions reveal deep misgivings about the very possibility of integration and the assumption that domination is an *inherent*, rather than learned behavior—thus ignoring Follett's contrary argument which is buttressed by philosophy, physics, biology, and psychology. Furthermore, they disregard Follett's explanation of a deeply nesting, broadly inclusive, networking federalism. Yes, everything happens in relatively small groups, but within this larger whole a-making.

It is more accurate to suggest that Follett believes power-with, integration, and all of her other prescriptions for practice are *possible* if society were run as a true democracy. Indeed, power-with is an assumption in Follett's understanding of integrative process and how it is applied to groups extending out to the global scope. In regard to applying integrative process to politics, historian Kevin Mattson (1998) seems to ignore the many instances in which Follett notes conflict, disruption, and disintegration as part and parcel of the integrative process, and acknowledges issues that cannot be integrated within the situation at hand. Other scholars argue that because of this admission, Follett provides only a partial theory (Fox 1968; Fry and Thomas 1996). This seems to be nit-picking as it is quite obvious based on her analysis of the three available alternatives—integration, compromise, and domination—she clearly believes compromise is the lesser of two evils and would be preferred over domination when integration fails. However, she also recognizes that learning to compromise is a lesser developmental step toward the capacity to integrate. At the other end of this debate, Child (2013) chides Follett for being too quick to see integration in situations where the appearance of consensus may occur only because groups become "internally coercive, and suppress opinions that deviate from those of the majority" (87). He clearly misses Follett's warnings against such inauthentic actions in her discussion of the crowd and that she identifies such situations as domination or imitation rather than integration.

On the issue of the crowd, Fry and Thomas (1996) suggest that Follett gives little concrete advice on how to transform crowds into groups. Yet, Follett's entire explication of integration as the intentional pursuit of circular response is geared toward that specific objective. She even presents it as a *method*: "Those who accept integration rather than compromise or domination as the law of social relations will seek the method" (Follett 2013c, 165) and then goes on to explain its component processes. In essence, atomistic individuals who form crowds, herds, and mobs can learn the method to become relational individuals who co-create groups.

Adding to the lack of faith in the potential of group processes, O'Connor (1996) criticizes Follett as being "almost obsessed with the concept of unity" (40). Likewise, Mattson (1998) characterizes her application of ontological circular response to social integration as imaginary: "People cannot always achieve unity. To uphold unity as a social good and attainable ideal is fine; to believe that unity is based on an objective law ignores reality. By creating a fictional law and by ignoring the fact that political conflict may often be agonal and strained, Follett weakened her more powerful and interesting ideas on the contingency of politics" (lv). These authors ignore that fact that Follett's argument about circular response is made at an ontological level—principles which *necessitate* a relational and dynamic reality—not a psychosocial law. At the psychosocial level, the process of integration is rife with conflict and unity is never *achieved*; it is simply a temporary endpoint of iterative integrative processes. Indeed, as Tonn (1996) notes, Follett "repeatedly acknowledges the difficulties involved in achieving unifying—difficulties she had personally experienced" (173).

Thus, an important element of the method of integration is to consider difference and conflict as an opportunity for constructive progress for both the individual and society. Yet, this is often mistaken, as noted in the discussion of negotiation above. Stivers (2006) supports this assessment, noting that even Dwight Waldo (see 1952, 96), one of Follett's staunch supporters in public administration, misunderstood her view of conflict—a core element of integrative process.

Follett considers conflict in economic action as well as political and organizational behavior. Thus, misunderstandings are also found in discussions of political economy, for which Follett was highly concerned in her search for a more democratic way of life. Kanter (1995) argues, "When Follett wrote that 'cut-throat' competition is beginning to go out of fashion' and that despite competition among firms, 'the cooperation between them is coming to occupy a larger and larger place,' she was wrong. ... At least in America. At least then" (xviii). Similarly, Mattson (1998) argues that Follett did not understand industry: "It is my contention that Follett was at her best when thinking not about private enterprise but about the nature of American politics and political life" (xxxi). Similarly, Roll and Thomas (2014) seem to chastise Follett's naivety in their insistence that contemporary economic literature finds that "collective action is much less likely to be a function of the group process or community coordination at levels larger than the community" (175) as otherwise there would be "significant incentives for members to free ride" (173).

However, it can be argued that Follett was only partially wrong in her ideas about political economy. She hoped that in the form of trade unions and other business-oriented cooperatives the group-spirit would thrive. Instead, what appeared initially as cooperation was merely a broadening of the "us" against a common "them" in the status quo competitive mode of association. While a business-against-society and capital-against-labor trend in which groups banded together for their shared self-interest without regard for the greater good has been the norm, when one looks at the Mondragon Corporation in the Basque region of Spain (Cheney 2001; Ormaechea 2001) and its recent expansion to North America in Cleveland-based cooperatives as an exemplar, examples of the cooperative competition Follett described continue to exist.

MISINTERPRETATION IN SUMMARY

Given these frequent problems of misinterpretation, "Follett's ideas constitute a difference that public administration has never integrated" (Stivers 2006, 475)—fully and accurately, in any case. Our argument has been that Follett's work is misinterpreted in both management and political theory because scholars simply do not understand this "difference"—her full philosophical grounding. However, we must also consider the likelihood that many scholars *disagree* with her relational process approach.

For example, Fry and Thomas (1996) argue that "Follett's writings are driven by a questionable philosophical premiss [*sic*]" (18). While they do not fully explain their meaning, this is exemplary of a typical claim made against Follett that she is too idealistic, or at least puts forward a "semi-utopian ideal" (Roll and Thomas 2014, 173). Stever (1986) characterizes her idealism as merely "shrewdly veneered" with pragmatism (274). Similarly, while Fry and Raadschelders (2014) temper their suggestion of idealism by noting Follett's own admittance that she was seeking a *possible* world as opposed to describing the *actual* world or an *ideal* world, they argue that her vision for change is based on two fundamental assumptions that they find unlikely: (1) attitudes must shift from desiring power-over to fostering power-with; and (2) interests must be formulated so as to permit integration. However, they describe the first assumption as "engaging in 'best-case' hypothesizing in assuming those baser instincts can be overcome" (Fry and Raadschelders 2014, 171). Of the latter, they insist that there will always be configurations of interests for which integration is not possible and "even if interests are in appropriate configuration, disagreement over objectives or the means to achieve those objectives may remain as an impediment to integrative solutions" (172).

Here, again, the authors' own static ontology, atomistic individualism, and positivist epistemology is showing, but without self-reflective declaration. The notion that anything is static or eternal—attitudes, interests, identities, or anything else—conflicts with Follett's relational process ontology. Therefore, such critiques need to be a well-constructed challenge to each of the philosophical foundations of Follett's argument—ontological assumptions, psychosocial theory, epistemological concepts, and beliefs grounded in relational process. Furthermore, the authors should identify their own philosophical assumptions in making such a critique. Therefore, it is important to situate our recapitulation of Follett's thinking in the "ontological turn" in social and political theory (Prozorov 2014a, xxviii).

IN SEARCH OF POLITICAL ONTOLOGIES

Perhaps because of the fierce hold the Newtonian/Cartesian ontology has on modern science, even the social sciences, theorists from a variety of disciplines are seeking to understand how ontological assumptions shape both knowledge and practice. While this is not the place to go into great detail, it is important to make note of this broader theoretical project because it underscores the need to make clear the ontology informing Follettian governance if it is to be affirmed and employed.

As social scientists we are often called to make suggestions for beneficial change—we cannot simply stop at description or even critique. We suggest that such recommendations should make clear the philosophical commitments that inform them (Stout and Love 2013a, b). As political theorist Robert Cox (1995) asserts, "the first task of a contemporary political theory is to *declare its ontology*" (36, emphasis added). Similarly, public administration theorist Gary Wamsley (1996) insists that ontological disclosure is the only appropriate platform from which one can make normative claims about governance. In other words, one must describe how one's understanding of existence *necessitates* the recommendations being made. Such commitments are not easily brushed aside and demand logical congruence all the way from beliefs to practices so that incongruence does not generate "ontological angst" (Evans and Wamsley 1999, 119).

Furthermore, Stephen White (2000) argues that in a dynamic, globalizing, pluralistic context that has become deeply fragmented and competitive and in which claims to truth and legitimacy are regularly contested, we must disregard ontologies which make *strong* claims for either a transcendent Whole or a static Is underlying positivist assumptions of Truth that drive practice. However, *weak* does not connote *thin*. Weak ontologies can provide a robust and detailed explication, and yet remain fluid in character as amendable normative affirmations. As an example, relational process ontology (Stout and Love 2013b) offers an alternative that assumes the possibility of both an element of authentic self and relational connection while being sufficiently dynamic to be non-colonizing and non-fundamentalist in its knowledge and prescriptions for practice.[2]

Follettian governance in particular implies a weak ontology that does not have hierarchical positions or any type of permanent unity, but which isn't atomistic or without governance either. It also suggests a dynamic state of being that supports ongoing change but does not allow representation through fixed social roles. As such, Follettian governance provides a better "weak" ontological grounding for global governance.

Similar affirmations of weak ontologies are nascent in the public administration literature, but are lacking depth and detail. For example, a panel at the 1999 American Political Science Association conference and a follow up journal symposium in *Administration & Society* launched an important dialogue on ontology in public administration, focusing primarily on concepts offered by Arendt and Heidegger (Farmer 2002a). These essays make problematic the prevailing individualist ontology that imagines being-in-the-world as fundamentally separate from everything and everyone else (Hummel 2002), as well as the notion of representation of either a political or expert nature (Stivers 2002b). If we are isolated individuals who must generate social space before any type of political relation is possible, how do we create social space? If we are worlds unto ourselves, how can anyone represent another?

Farmer suggests the solutions lie in changing our consciousness and our "understanding of self, others, and nature" (2002b, 125), but does not offer explanation. Hummel (2002) suggests the answers lie in understanding ourselves as "always in a social and physical context, in which our presence and its context are an inseparable whole" (103). Stivers (2008) takes up this point by suggesting that the political forms recommended by both Arendt and Follett are based on an ontology described by Heidegger's (1996) non-Cartesian view of reality in which being is experienced always in association with the world and others. In fact, all of existence is in an ontological state of Being-with, without separation and without a transcendent source. This explanation reflects relational aspects of Follett's ontological assumptions, but without necessarily indicating a dynamic state.

Howe (2006) asserts that the neutral, scientific ontology of liberalism leaves much to be desired as a basis for a public ethic—it offers neither intrinsic meaning nor transcendent purpose. Nor is there a sense of human connection. He provides a compelling argument for considering the enchanted materialism Bennett (2001) borrows from the ancient Greek Epicureans as an alternative basis for a non-rationalist ethic for public administration. He suggests that if we hold an aesthetic appreciation of all existence that we will make better judgments about collective action. This is not incongruent with Follett's ethics, but is not robust enough as a methodological framework.

There is also some discussion of ontology in the assumed condition of the subject in Lacanian psychoanalysis (Catlaw 2007; Catlaw and Jordan 2009; McSwite 2006). Catlaw (2007) also makes a call for an alternative to replace the political ontology of "*representation*" (2). He describes this as "a politics of the subject" in which: (1) neither unity nor atomism are acceptable; (2) radical difference must be accommodated within dynamic compositions; (3) becoming occurs through generative, situational processes; (4) governing is a process that cuts across human activity; (5) governing does not entail permanent social roles; and (6) governing focuses on facilitating the process (Catlaw 2007, 192-99). While these characteristics match Follettian governance (Love 2013), his project of explication has not yet materialized.

While these preliminary discussions of ontology and governance are encouraging, they by no means fully elucidate answers. We respectfully suggest that many of the alternatives proposed thus far are lacking in two fundamental ways. First, not all describe an ontological position that fully fits the collaborative approach. While Heidegger's understanding of *being-with* addresses relatedness, it does not fully accommodate an understanding of the dynamic process of *becoming* (Shaviro 2009). Nor does Heidegger reach beyond social reality to explain a non-Cartesian universe. Neither the ontological condition of the post-analytic Lacanian subject, nor the aesthetic mutual appreciation of enchanted materialism addresses the concept of innate relatedness. More promising is the description of what has been broadly labeled "relational ontology" as opposed to the predominant "individualist ontology" (Stout and Salm 2011).

Even more congruent with Follett's explication is the developing model of Integrative Governance (Stout and Love 2013a)—a conceptualization based on relational process ontology (Stout and Love 2013b). This ideal-type includes all the conceptual elements presented herein: ontology and language, psychosocial theory, epistemology, belief, ethics, political theory, economic theory, and administrative theory. However, added to Follett's ideas are a broad range of contemporary perspectives based on coherent concepts drawn from sources as diverse as biology, psychology, sociology, philosophy, theology, quantum physics, as well as Eastern, feminist, and indigenous spirituality. In the terms of Integrative Governance, relational process ontology makes a commitment to a notion of life as an ongoing process of becoming among interdependent beings, each of which is a unique expression of existence. We are a dynamic, mutually influencing multitude of unique but relating individuals. Such an ontology provides a logically coherent basis for practices that include all concerned individuals, allowing for equal mutual influence and change in an ongoing political process. These concepts are reflected in Follett's thinking.

In her own affirmation of her theory of governance, Follett explains, "I have been asked if this is a conservative or a radical point of view. It is both" (Follett 2013c, 188). She notes repeatedly that synthesis is the only lasting resolution of the contestations, paradoxes, and pathologies caused by the separation of any concept or thing into thesis and antithesis, like conservative versus radical theory. "Do we not find here too, as in every question where we go below the surface, that we wish to do away with atomism?" (188). Thus, at a philosophical level, Follettian governance is "better" because it is grounded in a "weak" ontological synthesis as opposed to a "strong" dominating or hybrid compromise ontology.

To explain the problem of ontological compromise, a hybrid would serve simply to reify or make static relational ontological assumptions thereby making process assumptions ineffectual (Stout and Love 2015b). Therefore, the ontology underlying Follettian governance demands full recapitulation. Suggesting that we can simply temper the mainstream political ontology with a little bit of relational process ontology is faulty logic: relational process ontology is fundamentally different from both collectivist and individualist ontologies. We cannot "leaven self-contained individualism with ensemble individualism, for once we enter the framework of the former, we have already defined our terms in ways that contradict their very essence within the framework of the latter" (Sampson 1988, 21). These differing ontological positions cannot coexist without ongoing competition for supremacy of one over the other. Similarly, representative authoritarian or pluralist forms of governance cannot coexist with participatory self-governance without inherent discord—when political leaders, public administrators, or the people are not in agreement, one must ultimately trump the others (Stout 2013b).

If we instead assume that a relational process approach to governance is ontologically necessary, then non-relational systems will eventually be replaced. However, given the strength of commitments to ontological positions, it is more likely that ontologies will continue to compete for primacy for some time. If public administration theorists wish to form some type of vanguard to foster a revolutionary transformation to collaborative governance (Stout 2009b), we must find the courage to lead the way to a necessarily and essentially different ontology. We must discover "*the will to will the common will*" (Follett 1998, 49) and generate pathways from those competing ontologies into the integrative process alternative Follett offers. This recapitulation of Follettian thinking is meant to assist this endeavor. It is our hope that more scholars and practitioners will recognize that "the scope of her vision was enormous, the tasks formidable" but that we will be "energized rather than discouraged" by the challenges (Tonn 1996, 173).

ENDNOTES

1. He does, however, exempt Enomoto's (1995) essay from this excoriation and we would agree based on his demonstrated grasp of the relational process ontology perspective.

2. The term authentic used herein refers to something that is self-originating as opposed to being externally imposed. It assumes the ontological possibility of an aspect of self that escapes social construction and/or transcendent ordering.

‍ 12 ‍

The Fruits of Follettian Thinking

Referring back to the method described in Chapter 1, we have completed the disaggregation of Follettian thinking for the purpose of explication in Chapters 2-9. Based on the further analysis of similarities in thought provided in Chapter 10, we feel it is fair to say that Whiteheadian process philosophy provides a coherent ontological foundation for Follettian thinking and, by extension, for related theories of collaborative and participatory administrative practice. Furthermore, in Chapter 11 we demonstrated how her ideas are misinterpreted based on ontological misunderstandings. Now, it is time for us to re-integrate her ideas into a cohesive whole with appropriate consideration of her relational process ontology. Here, we examine Follett's cross-cutting principles and the results they produce. With that understanding in hand, we consider how Follettian thinking is being employed in contemporary scholarship, as has also been noted in chapter endnotes throughout the book.

If we re-read Follett with an understanding of a *relational process ontology that embraces difference and seeks harmony*, then her prescriptions for political and administrative practice are not only quite logical, but necessary. In sum, this relational process ontology of co-creative becoming prefigures persons-in-community with an experiential, dynamic epistemology and process-oriented governance that would not enforce pre-determined values (in the sense of *a priori* forms of being) but instead replace them with a determining process (in the sense of becoming and learning) that seeks self-organizing coordinated harmony as opposed to domination and control. We need not enforce relatedness through order—

228

it is an ontological given. However, *we may foster or constrain it through our practices and institutional structures.*

This alternative ontological assumption causes us to think and act in relational terms as opposed to contractual terms—the world is not inhabited by disaggregated, atomistic individuals who must enter into externally ordered relation; it is composed of relating individuals who seek out one another to experience difference for enjoyment and creative development. But what we *can* do is consciously direct relating toward integration. This ontology's embrace of difference enables us to transform our understanding of conflict as a social problem to difference as an opportunity for a self-organizing, constructive, unifying, harmonizing, synthesizing process that generates shared power and progress. In fact, this is perhaps the key differentiation from liberal philosophy—rather than assuming conflict is a *problem* for social order, it is seen as creating the *opportunity* for individual and social progress. Administration thereby shifts from a permanent social role of authoritative director of order to a fluid social function of facilitating the harmonization of differences.

Together, these concepts negate the notion of representation, because while there is similarity based on relatedness, each expression of becoming, each individual within society is unique and cannot be replicated. No particular configuration can be held up as the "right" or "proper" expression of pure potentiality. Nor can any particular moment of expression be held as a static, authoritative point of balance. Therefore, ongoing participatory practice among complex networks of relationship becomes the necessary form through which harmonization of difference occurs—what Follett describes as deeply nesting, networking, and broadly inclusive federalism.

These are the basics of what can be called Follettian governance—facilitation of a mode of association through a relational process of becoming unique individuals, collectively engaged in an ongoing process of harmonizing differences through interlocking networks, to progress as both individuals and as society. However, as exemplified by the conductorless Orpheus Symphony Orchestra (Seifter and Economy 2001), those who "conduct" this process are chosen based on what is needed at the moment—choosing the role of leader or facilitator in accordance with the law of the situation and thereby opening the role to all participants in a self-organizing process of governance—one that is "located in every space, actualized through every interaction" (Catlaw 2007, 14). In other words, democracy becomes a way of life.

Follett's prescriptions for practice are grounded in democratic theory in a manner that informs both politics and organizational management—an ideal combination for collaborative governance as it is being practiced today (Stout and Love 2014, 2015a). Indeed, many public administration scholars use her theories to inform participatory practice and public engagement in collaborative governance (see for example, Elias and Alkadry 2011; King 2011; King, Feltey, and Susel 1998; King, Stivers, and Collaborators 1998; King and Zanetti 2005; Stivers 2000, 2006; Stout 2013b). Thus, we use the term "Follettian governance" (Stout and Staton 2011) to refer to the set of recommendations she makes for group coordination at any level of analysis, in either public or private settings.

Follettian governance is driven by three cross-cutting principles: integrative process, the situation, and the law of the situation. Follett formulates these three principles as they appear and reappear throughout the conceptual elements of her thinking from ontological assumptions to administrative practice. In turn, these three philosophical principles fundamentally alter the terms commonly used in ethics, political theory, economic theory, and administrative theory as shown in both her critique of standard approaches and affirmation of alternatives. The principles undergird a particular method or mode of association that is then applied to various social practices in order to produce democracy as a way of life that, in turn, produces progress for both the individual and society. Without a firm understanding of these principles, the terms she redefines can be easily misinterpreted and so the three principles warrant reiteration as points of reference.

Integrative process combines ontological assumptions, psychosocial theory, epistemological concepts, and a system of belief in a philosophical understanding of co-creative experience. The situation refers to the context in which integrative process occurs, assuming a federated structure of groups from the most intimate to the most global in scope. It is within these groups that knowledge is co-produced, ethics are co-determined, and political, economic, and administrative practices are collaboratively conducted. Finally, the law of the situation is what is discovered through the integrative process in which authority and ethics are established to guide co-creative action.

Taken together, these three principles inform her *method of integration* as applied to practice—the cornerstone of Follettian governance. If implemented accurately and adequately, Follett believes the method of integration will produce democracy as a way of life and progress for both the individual and society. To illustrate, Follett draws upon examples from community, political, and industrial life to show the nascent and decidedly non-utopian character of the method of integration in group governance. Yet, she is careful to note the limitations of the method both in terms of existing institutional barriers and the impossibility of integrating absolutely all desires successfully. Nevertheless, she feels certain we can do better living together than we do under standard practices of group governance. The following sections provide more detail on these principles, their application, and their results.

Integrative process

Integrative process is, put most simply, "the basic law of life" (Follett 2003c, 65). Integrative process "supports all life's structure and guides every activity" (302), from the metaphysical to the administrative. Integration is arguably Follett's foundational concept, which she applies equally to physical existence, the individual psyche, and groups of human beings in all social contexts (57). She explains that the dynamic ontological process of *circular response* or "the doctrine of circular or integrative behavior" (xv) can be found in chemistry, engineering, and relativity theory in physics (73-74) and is "the psychological term for the deepest truth of life" (116).

According to the relational process ontology from which she draws, there is nothing but integration among related parts comprising the whole of the universe: "reality is in the relating, in the activity-between" (Follett 2013c, 54). Integrative process seeks self-organizing coordinated harmony as opposed to externally imposed order. Therefore, integration is *relational* because it occurs between: different dimensions of the individual (physical, intellectual, emotional, spiritual, etc.); individuals and individuals in the group; individuals and the situation; the group and the situation; groups and groups; groups and groups and the situation; and so forth all the way out in interlocking sets to what she calls "the total situation" (55).

Furthermore, integration is a *process* because it never reaches a permanent point of stasis. Follett (2013c) insists "there is no result *of* process but only a moment *in* process" (60); therefore "the process must be emphasized rather than product, that the process is continuous" (102). Thus, rather than describing integrat*ion*, Follett (1919) often refers to "integrat*ing*" (576, emphasis added).

The situation

Using a systems approach long before such terminology existed Follett conceptualizes the environmental context as *the situation*. Situations are dynamic fields of mutual influence in which the factors "all together constitute a certain situation, but they constitute that situation through their relation to one another. They don't form a total situation merely by existing side by side" (Follett 2013h, 79). Follett suggests that the phrase "total relativity" is "rather clumsy," but she is "trying to express a total which shall include all the factors in a situation not as an additional total but as a relational total—a total where each part has been permeated by every other part" (79). Furthermore, the situation is dynamic because "there are 'progressive integrations'" (Follett 2013c, 146) in "what might be called the evolving situation" (55). Each "evolving situation" (55) interconnects with other situations in networking fashion, producing "the total situation" (55). Thus, the situation is both relational and dynamic.

This understanding of the whole informs her interpretation of federalism as a deeply nesting, networking, and broadly inclusive "whole a-making" (Follett 2013c, 102). Thus, the principle of the situation is also based on Follett's relational process ontology perspective that understands existence as holistic, dynamic, relational, and co-creative. Following, individuals are connected at an ontological level through mutual influence; however, conscious, active integration is necessary to foster the social bond for effective collective action. Follett's dynamic versions of circular response, psychoanalysis, and Gestalt underlie her understanding of true individuals with identities that are the integrative result of both internal and external forces—individuals are both self-determining and responsive to their environment. In sum, the situation and all within it—human and otherwise—are in dynamic, relational influence.

The law of the situation

From Follett's pragmatist perspective, to achieve the best individual and societal outcomes those acting within a given situation should be responsive to the immediate emergent situation, and, to the greatest degree possible, to the total situation as well. Follett conceives these dynamic contextual drivers of both instigation and adaptation as "the law of the situation" (Follett 2003j, 104). This includes all physical and social aspects of the situation, with consideration of those not actually present in the moment. As she explains, "We want to find the law of the situation in the situation and yet still be guided by law and not by personal or national whims or a narrow self-interest" (Follett 2013c, 152). Knowing when this law has been found must be sensed by the group and re-evaluated as the situation evolves.

The law of the situation is determined through specific ways of knowing, understanding, and finding agreement. Therefore, Follett explains this process in both epistemological and ethical terms. In Follett's pragmatist epistemology, knowledge is constantly being co-created and recreated through active experimentation and integration among those who employ what she refers to as a "scientific attitude of mind" (Follett 2013c, 29)—a willingness to see things in a new light, with alternative understandings. She argues, "Collective thinking must be reverenced as an act of creation" (Follett 1998, 372).

Through this approach to shared understanding, ethics is not the *substance* of the collective will but has the *process* of creating as its "germinating centre [*sic*]" (Follett 1998, 49). The process of generating an ethic is integrative and relational rather than procedural and formal, as it is in communicative ethics (Habermas and Cooke 1998). Through integration, a group ethic is generated that is mutualistic and in which all share responsibility for demanding and giving obedience through a sense of commitment that is experientially founded. Thus, obeying the law of the situation gives authority to the total situation, the situation, and the group process, as opposed to specific individuals, positions, or organizations. This method thereby rectifies power relationships in all social contexts: "If both sides obey the law of the situation, no *person* has power over another" (Follett 2003j, 105). This is the foundation of Follett's notion of shared power wherein "genuine power is power-with, pseudo power, power-over" (Follett 2013c, 189).

The method of integration

The group process of integration becomes the focal point of much of Follett's thinking. She explains integrating as the intentional process of creating "*functional unity*" (Follett 2013c, 256) among individuals actively engaging in circular behavior in any sector of society. Therefore, "there *is* a technique for integration" (Follett 2013b, 68). As she understands it, "the method of integration" (Follett 2013c, 178) is composed of a number of processual elements that are iterative rather than linear in nature. These elements include a disposition, a style of relating, a mode of association, and an approach to action.

Integrating begins with an attitude—a disposition that she describes as "*the will to will the common will*" (Follett 1998, 49). This perspective is grounded in a worldview based on relational process philosophy—a belief that the individual is fundamentally interconnected with everything else in the universe through a deeply nesting, widely inclusive network of becoming (Stout and Love 2013b). This relational disposition generates a cooperative style of relating and enables participatory interactions—or "*modes of association*" (Follett 1998, 147)—in which we feel an obligation to engage in public life and to consider others in all we do. Thus, the second characteristic of integrating is genuine participation: "You have to have participation before you can get co-operation" (Follett 2003g, 171).

In this participatory cooperation, the group co-produces knowledge, shared desire, purpose, choice of method, and so forth—in short, all activities common to the group decision-making process. In these activities, integrating seeks "the interpenetration of the ideas of the parties concerned" (Follett 2003l, 212). To achieve this end, integration occurs not through standard deliberation which tends toward debate among competing interests, but rather dialogic "interpermeation" (Follett 1998, 209) that includes "a cooperative gathering of facts" (Follett 2013c, 17) and "genuine discussion" that "is truth-seeking" (Follett 1998, 210) in the situation and in response to the law of the situation. Its synergistic effect produces more creative and effective methods because nothing is lost through domination or compromise: "By integrating these interests you get the increment of the unifying" (Follett 2013c, 45-46).

It "often takes ingenuity, a 'creative intelligence,' to find the integration" (Follett 2013b, 163). But from the perspective of *constructive conflict* (Follett 2003b), differing interests can be more easily integrated through the techniques of disintegration and revaluation. Disintegration is necessary in order to move from fully formulated *a priori positions* to the nuanced driving desires underneath. *Interests* are typically composed of a desire, an idea about how to get the desire met, and a passion to make it happen. Desire must be split from method in order to enable integration, which may be achieved either through change in the desire or change in the preferred method of fulfillment. Once divided, "revaluation is the flower of comparison" (38) that precipitates an organic change of opinion through dialogue and value comparison.

However, Follett (2013c) also notes that revaluation may occur in response to changes in the situation, changes in oneself, or new sources of knowledge. Regardless of the relational source, "through an interpenetrating of understanding, the quality of one's own thinking is changed" (Follett 2013c, 163). "The course of action decided upon is what we all together want, and I see that it is better than what I had wanted alone. It is what *I* now want" (Follett 1998, 25). Today, we would call this a consensus building process (Susskind, McKearnan, and Thomas-Larme 1999) or conflict resolution process (Forester 2009) that addresses both normative and causal beliefs (Sabatier 1988).

Because of this integration of desires and/or preferred methods, commitment to what is co-created is ensured not through consent or the binding authority of law or contract, "but in the fact that it has been produced by the community" (Follett 1998, 130); loyalty is *experientially* founded. Similarly, a sense of mutual responsibility is engendered by this shared ownership: "collective responsibility is not a matter of adding but of interweaving" (Follett 2013b, 75).

APPLICATION TO PRACTICE

Follett applies her principles of integrative process, the situation, and the law of the situation through her method of integration to political theory, economic theory, and administrative theory. In regard to political theory, Follett's experiences in the community centers movement made her "sure that democracy could be more than an abstract ideal. It must, she insisted, become a lived reality, a vigorous daily practice" (Mattson 1998, liv). Thus, Follett's primary concern is *modes of association* in human groups, preferring direct participation to representative forms of group governance at any scale and in any sector of society. She argues, "Majority rule is democratic when it is approaching not a unanimous but an integrated will" (Follett 1998, 142). Even a unanimous vote is not necessarily the will of the whole because it likely obscures some form of domination, even if only through passivity and imitation or compromise.

In what she calls "true democracy" (Follett 1998, 156), several familiar concepts are fundamentally redefined: (1) politics is a creative process of integration; (2) democratic values of freedom and equality are relational power-with; (3) the People is a dynamic, relational whole composed through a deeply nesting, broadly inclusive, and networking federalism; (4) representation and leadership are dynamic and determined by the law of the situation; and (5) the state is a convener and facilitator of integrative process.

Applying integrative process to economics and business, Follett sees power to be "the central problem of social relations" (Follett 2013c, xiii); including economic power among competitors as well as between consumer and producer, capital and labor, and industry and society. She envisions a new economic system that would have a purpose of creative production through cooperative competition and emergent self-governance. While markets would remain, they would be transformed into a functional unity with the same democratic operating principles as government.

Applying integrative process to administration in both political and economic endeavors, Follett envisions a scientific management in which coordination happens through "unifying" as "a process, not as a product" (Follett 2003m, 195). Thus, her two key principles of administrative theory are: (1) *authority* as a group process where all follow "what the situation demands" (Follett 2013b, 22) rather than as something that "filters down to those below" (Follett 2013a, 43); and (2) *functional unifying* in which interrelated parts are mutually and dynamically influencing. In essence, these two characteristics fundamentally change the *role* of the manager in pursuit of a new *goal* of scientific management: *coordinating the integrative process of unifying functions.*

Specifically, unity of command and managerial control are redefined as responsive authority and responsibility that are situation-determined; planning and decision-making are guided by participatory collaboration rather than managerial direction; functional division of labor becomes an ongoing process of integrative action; and hierarchical organizing style shifts to federalism and non-hierarchical coordination. The organizing style employs the form of true democracy—integrating federations of small groups—wherein participants are enabled to pursue coordinated activity with emergent and dynamic leadership based on the needs of the situation and the capacities of those involved—anyone can be a leader and an expert in "collective self-control" (Follett 2013h, 89).

DEMOCRACY AS A WAY OF LIFE

In her writings, Follett applies integrative process to community, government, and business settings, insisting that governance of all groups within the federated political economy should operate according to the method of integration. Adequate and accurate implementation of the method of integration in all spheres of society—government, market, and community—generates what Dewey would later call "democracy as a way of life" (Talisse 2003, 1).[1]

Thus, following the principle of the total situation, Follett's understanding of the whole demands that all artificial demarcations of societal sectors be eliminated. She observes, "We have a kind of time-theory of salvation: keep the debasing influences of industry to certain hours of the day, employ the others in some educational way, and if the race is keenly enough run the spiritualizing influences will win out. But we cannot split ourselves up like this, the eight-hour influence will continue into the leisure period; it is the eight-hour influences themselves that we must reckon with" (Follett 2013c, 87-88). This is particularly true in governance: "We have long thought of politics as entirely outside our daily life manipulated by those set apart for the purpose . . . We are now beginning to recognize more and more clearly that the work we do, the conditions of that work, the houses in which we live, the water we drink, the food we eat, the opportunities for bringing up our children, that in fact the whole area of our daily life should constitute politics. There is no line where the life of the home ends and the life of the city begins. There is no wall between my private life and my public life" (Follett 1998, 189). "Every single act of our life should be looked at as a social act" (368).

In this way, Follett's understanding of federalism begins with each individual integrating aspects of self within a dynamic, relational whole—the individual-in-community. From there, federalism moves out through all the various groups in which an individual acts, including family, work, and neighborhood. As noted in her explication of "true democracy," she describes these myriad and complex connections as "an infinite number of filaments" that "cross and recross and connect all my various allegiances" (Follett 1998, 312).

Therefore, "the task for politics, economics and jurisprudence is to provide those contacts, find those relations, which free in each the spiritual energy which, uniting each with each, gives us, on no conceptual plane but in our daily lives, a 'will of the people.' This reciprocal freeing, this calling forth of one from the other, this constant evocation, is the . . . life-process" (Follett 2013c, 130). By facilitating these connections, we will be able to "so democratize our industrial and our political methods that all will have a share in policy and in responsibility" (Follett 1998, 339). Therefore, "we need a new method: the group process must be applied to industrial groups as well as to neighborhood groups, to business groups, to professional societies—to every form of human association" or else "'industrial democracy' will fail exactly as so-called political democracy has failed" (Follett 1998, 325).

Follett (1998) explains, "I am talking of a new method of living by which the individual shall learn to be part of social wholes, through which he shall express social wholes" (180). For Follett, such true democracy is "the quintessential art of living,—what she later called 'creative experience.' ... the art of mutually creative human intercourse, of which ethics, politics, economics, sociology and social psychology were only applications or variations" (Cabot 1934, 80). In sum, Follett argues that when governance is based on integrative process—employing the method of integration within the situation, guided by the law of the situation—true democracy results.

PROGRESS AS CREATIVE COLLABORATION

Follett continues her argument by asserting that if true democracy were to become a way of life throughout all social activities, both the individual and society would progress. While the meaning of progress today may be quite narrow in terms of material ends, this was not the case during the Progressive Era. At that time, progress was conceived by some as a relational process through which all types of evolving human needs find greater expression and fulfillment (Stout 2010a). In this way, the creative and collaborative process of self-governance itself could become the signifier of progress, as opposed to static, pre-determined, material end-values like property, monetary value, or profit.

This difference begs some explanation. As traditionally conceived, progress has been measured in a materialist and individualist manner. In a zero-sum conceptualization of resources, the progress of the individual takes away from the progress of someone else; the progress of one nation limits the potential of another. Follett suggests these win-lose fictions cause the very conflict and competition feared by Hobbes and Locke. She insists, "the evolving situation, the 'progressive integrations,' the ceaseless interweaving of new specific respondings, is the whole forward movement of existence" (Follett 2013c, 134). Therefore, she challenges individualist assumptions in both her political and economic theories.

Referring back to the ontological and psychosocial principles she holds, Follett (1998) asserts that "association is the impulse at the core of our being" (193). But as always, she is concerned about the *mode* of that association. She tells a story about veterans saying that when they return from war they miss the fellowship of their comrades, and concludes, "If the essential characteristic of war is doing things together, let us begin to do things together in peace" (Follett 1998, 195). Rather than association for destruction, Follett seeks association for creation. Indeed, she suggests "progress implies respect for the creative process" (98).

Taken together, Follett's revised conceptualizations of democracy, federalism, creative production, cooperative competition, and emergent self-governance of the political economy enable her to transform our understanding of progress. For Follett (1998), "progress is not determined by economic conditions, by physical conditions, nor by biological factors solely, but more especially by our capacity for genuine coöperation" (93). Thus, "progress from one point of view is a continuously widening of the area of association" (193) and the rate of our progress will depend upon the degree to which we actualize co-creative democracy throughout all spheres of society.[2] Follett notes that she is not alone in this realization: "There are business men today who perceive that the *process* of production is as important for the welfare of society as the *product* of production" (Follett 2003d, 141). However, just as with competitive team spirit, the collaborative group spirit must be evolved: "Collective thinking must be reverenced as an act of creation. The time spent evolving the group spirit is time spent in creating the dynamic force of our civilization" (Follett 1998, 372).

Follett believes that progress will be fostered if we understand government as a community, the economy as a community, and community as a process. Therefore, "the study of community as process is absolutely necessary for the sound development of industry. And if we should have industrial democracy—but democracy is just this, productive interrelatings" (Follett 1919, 583). By adding the notion of interrelating into her understanding of progress, Follett's definition could be stated thus: *Progress is a co-creative process of integration among an ever widening whole.* Indeed, she asserts, "social progress is to be sure coadapting" (Follett 1998, 35). "Progress does not depend upon the similarity which we *find* but on the similarity which we *achieve*" (36). Thus, "the test of our progress is neither our likenesses nor our unlikenesses, but what we are going to do with our unlikenesses. Shall I fight whatever is different from me or find the higher synthesis?" (96).

However, Follett is not Pollyanna in her views—she notes repeatedly that integration is not easy and is not always possible: "coadapting means always that the fresh unity becomes the pole of a fresh difference leading

to again new unities which lead to broader and broader fields of activity"
(Follett 1998, 35). In other words, as noted in her other discussions of
integration, disruptions in integration that occur through the inclusion
of new perspectives and experiences cause the conflict that spurs creative
responses that produce new integrations. However, Follett argues that "the
next diversity will emerge on a higher social level—this is progress" (Follett 2013c, xiii). Together, the reciprocal responses of integration produce
progress in both the individual and the whole and so "we want the plus
values of the conflict" (xiv).

As noted in her application of integration in ethics, politics, and economics, the integration of difference is an ongoing challenge but a worthy
pursuit: "The task of coadaptation is unending" (Follett 1998, 93) and so
"progress is an infinite advance towards the infinitely receding goal of infinite
perfection" (51). But through that ongoing endeavor, "society flourishes
through the satisfaction of individual human desire, yet not through as many
as possible, but through interweaving human desires" (Follett 2013c, 49) in
what Follett calls "progressive integration" (160).

FOLLETTIAN THINKING IN CONTEMPORARY THEORY

Unlike many scholars who develop theoretical frameworks without empirical grounding or practical application, Follett's thinking is grounded in
real world practice. Although her theories are built from experiences now a
century old, Salimath and Lemak (2004) argue that Follett's work "remains
contemporary for it is rooted in her keen ability to grasp the complexities
inherent in the human services enterprise" (1291). Indeed, Maddock and
Mcalpine (2006) suggest that "Mary Follett was so far ahead of her time
that she is still to be discovered as a pivotal thinker about democracy as a
process and about the role of leaders in that process" (44). Thus, although
her "profound insights have been ignored by modern scientists and policy
advisors alike" (Kakabadse et al. 2013, 80) for decades, Follett is indeed
being rediscovered, particularly in fields of practice that seek to integrate
theory and practice in *praxis.*

There is a growing consensus that such communities of practice can best
thrive when embracing a Follettian approach to achieving a diverse unity
(Novicevic et al. 2007) by allowing differences to emerge, confront one
another, and seek integration in an evolving, situated group of professionals.
This keeps applied disciplines responsive to changing conditions and

new knowledge, contributing to building learning organizations (Senge 1990; Senge 1994), and allowing groups of all kinds to network and evolve effectively in a global environment (Gehani and Gehani 2007). Thus, Follettian concepts can increasingly be found in contemporary theory in applied disciplines such as public administration, organizational management, mediation and negotiation, and social work. Here we highlight some examples from these fields' literatures that share our understanding of integrative process, its application to practice, democracy as a way of life, and progress as creative collaboration.

Governance

At the broadest scale, Follett's ideas are applied to the governance and administration of any type of organization—government, business, or nonprofit. For example, Morton and Lindquist (1997) argue that Follett's ideas could help build a coherent theoretical foundation for public administration. Because of her emphasis on integrative process, Follett's ideas consistently demand increased ongoing authentic participation in all aspects of social life, leading some to dub her not only the "prophet of management" but also the "prophet of participation," presaging "the effort to create a more democratic public administration through citizen engagement" (Morse 2006, 8) as well as to enhance "the efficiency and effectiveness of government" (Morse 2006, 10).

The growing emphasis on participatory democracy reiterates Follett's call for practices that not only yield better and more democratic results, but also "fulfills the spirit" (Cunningham 2000). Indeed, Mathews (2014) argues that a desire for such democratic participation is nascent within all of us. Thus, there is growing recognition that Follett's work provides a robust foundation for moving us from a reliance on representative governmental institutions to a model of governance as "multilevel coordination rather than authoritative decision-making" (Wachhaus 2014, 574), a "dynamic process rather than a structure" (589). This is perhaps best reflected in some articulations of what has been termed "New Governance" which is "not a static, but a dynamic set of social relations" (Cohen 2008, 517) in which "the state [is] not . . . a central and coercive power, but rather a convener, funder, catalyst, coordinator, and supervisor, and also a participant" (513).

This governance process begins at the local level with agencies utilizing participatory processes, the creation and strengthening of neighborhood associations, and co-creative community development activities. Indeed, a case study of this mix of activities can be found in Tempe, Arizona (see Stout 2010b). Such a micro-level focus on community as process is the most basic building block for developing Follett's sense of "deep" democracy; integrative action must be produced all the way down to the daily interactions between neighbors in what we describe today as building social capital (Morse 2006, 10). For instance, seeing schools as the center of neighborhood systems, Follett makes "specific recommendations on how to organize local community activities so as to make better use of existing facilities, such as the use of school premises out of hours, and her views on how community activism can provide greater substance to the democratic process" (Child 2013, 90). As such, she re-envisions the relationship between these local public institutions and the community, articulating ways they can foster participation and build community ties and democratic skills. Roll and Thomas (2014) explain that this entails "one of the chief insights of her work"; that communities will "develop their own means of creating institutions" (174). Thus, according to Morse (2006), such an approach fulfills Follett's requirement that "an authentic democracy is one in which everyone participates in self government" (10).

However, Follett's approach to governance does not stop at the micro-level of neighborhoods; she sees these local efforts interlocking outward to form larger political units to produce what Barber (1984) calls "strong democracy." As Roll and Thomas (2014) note, "by allowing self-government, the interests of a community integrate with society as a whole" (175). This process is explicated in Follett's deeply nesting, broadly inclusive federated networks in which micro and macro social processes are intricately intertwined (Cohen 2008) and "small-scale changes provide scaffolding for large-scale changes" (Ansell 2011, 52). As Mendenhall, Macomber, and Cutright (2000, 203) explain, "Follett believed that experimentation and theoretical understanding should serve the purpose of assisting the moral and social progress of the human community" (203). For this reason, Mathews (2014) likens Follett's description of governance to an ecological system—each element within the system influences the others in a way that improves (or disrupts) the health of the political system. This connection between micro-level community actions and macro-level impacts reflects Follett's description of federalism.

These prescriptions for authentic participation in self-governance also have profound implications for the roles of public agencies and public administrators. Indeed, as Ansell (2011) explains, in collaborative governance public agencies are transformed into "a central linchpin in building consent for public problem-solving" (18), making them a "nexus of democracy and governance" (3). Roll and Thomas (2014) explain that these agencies fulfill Follett's prescriptions for participatory administration "by bringing people and organizations together to the table in public service decisions" (176). Gabriele (2013) cautions, however, that these interactions must be integrative, recognizing that "ongoing exchanges between administrators and citizens will naturally vary, change, and adapt as external circumstances do" (7). This has profound implications not only for the process but also for relationships within community. As Morse (2006) notes, when such public interactions are part of an ongoing process of participation in which all are subject to the law of the situation, there is a blurring of us-them distinctions between citizens and administrators. As a result, administrators are seen "as citizens, albeit citizens with special responsibilities" (24).

Management and administration

As Follett began studying labor relations, she moved from the macro of society's governance to the micro of organizational management. Here, Follett refined her ideas about constructive conflict and integration within industry, again using a perspective of democracy as a way of life. As noted in Chapter 9, it was perhaps during this period that she reached the height of her popularity as a lecturer, speaker, consultant, and even presidential advisor. Leading management scholars at the time were so fond of her work that they published what lectures could be found posthumously in collected volumes. Her ideas continue to resonate within various areas of management scholarship: stakeholder theory, human resource development, and leadership studies. As Aupperle (2007) notes, "one would be hard pressed to identify any management scholar who has had as many seminal contributions to the field of management" (363) and Stewart (1996) insists, it is still the case that "what she has to say is relevant" (177) as "Follett had already said much of what [was] being written in the 1990s" (178).

Although later in her career she explicitly studied private firms, Follett's understanding of integrative unity within and among firms was rooted in her own community work in Boston. This grounding in practical experience leads McLarney and Rhyno (1999) to suggest Follett "may have been one of the first action researchers" (302). Indeed, Damart (2013) argues that it was Follett's practical experience in the community centers and working with business firms in the area that allowed her to understand the interrelations that exist not only within an organization but between that organization and its environment—all interacting as part of a total situation.

This systems view can be found today in stakeholder theory, which combines organizational theory and business ethics to help managers address the varying interests of those who are impacted by organizational operations (Freeman 1984) within a network of interrelating actors in a "business ecosystem" (Moore 1993). While Follett is not mentioned in the traditional stakeholder literature, Melé (2007) notes the overlap in ideas as Follett "mentions a number of groups related to the firm to whom the manager has to pay heed, and with whom he or she has to maintain human relations" (416). Similarly, Schilling (2000) argues Follett's descriptions of integrative process "are very useful in understanding the way the firm's actions towards any single stakeholder affect the whole system and elicit feedback effects to the firm" (227). Indeed these ideas are considered "the main tenet, if not the definition, of stakeholder theory" (Schilling 2000, 230) or the "seminal approach to stakeholder theory" (Melé 2007, 405).

In recognizing firms as part of a larger system, stakeholder theory is related to issues of corporate social responsibility (Melé 2007) which emphasizes "institutional actions and their effect on the whole social system" (Davis 1967, 46). As such managers are not only encouraged to consider how the situation impacts their actions, but how their actions in turn impact the total situation. This requires careful consideration of the interests of all stakeholders within the system (Melé 2007). Applying the method of integration, Schilling (2000) explains socially responsible managers must seek to change relations among stakeholders, allowing for behaviors to evolve so that "each individual is . . . helping to create the whole of society (and being mutually created by society) via a number of pathways" including firm actions (230). This process links corporate social responsibility to a Follettian notion of social progress by utilizing the method of integration across the diverse pool of stakeholders within the social system for cross-fertilization (Schilling 2000).

Follett's examination of the interpermeation of various stakeholders also demonstrates their overlapping interests in addressing social problems, particularly "wicked problems" (Rittel and Webber 1973). Again, Follett's experiences in Boston provide a key foundation for her insights. Gabriele (2013) asserts that in this community work, "settlement women created networks anchored in democratic principles" (2) in which "by working in tandem to make decisions, network actors engage in Follett's concept of circular response management" (9-10). Thus, Follett also provides the foundation for inter-organizational collaboration in the areas of collaborative public management and public network management. Indeed, Roll and Thomas (2014) argue there is a clear "common ground between Follett's vision and the modern push toward understanding networks" (175) and that the contemporary "literature on inter-organizational networks also advances Follett's ideas in key ways" (179).

Moving from this broader system to the firm itself, Melé (2007) explains that Follett also develops a notion of corporate responsibility that applies internally to the organization. Here, an argument is made for democratic participation in the workplace where "being responsible to the functional whole gives workers a sense of service to the community" (Melé 2007, 416) of the organization. Indeed, as Weinberg (1996) explains, management theory must make adjustments to recognize "the essential humanness of organization," a change that "requires a consciousness of this reality . . . that the interpersonal dynamics that support and those that undermine can be identified and understood" (178). Making this change necessitates "envisioning new patterns of relating among employees and between them, their managers, and the situation of their work" (Weinberg 1996, 177).

Thus, following Follett, managers recognize that organizations are dynamic entities that are continually created and recreated along with the individuals who comprise them (Weinberg 1996). As such, Follett's prescriptions for organizational dynamics follow her prescriptions for governance: *democratic participation*. Child (2013) argues these recommendations are "in tune with the growing inversion of the traditional hierarchical organization 'pyramid' in the possession of knowledge and problem solving" (89), and Eylon (1998) uses Follett's ideas to transform our understanding of workplace empowerment as a delegation or sharing of power to enabling each person to function according to the law of the situation.

This is applied not only to operational workplace policies and procedures but also to issues of workplace justice. Melé (2007) notes, while Follett did not write on management ethics specifically, her ethical principles can be successfully applied in that context. For instance, Barclay (2005) explains that Follett's integrative process provides a method for managers and employees to "jointly develop definitions of fairness" such as workshops, feedback sessions, and one-on-one meetings rather than simply taking unilateral steps to understand employee complaints and provide top-down "fixes" for perceived injustices (747). Indeed, Barclay (2005) argues that

Follett's approach is even "somewhat more extreme than contemporary researchers" because integration both empowers employees and increases a sense of interpersonal justice by ensuring "all concerned parties are involved and understand why a particular decision was made" (743). Thus, "integrative unity creates a common understanding of 'justice' and aligns the interests of the parties involved" (Barclay 2005, 747). Child (2013) argues this approach is likely to be highly effective "both in quality of innovation it provides and in the level of employee commitment it generates" (89). As such "current motivational research owes a great debt to Follett's work and incorporates many of her concepts" (Roll and Thomas 2014, 180).

Barclay (2005) further argues that Follett's situation a-making expands organizational justice by understanding ethics as a "dynamic and contextual process" (751). Integrative process helps management theorists see that ideas of justice are not merely differences in static perspectives (e.g., manager versus employee), but that conceptions of justice are impacted by a reciprocal interplay between parties within the situation. Thus, managers should be trained in the method of integration to help them foster organizational justice (Barclay 2005) and other aspects of administration (Wheelock and Callahan 2006).

These ideas are being further expanded beyond traditional understandings of workplace justice to recognize that organizations can play a part in fostering human growth and potential for the individuals in the organization. Johnson (2007), for instance, refers to the workplace as chalice for spiritual growth and expression, arguing that "Follett saw relating as the means to achieving spirituality in individuals, the workplace and in other realms of society" (436). Nickel and Eikenberry (2006) argue that in this democratic approach to management, Follett presages a feminist "discursive rather than non-discursive" approach to management (373). Morton and Lindquist (1997) also liken this dialogic approach to "feminist approaches to the ethical resolution of conflict, which focuses on dialectical communication between participants to reach an integrative solution that attends to the needs of all," again demonstrating how Follett's ideas presage contemporary feminist theory (363). Banerjee (2008) likewise links her understanding of power-with to feminist theory and activism and Kaag (2008) argues that in her description, and affirmation, of power-with, Follett "anticipates the writing of Simone de Beauvoir, Hannah Arendt, and Gloria Anzeldua in suggesting that violence is antithetical to power insofar as violence seeks to destroy relationships" (150). Thus, Stivers (1996) suggests that the values displayed by Follett's approach to management can be classified as "cultur-ally 'feminine'" (163).

Considering how these elements impact organizational design, Whee-lock and Callahan (2006) note that Follett's ontology, epistemology, and axiology emphasize and integrate the three touchstone elements of Human Resource Development (HRD) theory: people, organization, and learning. They explain that "the HRD practitioner operating from Follett's perspec-tive uses adult learning to facilitate the development of the individual and the organization through group work so that an integrated unity is accom-plished" (Wheelock and Callahan 2006, 268). Indeed, as Parker (1984) argues, Follett was prescient in her realization "that in dealing with person-nel" managers must understand that "human and technical problems could never be completely separated and that an organization's standards must be allowed much more elasticity" (739). In other words, goals, technology, and individual roles within the organization are part of the evolving situation and managers must always consider how each of these elements change and interact within the situation. As such Novicevic et al. (2007) suggest that this helps us better understand organizational learning as "a relational process" (374) and Morton and Lindquist (1997) note that Follett was "enthralled by the practical and experimental nature of learning in business; she found it vital and action oriented" (352). In sum, Child (2013) sees the foundations of organizational development in Follett's emphases on "how team-working can enhance innovation, particularly in its capacity to integrate a diversity of member contributions and viewpoints" and mechanisms for coping with conflict within the organization" (89).

Organization theory is also beginning to recognize the role of the manager as a leader who fosters multiple or shared leadership through non-hierarchical methods of power-with (Wheelock and Callahan 2006). Wheelock and Callahan (2006) note that while there are similarities between Follett's approach to management and others in the field, she "introduces new thoughts regarding participatory organizations, communication, and leadership" (266). These critical changes lead McLarney and Rhyno (1999) to believe Follett's philosophy provides a new understanding of leadership, moving from a particularist focus on lead*ers* to a group focus on leader*ship*. Furthermore, they compare Follett's approach with Westley and Mintzberg's (1989) "visionary leadership" (1), arguing that Follett presages the model's emphasis on the interrelationship between leader and group: the leader must evoke participation from team members who are part of the process of integration. As Follett notes, leadership and followership are in reciprocal relationship within the group.

Following this Follettian notion of leadership, Wheelock and Callahan (2006) insist the HRD practitioner must keep "at the forefront the importance of developing leaders who institute horizontal authority, functional leadership, teamwork, power-with, and the law of the situation" (268). Gehani and Gehani (2007) go so far as to say that leaders who understand how to use power-with to evoke such participation are "better prepared even today to run a dynamic knowledge-based firm" such as the myriad "innovative global enterprises in the 21st century" (400). In this sense, Follett's version of the visionary leader is one that must also be able to foster ongoing integration, a skill that requires the ability to act as facilitators or negotiators rather than directors (Maddock and Mcalpine 2006). It is to Follett's influence in the field of negotiation that we now turn.

Negotiation

Negotiation is a "process that pervades every level of human interaction" (Kolb 1996, 339). Therefore, while it is a distinct field of practice, it is applied in all types of group contexts. The negotiation literature has been fundamentally influenced by Follett; indeed, Kolb (1996) dubs her "the mother of the contemporary field" (339) and Drucker (1995) asserts, "If Mary Parker Follett is known today at all, it is for her 'Constructive Conflict'" (4). Some have suggested that it is this valuable contribution to negotiation that has driven Follett's resurgence in popularity more generally (Fry and Thomas 1996; Melé 2007). Davis (1991) insists that Follett's emphasis on the malleability of facts and multiplicity of perspective, and therefore the need for dialogue between multiple parties (experts, decision-makers, lay-people), "might have been describing a modern-day public policy mediation or negotiated investment strategy" (137). Follett's ideas continue to provide guidance to this area of negotiation as her "often humorous and always thought-provoking analysis serves as a useful 'checklist' for today's negotiators, mediators, arbitrators, facilitators, and factfinders," insisting that "her approach is especially valuable to those involved in complex negotiations" (Davis 1991, 131).

Cohen (2008) explains the practice of negotiation links to theories of New Governance as a facilitative practice. In essence, both theories mirror Follett's prescriptions for employing the method of integration and its elements of constructive conflict. Follett recognizes that integrative process within the total situation a-making will enable local negotiations to "scale up" to the national or even global level. Thus, the negotiation literature, which provides detailed analysis of how to apply the concept of constructive conflict in practice at the micro level is essential to the macro level of Follett's deeply-nesting federalism.

Regardless of the scale of application, negotiation is generally split into two primary approaches based on the work of Walton and McKersie (1965): distributive negotiation and integrative negotiation. The former assumes a static pool of resources in a zero-sum game in which individuals' interests are in competition with one another. The latter assumes a dynamic situation and uses "principled bargaining" inspired by Follett's recommendation of integration as a preferred method to either domination or compromise when addressing conflict (Kolb 1996; Shapiro 2012). Integrative negotiation begins with the assumption that "a higher joint benefit is possible than through compromise" and negotiators seek to find "third way" options that can integrate the interests of the negotiating parties rather than seek domination or compromise based on existing positions (Kolb 1996, 341).

The integrative approach to bargaining has five primary assertions: (1) compromise is neither ideal nor necessary; (2) power relations affect conflict resolution; (3) conflict is functional and necessary; (4) interpersonal dynamics play an important role in conflict negotiations; and, (5) conflict situations can, and should, be approached in a joint manner (Jones-Patulli 2011, 6). This approach clearly reflects "Follett's views on conflict and integrative unity" and as such "she is known as a leader in integrative negotiations" (Wheelock and Callahan 2006, 266). Indeed, the approach and its label are derived from Follett's method of integration (Pruitt and Lewis 1975) even though it was appropriated and popularized by Fisher and Ury (1991).[3]

Integrative bargaining assumes *interdependent* negotiators rather than particularist notions of interests (Kolb 1996). Indeed, Kolb (1996) insists that it is in this shift from individual interests to *relationships*, that bargaining can be considered integrative in the Follettian sense. This emphasis on relationship in negotiations creates an atmosphere of connectedness, emphasizing a sense of interdependence and trust in which negotiations can generate more fruitful outcomes because facilitators understand that not only the facts of the situation are malleable and subject to multiple interpretations (Davis 1991) but also that goals and interests are likewise unfixed (Kolb 1996). Thus, just as fact-finding and interpretation is a joint affair, so is the uncovering and determination of interests and goals. This collaborative approach leads Morton and Lindquist (1997) to argue that Follett's integrative method aligns with feminist approaches to conflict resolution which "advocate alternative methods to generate creative solutions that attend to the needs and interests of each participant" (366), reinforcing attention to organizational justice as discussed above.

Cohen (2008) cautions, however, that existing social hierarchies and power imbalances may be elements of the situation and thus shape individuals, interests, and social interactions; therefore, integrative processes must be mindful of these potential imbalances within relationships to prevent reinforcing power-over in the name of power-with. Furthermore, there is also a concern that elements of particularism remain not only in distributive negotiation, but in the integrative negotiation literature as well. Thus, some are now suggesting Follett's imprint can perhaps be better implemented in a more contemporary successor: *collaborative* negotiation (Cohen 2008). In collaborative negotiation parties work together to understand individual and collective interests and generate solutions that meet the situational interests of all parties (Lewicki, Saunders, and Barry 2003).

Like Follett, negotiation practitioners insist that circular response without intentional integration is problematic and therefore negotiation practitioners seek to train individuals in the skills needed to become "self-reflexive agents" (Cohen 2008, 523), a realization that has implications "at both the micro and macro level" (Schilling 2000, 224). Remembering Cohen's connection between New Governance and negotiation, we see that both literatures reject a zero-sum game in negotiations and instead recognize that the individuals, resources, interests, and desires in any situation are relationally determined and therefore dynamic rather than static—all may expand or contract together rather. Further, both literatures assume a relational individual engaged in "perceptual feedback loops" (Cohen 2008, 524) that function according to Follett's concept of integrative process. The field of social work pulls together these macro and micro assumptions and puts these prescriptions into practice at the individual and family level of analysis. It is to this area of the literature we now turn.

Social work

Recalling that Follett's theory building began in the direct practice of social work in her activities around "founding, developing, and leading the community centres movement" during the Progressive Era (Phillips

2010, 50), "her experience clearly played a large role in her thinking, providing empirical evidence of how people work best together" (Maddock and Mcalpine 2006). Indeed, it makes sense that her philosophy would be grounded in her social work experience; a vantage point from which she could understand functional unity in groups, engage in integrative negotiation, see various family and community members impacting one another in circular response, and recognize that micro-level actions ripple out into the macro-level political and social spheres. And yet, "while others have worked in community development, few have connected their experience and thinking to the state and its governance arrangements, nor have they so clearly related social organisation [*sic*] and political institutions to psychology and social relationships" (Maddock and Mcalpine 2006). Therefore, Follett offers a uniquely holistic view of social work, the bulk of which occurs at the nexus between government and community in the nonprofit sector—the predominant site of social work.

While we have seen that Follett's ideas have broad implications, it is useful to see how they are being applied *within* the field of social work since they are so heavily influenced by her social work experience. While discussion of her work is not widely found in the social work literature, Selber and Austin (1997) argue that Follett's management concepts are particularly fruitful for the field because her philosophy provides robust support for central concepts "such as a strengths perspective and recognition of the worth of each person," the appreciation of diversity, and focus on the empowerment of individuals (12). Her method of integration itself—the breaking of wholes into component parts and examining differences for deeper understanding of the total situation—parallels precisely the "social work problem-solving model" (12).

More specifically, Cohen (2011) draws on Follett to improve established approaches to social work, such as the standard "authority-based practice" (ABP) and emerging paradigm of "evidence-based practice" (EBP). He argues that such methods assume static, well-defined problems and rely almost explicitly on empirical data to understand problems to determine fixed, categorical solutions. These approaches also rely on top-down implementation based either on positional authority or technical expertise, respectively. In contrast, he insists "the social systems in which social workers must engage are embedded in *turbulent environments*, in which dynamic processes arise from the interactions with other social systems and from changes in environment" (341)—an understanding well-supported by Follett's descriptions of integrative process within the situation. In this context, Cohen (2011) calls for a creative and integrative approach in which problem-solving is a process of discovery involving the social worker, client, and client system "with the aim of creating a desired future for clients within the context of their total situation" (342). Like Follett, Cohen stresses that these processes are non-linear and iterative with no clear culmination, "with the various aspects appearing over and over again" (343).

To better fit these assumptions, Cohen (2011) draws upon the work of Follett, Dewey, and Simon to craft an approach to social work he calls design-based practice (DBP). This approach: (1) sees knowledge creation as a joint and experiential process; (2) assumes a dynamic environment; (3) desired goals are discovered and refined through ongoing integration and joint evaluation; and (4) empowers clients using reflective and interactive process. Each of these components is clearly reflective of Follett's philosophical commitments and nicely amends Simon's approach to bounded rationality. Thus in this approach "design" does not mean *orchestrated*, but, drawing from Follett's facilitative leadership, is rather a purposeful and reflective process in which the designed plan of action in any given situation is jointly determined and adjusted through an ongoing process of integration. Such an approach is "more attuned to the complexities of the contextual environment in which social work operates and to the challenges facing the field of social work in the future" (Cohen 2011, 338).

Reflecting this connection, Cohen further aligns DBP with Follett's components of organizational leadership (evoking, interacting, integrating, emerging), while adjusting her approach slightly. He similarly identifies four key elements: (1) Evoking—the social worker draws "out the perceptions, assumptions, and desires of the client, the practitioner, and major stakeholders with respect to the client's situation"; (2) Integrating—"identifying the alternative representations or scenarios for action and then creating a unifying design through reciprocal interaction and mutual adjustment"; (3) Emerging—"the client or client system begins to try out or experiment with new behaviors, organizational forms or structures that are consistent with the unifying design"; and (4) Adapting—continually re-evaluating and adjusting to the changing situation through creative and innovative means (Cohen 2011, 343). This process employs the integrative method to work with clients and client systems in a way that is beneficial for all involved.

Unfortunately, Cohen (2011) notes that such an explicitly integrative design-oriented approach has not yet become prominent in schools of social work. Instead, students are still taught to "describe, understand, and criticize systems, but not to design or redesign them" (344). Yet social work is focused on improving the situations of its clients by understanding and improving *relationships* as a means of bringing forth change—both for individuals and for their groups (Cohen 2011). This is precisely what Follett's philosophy brings to social work in concrete terms; providing real guidance for social workers to act as change agents, to "use this relationship as a foundation for engaging clients in designing their own desired futures and monitoring their progress" (345). We concur, adding only the clarification that per Follettian thinking monitoring should be a joint affair.

SUMMARY

It is clear that the fruits of Follettian governance are as desirable today as they were upon their introduction and discussion in the decades leading up to World War II. This resurgence of interest in integrative process and its applications to practice in governance, management and administration, negotiation, and social work is encouraging because of the promise it holds for generating democracy as a way of life and progress through creative collaboration. Thus, in Chapter 13 we consider such affirmation in light of the contemporary context.

ENDNOTES

1. Here again, Follett presages the vision of relational sociology: "It brings about a complex citizenship that operates by valorizing the principle of relationality applied to all of society's spheres" (Donati 2014, 113).

2. As noted by Stout (2010a), public intellectual and businessman Henry George (1929) shares this holistic interpretation of progress.

3. Despite developing an approach to negotiation that clearly draws from Follett, and using one of her well-known stories as an illustration in their book, Fisher and Ury (1991) do not credit Follett as an influence in their acclaimed book other than to recognize her as the source of the case example in their foreword.

❧ 13 ❧

An Affirmation of Follettian Governance: Why Now?

In Chapter 1, we suggested that the contemporary milieu is more welcoming and fitted to what we call Follettian governance (Stout and Staton 2011) than prior historical moments. Roll and Thomas (2014) concur, suggesting that Follett's vision of the New State "is today more realistic than at the time of its conception" (180). This chapter discusses the contemporary condition in more detail, carefully considering some of changes that have taken place as our world becomes increasingly globalized and a market-oriented worldview becomes more pronounced. We highlight some of the current crises in the social and governance spheres, as well as resistance movements that are emerging in response to these crises. This is carefully considered both empirically and theoretically, followed by an assertion that Follettian thinking is more fruitful in this context than other approaches. We currently see a time when Follett's ideas provide a better foundation for democracy as a way of life—for *everyone*.

THE CONTEMPORARY CONTEXT OF GLOBALIZATION

Reiterating from Chapter 1, Follett (2003e) claimed society in the early 1900s was in desperate condition due to: "(1) exploitation of our natural resources whose day is now nearly over; (2) keener competition; (3) scarcity of labour [sic]; (4) a broader conception of the ethics of human relations; (5) the growing idea of business as a public service which carries with it a sense of responsibility for its efficient conduct" (122). In these five succinct points, Follett articulates the crises of environmental, social, and economic sustainability that were emerging after the Industrial Revolution. Her ideas for governance were developed with these kinds of challenges in mind, yet have never been adequately considered or applied to the very problems she directly addresses. Indeed, in the wake of globalization, the problems Follett sought to address have only grown in urgency.

There appears to be rather widespread agreement that the forces of globalization have impacted every natural and societal system. Drawing from a sample of theoretical physics, new materialism, process theology, post-humanism, sociology, and political theory, we can see that the human predicament is rife with crises. As theoretical physicist David Bohm (2004) succinctly puts it, "What are the troubles of the world? They seem so many that we can hardly begin even to list them" (55). However, we generally categorize them as environmental, economic, and social issues, with particular emphasis on "the major problems of climate change, global inequality, and warfare that face the world today" (Edwards 2010, 297). In each of the crises outlined below, while the conditions seem bleak, we also note emerging responses.

Environmental crisis

The umbrella under which environmental concerns have become collected is still generally the issue of climate change. At the time of this writing, while political arguments about its causes continue, it is generally accepted that the impacts of climate change resonate around the globe, "from melting glaciers, sea ice and tundra, to extreme weather events and drought" (Randolph 2012, 127). In the long term, such changes threaten human habitations. As Speth (2008) warns: "If you take an honest look at today's destructive environmental trends, it is impossible not to conclude that they profoundly threaten human prospects and life as we know it on the planet" (17). In the short term, climate change exacerbates stressors in the economy due to "higher fossil fuel and electricity prices" (Randolph 2012, 127). Awareness of the environmental crisis aggravated by pollution is augmented by the contemporary understanding of the impacts of agricultural and industrial practices that wreak havoc on human health and biodiversity at local, regional, and global levels. Indeed, the critical nature of the environmental impacts currently underway have led many biologists to argue that a sixth mass extinction is already underway; one that is driven by such human activity (Barnosky et al. 2011).

Philosophically, these practices are largely driven by market economic assumptions that view natural resources as merely boundless means to profit.

Demand for an ever-increasing quality of life—as determined by Western standards—for ever-increasing numbers of people, results in mass harvesting of natural resources without attention to system limitations or impact on the overall ecosystem. Such practices, driven by both profit and demand are often operated by large multinational corporations.

For instance, the widely publicized 2010 oil spill from BP's *Deepwater Horizon* oil rig, occurred in part due to "a series of cost-cutting moves" on the part of BP and its contractors (Freudenburg and Gramling 2011, 15) and the catastrophe "initiated a previously unknown category of marine pollution" (Somasundaran et al. 2014, 19) the full impacts of which will not be known for some time. The use of hydraulic fracturing to reach ever more remote sources of natural gas have profound health impacts on local communities and wildlife populations through soil and water contamination (Kassotis et al. 2014; Osborn et al. 2011). The process is known to cause microearthquakes and not only has the number of events been increasing in areas with historically low risks, as the wells become deeper the severity of earthquakes induced are also increasing (Ellsworth 2013).

This demand for inexpensive products has also led to large scale agricultural production which, while it has "been successful in increasing food production, it has also caused extensive environmental damage" (Foley et al. 2005, 570). Industrial farm animal production (IFAP) seeks to maximize profit by raising food animals in highly compact and often enclosed environments (concentrated animal feedlot operations). This high concentration of animals results in increased use of antibiotics and production of animal waste, polluting surrounding soil and water (Halden and Schwab 2008; Mallin and Cahoon 2003). These high-density operations also place unsustainable pressures on land and water resources to feed the livestock, resulting in nutrient depletion in topsoil, soil erosion and global deforestation (Halden and Schwab 2008) and have been calculated to have a larger impact on global warming than the transportation sector (Steinfeld et al. 2006). Intensive animal and agricultural production practices for food production utilize high levels of both pesticides and nitrogen-rich fertilizers and is linked to pollution and degradation of soil, eutrophication of water ways that causes toxic algal blooms in critical water sources, loss of biodiversity, and smog (Kane et al. 2014; Mallin and Cahoon 2003; Tilman et al. 2002). These impacts compromise the health of the global ecosystem. Despite the growing understanding of the widespread harmful impacts of energy and food production, such practices continue to be encouraged by an economic model based on the assumption of limitless growth (Kakabadse et al. 2013; Roy and Crooks 2011), which relegates the impacts on critical natural factors such as the ozone layer, underground aquifers, topsoil quality, and biodiversity to the status of externalities not quantified or considered in the system. Indeed, such "externalities" have profound *internal* implications for life on this planet. As zoologist and environmentalist David Suzuki argues, "that economy is not based in anything like the real world" (as quoted in Roy and Crooks 2011).

Due to the environmental crises of climate change and loss of biodiversity, the human *condition* has become a *predicament*—a devastating system that has led us to the brink of ecological disaster that reveals the delicate balance of the ecosystem; what Connolly (2013) characterizes as "the fragility of things." Indeed, the effects of pollution, loss of biodiversity, and climate change are not, and cannot be isolated; these crises threaten everyone, regardless of nationality. This unsustainable system creates widespread "disruptive effects on our economic and social systems, which now must bear the costs of conversion to a low-carbon, green economy" (Randolph 2012, 127).

Thus, while Follett was apt in her identification of the exploitation of our natural resources as a key problem, rather than subsiding as knowledge of the problem grew, these processes unfortunately continue to be exacerbated by the very sociopolitical conditions she criticized nearly one hundred years ago: hierarchy (domination over nature) and competition (exploitation for profit). Accordingly, the human predicament is typically attributed to the technological and financial practices of advanced capitalism, or more delicately framed as "the vagaries of the international economy" (Coole and Frost 2010b, 16). In short, the development machine "encounters structural limitations in its external and internal environments" (Donati 2014, 19). Its external limits are the natural environment's capacity to accommodate our practices. Today, these issues "acquire an urgency unimaginable just a generation ago" (Coole and Frost 2010b, 16).

Awareness of these crises "inaugurates a negative or reactive form of pan-human planetary bond, which recomposes humanity around a commonly shared bond of vulnerability, but also connects the human to the fate of other species" (Braidotti 2013, 111). Political theorist William Connolly (2011) refers to this situation as the "human estate" (5)—a particular world of concern as opposed to all other force-fields of becoming. While the earth's geological world may not be concerned with the human estate, we must be quite concerned with its sustainability. As such, responses in contemporary physical and social sciences increasingly "rest on an enlarged sense of inter-connection between self and others, including the non-human or 'earth' others" (Braidotti 2013, 47-48)—a perspective that has been called a "*zoe*-egalitarianism*" (71) in reference to Life or existence writ large.

Contemporary social sciences and humanities argue that our very survival demands that we reclaim an understanding of existence beyond human consciousness and perception to become embodied and embed-ded in nature once again. This is beginning to happen in concrete ways through broad public recognition of the concept of our individual and collective carbon footprints and specific actions that can be taken individu-ally to mitigate them. By applying non-hierarchical, collaborative efforts, still larger strides can be achieved. For instance resource management can be enhanced by creating volunteer opportunities "in implementation of natural resource projects, such as watershed monitoring, trail maintenance, habitat enhancement, and stream bank restoration" (Randolph 2012, 132). Likewise, planning for natural hazards mitigation is beginning to include collaborative community efforts in "(1) planning for long-term social, economic, and environmental sustainability, and (2) taking immediate action to strengthen neighborhood and organizational capacity" (135). Such efforts are best exemplified currently in the ICLEI—Local Govern-ments for Sustainability network (formerly the International Council of Local Environmental Initiatives)—with its various programs for developing resilient, sustainable urban areas.

Economic crisis

As noted above, economic growth faces limitations in the form of natu-ral resources, but our economic systems face internal limitations as well (Donati 2014). The internal limitations of the current approach to eco-nomic development peaked most recently in the global economic crisis of 2008 and the following recession through 2012 or beyond, depending on one's perspective. Indeed, the exacerbating conditions underlying the global financial crisis (GFC) are the very same as those driving our contemporary environmental crisis: an "institutional order of the whole society" (Donati 2014, 73) that is based on an assumption of limitless progress and growth. In response to this observation, Kakabadse et al. (2013) argue that "the roots of the current GFC can be seen in the wave after wave of neo-liberal ideological projections capturing government policy since the days of Thatcher and Reagan in the late 1970s" (81). Indeed, the supposition of endless resources, and the pitting of liberal competition and profit against socialist solidarity and redistribution leads sociologist Pierpaolo Donati (2014) to conclude that the crash was due to the fact that economic systems based in a tension between freedom (individualism) and control (holism) *"are not sustainable as long-term systems"* (45).

By manipulating the very dualism Follett critiques, these neoliberal strains of free market capitalism are able to use fear of strong centralized control and the current wave of globalization to become a hegemonic force for global movement toward deregulation and the hollowing out of governments (Love 2013). The result is a spreading ideology wherein the political economy is seen as the only or best type of self-organizing and self-regulating system (Connolly 2013). Yet, it is one that "leads to moral/ ethical pervasions spawning rapacious greed and corruption" (Kakabadse et al. 2013, 81). Thus, instead of diversifying economic and social perspectives, globalization has been driven by market ideology and tends to homogenize cultures: "It is an ideology that defines basic expectations about the roles and behaviors of individuals and institutions" (Kettl 2000, 490). The resulting movement has been one that focuses on "deregulation as a form of freedom" in which "global corporatism and the 'utopia' of unlimited consumption prevail" (Kakabadse et al. 2013, 81).

This hegemonic argument is difficult to deny, as the key actors in globalization and the push toward international governance include the World Bank, the International Money Fund, various United Nations initiatives, the Organization for Economic Cooperation and Development, and the G-20 (Fremond and Capaul 2002; Kettl 2000). These organizations wield strong influence over public policy on international debt, aid, and trade, and generally attach requirements to grants of favorable trade status and development assistance. In their shared model, governments are supported based on democratic accountability, political stability, safety and security, effectiveness, lack of regulatory burden, rule of law, and lack of corruption (Fremond and Capaul 2002). According to these groups, good governance is defined as "transparency and accountability in government, economic liberalization and privatization, civil society participation, and respect for human rights, democracy and the rule of law" (Collingwood 2003, 55). In other words, the role of government is to ensure "the rights of outside suppliers of equity finance to corporations are protected and receive a fair return" (Fremond and Capaul 2002, ii). Such policies use power imbalances and economic need to force capitalist market policies on populations regardless of whether such economic and governance structures are culturally appropriate.

Despite the negative global impact of such policies, in the face of the financial crises that ensue, this system continues to respond with more of the same; thus, attempts to recapture the runaway impacts that led to the global financial crisis necessarily fail to adequately mitigate the problem. Indeed, in the societies whose neoliberal policies sparked the GFC, Kakabadse et al. (2013) argue that economic responses to the crash double-down on these market forces and thus merely exacerbate the original problems that created it. These responses build in additional incentives for continued greed and corruption through policies such as "too big to fail," regulatory capture, and ongoing failures in corporate governance that do not to see past the hegemonic "group think" of the (ostensibly) free market mentality. As a result, the GFC not only increased economic disparities in the short-term but policies addressing it continue to fuel asymmetries, injustices, and resentments both within and among regions, fostering the "long-term and increasing gap between rich and poor [that] is sometimes called 'global apartheid'" (Griffin 2007, 104). These conditions amplify global antagonisms and hostilities that impact both state and market processes, bleeding out into all social roles (Connolly 2011).

In response to growing awareness of these disparities, as well as the widespread impact of the crisis, Connolly (2013) suggests that the economic crash produced a sort of cultural disbelief—how could government and the market allow this to happen? He argues that if we make "a critical account of the expansion, intensification, and acceleration of neoliberal capitalism, you may be brought face-to-face with the fragility of things today—that is, with growing gaps and dislocations between the demands neoliberalism makes upon several human activities and nonhuman fields and the capacities of both to meet them" (10). With the capitalist system failure and alternatives being practiced in various social movements, he believes we may be at a turning point in political economy quite similar to where religion stood before the Enlightenment and where the physical sciences stood as the Newtonian system began to collapse into quantum and complexity theory. Prozorov (2014b) agrees, noting that the Occupy movement exemplifies a promising "emancipatory, egalitarian and communitarian orientation" (xx).

More specifically oriented toward economic action, community development initiatives that seek to link the micro and macropolitical have been carried forward by groups like the Industrial Areas Foundation (IAF) and the Local Initiatives Support Corporation (LISC). These large non-government organizations share a common value of the importance of supporting grassroots-driven community building and the interrelating among people and place. Similarly, alternative economic systems based in cooperative competition are well established by the Mondragon Corporation of federated worker cooperatives in the Basque region of Spain (Cheney 2001; Ormaechea 2001). This Mondragon model has begun to spread, and can be seen in emerging efforts in the United States such as the Ever-green Cooperatives Initiative of Cleveland, Ohio which has sparked what is becoming known as "the Cleveland model," an approach that "focuses on economic inclusion and building local economy from the ground up" (Howard, Kuri, and Lee 2010, 3).

Social crisis

The result of this globalizing economic force has been an "Economization of the World" (Waldo 1988, 931) through which all forms of social relationship become transactions with an economic or market-like character (Ramos 1981). Some describe this globalization as a force that produces what could be called an "economic polity" as opposed to a political economy (Wolin 1981, 31). As such, many feel globalization "is increasingly forcing us to live in an economy rather than a society" (Smadja 2000, 64).

Most contemporary critical social theory perspectives see advanced capitalism driving the human predicament: "all living species are caught in the spinning machine of the global economy" in which natural resources and living organisms alike are commodified in a "bio-technological indus-trial complex" (Braidotti 2013, 7). This machine has, in many ways, taken on a life of its own such that the "contemporary global condition that now exceeds the control of any market system, state, or network of states" (Connolly 2011, 127). In this economized worldview, the citizen's role in government has almost disappeared—governance has been de-politicized (Stivers 2008) and we have replaced civic virtue with "civic commercial-ism" (Ventriss 1991, 121). We have become little more than "citizens of corporate-nations" (King and Zanetti 2005, 21).

In this market-dominated context, producers are actually in control of exchange (Thorne, 2010) rather than consumers, as rhetorically promised. Indeed, Debord (1994) likens the neoliberal marketplace to a flashy spectacle because it is intended to distract and mislead the consumer in order to hide power imbalances. The market-oriented policies and rhetoric of neoliberalism thus work to make concentrated power within the globalizing market invisible while creating a visible, though false, sense of individual empowerment (Thorne & Kouzmin, 2004, 2006). This "colonization of the life-world" (Habermas 1989, 54) has allowed the infiltration and hegemony of market values throughout all social institutions and the corresponding loss of other values is damaging political and civic life.

In the neoliberal marketplace of late capitalism, individuals are ostensibly free to consume as they choose. However, "the dynamics of consumption actually render the individual more rather than less vulnerable to control" (Barber, 2007, p. 36). Even as the consumer strives to construct identity through consumption, she remains fragmented through the proliferation of niche markets. Indeed, the "choices" offered by the market are disempowering because they are manipulated and multiplied, often drowning out authentic needs with manufactured needs (Marcuse, 1964). Individual consumers become increasingly subject to manipulation by market forces (Barber, 2007; McSwite, 1997), vulnerable to such manipulation because their yearning for stable identity (Kinnvall, 2004). As a result, identity politics further divides and separates individuals across various characteristics, and broadly inclusive communities disappear.

Yet, as Bauman (2001) explains, "this blatantly conflicts with everyday experience in (and sociological studies of) the worlds of work, family and local community, which show the individual is not a monad but is self-insufficient and increasingly tied to others, including at the level of world-wide networks and institutions" (xxi). This networking results in a strange conundrum in which, despite the degradation of community, we are more connected via communications technologies than ever before. But, as theoretical physicist David Bohm (2004) argues, "in spite of this worldwide system of linkages, there is, at this very moment, a general feeling that communication is breaking down everywhere, on an unparalleled scale" (1). By this he means our capacity for actual *dialogue*—the listening and mutual understanding that enables integrative change—is less rather than more. We are more diverse and less connected than ever before and have fewer skills to "make common" (e.g., communicate) shared meanings. Thus, while "society is based on shared meanings, which constitute the culture. . . . at present, the society at large has a very incoherent set of meanings" (32).

Bohm argues that this is because Western languages and worldviews actually disable our abilities to be open, withhold judgment, and allow shared meanings to emerge. We use discussion to analyze and fragment meanings and debate to proliferate our own understandings. Unfortunately, this is "not merely making divisions, but it is breaking things up which are not really separate" (Bohm 2004, 56). And, as social agreements about everything from language meanings to identity and political ideology break down, the human condition is rapidly becoming that of the *fragmented individual* (Love 2012)—an isolated and de-centered self that is at the effect of many shifting social constructions of identity that have less and less to do with an authentic essence of one's own. This condition corresponds with the social type of atomism (Douglas 1996) in which there is no group and thus no social order.

Beck and Beck-Gernsheim (2001) describe the sociological impact of this spreading neoliberal ideal as "individualization"—a paradoxical situation in which self-sufficiency is rhetorically espoused but increasingly less feasible. Indeed, our globalized postmodern society is increasingly experienced as "'paradoxical community': a community made by people without any real community" (Donati 2014, 13), or a "a paradoxical collectivity of reciprocal individualization" (Bauman 2001, xxi). As Bauman (2001) explains, "Neoliberal economics rests upon an image of the autarkic human self. It assumes that individuals alone can master the whole of their lives, that they derive and renew their capacity for action from within themselves" (xxi). As such, coexistence cannot be achieved from the atomistic, binary perspective of individualism. Nor can a collective culture be achieved through our standard attempts to balance freedom and control which prevent society from "developing new meaningful and stable relations" (Donati 2014, 5). Thus, while globalization is increasingly bringing more people into an ever-widening economic community, the "ethic of individual self-fulfillment and achievement" is fracturing all other communities, creating "an age in which the social order of the nation state, class, ethnicity and the traditional family is in decline" (Beck and Beck-Gernsheim 2001, 22). This leads to "a society where no one is any longer recognizable by anyone else, [and] each individual is necessarily unable to recognize his own reality" (Debord 1994, 152).

To address this paradoxical situation in which the individual is empowered rhetorically while disempowered economically, socially, and politically, where communication technology is advancing means of self-expression while communication between individuals is atrophied, we must seek a "posthuman politics" (Braidotti 2006) that recognizes the primacy of relation, interdependence, and *life* writ large. Because we still waiver among eternal or lifeless ontologies, posthumanist Rosi Braidotti (2003) argues "our public morality is simply not up to the challenge of the scale and complexity of damages engendered by our technological advances. This gives rise to a double ethical urgency: firstly, how to turn anxiety and the tendency to mourn the loss of the natural order into effective social and political action, and secondly, how to ground such an action in the responsibility for future generation, in the spirit of social sustainability" (112-13). We must "start from the empirical imperative to think global, but act local, to develop an institutional frame that actualized a posthuman practice that is 'worthy of our times'" (Braidotti 2011, 177). This must be done without cynicism or nihilism, with a metapolitics beyond resistance that "maintains the possibility of political transformation without articulating any [substantive] universal principles that would prescribe its direction" (Prozorov 2014a, 45).

Such an affirmative "politics of becoming" (Connolly 1999) must be based on an "affirmative ethics . . . based on the praxis of constructing positivity" (Braidotti 2013, 129) that is "grounded in a sense of responsibility and inter-generational accountability" (192). Connolly (2013) agrees but notes that this affirmative perspective "seems insufficiently articulated in radical theory today" (31). Similar to Donati (2014), he argues that none of the ideological positions promoted thus far are sufficient to meet the contemporary condition: "Neither neoliberal theory, nor socialist productivism, nor deep ecology, nor social democracy in its classic form" (37). Prozorov (2014a) agrees, arguing that all attempts to combine or balance community, equality, and freedom have failed.

At the individual level, rather than staking claims through identity politics, people are exploring their own subjectivities and their differences with cultural others to find ways of living *together* while maintaining important differences such as gender, class, race, ethnicity, age, and sexual orientation. Through efforts like Occupy Together, social movements of resistance and refusal are growing and linking up to locate strategic sites of social and political action to pursue productive change to structural systems through "vibrant pluralist assemblage acting at multiple sites . . . rather than . . . a mere electoral constellation" (Connolly 2013, 41). As the Commission on Global Governance argues, "the emergence of a global civil society, with many movements reinforcing a sense of human solidarity, reflects a large increase in the capacity and will of people to take control of their own lives" (Carlsson and Ramphal 1995, 335). While increasingly globalized interconnection through technology may face the difficulties highlighted above, due in part to these advances, "more and more people have begun to realize that there are many other worlds, other forms of life, other faiths, other worldviews and perspectives. That is to say there is wisdom, truth, and beauty in other traditions, in other places" (Wang 2012, 44).

Summary

Clearly, the crisis of sustainability confronted at environmental, economic, and social fronts demands a theoretical response. Furthermore, it is certain that Follett saw the writing on the wall even in her own time, in her curiously prescient manner. While it is clear that received social, economic, and political theories have contributed to these crises, alternatives that merely critique cannot help build that which the social movements seek. Therefore, we must consider all three types of theoretical response—to perpetuate received approaches through incrementalism, to attempt tearing down the master's house with his own tools (critique toward reform), or to craft new tools altogether (affirmation of transformation). Here, we will consider the current conversation in governance theory in comparison with Follett's thinking on how to respond to the contemporary context of globalization.

CONTEMPORARY GOVERNANCE THEORY[1]

What society believes governance to be changes over time and across place. We find ourselves in a contemporary governance context in which there is less organizational hierarchy and control within the institutions of society, but there is more competition. We have not eliminated the original institutions, but rather changed the rules of engagement from what might be described as the authoritative dictates of classical conservative liberalism to the pluralist and market-like transactions of modern liberalism and neoliberalism. As noted in the discussion of the contemporary context, we may seem to be significantly more autonomous from hierarchical domination, but we are prevented from forming social bonds due to the overwhelming competitive spirit imbuing the political economy (Stout 2010a). And yet, we also have not escaped the shared assumption of all forms of liberalism: that we can be collectively represented by either people or ideas.

Most Western democracies hold sovereign prerogative within the state or federated states because it empowers the representatives and administrators who comprise the state and control its laws (Ostrom 1989).

Sovereignty represents political power—the power to decide and to act not only for oneself, but in a manner that affects others. The sovereign is "above or superior to all others; chief; greatest; supreme . . . supreme in power, rank, or authority . . . holding the position of ruler; royal; reigning . . . independent of all others" (Neufeldt 1996, 1283). When those with authority to act on behalf of the government are for all intents and purposes the principal authority for the jurisdiction, the jurisdictional members are denied their full sovereignty.

Clearly, this is the meaning of sovereignty that governance theory cannot seem to escape. By establishing a representative system of government, we have retained symbolic sovereignty within the independent individual while imbuing institutions of the state with functional political authority through the supposedly voluntary will of an abstraction called the People (Catlaw 2007). Through this system all those who are considered citizens are able to choose their representatives and temporarily lend their sovereignty to them until the next election. This political authority is then delegated at least in some part to public administrators who are made answerable through various mechanisms. Through increasing intersectoral and international partnerships of various types, this sovereignty is "lent" even further, with even less electoral control. Yet, the human and social conditions outlined above deny the possibility of objectivity of any kind, ensuring a corollary impossibility of representation of any type (Sarup 1989).

Rather than empowering self-government, this process deepens tensions between the rhetorically sovereign individual and a functionally sovereign representative state, creating, exacerbating and augmenting the paradoxical nature of individualism felt in the social context. There the supposed fully self-sufficient individual is cut off from the community; in the context of representation, self-governing voice exists only *through* community, and yet individualization breeds expectations of *"individual representations of the People"* (Catlaw 2007, 181). However, when sovereignty is handed over through systems of representation the individual subsequently finds herself under the purview of authority given to another entity (White 1990), and increasingly does not see herself in the "mirror" of representation subsequently put forth (Catlaw 2007). Catlaw (2007) depicts the impact of this dissociation quite clearly; as we become increasingly individualized, "we see the collapse of the mass into the individual" (181). This echoes Follett's understandings of imitation in crowds and her critique thereof.

With the alienating tendencies of the social context highlighted above exacerbated by the dissociative pathology of representation, apathy can be expected with corresponding erosion of participation, leaving individuals isolated under the authority of the sovereign. This allows power to concentrate in the hands of a few "sovereign Individuals," elevated by their relative power within the market and, therefore, within the political sphere (Thorne 2010). This gives rise to the "society of control" (Catlaw 2007, 156), where control is omnipresent in both centralized and decentralized forms and individuals are disempowered. In this atmosphere, neoliberal policies continue to amplify the ontology of individualism, acting as a "midwife [to] a new world order" (Witt 2010, 924).

In the contemporary context, then, *governments* themselves are increasingly decentered among other actors across sectors. "Government—the State—is no longer the defining ingredient" (Stivers 2008, 104). Again, as part of neoliberal reforms, a key element of this phenomenon is the push toward government load-shedding of functions and privatization of delivery exemplified in reform movements like reinventing government (Gore and Clinton 1993; Osborne & Gaebler 1992) and the New Public Management (Hood 1996). In short, the public good is increasingly co-produced by governments, corporations, and a variety of nonprofit Non-Governmental Organizations (NGOs) through contracting out or elimination of government functions altogether. In fact, by 2005 in the U.S., direct provision of goods and services by the federal government accounted for only five percent of its overall activity (Salamon 2005). In local governments, for which direct services account for a higher level of government activity, over a quarter of all services have been privatized—with government contracting seeing sector growth even through the 2008 recession (Epstein 2013). However, it is clear to many that privatization "is not merely another management tool but a basic strategy of societal governance. It is based on a fundamental philosophy of government and of government's role in relation to the other essential institutions of a free and healthy society" (Savas 2000, 328). In broad brushstrokes, this is a philosophy that rejects the notion of publicness and embraces the expansion of market values to achieve the common good. Because of this shifting philosophy, the entire notion of publicness has come into question (Bozeman and Bretschneider 1994; Emmert and Crow 1988; Wettenhall 2001).

Considering the combined implications of *publicness* as questionable, the prevalence of privatization, and increasing globalization and its attendant marketplace ethos, the context of governance is no longer exclusively the government agency or even nation, but rather an intersectoral, international process that is characterized more by capitalist markets operating with government support, as opposed to democracy. To the inter*sectoral* complexity, we must also add international blurring. The nation-state is rapidly losing its status as the "locus of governance for collective life . . . events have fueled a global connectedness or interdependence that transcends national boundaries and is manifested in financial, political, environmental, technological, and cultural ways" (Yoder and Cooper 2005, 298). This has significant implications for both governance theory and practice that have only begun to be explored—issues that "spill over onto the most basic questions of American governance" (Kettl 1993, 211).

However, this is a narrow view of the role of government that doesn't necessarily fit all cultural perspectives (Brinkerhoff and Goldsmith 2005). Most basically, those affirming alternatives argue that "neither hierarchy nor markets are appropriate forms of governance" (Marsh 1998, 8). Despite this, Connolly (2011) argues we cannot simply forego the state as an institution due to the current hegemony of neoliberal markets. However, we must marry state politics with micropolitics to achieve not only social, but economic and environmental sustainability in the face of the current fragility of things. The new welfare state "must permit greater social differentiation while assuring greater integration. In other words, it must seek a less state-based society while offering more coordination and political direction towards the common good of the entire society" (Donati 2014, 79).

To achieve this, as noted long ago: "An important distinction is to be made between the locus of decision and the mode of calculation" (Wildavsky 1979, 123). As the sector where governance happens becomes less important, how decisions are made becomes more important—the degree to which the process is democratic is of core concern. For example, citizens of European nations are not so upset about the idea of the Union making international policy decisions—they are concerned that these decisions are in the hands of appointed experts rather than political deliberation (Kettl 2000). Thus, scholars urge politicians to "play a key role in efforts to ensure the democratic anchorage of governance networks" (Sørensen and Torfing 2005a). In short, governance demands a reframing of democracy, civic agency, and politics (Boyte 2005)—a project Follett understands as integrative process throughout all sectors of social life.

Publicness must be therefore be reaffirmed and may be measured by "commitment to the common good and civic involvement" (Carino 2001, 60). Indeed, Follett (1998) recognizes that the further we get from engaging such participatory deliberations, the less democratic governance becomes. Participatory practices enable governance as a function of both moral and instrumental choice. It is this mode of governance that "provides the link between theories of communicative action, deliberative democracy, and new forms of global governance" (Risse 2004, 293). These approaches can help us determine "how to design and manage the immensely complex collaborative systems" (Salamon 2005, 10-11), and in doing so "holds out the possibility that improved participation and dialogue can fill the gaps that have appeared in the ideals and practices of representative and responsible government" (Bevir 2012, 110). Participatory governance practices must accommodate cultural diversity, non-rational human behavior, and demands for inclusive citizenship beyond mere consumer choice (Kelly 1998). They must also reach into theories of political economy as the new paradigm in order to address "big issues" like democratization, societal equity, and ethics (Klingner 2004).

This notion of the degree to which governance includes direct engagement in democratic deliberation was conceptualized by Arnstein (1969) in her Ladder of Participation model: "Participation of the governed in their government is, in theory, the cornerstone of democracy" (216). Using evaluations of participation practices in urban revitalization, she identified a typology that includes nonparticipation (manipulation and therapy), tokenism (informing, consultation, and placation), and citizen power (partnership, delegation, and control) (Arnstein 1969). In pointing to the issue of decision making power, she revealed "the central issue of the participation debate" (Fagence 1977, 122). Empirical studies support this claim (see for example, Kathlene and Martin 1991; Stout 2010b). To be authentic, participation efforts must represent a "genuine devolution of authority" (Carley and Smith 2001, 198). Therefore, co-production cannot be repressive or reflect the inauthentic characteristics of co-optation (Selznick 1949). Follett recognizes these direct practices as the only true democracy.

Much of the contemporary literature attempting to address these governance issues is focused on network theory and collaboration. Within this literature, two distinct types of collaborative governance are discussed: (1) *organizational* collaboration amongst formal actors, often as a means of more effectively coordinating resources in response to complex policy problems (see for example, Agranoff 2006, 2008; Agranoff and McGuire 1998; Ansell and Gash 2008; Bingham and O'Leary 2008; Fung 2006; Hartley, Sørensen, and Torfing 2013; Hertting and Vedung 2012; Kettl 2006; Koppenjan and Klijn 2004; Milward and Provan 1998; Provan and Kenis 2008; Sørensen and Torfing 2005b); and (2) *community* collaboration between organizational actors and the general public (see for example, Bingham, Nabatchi, and O'Leary 2005; Box 1998; Bryer 2009; Cooper, Bryer, and Meek 2006; Nabatchi 2010, 2012). In some initiatives the two types are combined and in all, "the purpose of collaboration is to generate desired outcomes together that could not be accomplished separately" (Emerson, Nabatchi, and Balogh 2012, 14).

However, the theory informing these two streams of collaborative governance differ on important points based on the emphasis of instrumental versus democratic outcomes. Unlike Follett, they do not typically weave together these strands of management and political theory. Ostensibly, the instrumental value produced by collaboration is generated by the removal of hierarchical command and control structures as well as the excessive competition of markets. Instead, collaboration offers an egalitarian, networked style of organizing collective action—or *mode of association*—amongst actors who are motivated to work cooperatively. Yet, we also know that in their attempts to collaborate these actors bring to the table power dynamics grounded in their relative social, economic, and organizational status (Cohen 2008; Sabatier and Jenkins-Smith 1999), and can reinforce "the privileging of strong and resourceful elites" rather than furthering democratic values (Sørensen and Torfing 2009, 234). Following Follett, we argue that these power dynamics also carry forward attitudinal *dispositions* and *relational styles* that produce interpersonal dynamics more appropriate to hierarchical and competitive modes of association, hindering the collaborative capacity of the group.

Therefore, in assessing the instrumental value produced by network style organizing and collaborative governance (e.g., cost-efficiency, effectiveness, and degree of innovation), we must analyze the degree to which democratic values (e.g., participatory democracy) are enacted within the network and in interactions with the context (Sørensen and Torfing 2009). We argue that the relational dispositions and dynamics associated with participatory democracy are precisely the characteristics that foster successful instrumental outcomes—individual and societal progress.[2] Understanding and effectively using the integrative method at the micro level is necessary to achieve social progress at the macro level (Cohen 2008). In short, the most fruitful instrumental outcomes are produced only through the efforts of the group; only through integrative experience can the efforts of the group produce the most creative and successful outcomes. Ergo, to achieve the greatest instrumental outcomes we must first have the highest level of integrative collaboration.

In our contemporary context, governance "is spread throughout a global ecosystem" in which "processes and structures continually interact and a new order emerges in response to disruptions" (Crosby 2010, s71). Globalization is becoming "thick" through increasing density of intersectoral organizational networks engaging in governance activities that reach beyond national borders (Keohane and Nye 2000, 108). As such there is potential for "a scaling up of the principles and techniques of collaborative problem solving to matters of national and global concern" (Cohen 2008, 505). From this scaling up a "multilevel 'constitutional process'" emerges (Ansell 2011, 61), in which multiple "functional contracts" are created "simultaneously rather than a single monolithic social contract" (Wachhaus 2014, 585). This significantly alters the concepts of sovereignty and social contract, redefining them for a globalized world. The outcome of these prescriptions is a blurring of boundaries across all levels of society and the associated call to think globally while acting locally, and as O'Connor (2000) suggests, "in a time characterized by the idea of 'boundarylessness', Follett has much to teach" (167).

Indeed, to adequately address the problems of contemporary governance, governance theory must ask the right questions: How egalitarian are the relationships among actors? Do the rules of engagement match the integrative characteristics of collaboration, or do behaviors grounded in hierarchy or competition limit outcomes to domination or compromise? How do we develop collaborative capacity?

Follettian thinking is an excellent source from which to generate such questions and answers and is beginning to be used precisely in this fashion (Bartels 2013, 2014). Because she draws from both political and organizational theory to frame the manner in which integrative process permeates all social action, she is uniquely positioned to close the theoretical gap between instrumental and democratic outcome objectives. Furthermore, as noted in Chapter 12, she is unique in her efforts to provide practical examples and suggestions for practice (Child 2013). Indeed, Follett is not only a key theorist of governance, management, negotiation and social work, she is recognized as a founder of the field of public administration

(Fry and Raadschelders 2014). Many scholars use her theories to inform public engagement in collaborative governance (see for example, Elias and Alkadry 2011; King 2011; King, Feltey, and Susel 1998; King and Zanetti 2005; Stivers 2000; Stout 2013b), and to augment our understandings of interrelations within networks (Gehani and Gehani 2007).

Linking these micro-level relationships to macro-level networks and governance within a global context requires a new understanding of public agencies and the blurring of institutional boundaries (Roll and Thomas 2014; Wachhaus 2014). New institutionalism suggests that institutions should be understood as rules of the game that structure action, rather than as actual organizations (North 1990). Thus, the focus shifts to actors, relationships, and actions beyond the boundaries of individual agencies or even systems of government. This shift to a focus on relationship requires a clear understanding of how literatures pertaining to micro structures and macro governance, respectively, can inform one another (Cohen 2008). Indeed, the intent to "actively involve the public *in the process* of governing" (Wachhaus 2014, 588) "can and should be incorporated" into "institutional design" (Cohen 2008, 513). This can be fostered by micro-level literatures which provide "a theory and a set of prescriptions for dealing with microinteractions that [governance theorists] currently lack" (514). Likewise, attention to macro-level impacts places micro-level "problem-solving techniques into a macropolitical context" (514).

CONCLUSION

While the contemporary circumstances are certainly dire, they are by no means immutable. When individuals and groups feel dominated or alienated, there are several common responses—refuse and resist, join the competition, acquiesce voluntarily, or succumb. However, there is another possibility in which one seeks to co-create a sense of identity that is cohesive and dynamic—not through domination or compromise, but rather through intentional social process—what Follett calls the method of integration. Despite failed attempts to instantiate such approaches to participatory governance, citizens continue to demand it from their own governments.

A successful and sustainable response to the crises we face requires fundamental changes to the manner in which we shape individual and collective action together. In other words, we may no longer consider our situation as an objective *condition* subject to divine salvation or remediation via better scientific and technological knowledge, but rather as a complex and changing *predicament* in which we are fully implicated (Connolly 2011). Follett's comprehensive approach provides a basis from which to address "the fundamental challenge" of working "out what is involved in construing the world as a world of processes rather than things and then reformulate both the natural and the human sciences on this foundation" (Gare 2000, 5). Follett's descriptions of the total situation set the stage for understanding how human actions are an intricate part of natural, social, and economic global processes that can either negatively or positively impact the crises we are currently experiencing. Thus, her ideas help us understand both the driving forces underlying contemporary crises, as well as the potential for addressing them.

While globalization is often described in its negative attributes, it is also responsible for a radical pluralizing effect as noted above at the end of each subsection on the contemporary context. Seeing environmental, economic, and social alternatives, many actual people are taking an affirmative approach to refusal. Much like Follett, to make effective criticism *and* take positive action (Fraser and Nicholson 1988) these movements pair critique and resistance with pragmatic affirmation that is not dominating in its prescriptions, but rather tentative and culturally inclusive. As noted in the popular phrase, "think globally, act locally", these new movements seek responses to social, economic, and environmental challenges that consider and accommodate all.

We argue that Follettian thinking bolsters such responses to the crises described above, bringing them into the actual functions of micropolitics, the state, and global action—the practices of governance throughout society. Follett provides what is arguably the most robust formulation of participatory democracy in her understanding of integrative process. Her ideas clarify the relational disposition, cooperative style of relating, and participatory mode of association that together produce the most fruitful collaborative dynamics. These understandings better explain how the desired outcomes of collaboration are either fostered or constrained in governance practices. Her formulation of integrative process, democracy as a way of life, and progress as creative collaboration can contribute greatly to the development of governance theory.

Indeed, what we see today in various environmental, economic, social, and governance crises can all be traced to the dualism and its many permutations Follett critiques. She was hopeful that this dichotomous perspective would be rejected and a process-based synthesis embraced instead. However, she would not be surprised by the current climate given that the tension between hierarchy and competition has remained unchanged within the growing hegemonic nature of global competition. But it is not too late to return to her prescriptions—indeed, we must do so if the crises described above are to be mitigated rather than exacerbated.

This shift in perspective requires a dialogue among physical science, social science, philosophy, and theology so that we can both recognize and protect ourselves from life's dangers while investing in existential affirmation (Connolly 2011). Follett's interdisciplinary approach presages this recommendation and provides a foundation from which to address our contemporary intersectoral, international governance context. How to foster this approach must be carefully considered. It is to this task we turn in Chapter 14.

ENDNOTES

1. This section draws liberally from Stout (2013b) and Stout, Bartels, and Love (2014).

2. This assertion echoes the arguments of many during the Progressive Era (see Stout 2010a).

֍ 14 ֎

Implementing Follettian Governance

For Follettian governance to become a reality, the political and administrative theorists promoting her approach (or one similar to it) must come to terms with the full implications of attempting implementation. Pragmatically, we must develop a common language that both expresses the concepts comprehensively while bringing them into contemporary nomenclature. For example, the term *harmonization*, while meaning to Follett the difficult process of integrating difference in order to live together, in today's world sounds utopian in nature. If theorists promoting these concepts can develop shared terminology to express the processes of this form of governance, momentum will be easier to build.

However, we also agree with Follett; regardless of terminology it can be very difficult to shift outlooks in practice because it will "mean a real change in attitudes" (Mintzberg 1995, 204). In her later management papers, Follett tells a story of having a problem with the phone company. Each time she has difficulty with a representative or is unable to get a satisfactory resolution, she asks for the person "over" the individual she is speaking with. Upon reflection, she admits being embarrassed by her actions. She says: "You see, in spite of all my principles, I was so used to the old way of thinking that I couldn't adjust myself quickly to a different way of thinking. I wanted someone who had the authority to boss, so I kept straight on in this search for someone above others instead of asking: 'What particular job is this?'" (Follett 2013a, 39). Thus, she demonstrates that each of us is prone to make the mistake of reverting to "the old idea" (Follett 2003n, 290) and must maintain a self-reflective vigilance.

We agree with the assessment that each decade's wave of ever more humanistic management and ever more participatory governance reflects a "slow, episodic movement toward the new organization, with periods of plateauing between the waves of interest and enthusiasm. Given the sweeping nature of the change in question, nothing less than total cultural change, what else could reasonably be expected? Organizational inertia is enormous; change is painful" (Lawrence 1995, 295). But despite the challenge it represents to make such a transformational shift, we believe that if we are to pursue global governance in an authentically democratic manner, we must co-create the deeply nesting, networking, and broadly inclusive federalism Follett proposes—one that is grounded in relational process ontology.

Ushering in such a new "state" will require more than theoretical exploration. We must take Follett's advice in regard to practice and begin the developmental process required to instantiate Follettian governance. Toward this end, the method of integration, fully informed by her three principles of integrative process, the situation, and the law of the situation, must be learned, developed, and practiced by individuals and groups in all spheres of social action. It is these everyday micro-practices that will ultimately reshape the macro-modalities (structures), as noted by Foucault (1977) and Bourdieu (Swartz 2003).

INTEGRATION AS A SKILL

Integrative process—this new relational disposition, cooperative style of relating, and participatory mode of association—and its method of integration are not innate social skills. Therefore, training for integrative process must be established just as for any other art, trade, or life skill. Furthermore, successful integration requires that *all* people obtain the skill. "We can never reform American politics from above, by reform associations, by charters and schemes of government. Our political forms will have no vitality unless our political life is so organized that it shall be based primarily and fundamentally on spontaneous association" (Follett 1998, 202). Unfortunately, for the most part we are trained in the skills of hierarchy and competition. Therefore Follett argues, "If we want a nation which shall be really self-governed not just nominally self-governed, we must train up our young people in the ways of self-direction" (371) and "make them see that education is for life" (370).

While we may have an ontological predisposition toward relational social and creative experience, conscious and purposeful integration is a skill that must be learned and practiced, or learned by doing: "No training for democracy is equal to the practice of democracy" (Follett 1998, 366). Even if these qualities are facilitated and generated through interactions within a given group, as the participants interact iteratively with other situations in the existing political economy, tensions with mismatched styles of relating may remain. For example, participants often lack the capacity to break with habitual patterns of communication and adapt the course of their conversations to the law of the situation (Bartels 2014); they must become "experience conscious . . . aware that significant things *are* going on in [their lives]" (Follett 1970, 140).

To overcome these habits of hierarchy and competition, effective collaboration requires attitudinal and skill development appropriate to what Follett (1998) describes as "true democracy" (156). In regard to attitudes, integration requires the willingness and readiness to work with other people: "that we are ready to sacrifice individual interests to the general good, that we have a fully developed sense of responsibility" (366). Dispositions, while formed from infancy onward, can be changed through attitudinal development. Follett herself notes that training for a relational disposition, cooperative style of relating, and participatory mode of association is possible. "William Blake said: 'True education lives in the cultivation of imagination.' Yes, in the quickening of imagination, the widening of sympathy, the training of emotion. I believe our emotions have as legitimate an influence on our life as our thinking, but they also need the right kind of cultivating" (Follett 1970, 146).

Today, we would refer to development of such understanding as "emotional intelligence" (Goleman 1995) which includes both *interpersonal intelligence* (the capacity to understand the intentions, motivations, and desires of other people) and *intrapersonal intelligence* (the capacity to understand oneself, to appreciate one's feelings, fears, motivations, and desires) (Gardner 1983).[1] Developing both interpersonal and intrapersonal emotional intelligence is critical for integration as these capacities facilitate the ability to understand one's own emotional responses as well as perceive the situation from the perspectives of others (Goleman 1995) through "self-awareness, motivation, self-regulation, empathy, and adeptness in relationships" (Goleman 2011, 24). As Bohm (2004) notes, this "requires *sensitivity*—a certain way of knowing how to come in and how not to come in, of watching all the subtle cues and the senses and your response to them—what's happening inside of you, what's happening in the group" (45). This type of awareness "involves the senses, and also something beyond. . . . It's perception of meaning . . . a more subtle perception" (Bohm 2004, 46). Furthermore, fostering such skills is necessary to promote cooperative styles of relating, which include the ability to form a shared purpose; to act together without formal mandates, rules, and censures; and to meet conflict and difference with ongoing collective problem-solving.

Bohm (2004) describes this as occurring through a sort of suspension that opens our mind to interweaving with others rather than defending our own perspective, jointly developing an emergent understanding of complex and unpredictable situations as well as mutual trust that we will learn what we do not yet know from our ongoing conversations. Suspension involves being conscious of thoughts, feelings, and reactions without acting on them but rather contemplating their meanings. This requires development of a capacity for dialogue. Rather than listening "in an ego-driven way, shaping what comes to us so that it fits our existing ideas, channeling it according to our needs and desires," skillful listening can "encourage the kind of compassion that comes when we relinquish oversimplification and the urge to impose premature diagnoses of our own on complex problems" (Stivers 1994, 366). Such active listening implies giving respectful attention to others, acknowledging difference and the willingness to learn, and fostering recognition, responsiveness, humility, inclusion, moral sensibility, and self-development. In sum, "dialogue is the collective way of opening up judgments and assumptions" (Bohm 2004, 53) that "actually gets at the root of our problems and opens the way to creative transformation" (27).

These cooperative styles of relating can be cultivated in a variety of ways.[2] A powerful approach is facilitated dialogue that creates conditions in which participants feel safe to share their deeply held values, feelings, and experiences. Participants learn to listen to what others are really saying, and to become aware of the assumptions and thought processes triggered by what others are saying and inquire how these limit their ability for integrating (Argyris 1970; Schein 2003). Another effective method of developing collaborative capacity is by mediating negotiations in situations of conflict or disagreement. Mediators can use a set of facilitative strategies and practices to encourage participants to focus their energy on discovering their own and shared interests and work towards joint decisions everyone can agree with (Forester 2006, 2009). Yet another approach is using creative formats that challenge participants to step out of their comfort zone and reflect on their habitual practices. For example, role playing can enable participants to consider practices that would normally not be conceivable for their organizations, experience the lived realities of other participants, and imagine new, creative collaborative scenarios (Innes and Booher 1999).

Finally, participatory modes of association require "that we are trained in initiative and action" (Follett 1998, 366). We must learn the skills of dialogue and "participatory thought" (Bohm 2004, 99) in order to create together shared understandings and meanings so that action then becomes effective. Bohm (2004) recommends that while we may need to begin with facilitated dialogue, the function of the facilitator is "to work himself out of a job" (17). "The group process must be learnt by practice" and is "to be acquired only through those modes of living and acting which shall teach us how to grow the social consciousness" (Follett 1998, 363). "These then are the lessons which we hope group activities will teach—solidarity, responsibility and initiative,—how to take one's place worthily in a self-directed, self-governing community" (368). Indeed, integrative process must become part of family life, school life, organized recreation, club life, civic life, and work life. However, given the heterogeneous nature of neighborhoods Follett targets them as the most fruitful training ground for true democracy.

NEIGHBORHOOD AS CONSERVATORY

As was being practiced in the self-governance of settlement houses and community centers during the Progressive Era, people must learn through practice to participate in the process of collective thinking, deciding, and action. Follett believes "the neighborhood group gives the best opportunity for the training and for the practice of citizenship" (Follett 1998, 339). Neighborhood organizations "do not exist merely for the satisfaction of neighborhood needs, for the creating of a community bond, for the expression of that bond in communal action,—they also give the training necessary to bring that activity to its highest fulfilment [sic]. We all need not merely opportunities to exercise democracy, but opportunity for training in democracy" (207).

Follett explains that if we stick to family and friend or peer work groups alone, we may not have the need to learn the skill of integration: "That very homogeneity which we nestle down into and in which we find all the comfort of a down pillow, does not provide the differences in which alone we can grow. We must know the finer enjoyment of recognized diversity" (Follett 1998, 199). Conversely, "in a neighborhood group you have the stimulus and the bracing effect of many different experiences and ideals" (196). "In a more or less mixed neighborhood, people of different nationalities or different classes come together easily and naturally on the ground of many common interests: the school, recreational opportunities, the placing of their children in industry, hygiene, housing, etc. Race and class prejudices are broken down by working together for intimate objects" (197). Furthermore, "the fluctuating population of neighborhoods may be an argument against getting all we should like out of the neighborhood bond, but at the same time it makes it all the more necessary that some organization should be ready at hand to assimilate the new-comers and give them an opportunity of sharing in civic life as an integral, responsible part of that life" (201).

This heterogeneity is one reason Follett recommends that neighborhoods be considered the basis of political life. "I learn my relation to society by coming into contact with a wide range of experiences, of people, by cultivating and deepening my sympathy and whole understanding of life" (Follett 1998, 193). Neighborhoods are the locus of day-to-day life and where many personal interests are most directly experienced and contradicted. "If the neighborhood group is to be the political unit, it must learn how to gather up into significant community expression these more partial expressions of individual wants" (201). These practical applications of integration at a small scale provide the training necessary to integrate more complex and broad-reaching desires and differences. "We shall never know how to be one of a nation until we are one of a neighborhood. And what better training for world organization can each man receive than for neighbors to live together not as detached individuals but as a true community" (202).

Through this approach, "neighborhood organization gives us a method which will revolutionize politics" (Follett 1998, 203). Furthermore, neighborhood organizations provide the venue through which to act: "those forms within which good citizenship can operate, by making it possible to acquire the habit of good citizenship by the practice of good citizenship" (339). As an active member of the community centers movement, Follett saw how such associations can "release the potential values of neighborhood life, to find a channel for them to flow in, to help people find and organize their own resources" (205). Through this process, "what we hope neighborhood organization will do for the development of responsibility is this: that men will learn that they are not to *influence* politics through their local groups, they are to *be* politics" (Follett 1998, 240).

Therefore, the movement's "proposal is that people should organize themselves into neighborhood groups to express their daily life, to bring to the surface the needs, desires and aspirations of that life, that these needs should become the substance of politics, and that these neighborhood groups should become the recognized political unit" (Follett 1998, 192). Neighborhood organizations can become conservatories of democracy through the practice of integration and collective action. Follett recommends five basic methods for doing so: (1) regular meetings of neighbors to discuss neighborhood civic issues as well as meetings to address specific objectives; (2) practicing genuine discussion toward integration during meetings; (3) learning from one another and others through lectures, classes, and clubs; (4) taking on increasing responsibility for neighborhood life; and (5) establishing connections between the neighborhood and city, state, and national governments (204-05).

Sadly, Follett admits, "a free, full community life lived within the sustaining and nourishing power of the community bond, lived for community ends, is almost unknown now" (Follett 1998, 200), and we argue that this still seems to be the case. What prevents democratization from happening?

> It all comes down to our fear of men. If we could believe in men, if we could see that circle which unites human passion and divine achievement as a halo round the head of each human being, then social and political reorganization would no longer be a hope but a fact. The old individualism feared men; the corner-stone of the new individualism is faith in men. . . . We are beginning to realize that the redemptive power is within the social bond, that we have creative evolution only through individual responsibility. (Follett 1998, 341)

THE ACADEMY AS CONSERVATORY

To overcome these fears and develop the social bond, we argue that professional degree programs that develop practitioners who work with the public—public administration, social work, planning, education, law, business, and so forth—employ the practice of developing a strong philosophical grounding for practice and extend that endeavor to include a variety of perspectives, not simply the mainstream instrumental approaches based on static, individualist ontologies or the radically collectivist and individualist alternatives. Follett's theory of integrative process is clearly differentiated from the dialectically opposing One/Many perspectives it seeks to synthesize and supplant. Therefore, we respectfully submit that students, particularly in fields of applied practice, should be introduced to her work so that they may consider how integrative process might improve their own practice. Selber and Austin (1997) appear to agree, arguing that Follett's "management concepts should be included in social work curricula" (10).

Follett recommends that formal education for applied practice include three methods: "(1) through the subject we are occupied with, (2) through activities devised for the classroom group, (3) through using outside group activities for our students to experiment with, observe and report on in class" (Follett 1970, 142).[3] Each will be considered in the discussion that follows, using public administration as the example.[4]

In regard to subject matter, public administration as a field of study has grappled with its role in theory building and the production of knowledge as a field of academic study, juxtaposed to its role as a field of professional practice. This has been described in the past as an "intellectual crisis" (Ostrom 1989) that has led to numerous critiques of the field's scholarly preference for the descriptive case study as opposed to more theoretically driven analysis, meta-analysis, or advanced quantitative analysis (Cleary 1992, 2000; Houston and Delevan 1990; McCurdy and Cleary 1984; O'Connor 2000; Perry and Kraemer 1986; Stallings 1986; Stallings and Ferris 1988; White 1986; Wright, Manigault, and Black 2004). In short, public administration often wonders if it is an academic discipline in the received sense of the term. Perhaps due to this almost existential angst, there has been an increasing trend toward celebrating the practitioner backgrounds of many "pracademics" (Posner 2009) and calls from both academic and professional sides of the discipline to build better bridges between theory and practice.

Evidence of the desire to more productively bridge the work of academics and practitioners is reflected in adoption of a series of special sections of *Public Administration Review* over the past decade, including: (1) The Reflective Practitioner; (2) Academic–Practitioner Exchange; (3) Theory to Practice; (4) Administrative Profile; and (5) Administrative Case Study. As an example, the intent of the Theory to Practice series was to increase interaction between practitioners and academics in research, theory development, and curriculum (Raadschelders and Lee 2011). The legacy of the Theory to Practice series is an uncommon exchange of evidence, perspectives, and application on the key issues in public management between academics and practitioners (Durant and Durant 2012).

In August, 2008, the academic journal *Administrative Theory & Praxis* initiated a series on "Reflections on Theory in Action," calling for papers that "reflect on theory and when efforts are made to put this theory into action in order to learn, change, or innovate" (Kensen 2008, 140-41). In the initiating article of the series, then editor and public administration theorist Thomas Catlaw (2008) notes, "there is probably not a word that does as much as work—or causes as much trouble—in public administration as the word practical . . . It pins together the various domains that comprise 'public administration.' At this node, academic scholarship should inform administrative practice; university-based education should be practical and help practicing administrators to solve 'real world' problems or applied in a hypothetical, imagined, or actual administrative context" (518).

Therefore, practical is generally taken to mean "capable of being put into use, of being put into practice" (Catlaw 2008, 517). It follows that theory can be understood as "potential action under consideration" (Miller and King 1998, 54). However, as Catlaw (2008) points out, we are talking not only about instrumental usefulness, but offering value because it is "*interesting*. It is an idea, instrument, or bit of knowledge that resonates with us" (527). Indeed, it has been suggested that "educating MPA [Master of Public Administration] students to competency in theory adds at least three potential aspects to their capacity for effective administrative action: richness of perspective, flexibility of attention, and modesty" (McSwite 2001, 112). As a result, theory can help build universal competencies in terms of knowledge, skills, abilities, *and* attitudes (KSAs). This offers particular value in light of the recent addition to the standards for public administration competence of the ability to "articulate and apply a public service perspective" (NASPAA 2009, 7). In developing such attitudes, MPA programs are designed for professional socialization (Stout 2009a).

This renewed emphasis on philosophy is suited to Follettian thinking. In his introduction to *The New State*, Lord Haldane (1920) offers extensive discussion of education. Haldane, as would Mary Follett and John Dewey, argues that education cannot be limited only to technical and applied knowledge bent simply toward production. Instead, it must include philosophy, social science, and the arts and humanities so that "an educated democracy would gradually become a democracy inspired" (Haldane 1920, xxiv). Only through such perspective can we hope to "change the temper" and "double the efficacy of Miss Follett's principle of group organization" (Haldane 1920, xxv). This must be done by reinforcing the connection between education and experience, to help students become life-long learners through continued self-reflection (Wheelock and Callahan 2006), whereby they can connect what they learn in the classroom to what they experience in their organizations and communities (Dewey 1997).

To change the dispositions already inculcated in individuals by the time they reach university study, they must be exposed to alternative perspectives in a manner that encourages and enables individual choice-making among theories and prescriptions for practice. This can be a difficult proposition given the choices among textbooks and journal publications—Follett's and similar ideas are much less common offerings. However, at least one graduate text has been developed specifically for this purpose of exposure to alternatives and individual choice-making—*Logics of Legitimacy: Three Traditions of Public Administration Praxis* (Stout 2013b),[5] and we are hopeful, given Follett's re-emergence within various fields of practice noted in Chapter 11, that more texts will follow suit. By providing students with a variety of theories and prescriptions for practice, such texts give necessary theoretical grounding for the range of activities required by the field of practice, along with distinctive approaches to those activities. This diversity is crucial to prepare students for the divergent perspectives they are certain to encounter in practice. However, to bring these abstract ideas to life, classroom exercises must be employed.[6]

In her discussion of the student-teacher relationship, Follett (1970) argues, "The essential point around which I hope this paper all centers is that the leadership of the teacher consists in his relating his student to the life of the community. He should show him his relation to the world's needs" (147). Because many students now enter professional degree programs directly from an undergraduate degree program, the likelihood of having a sense of "the world's needs" from personal or professional experience can be quite limited. Indeed, even those with practical experience may be similarly limited unless they have moved beyond the circles of family, friends, and work as noted above. Therefore, film illustration and discussion as well as role-play exercises can be used to provide a window on that world from the classroom.[7] MPA students who have taken part in such classroom exercises report finding them useful for this purpose: "Film illustrations were wonderful use of displaying concepts . . . I think they were very helpful to understand each of the traditions in action" (Anonymous, 2012). Alternatively, in programs with students who are in-service professionals, it is important to draw out (evoke) their various experiences in classroom discussions and activities so that they might reflect on their own experiences in comparison with those of their classmates.

In order to foster co-learning and begin the process of building integrative skills, having students work in pairs or teams to analyze examples—from either "reel life" or their own experiences—allows them to work together to consider what philosophical assumptions are at play and perhaps in conflict. To contextualize to public administration practice, student teams can then design experiential exercises (role playing) that demonstrate the governance roles of elected representatives, expert administrators, and affected citizens in a process appropriate to those assumptions.[8,9] Such role playing activities are critical pedagogical tools because making connections between theory and experience is a critical component to long-term learning (Dewey 1997; Sogunro 2004).

Following the experience, guided reflective discussion with each student noting how it "feels" to play the different roles and assessing the pros and cons of the approach based on those experiences contributes to praxis. This pedagogical approach can help students connect theory with experience through the kind of reflection that is critical to becoming reflexive practitioners (Schön 1983). Such an approach enables students to discover distinct approaches to public service and builds on "a way to enhance learning that has been advanced for decades" (Ash and Clayton 2004, 137). Combined with diverse approaches to the subject matter, rather than being socialized into one particular approach to the profession, students are exposed to the landscape from which they may make their own informed choices and are given opportunities to practice doing so within the safety of the classroom. This intimate understanding of the choice-making involved in adopting a particular perspective sensitizes students to the problems of diversity in the process of practice, particularly when the perspectives of various actors and stakeholders differ.

According to Follett's model, from this initial window on the world, students must then be brought into that world for actual experience. It is critical to move from theory to practice in more than carefully designed classroom and mental exercises. The real world is unpredictable and ambiguous and tests our espoused theories with action (Argyris and Schon 1978). Therefore, MPA faculty increasingly use pedagogical techniques designed to bridge theory to practice in the real world (Bushouse, et al. 2011; Cunningham

1997; Killian 2004; Kramer 2007). Internships, capstone projects, and service learning experiences are commonly used in practice fields. Such field-based approaches are particularly valuable in professional fields that serve the public. Public service is in many ways a "contact sport" that requires the ability to thrive in a dynamic and unpredictable environment and the capacity to make emergent decisions to facilitate collective action.

Many MPA programs require internships, especially for pre-service students or in-service students wishing to change areas of specialization. Because these types of advanced degrees are designed to prepare professionals for career work, actual experience is necessary to help students successfully transfer theory to practice. MPA internships place students in a range of institutions, including local governments, state and federal agencies, as well as non-profit organizations, healthcare agencies, and other organizations that enable public service. Placements are chosen based on career goals and an appropriate fit of responsibilities to skill development. Particular learning outcomes are identified, requiring an agreement among the faculty advisor, the student, and the internship supervisor. Students are required to complete a specified number of contact hours (for example, 500 hours) with the placement organization. Timesheets typically track the number of contact hours, type of activity, and learning outcomes. This fieldwork is generally supervised by a faculty advisor, as well as a direct supervisor in the placement itself. Sometimes, a report or presentation on key internship experiences and their link to MPA program objectives are also required.

Many MPA programs also adopt capstone courses to help students successfully transition from learning to practice. Capstone courses provide not only an opportunity to bridge theory to practice (McGaw and Wechsler 1999; Reid and Miller 1997), but also to weave together acquired public service competencies to address "real-world" issues in public administration. Capstone courses provide an opportunity for students to apply their own leadership and management knowledge, skills, and attitudes to the implementation of a public service project. These projects are often service learning activities that bring the foundational theories learned in prior courses into actual practice in the field. In essence they integrate the competencies through experience. Projects are often fraught with ambiguity, conflicting ideas, and unanticipated changes. Students learn to deal with such challenges successfully, and can learn from the process even with less than hoped-for project results.

Service learning projects that place students in organizational and community settings have been effectively used in variety of public administration programs to link course material and theory to practice (Bushouse and Morrison 2001; Dicke, Dowden, and Torres 2004; Imperial, Perry, and Katula 2007; Lambright 2008; Lambright and Lu 2009; Stout 2013a) while also producing real value in organizations and communities (Newcomer and Allen 2010; Plein and Morris 2005; Waldner and Hunter 2008). Thus, service-learning is "designed to promote academic enhancement, personal growth, and civic engagement" (Ash and Clayton 2004, 138). Service-learning approaches must also avoid promotion of hierarchical relationships with community partners. Care must be taken to utilize the process of integration, bringing together the diverse perspectives of experts, practitioners, students, and community members.

Follett would likely concur emphatically on this point, following her model of practice to academy to practice again. For example, in his discussion of education, Lord Haldane did not envision the learning relationship as an activity conducted solely in the halls of universities. He and Follett both believed university professors should take such learning into the real world; to "devote themselves to this new and extra-mural work" of community education (Haldane 1920, xxii) and research sabbaticals (Follett 1970). In today's institutions of higher learning, this type of education is offered through professional (as opposed to academic discipline) degree programs, continuing education and lifelong learning courses, outreach programs, and applied research offered through universities, exemplified by the extension services of U.S. Land Grant colleges and universities.

However, in the rush to provide hands-on and real-world experiences that apply course concepts and theories through internships and service learning, there can often be an absence of active reflection. Yet such reflection on experience is what enables students to make sense of what is happening, consciously link it to theory, and integrate it most fully into their acquired knowledge (Ash and Clayton 2004; Cunningham 1997). Analytical reflection on those experiences fosters critical thinking and the linkage of theory and practice (Collier and Williams 2005). Active reflection also supports the "double loop learning" (Argyris and Schon 1978) so sought after in organizational contexts, enabling the learner to adopt, adjust, or reject theory based on experience. Therefore, Bushouse et al. (2011) argue "faculty should provide public administration students with ample opportunities to link theory with practice through reflection. Instructors should be prepared to take an active role in facilitating the reflection process and should not assume that students will be able to make the linkages between theory and practice on their own" (Bushouse et al. 2011, 106).

Integrative theory seminars, integrative practice seminars, and service-learning through internships and capstone projects can provide opportunities for guided reflection as students discover theory, articulate their own public service perspective, and apply both knowledge and attitudes in practical skill-building. Active reflection can be encouraged in a variety of pedagogical approaches and assignments, including lecture discussion, role-playing exercises, case analysis, both informal and formal writing assignments, and peer, faculty, and client feedback. In all, these activities develop "the reflective practitioner" (Schön 1983).

Together, a pedagogical approach that combines in-class and field experience with theory and reflection achieves what Follett views as a key mentoring role of teacher to student:

> One opportunity that the teacher has of showing the student his relation to the worlds needs is when, as so often happens, he helps him choose his purpose in life. While he should never choose it for him, since that is the very core of individuality—the distinct and separate purpose of each man—yet the teacher can help him by showing him that there are always two factors which should determine his choice: his own bent, and also how he can best make his contribution to the common life. Moreover, he can show his student the relation of his own purpose to larger purposes, the relation of his daily acts to the community life, the relation of any part to as large a whole as the student is capable of understanding. (Follett 1970, 147)

The approach described here meets the spirit and purpose of Follettian epistemological concepts. In higher learning, "student and teacher are comrades on a journey of discovery on which both recognise [sic] that there is no finality, and that what signifies is not a body of rigid and complete truth, for there is none such, but the search after truth, and the expansion and freedom of spirit which such search gives" (Haldane 1920, xix). Follett spoke on this relationship in her lecture on "The Teacher-Student Relation" as an aspect of leadership. There, she argues, "The greatest service a teacher can render the student is to increase his freedom—his free range of activity and thought and his power of control. . . . The teacher releases energy, frees potentialities, but within method within the laws of group activity and group control" (Follett 1970, 137-38). Of course, by the latter points, Follett means the law of the situation that guides all leadership and followership in the situated, integrative process of group activity.

It must be noted that coproduced learning and service learning require a greater commitment on the part of both students and faculty. These types of approaches prepare students for real-world expectations of self-direction, team work, and inter-organizational collaboration (Killian 2004) and build both research and management skills (Whitaker and Berner 2004). However, such approaches are also highly ambiguous and lead to higher levels of stress and unpredictability (Jacoby 2003). Therefore, they represent somewhat of a risk on the part of faculty, particularly those still on the road to tenure and promotion (Boyer 1990, 1996). However, they prepare students to begin the "continuous life-long process" of joint learning and reflection that are necessary for integration (Wheelock and Callahan 2006, 267). In sum, we believe that the rewards for both students and faculty far outweigh the cost of the pedagogical ingenuity and effort required for coproduced learning and service learning experiences. Therefore, we heartily recommend the approach to other faculty engaged in the endeavor of developing practitioners who serve the public.

FINDING THE WILL TO AFFIRM

In closing, we would like to consider the challenge involved in affirming Follettian governance as scholars of the social sciences. We propose this endeavor in a time when positivist prescriptions for practice based on empirically derived theory continue to hold sway, while critical theory nips at the margins and points out the folly in such attempts at incremental change and sometimes calls for utopian alternatives. However, much critical theory is grounded in existential resentment and we agree with Connolly (2011) that "a cynic is often an authoritarian who rejects the current regime of authority" (55). In Follett we find not only a robust critique of the way it has been done but an alternative that avoids the trap of absolutism. Its dynamic relational grounding enables us to "act upon this faith while folding an appreciation of its comparative contestability" (112). We believe Follettian thinking can help us to put "practices of the self, ethics, micropolitics, and macropolitics . . . into the fray in ways that support each other" (Connolly 2013, 130). Thus, we affirm Follettian thought in contemporary governance theory.

Braidotti (2013) has considered a similar intention to affirm a vital materialism in the humanities: "This project requires more visionary power or prophetic energy, qualities which are neither especially in fashion in academic circles, nor highly valued scientifically" (191). It requires a "faith in the creative powers of the imagination" (191) that is not typically allowed in the academy. Nevertheless, "prophetic or visionary minds are the thinkers of the future. The future as an active object of desire propels us forth and motivates us to be active in the here and now of a continuous present that calls for both resistance and the counter-actualization of alternatives" (191). Connolly (2011) agrees, arguing that political theorists must take on the methods of the *seer* that are common to all sorts of onto-philosophical traditions. Using intuition, seers can perceive "how crucial shifts in the pace of events and the timing of responses are to the world" (153). He argues that while this sensitivity or disposition is rare, it can be cultivated and should be; it is essential to creative thinking in a world of becoming in "the formation of new maxims, judgments, concepts, and strategies at untimely moments when a collection of old precepts, habits, and standards of judgment are insufficient to an emerging situation" (164). Indeed, we must be "passionately committed to writing the prehistory of the future . . . This is the horizon of sustainable futures" (Braidotti 2010, 216-17).

Our point is this: the contemporary predicament is not a foregone historical conclusion, nor is our possible response to it necessarily incremental. It is simply one world among possible worlds that we might co-create (Braidotti 2013) and it could have happened otherwise (Connolly 2013). To unabashedly affirm an alternative response to current conditions "provides one way to act resolutely in the world while warding off individual and collective drives to existential resentment" (Connolly 2011, 6). Such steadfast affirmation need not be colonizing or hegemonic. Indeed *integrative process* is inherently not dominating or subjugating because it is constantly open to difference and the difficult challenge of integration.

Thus, we join Connolly (2011) in what he claims is "a growing contingent who think that a perspective defined by active examination of becoming can make positive contributions to explorations of spirituality, economic, political action, poetic experience, and ethics" (8). Furthermore, we admit that this may require a "radical, pluralist assemblage" (Connolly 2013, 137) acting "in more militant, visible, creative and inspirational ways" (Connolly 2011, 144). We believe such an assemblage would benefit from the inclusion of scholars and that our role performance as such should have the freedom to shift from critique to affirmation. Following Connolly's (2013) prescription, we should be allowed to combine process philosophy, pragmatist experimentation, and reflexivity in caring for the world, cultivating a capacity to dwell sensitively in significant moments, ushering in new concepts and practices experimentally, and periodically reflecting on those interventions to ensure they are working. In Follett's own words,

> the task given us to-day is to revalue all the world values, to steer straight on and on into the unknown—a gallant forth-faring indeed. But conscious evolution, the endless process of a perfect coordinating, demands vital people. War is the easy way: we take to war because we have not enough vitality for the far more difficult job of agreeing . . . We have to be higher order of beings to do it—we become higher order of beings by doing it. And so the progress goes on forever: it means life forever in the making, and the creative responsibility of every man. (Follett 1998, 103)

It is precisely this challenging creative process that inspires Follett. She is invigorated by the prospects of relational process philosophy as applied to actual groups: "I am interested—more interested than anything else in the world—in these correspondences in thinking between scientists, philosophers, and business managers, because such correspondences seem to me a pretty strong indication that we are on the right track" (2003m, 199). Follett feels that the coordinating of group efforts within organizations provides illustration of these cross-disciplinary discoveries and refutes a growing social angst. Indeed, rather than going along with the chorus that claims "we are living in a barren age" of "degeneration" (Follett 2003a, 94), Follett insists that we must not "make the mistake of connecting creativeness always and inevitably with individuals" but "may now enter on a period of collective creativeness if we have the imagination to see its potentialities, its reach, its ultimate significance, above all if we are willing patiently to work out the method" (94).

Follett believes that most others would share her passion if it were made widely known: "Surely with the world in its present condition we have a task before us which may indeed appeal to the constructive passion in any man—in every man" (Follett 2013h, 89). We agree, and assert that Follettian governance of our global society will lead to the most fruitful outcomes for all. Therefore, let us heed her call to public service:

The spirit of a new age is fast gripping every one of us. The appeal which life makes to us to-day is to the socially constructive passion in every man. This is something to which the whole of me can respond. This is a great affirmative. Sacrifice sometimes seems too negative, dwells on what I give up. Service sometimes seems to emphasize the *fact of* service rather than the *value* of the service. Yet service and sacrifice are noble ideals. We cannot do without them. Let them, however, be the handmaids of the great purpose of our life, namely, our contribution to that new world we wish to see rise out *of* our present chaos, that age which shall bring us individual freedom through collective control. (Follett 2003f, 314)

ENDNOTES

1. Gardner's (1983) focus is on what he terms "multiple intelligences" rather than just emotional intelligence. Intrapersonal and interpersonal intelligence, which have been linked to Goleman's (1995) idea of emotional intelligence, are just two of the seven types of intelligence identified by Gardner's theory of multiple intelligences.

2. On this issue of nurture versus nature, Whitehead would agree: "Little children are not selfish Benthamite utilitarians, constantly calculating their own advantage, although they readily learn such social skills. Nor are they Rousseau's primitives, naturally altruistic in their dealings with others, although they can readily be taught these skills as well" (Allan 1993, 275).

3. We would like to thank West Virginia University MPA student Jessica Fowler for bringing this article to our attention in an assignment.

4. This section draws liberally from Stout and Holmes (2013).

5. This text presents three Traditions within U.S. administrative practice— Constitutional, Discretionary, and Collaborative. Within each Tradition, a broad literature review is provided that traces the historical, philosophical, and intellectual foundations of logically aligned prescriptions for practice, including consideration of: political ontology, political authority and scope of administrative practice, criteria for proper behavior, decision making approaches, organizing styles, the assumed characteristics of the governance context, and the resulting role conceptualization of the practitioner. Taken together, several patterns in how these issues are approached (*logics of legitimacy*) channel administrative behavior into three distinct role types: Bureaucrat, Entrepreneur, and Steward. These differences are critical to both professional socialization and practice.

6. The approach prescribed here is based on a method utilized in the MPA program at West Virginia University and has been described in detail elsewhere (Stout and Holmes 2013).

7. Films are a helpful way to approach case study, particularly for pre-service students with less direct experience to contextualize traditional case analysis (Stout, 2011; Goodsell and Murray, 1995; Eagan, 2011).

8. If using *Logics of Legitimacy* (Stout 2013b), students would design these activities according to the Tradition identified: Constitutional, Discretionary, or Collaborative; the last of which is largely informed by Follett's thinking.

9. In the field of social work, experiential exercises might consider the practitioner, the client, and other stakeholders such as family or community members.

Works Cited

Agranoff, Robert. 2006. "Inside Collaborative Networks: Ten Lessons for Public Managers." *Public Administration Review* 66: 56-65. doi: 10.1111/j.1540-6210.2006.00666.x.

Agranoff, Robert. 2008. "Enhancing Performance through Public Sector Networks: Mobilizing Human Capital in Communities of Practice." *Public Performance & Management Review* 31 (3): 320-47. doi: 10.2307/20447680.

Agranoff, Robert, and Michael McGuire. 1998. "Multinetwork Management: Collaboration and the Hollow State in Local Economic Policy." *Journal of Public Administration Research and Theory* 8 (1): 67-91.

Allan, George. 1993. "Process Ideology and the Common Good." *The Journal of Speculative Philosophy* 7 (4): 266-85.

Ansell, Chris, and Alison Gash. 2008. "Collaborative Governance in Theory and Practice." *Journal of Public Administration Research and Theory* 18 (4): 543-71. doi:10.1093/jopart/mum032.

Ansell, Christopher. 2011. *Pragmatist Democracy: Evolutionary Learning as Public Philosophy.* New York: Oxford.

Appleby, Paul H. 1945. *Big Democracy.* New York: Knopf.

Arendt, Hannah. (1958) 1998. *The Human Condition.* Reprint. Chicago: University of Chicago Press.

Argyris, Chris. 1970. *Intervention Theory and Method: A Behavioral Science View.* Reading, MA: Addison-Wesley.

Argyris, Chris, and Donald A. Schon. 1978. *Organizational Learning: A Theory of Action Perspective.* Reading, MA: Addison-Wesley.

Arnstein, Sherry. 1969. "A Ladder of Citizen Participation." *Journal of the American Institute of Planners* 35 (3): 216-24.

Ash, Sarah L., and Patti H. Clayton. 2004. "The Articulated Learning: An Approach to Guided Reflection and Assessment." *Innovative Higher Education* 29 (2): 137-53.

Aupperle, Kenneth E. 2007. "Introduction: Mary Parker Follett—A Bridge Over Management's Troubled Waters." *International Journal of Public Administration* 30 (4): 363-66.

Banerjee, Amrita. 2008. "Follett's Pragmatist Ontology of Relations: Potentials for a Feminist Perspective on Violence." *Journal of Speculative Philosophy* 22 (1): 3-11.

Barber, Benjamin. 1998. "Foreword." In *The New State: Group Organization the Solution of Popular Government*, xiii-xvi. University Park, PA: Pennsylvania State University Press.

Barber, Benjamin R. 1984. *Strong Democracy: Participatory Politics for a New Age*. Berkeley, CA: University of California Press.

Barclay, Laurie J. 2005. "Following in the Footsteps of Mary Parker Follett: Exploring How Insights from the Past Can Advance Organizational Justice Theory and Research." *Management Decision* 43 (5/6): 740-60.

Barnosky, Anthony D., Nicholas Matzke, Susumu Tomiya, Guinevere O. U. Wogan, Brian Swartz, Tiago B. Quental, Charles Marshall, Jenny L. McGuire, Emily L. Lindsey, Kaitlin C. Maguire, Ben Mersey, and Elizabeth A. Ferrer. 2011. "Has the Earth's Sixth Mass Extinction Already Arrived?" *Nature* 471.

Bartels, Koen P. R. 2014. "Communicative Capacity: The Added Value of Public Encounters for Participatory Democracy." *The American Review of Public Administration* 4, 656-74 doi: 10.1177/0275074013478152.

Bartels, Koen P. R. 2013. "Public Encounters: The History and Future of Face-to-Face Contact Between Public Professionals and Citizens." *Public Administration* 91 (2): 469-83. doi:10.1111/j.1467-9299.2012.02101.x.

Bauman, Zygmunt. 2001. "Individually Together." In *Individualization: Institutionalized Individualism and Its Social and Political Consequences*, edited by Ulrich Beck and Elisabeth Beck-Gernsheim, xiv. Thousand Oaks: Sage Publications.

Beck, Ulrich, and Elisabeth Beck-Gernsheim. 2001. *Individualization: Institutionalized Individualism and Its Social and Political Consequences*. Vol. 13. Thousand Oaks: Sage Publications.

Bennett, Jane. 2001. *The Enchantment of Modern Life: Attachments, Crossings, and Ethics.* Princeton, NJ: Princeton University Press.

Bennis, Warren. 1995. "Thoughts on 'The Essentials of Leadership.'" In *Mary Parker Follett, Prophet of Management: A Celebration of Writings from the 1920s,* edited by Pauline Graham, 177-81. Washington, D.C.: Beard Books.

Bergson, Henri. (1913) 2001. *Time and Free Will: An Essay on the Immediate Data of Consciousness.* Translated by F. L. Pogson. Reprint. 3rd ed. Mineola, NY: Dover Publications.

Bergson, Henri. (1946) 2007. *The Creative Mind: An Introduction to Metaphysics.* Reprint. Mineola, NY: Dover.

Bergson, Henri. (1896) 2010. *Matter and Memory.* Translated by Nancy Margaret Paul and Palmer W. Scott. Reprint. Digireads.com Publishing.

Bergson, Henri, and Arthur Mitchell. (1911) 1920. *Creative Evolution.* Reprint. London: Macmillan and Company, Ltd.

Bevir, Mark. 2012. *Governance: A Short Introduction.* Oxford: Oxford University Press.

Bingham, Lisa Blomgren, Tina Nabatchi, and Rosemary O'Leary. 2005. "The New Governance: Practices and Processes for Stakeholder and Citizen Participation in the Work of Government." *Public Administration Review* 65 (5): 547-58.

Bingham, Lisa Blomgren, and Rosemary O'Leary. 2008. *Big Ideas in Collaborative Public Management.* Armonk, NY.: M. E. Sharpe.

Bohm, David. 1980. *Wholeness and the Implicate Order.* London: Routledge & Kegan Paul.

Bohm, David. 2004. *On Dialogue.* New York: Routledge.

Boje, David M., and Grace Ann Rosile. 2001. "Where's the Power in Empowerment? Answers from Follett and Clegg." *Journal of Applied Behavioral Science* 37 (1): 90-117.

Box, Richard C. 1998. *Citizen Governance: Leading American Communities into the 21st Century.* Thousand Oaks, CA: Sage Publications.

Box, Richard C. 2008. *Making a Difference: Progressive Values in Public Administration.* Armonk, NY: M. E. Sharpe.

Boyer, Ernest L. 1990. *Scholarship Reconsidered: Priorities of the Professoriate.* Edited by Carnegie Foundation for the Advancement of Teaching. New York: John Wiley & Sons.

Boyer, Ernest L. 1996. "The Scholarship of Engagement." *Journal of Public Service and Outreach* 1: 11-20.

Boyte, Harry C. 2005. "Reframing Democracy: Goverance, Civic Agency, and Politics." *Public Administration Review* 65 (5): 536-46.

Bozeman, Barry, and Stuart Bretschneider. 1994. "The 'Publicness Puzzle' in Organization Theory: A Test of Alternative Explanations of Differences between Public and Private Organizations." *Journal of Public Administration Research and Theory* 4 (April): 197-223.

Braidotti, Rosi. 2006. *Transpositions: On Nomadic Ethics.* Cambridge: Polity Press.

Braidotti, Rosi. 2010. "The Politics of 'Life Itself' and New Ways of Dying." In *New Materialisms: Ontology, Agency, and Politics*, edited by Diana Coole and Samantha Frost, 201-18. Durham, NC: Duke University Press.

Braidotti, Rosi. 2011. *Nomadic Theory: The Portable Rosi Braidotti.* New York: Columbia University Press.

Braidotti, Rosi. 2013. *The Posthuman.* Cambridge, MA: Polity Press.

Brigg, Morgan. 2007. "Biopolitics Meets Terrapolitics: Political Ontologies and Governance in Settler-Colonial Australia." *Australian Journal of Political Science* 42 (3): 403-17.

Brinkerhoff, Derick W., and Arthur A. Goldsmith. 2005. "Institutional Dualism and International Development: A Revisionist Interpretation of Good Governance." *Administration & Society* 37 (2): 199-224.

Bryer, Thomas A. 2009. "Explaining Responsiveness in Collaboration: Administrator and Citizen Role Perceptions." *Public Administration Review* 69 (2): 271-83. doi:10.1111/j.1540-6210.2008.01973.x.

Bushouse, Brenda K., Willow S. Jacobson, Kristina T. Lambright, Jared J. Llorens, Ricardo S. Morse, and Ora-orn Poocharoen. 2011. "Crossing the Divide: Building Bridges between Public Administration Practitioners and Scholars." *Journal of Public Administration Research and Theory* 21 (Supplement 1): i99-i112.

Bushouse, Brenda K., and Sara Morrison. 2001. "Applying Service Learning in Master of Public Affairs Programs." *Journal of Public Affairs Education* 7 (1): 9-17.

Cabot, Richard C. 1934. "Mary Parker Follett, An Appreciation." *The Radcliffe Quarterly* 18 (2): 80-82.

Calas, M., and L. Smiricich. 1996. "Not Ahead of Her Time: Reflection on Mary Parker Follett as Prophet of Management." *Organization* 3 (1): 147-52.

Carino, Ledvina V. 2001. "Private Action for Public Good? The Public Role of Voluntary Sector Organizations." *Public Organization Review: A Global Journal* 1: 55-74.

Carley, Michael, and H. Smith. 2001. "Civil Society and New Social Movements." In *Urban Development and Civil Society: The Role of Communities in Sustainable Cities*, edited by Michael Carley, P. Jenkins and H. Smith. London: Earthscan.

Carlsson, Ingvar, and Shridath Ramphal. 1995. Our Global Neighborhood: The Report of the Commission on Global Governance. Oxford: The Commission on Global Governance.

Catlaw, Thomas J. 2005. "Constitution as Executive Order: The Administrative State and the Political Ontology of We the People." *Administration & Society* 37 (4).

Catlaw, Thomas J. 2007. *Fabricating the People: Politics & Administration in the Biopolitical State.* Tuscaloosa, AL: University of Alabama Press.

Catlaw, Thomas J. 2008. "What's the Use in Being Practical?" *Administrative Theory & Praxis* 30 (4): 515-29.

Catlaw, Thomas J., and Gregory M. Jordan. 2009. "Public Administration and 'The Lives Of Others': Toward an Ethics of Collaboration." *Administration & Society* 41: 290-312.

Cheney, George. 2001. "Mondragon Cooperatives." *Social Policy* 32 (2): 4-9.

Child, John. 1969. *British Management Thought: A Critical Analysis.* London: George Allen and Unwin Ltd.

Child, John. 1995. "Follett: Constructive Conflict." In *Mary Parker Follett, Prophet of Management: A Celebration of Writings from the 1920s*, edited by Pauline Graham, 87-95. Washington, D.C.: Beard Books.

Child, John. 2013. "Mary Parker Follett." In *The Handbook of Management Theorists*, edited by Morgan Witzel and Malcolm Warner, 74-93. Oxford: Oxford University Press.

Chrislip, David D. 2002. *The Collaborative Leadership Fieldbook: A Guide For Citizens And Civic Leaders.* San Francisco: Jossey-Bass.

Christ, Carol P. 2003. *She Who Changes: Reimagining the Divine in the World.* New York: Palgrave MacMillan.

Cleary, Robert E. 1992. "Revisiting the Doctoral Dissertation in Public Administration: An Examination of the Dissertations of 1990." *Public Administration Review* 52 (1):55-61.

Cleary, Robert E. 2000. "The Public Administration Doctoral Dissertation Reexamined: An Evaluation of the Dissertations of 1998." *Public Administration Review* 60 (5):446-55.

Cobb, John B., Jr. 1975. *Christ in a Pluralistic Age*. Philadelphia: Westminster Press.

Cobb, John B., Jr. 1982. *Process Theology as Political Theology*. Philadelphia: Westminster Press.

Cobb, John B., Jr. 1994. *Sustaining the Common Good. A Christian Perspective on the Global Economy*. Cleveland: Pilgrim Press.

Cobb, John B., Jr. 2002. *Postmodernism and Public Policy: Reframing Religion, Culture, Education, Sexuality, Class, Race, Politics and the Economy*. Albany: State University of New York Press.

Cobb, John B., Jr. 2004. "Thinking with Whitehead about Nature." In *Whitehead's Philosophy: Points of Connection*, edited by J. Polanowski and D. Sherburne. Albany: State University of New York Press.

Cobb, John B., Jr. 2008. *Whitehead Word Book*. Claremont, CA: P&F Press.

Cobb, John B., Jr., and David Ray Griffin. 1976. *Process Theology: An Introductory Exposition*. Louisville, KY: Westminster Press.

Cohen, Amy J. 2008. "Negotiation, Meet New Governance: Interests, Skills, and Selves." *Law & Social Inquiry* 33 (2):503-62.

Cohen, Burton J. 2011. "Design-based Practice: A New Perspective for Social Work." *Social Work* 56 (4):337-46.

Collier, Peter J., and Dilafruz R. Williams. 2005. "Reflection in Action: The Learning-Doing Relationship." In *Learning Through Serving*, edited by Christine M. Cress, Peter J. Collier and Vicki L. Retenauer, 83-97. Sterling, CA: Stylus.

Collingwood, V. 2003. "Assistance with Fewer Strings Attached." *Ethics and International Affairs* 17 (1):55-68.

Connolly, William E. 1999. *Why I Am Not a Secularist?* Minneapolis, MN: University of Minnesota Press.

Connolly, William E. 2011. *A World of Becoming*. Durham, NC: Duke University Press.

Connolly, William E. 2013. *The Fragility of Things: Self-Organizing Processes, Neoliberal Fantasies, and Democratic Activism*. Durham, NC: Duke University Press.

Coole, Diana, and Samantha Frost. 2010a. "Introducing the New Materialisms." In *New Materialisms: Ontology, Agency, and Politics*, edited by Diana Coole and Samantha Frost, 1-43. Durham, NC: Duke University Press.

Coole, Diana, and Samantha Frost, eds. 2010b. *New Materialisms: Ontology, Agency, and Politics*. Durham, NC: Duke University Press.

Cooper, Terry L., Thomas A. Bryer, and Jack W. Meek. 2006. "Citizen-Centered Collaborative Public Management." *Public Administration Review* 66: 76-88. doi:10.1111/j.1540-6210.2006.00668.x.

Cox, Robert W. 1995. "Critical Political Economy." In *International Political Economy: Understanding Global Disorder*, edited by Bjorn Hetne. Halifax, Nova Scotia: Fernwood Publishing.

Crosby, Barbara C. 2010. "Leading in the Shared-Power World of 2020." *Public Administration Review* 70 (s1): s69-s77.

Cunningham, Bob. 1997. "Experential Learnng in Public Administration Education." *Journal of Public Affairs Education* 3 (2): 219-27.

Cunningham, Robert. 2000. "The New State." *Journal of Organizational Change Management* 13 (1): 89-91.

Daly, Herman, and John B. Cobb, Jr. 1990. *For the Common Good: Redirecting the Economy Toward Community, the Environment, and a Sustainable Future*. Boston: Beacon Press.

Damart, Sébastien. 2013. "How Mary Follett's Ideas on Management Have Emerged: An Analysis Based on Her Practical Management Experience and Her Political Philosophy." *Journal of Management History* 19 (4): 459-73.

Davis, Albie M. 1991. "Follett on Facts: Timely Advice from an ADR Pioneer." *Negotiation Journal* 7 (2): 131-38.

Davis, Keith. 1967. "Understanding the Social Responsibility Puzzle." *Business Horizons* 10 (4): 45-50.

Debord, Guy. 1994. *The Society of the Spectacle*. New York: Zone Books.

Deleuze, Gilles. 1992. *The Fold: Leibniz and the Baroque*. Translated by Tom Conley. Minneapolis, MN: University of Minnesota Press.

Deleuze, Gilles. 2001. *Pure Immanence: Essays on a Life*. Translated by Anne Boyman. New York: Zone Books.

Deleuze, Gilles, and Felix Guattari. 1987. *A Thousand Plateaus: Capitalism and Schizophrenia*. Translated by Brian Massumi. New York: Continuum.

Deming, W. Edwards. 2000. *Out of the Crisis*. Cambridge: MIT Press.

Desmet, Ronny. 2007. Whitehead and the British Reception of Einstein's Relativity: An Addendum to Victor Lowe's Whitehead Biography. Claremont, CA: Center for Process Studies.

Dewey, John. 1896. "The Reflex Arc Concept in Psychology." *Psychological Review* 3 (4): 357-70.

Dewey, John. 1920. *Reconstruction in Philosophy*. Princeton, NJ: H. Holt.

Dewey, John. 1934. *A Common Faith*. New Haven, CT: Yale University Press.

Dewey, John. (1938) 1997. *Experience and Education*. New York: The Macmillan Company.

Dicke, Lisa, Sara Dowden, and Jodi Torres. 2004. "Successful Service Learning: A Matter of Ideology." *Journal of Public Affairs Education* 10 (3): 199-208.

Donati, Pierpaolo. 2014. *Transcending Modernity: The Quest for a Relational Society*. Bologna: University of Bologna, Cesis-Department of Sociology and Business Law.

Douglas, Mary. (1970) 1996. *Natural Symbols: Explorations in Cosmology*. New York: Routledge.

Drucker, Peter F. 1995. "Introduction." In *Mary Parker Follett, Prophet of Management: A Celebration of Writings from the 1920s*, edited by Pauline Graham, 1-9. Washington, D.C.: Beard Books.

Dumas, Angela. 1995. "Reflections on Design and the Third Way." In *Mary Parker Follett, Prophet of Management: A Celebration of Writings from the 1920s*, edited by Pauline Graham, 205-11. Washington, D.C.: Beard Books.

Durant, Robert F., and Jennifer R. S. Durant, eds. 2012. *Debating Public Administration: Management Challenges, Choices, and Opportunities*. Boca Raton, FL: CRC Press.

Edwards, Jason. 2010. "The Materialism of Historical Materialism." In *New Materialisms: Ontology, Agency, and Politics*, edited by Diana Coole and Samantha Frost, 281-98. Durham, NC: Duke University Press.

Elias, Maria Veronica, and Mohamad G. Alkadry. 2011. "Constructive Conflict, Participation, and Shared Governance." *Administration & Society* 43 (8): 869-95.

Ellsworth, William L. 2013. "Injection-Induced Earthquakes." *Science* 341 (12 July).

Emerson, Kirk, Tina Nabatchi, and Stephen Balogh. 2012. "An Integrative Framework For Collaborative Governance." *Journal of Public Administration Research and Theory* 22 (1): 1-29. doi:10.1093/jopart/mur011.

Emmert, Mark A., and Michael M. Crow. 1988. "Public, Private and Hybrid Organizations: An Empirical Examination of the Role of Publicness." *Administration and Society* 20 (2): 216-44.

Enomoto, Tokihiko. 1995. "The Individual in the Group." In *Mary Parker Follett, Prophet of Management: A Celebration of Writings from the 1920s*, edited by Pauline Graham, 240-45. Washington, D.C.: Beard Books.

Epstein, Wendy Netter. 2013. "Contract Theory and the Failure of Public-Private Contracting." *Cordozo Law Review* 34: 2211-259.

Escobar, Oliver. 2011. "Public Dialogue and Deliberation: A Communication Perspective for Public Engagement Practitioners." In, ed Edinburgh Beltane. Edinburgh, Scotland: Beacons for Public Engagement.

Evans, Karen G., and Gary L. Wamsley. 1999. "Where's the Institution? Neoinstitutionalism and Public Management." In *Public Management Reform and Innovation: Research, Theory, and Application*, edited by George H. Frederickson and Jocelyn M. Johnston, 117-44. Tuscaloosa, AL: University of Alabama Press.

Eylon, Dafna. 1998. "Understanding Empowerment and Resolving Its Paradox: Lessons from Mary Parker Follett." *Journal of Management History* 4 (1): 16.

Fagence, M. 1977. *Citizen Participation in Planning*. New York: Pergamon Press.

Farmer, David John. 2002a. "Introduction." *Administration & Society* 34: 87-90.

Farmer, David John. 2002b. "Questions." *Administration & Society* 34: 125-29.

Fisher, Roger, and William Ury. 1991. *Getting to Yes: Negotiating Agreement without Giving In*. Second edition. New York: Houghton Mifflin Company.

Foley, Jonathan A., Ruth DeFries, Gregory P. Asner, Carol Barford, Gordon Bonan, Stephen R. Carpenter, F. Stuart Chapin, Michael T. Coe,

Gretchen C. Daily, Holly K. Gibbs, Joseph H. Helkowski, Tracey Holloway, Erica A. Howard, Christopher J. Kucharik, Chad Monfreda, Jonathan A. Patz, I. Colin Prentice, Navin Ramankutty, and Peter K. Snyder. 2005. "Global Consequences of Land Use." *Science* 309 (22 June): 570-74.

Follett, Mary Parker. 1896. *The Speaker of the House of Representatives.* New York: Longmans, Green and Co.

Follett, Mary Parker. 1918. *The New State: Group Organization the Solution of Popular Government.* New York: Longmans, Green and Co.

Follett, Mary Parker. 1919. "Community Is a Process." *Philosophical Review* 28 (6): 576-88.

Follett, Mary Parker. 1924. *Creative Experience.* New York: Longmans, Green and Co.

Follett, Mary Parker. 1926. "Some Methods of Executive Efficiency." In *Proceedings of the Twenty-Third Lecture Conference tor Works Directors, Foremen and Forewomen*, edited by Oxford Ballioll College, 72-76. York: Yorkshire Printing Works.

Follett, Mary Parker. 1970. "The Teacher-Student Relation." *Administrative Science Quarterly* 15 (2): 137-48.

Follett, Mary Parker. (1918) 1998. *The New State: Group Organization the Solution of Popular Government.* University Park, PA: Pennsylvania State University Press.

Follett, Mary Parker. (1942) 2003a. "Business as Integrative Unity." In *Dynamic Administration: The Collected Papers of Mary Parker Follett*, edited by Henry C. Metcalf and Lyndall Urwick, 71-94. New York: Routledge.

Follett, Mary Parker. (1942) 2003b. "Constructive Conflict." In *Dynamic Administration: The Collected Papers of Mary Parker Follett*, edited by Henry C. Metcalf and Lyndall Urwick, 30-49. New York: Routledge.

Follett, Mary Parker. (1942) 2003c. "The Giving of Orders." In *Dynamic Administration: The Collected Papers of Mary Parker Follett*, edited by Henry C. Metcalf and Lyndall Urwick, 50-70. New York: Routledge.

Follett, Mary Parker. (1942) 2003d. "How Must Business Management Develop in Order to Become a Profession." In *Dynamic Administration: The Collected Papers of Mary Parker Follett*, edited by Henry C. Metcalf and Lyndall Urwick, 132-45. New York: Routledge.

Follett, Mary Parker. (1942) 2003e. "How Must Business Management Develop in Order to Possess the Essentials of a Profession?" In *Dynamic Administration: The Collected Papers of Mary Parker Follett*, edited by Henry C. Metcalf and Lyndall Urwick, 117-31. New York: Routledge.

Follett, Mary Parker. (1942) 2003f. "Individualism in a Planned Society." In *Dynamic Administration: The Collected Papers of Mary Parker Follett*, edited by Henry C. Metcalf and Lyndall Urwick, 295-314. New York: Routledge.

Follett, Mary Parker. (1942) 2003g. "The Influence of Employee Representation in a Remoulding of the Accepted Type of Business Manager." In *Dynamic Administration: The Collected Papers of Mary Parker Follett*, edited by Henry C. Metcalf and Lyndall Urwick, 167-82. New York: Routledge.

Follett, Mary Parker. (1942) 2003h. "Leader and Expert." In *Dynamic Administration: The Collected Papers of Mary Parker Follett*, edited by Henry C. Metcalf and Lyndall Urwick, 247-69. New York: Routledge.

Follett, Mary Parker. (1942) 2003i. "The Meaning of Responsibility in Business Management." In *Dynamic Administration: The Collected Papers of Mary Parker Follett*, edited by Henry C. Metcalf and Lyndall Urwick, 146-66. New York: Routledge.

Follett, Mary Parker. (1942) 2003j. "Power." In *Dynamic Administration: The Collected Papers of Mary Parker Follett*, edited by Henry C. Metcalf and Lyndall Urwick, 95-116. New York: Routledge.

Follett, Mary Parker. (1942) 2003k. "The Psychology of Conciliation and Arbitration." In *Dynamic Administration: The Collected Papers of Mary Parker Follett*, edited by Henry C. Metcalf and Lyndall Urwick, 230-46. New York: Routledge. .

Follett, Mary Parker. (1942) 2003l. "The Psychology of Consent and Participation." In *Dynamic Administration: The Collected Papers of Mary Parker Follett*, edited by Henry C. Metcalf and Lyndall Urwick, 210-29. New York: Routledge.

Follett, Mary Parker. (1942) 2003m. "The Psychology of Control." In *Dynamic Administration: The Collected Papers of Mary Parker Follett*, edited by Henry C. Metcalf and Lyndall Urwick, 183-209. New York: Routledge.

Follett, Mary Parker. (1942) 2003n. "Some Discrepencies in Leadership Theory and Practice." In *Dynamic Administration: The Collected*

Papers of Mary Parker Follett, edited by Henry C. Metcalf and Lyndall Urwick, 270-94. New York: Routledge.

Follett, Mary Parker. (1949) 2013a. "The Basis of Authority." In *Freedom and Co-Ordination: Lectures in Business Organization by Mary Parker Follett*, edited by Lyndall Urwick, 34-46. Abingdon: Routledge.

Follett, Mary Parker. (1949) 2013b. "Co-ordination." In *Freedom and Co-Ordination: Lectures in Business Organization by Mary Parker Follett*, edited by Lyndall Urwick, 61-76. Abingdon: Routledge.

Follett, Mary Parker. (1949) 2013c. *Creative Experience*. Peabody, MA: Martino Fine Books.

Follett, Mary Parker. (1949) 2013d. "The Essentials of Leadership." In *Freedom and Co-ordination: Lectures in Business Organization by Mary Parker Follett*, edited by Lyndall Urwick, 47-60. Abingdon: Routledge.

Follett, Mary Parker. (1949) 2013e. *Freedom and Co-ordination: Lectures in Business Organization, Routledge Library Editions: Organizations*. New York: Routledge.

Follett, Mary Parker. (1949) 2013f. "The giving of orders." In *Freedom and Co-ordination: Lectures in Business Organization by Mary Parker Follett*, edited by Lyndall Urwick, 16-33. Abingdon: Routledge.

Follett, Mary Parker. (1949) 2013g. "The Illusion of Final Authority." In *Freedom and Co-ordination: Lectures in Business Organization by Mary Parker Follett*, edited by Lyndall Urwick, 1-15. Abingdon: Routledge.

Follett, Mary Parker. (1949) 2013h. "The Process of Control." In *Freedom and Co-ordination: Lectures in Business Organization by Mary Parker Follett*, edited by Lyndall Urwick, 77-89. Abingdon: Routledge.

Ford, Lewis S. 1977. "An Appraisal of Whiteheadian Nontheism." *Southern Journal of Philosophy* 15 (1): 27-35.

Forester, John. 2006. "Making Participation Work When Interests Conflict: Moving from Facilitating Dialogue and Moderating Debate to Mediating Negotiations." *Journal of the American Planning Association* 72 (4): 447-56.

Forester, John. 2009. *Dealing with Differences: Dramas of Mediating Public Disputes*. Oxford: Oxford University Press.

Foucault, Michel. 1977. "Nietzsche, Genealogy, History." In *Language, Counter-Memory, Practice: Selected Essays and Interviews*, edited by D. F. Bouchard. Ithaca: Cornell University Press.

Foucault, Michel. 1978. *The History of Sexuality*. III vols. Vol. I. New York: Pantheon Books.

Fox, Elliot M. 1968. "Mary Parker Follett: The Enduring Contribution." *Public Administration Review* 28 (6): 520-29.

Fraser, Nancy, and Linda Nicholson. 1988. "Social Criticism without Philosophy: An Encounter between Feminism and Postmodernism." *Theory, Culture & Society* 5: 373-94.

Freeman, R. Edward. 1984. *Strategic Management: A Stakeholder Approach*. Boston: Pitman.

Fremond, Olivier, and Mierta Capaul. 2002. The State of Corporate Governance: Experience from County Assessments. In *Policy Research Working Paper*. Washington, D.C.: The World Bank.

Freudenburg, William R., and Robert Gramling. 2011. *Blowout in the Gulf: The BP Oil Spill Disaster and the Future Of Energy in America*. Cambridge: MIT Press.

Fry, Brian R. 1989. *Mastering Public Administration: From Max Weber to Dwight Waldo*. 1st ed: Seven Bridges Press, LLC.

Fry, Brian R., and Jos C. N. Raadschelders. 2008. *Mastering Public Administration: From Max Weber to Dwight Waldo*. 2nd ed. Washington, D.C.: CQ Press.

Fry, Brian R., and Jos C. N. Raadschelders. 2014. *Mastering Public Administration: From Max Weber to Dwight Waldo*. 3rd ed. Washington, D.C.: CQ Press.

Fry, Brian R., and Lotte L. Thomas. 1996. "Mary Parker Follett: Assessing the Contribution and Impact of her Writings." *Journal of Management History* 2 (2): 11.

Fuller, R. Buckminster. 1975. *Synergetics: Explorations in the Geometry of Thinking*. London: Macmillan Publishing Co. Inc.

Fung, Archon. 2006. "Varieties of Participation in Complex Governance." *Public Administration Review* 66: 66-75.

Gabriele, Kathryn R. 2013. "Lessons from a Buried Past: Settlement Women and Democratically Anchored Governance Networks." *Administration & Society*. doi:10.1177/0095399713481600.

Gadamer, Hans-Georg. 1997. *Truth and Method*. 2nd ed. New York: Continuum.

Gardner, Howard. 1983. *Frames of Mind: The Theory of Multiple Intelligences*. New York: Basic Books.

Gare, Arran. 2000. "Human Ecology, Process Philosophy, and the Global Ecological Crisis." *Concrescence: The Australian Journal of Process Thought* 1: 1-11.

Gehani, R. Ray, and Rashmi Gehani. 2007. "Mary Parker Follett's Constructive Conflict: A "Psychological Foundation of Business Administration" for Innovative Global Enterprises." *International Journal of Public Administration* 30 (4): 387-404.

George, Claude S. Jr. 1972. *The History of Management Thought.* 2nd ed. Englewood Cliffs, NJ: Prentice-Hall.

George, Henry. (1879) 1929. *Progress and Poverty, the Remedy: An Inquiry into the Causes of Industrial Depressions and the Increase of Want with Increase of Wealth, The Modern Library.* New York: Random House.

Giddens, Anthony. 1984. *The Constitution of Society: Outline of the Theory of Structuration.* Berkeley University of California Press.

Gilligan, Carol. 1982. *In a Different Voice.* Cambridge, MA: Harvard University Press.

Goleman, Daniel. 1995. *Emotional Intelligence: Why It Can Matter More Than IQ.* New York: Bantam Books.

Goleman, Daniel. 2011. *Working with Emotional Intelligence.* New York: Bantam Dell.

Gore, Al, and Bill Clinton. 1993. From Red Tape to Results: Creating a Government That Works Better and Costs Less. Washington, D.C.: U.S. Government Printing Office.

Grady, Robert C. 2002. The Demise and Restoration of Pluralism in Early Political Science In *Southern Political Science Association Annual Meetings.* Savannah, Georgia.

Graham, Daniel W. 2002. "Heraclitus and Parmenides." *Presocratic Philosophy: Essays in Honour of Alexander Mourelatos*: 27-44.

Graham, Pauline. 1995a. "Mary Parker Follett (1868-1933): A Pioneering Life." In *Mary Parker Follett, Prophet of Management: A Celebration of Writings from the 1920s*, edited by Pauline Graham, 11-32. Washington, D.C.: Beard Books.

Graham, Pauline, ed. 1995b. *Mary Parker Follett, Prophet of Management: A Celebration of Writings from the 1920s.* Washington, D.C.: Beard Books.

Greenleaf, Robert. 1982. *Servant As Leader.* Indianapolis, IN: Robert K. Greenleaf Center.

Griffin, David Ray, ed. 1988. *Spirituality and Society: Postmodern Visions.* Albany: State University of New York Press.

Griffin, David Ray. 2001. *Reenchantment without Supernaturalism: A Process Philosophy of Religion.* Ithaca: Cornell University Press.

Griffin, David Ray. 2007. *Whitehead's Radically Different Postmodern Philosophy: An Argument for its Contemporary Relevance.* Albany, NY: State University of New York Press.

Gulick, Luther, and Lyndall Urwick, eds. 1937. *Papers on the Science of Administration.* New York: Institute of Public Administration.

Habermas, Jürgen. 1984. *The Theory of Communicative Action, Vol. 1: Reason and the Rationalization of Society.* Translated by T. McCarthy. Boston: Beacon Press.

Habermas, Jürgen. 1989. *The Structural Transformation of the Public Sphere: An Inquiry into a Category Of Bourgeois Society.* Cambridge: MIT Press.

Habermas, Jürgen. 1998. *Between Facts and Norms.* Cambridge, MA: MIT Press.

Habermas, Jürgen, and Maeve Cooke, eds. 1998. *On the Pragmatics of Communication, Studies in Contemporary German Social Thought.* Cambridge, MA: MIT Press.

Haldane, Richard Burdon. 1920. "Introduction." In *The New State: Group Organization the Solution of Popular Government*, edited by Mary Parker Follett. New York: Longmans, Green and Co.

Halden, Rolf U., and Kellog J. Schwab. 2008. Environmental Impact of Industrial Farm Animal Production. Pew Commission on Industrial Farm Animal Production.

Harmon, Michael M. 2006. *Public Administration's Final Exam: A Pragmatist Restructuring of the Profession and the Discipline.* Tuscaloosa, AL: University of Alabama Press.

Harmon, Michael M., and O. C. McSwite. 2011. *Whenever Two or More Are Gathered: Relationship as the Heart of Ethical Discourse.* Edited by Camilla Stivers, *Public Administration: Criticism & Creativity.* Tuscaloosa, AL: The University of Alabama Press.

Hartley, Jean, Eva Sørensen, and Jacob Torfing. 2013. "Collaborative Innovation: A Viable Alternative to Market Competition and Organizational Entrepreneurship." *Public Administration Review* 73 (6): 821-30. doi:10.1111/puar.12136.

Hegel, Georg W. F. (1807) 1977. *Phenomenology of Spirit.* Translated by

Arnold V. Miller. Oxford: Clarendon Press.

Heidegger, Martin. 1996. *Being and Time*. Translated by J. Stambaugh. Albany, NY: State University of New York Press.

Hendriks, Frank. 2010. *Vital Democracy: A Theory of Democracy in Action*. New York: Oxford University Press.

Henton, Douglas, John Melville, and Kimberly Walesh. 1997. *Grassroots Leaders for a New Economy: How Civic Entrepreneurs are Building Prosperous Communities*. San Francisco: Jossey-Bass.

Hertting, Nils, and Evert Vedung. 2012. "Purposes and Criteria in Network Governance Evaluation: How Far Does Standard Evaluation Vocabulary Take Us?" *Evaluation* 18 (1): 27-46.

Holt, Edwin B. (1919) 1925. *The New Realism*. New York: Macmillan.

Hood, Christopher. 1996. "Exploring Variations in Public Management Reform of the 1980s." In *Civil Service Systems in Comparative Perspective*, edited by H. A. Bekke, James L. Perry and T. A. Toonen, 268-87. Bloomington, IN: Indiana University Press.

Houston, David J., and Sybil M. Delevan. 1990. "Public Administration Research: An Assessment of Journal Publications." *Public Administration Review* 50: 674-81.

Howard, Ted, Lillian Kuri, and India Pierce Lee. 2010. The Evergreen Cooperative Initiative Of Cleveland, Ohio: Writing the Next Chapter for Anchor-Based Redevelopment Initiatives. In *The Neighborhood Funders Group Annual Conference*. Minneapolis, MN.

Howe, Louis E. 2006. "Enchantment, Weak Ontologies, and Administrative Ethics." *Administration & Society* 38 (4): 422-46.

Hummel, Ralph P. 2002. "Critique of "Public Space"." *Administration & Society* 34: 102-07.

Hunt, Rockwell D. 1937. "Co-opetition." *Los Angeles Times*, November 20, A.

Husserl, Edmund. (1931) 1982. *General Introduction to a Pure Phenomenology*. Translated by F. Kerston. Boston: Kluwer.

Imperial, Mark T., James L. Perry, and Michael C. Katula. 2007. "Incorporating Service Learning into Public Affairs Programs: Lessons from the Literature." *Journal of Public Affairs Education* 13 (2): 243-64.

Innes, J. E., and D. E. Booher. 1999. "Consensus Building as Role Playing and Bricolage." *Journal of the American Planning Association* 65 (1): 9-26.

Irvine, Andrew D. 2010. Alfred North Whitehead. In *Stanford Encyclopedia of Philosophy*. Stanford, CA: Stanford University Metaphysics Research Lab.

Jacoby, Barbara. 2003. "Fundamentals of Service Learning Partnerships." In *Buildng Partnerships for Service Learning*, edited by Barbara Jacoby, 1-29. San Francisco: John Wiley & Sons.

James, William. 1907. *Pragmatism: A New Name for Some Old Ways of Thinking*. Cambridge, MA: Harvard University.

James, William. 1909. *A Pluralistic Universe*. New York: Longmans, Green.

James, William. (1907) 1955. *Pragmatism and Four Essays from The Meaning of Truth*. New York: Meridian Books.

Johnson, Avis L. 2007. "Mary Parker Follett: Laying the Foundations for Spirituality in the Workplace." *International Journal of Public Administration* 30 (4): 425-39.

Jones-Patulli, Jennifer. 2011. Reconciling the Carrot and the Stick: An Intellectual History of Integrative Bargaining in 20th Century American Organizational Relations. In *CRC Working Paper*. Ottawa, Ontario, Canada: Saint Paul University.

Kaag, John. 2008. "Women and Forgotten Movements in American Philosophy: The Work of Ella Lyman Cabor and Mary Parker Follett." *Transactions of the Charles S. Peirce Society* 44 (1): 134-57.

Kagan, Shelly 1998. *Normative Ethics*. Boulder, CO: Westview Press.

Kakabadse, Andrew, Alexander Kouzmin, Nada K. Kakabadse, and Nikolai Mouraviev. 2013. "Auditing Moral Hazards for the Post-Global Financial Crisis (GFC) Leadership." In *State Crimes Against Democracy: Political Forensics in Public Affairs*, edited by Alexander Kouzmin, Matthew T. Witt and Andrew Kakabadse. New York: Palgrave Macmillan.

Kane, Douglas D., Joseph D. Conroy, R. Peter Richards, David B. Baker, and David A. Culver. 2014. "Re-eutrophication of Lake Erie: Correlations between Tributary Nutrient Loads and Phytoplankton Biomass." *Journal of Great Lakes Research*. doi:10.1016/j.jglr.2014.04.004.

Kanter, Rosabeth Moss. 1995. "Preface." In *Mary Parker Follett, Prophet of Management: A Celebration of Writings from the 1920s*, edited by Pauline Graham, xiii-xix. Washington, D.C.: Beard Books.

Kassotis, Christopher D., Donald E. Tillitt, J. Wade Davis, Annette M. Hormann, and Susan C. Nagel. 2014. "Estrogen and Androgen

Receptor Activities of Hydraulic Fracturing Chemicals and Surface and Ground Water in a Drilling-Dense Region." *Endocrinology* 155 (3): 897-907.

Kathlene, L., and J. A. Martin. 1991. "Enhancing Citizen Participation: Panel Designs, Perspectives, and Policy Formation." *Journal of Policy Analysis and Management* 10 (1): 46-63.

Katz, Daniel, and Robert Louis Kahn. 1978. *The Social Psychology of Organizations*. Vol. 2d. New York: Wiley.

Keller, Catherine. 2003. *Face of the Deep: A Theology of Becoming*. New York: Routledge.

Kelly, Rita Mae. 1998. "An Inclusive Democratic Polity, Representative Bureaucracies, and the New Public Management." *Public Administration Review* 58 (3): 201-08.

Kensen, Sandra. 2008. "Reflections on Theory in Action: An Introduction and Invitation to Participate." *Administrative Theory & Praxis* 30 (10): 139-42.

Keohane, R. O., and J. S. Nye. 2000. "Globalization: What's New? What's Not? (And So What?)." *Foreign Policy* 118 (Spring): 104-19.

Kettl, Donald F. 1993. *Sharing Power: Public Governance and Private Markets*. Washington, DC: Brookings Institution.

Kettl, Donald F. 2000. "The Transformation of Governance: Globalization, Devolution, and the Role of Government." *Public Administration Review* 60 (6): 488-97.

Kettl, Donald F. 2006. "Managing Boundaries in American Administration: The Collaborative Imperative." *Public Administration Review* 66 (s1): 10-19.

Killian, Jerri. 2004. "Pedagogical Experimentation: Combining Traditional, Distance, and Service Learning Techniques." *Journal of Public Affairs Education* 10 (3): 209-24.

King, Cheryl Simrell, ed. 2011. *Government Is Us 2.0*. Armonk, NY: M. E. Sharpe.

King, Cheryl Simrell, Kathryn M. Feltey, and Bridget O. Susel. 1998. "The Question of Participation: Toward Authentic Participation in Public Administration." *Public Administration Review* 58 (4): 317-26.

King, Cheryl Simrell, Camilla Stivers, and Collaborators, eds. 1998. *Government Is Us: Public Administration in an Anti-Government Era*. Thousand Oaks, CA: Sage Publications.

King, Cheryl Simrell, and Lisa A. Zanetti. 2005. *Transformational Public Service: Portraitsof Theory in Practice*. Armonk, NY: M. E. Sharpe.

Klingner, Donald E. 2004. "Globalization, Governance, and the Future of Public Administration: Can We Make Sense Out of the Fog of Rhetoric Surrounding the Terminology?" *Public Administration Review* 64 (6): 737-43.

Kolb, Deborah M. 1996. "The Love for Three Oranges or: What Did We Miss about Ms. Follett in the Library?" *Negotiation Journal* 11 (4): 339-48.

Koppenjan, Joop, and Erik-Hans Klijn. 2004. *Managing Uncertainties in Networks*. London: Routledge.

Kramer, Robert. 2007. "How Might Action Learning Be Used to Develop the Emotional Intelligence and Leadership Capacity of Public Administrators?" *Journal of Public Affairs Education* 13 (2): 205-42.

Krupp, Sherman R. 1961. *Pattern in Organization Analysis: A Critical Examination*. New York: Holt, Rinehart and Winston.

Lambright, Kristina T. 2008. "Lessons Outside of the Classroom: Examining the Effectiveness of Service Learning Projects at Achieving Learning Objectives." *Journal of Public Affairs Education* 14 (2) :205-17.

Lambright, Kristina T., and Yi Lu. 2009. "What Impacts the *Learning* in Service Learning? An Examination of Project Structure and Student Characteristics." *Journal of Public Affairs Education* 15 (4): 425-44.

Lasswell, Harold D. 1950. *Politics: Who Gets What, When, How*. New York: McGraw-Hill.

Lawrence, Paul R. 1995. "Epilogue." In *Mary Parker Follett, Prophet of Management: A Celebration of Writings from the 1920s*, edited by Pauline Graham, 291-96. Washington, D.C.: Beard Books.

Lewicki, Roy, David Saunders, and Bruce Barry. 2003. *Negotiation*. 4th ed. Boston: McGraw Hill Irwin.

Lewin, Kurt. 1958. *Group Decision and Social Change*. New York: Holt, Rinehart and Winston.

Lishner, David A., C. Daniel Batson, and Elizabeth Huss. 2011. "Tenderness and Sympathy: Distinct Empathic Emotions Elicited by Different Forms of Need." *Personality and Social Psychology Bulletin* 37 (5): 614–25.

Loomer, Bernard. 1976. "Two Conceptions of power." *Criterion* 15 (1): 7-29.

Love, Jeannine M. 2008. "The Rugged Individualist Club." *Administrative Theory & Praxis* 30 (4): 424-49.

Love, Jeannine M. 2012. "From Atomistic to Interwoven: Utilizing a Typology of i/Individualisms to Envision a Process Approach to Governance." *Administrative Theory & Praxis* 34 (3): 362-84.

Love, Jeannine M. 2013. "A Society of Control: The Paradox of the People and the Individual" *Public Administration Quarterly* 37 (4), 576-93.

Luhmann, Niklas. 1995. *Social Systems.* Stanford: Stanford University Press.

Maddock, Su, and Marion Mcalpine. 2006. "An Inspiration for Tme: Mary Parker Follett (1968-1933)." *The British Journal of Leadership in Public Services* 2 (2): 44-48.

Mallin, Michael A., and Lawrence B. Cahoon. 2003. "Industrial Animal Production: A Major Source of Nutrient and Microbial Pollution." *Population and Environment* 24 (5): 369.

Mansbridge, Jane J. 1998. "Mary Parker Follett: Feminist and Negotiator." In *The New State: Group Organization the Solution of Popular Government,* xvii-xxviii. University Park, PA: Pennsylvania State University Press.

Marcuse, Herbert. 1972. *Counterrevolution and Revolt.* Boston: Beacon Press.

Marsh, David. 1998. "The Development of the Policy Network Approach." In *Comparing Policy Networks,* edited by David Marsh, 3-17. Philadelphia: Open University Press.

Mathews, David. 2014. *The Ecology of Democracy: Finding Ways to Have a Stronger Hand in Shaping Our Future.* Dayton, OH: Kettering Foundation Press.

Mattson, Kevin. 1998. "Reading Follett: An Introduction to *The New State.*" In *The New State: Group Organization the Solution of Popular Government,* xxviv-lix. University Park, PA: Pennsylvania State University Press.

Maturana, Humberto R., and Francisco Varela. (1987) 1992. *The Tree of Knowledge: The Biological Roots of Human Understanding.* 2nd Ed. Boston: Shambhala Publications.

McCurdy, Howard E., and Robert E. Cleary. 1984. "Why Can't We Resolve the Research Issue in Public Administration?" *Public Administration Review* 44 (1): 49-55.

McGaw, Dickenson, and Louis Wechsler. 1999. "Romancing the Capstone: The Jewel of Public Value." *Journal of Public Affairs Education* 5 (2): 89-105.

McGregor, Douglas. 1960. *The Human Side of Enterprise.* New York: McGraw-Hill.

McLarney, C., and Shelley Rhyno. 1999. "Mary Parker Follett: Visionary Leadership and Strategic Management." *Women in Management Review* 14 (7): 292-304.

McSwite, O. C. 1997. *Legitimacy in Public Administration: A Discourse Analysis.* Thousand Oaks, CA: Sage Publications.

McSwite, O. C. 2001. "Theory Competency for MPA-Educated Practitioners." *Public Administration Review* 61: 111-15.

McSwite, O. C. 2006. "Public Administration as the Carrier of the New Social Bond." *Administrative Theory & Praxis* 28 (2): 176-89.

Melé, Domènec. 2007. "Ethics in Management: Exploring the Contribution of Mary Parker Follett." *International Journal of Public Administration* 30 (4): 404-24.

Mendenhall, Mark E., James H. Macomber, and Marc Cutright. 2000. "Mary Parker Follett: Prophet of Chaos and Complexity." *Journal of Management History* 6 (4): 191.

Mesle, C. Robert. 2008. *Process-Relational Philosophy: An Introduction to Alfred North Whitehead.* West Conshohocken, PA: Templeton Foundation Press.

Metcalf, Henry C., and Lyndall Urwick, eds. 1942. *Dynamic Administration: The Collected Papers of Mary Parker Follett.* New York: Harper & Brothers Publishers.

Metcalf, Henry C., and Lyndall Urwick, eds. 2003. *Dynamic Administration: The Collected Papers of Mary Parker Follett.* New York: Routledge.

Miller, Hugh T., and Cheryl Simrell King. 1998. "Practical Theory." *American Review of Public Administration* 28: 43-60.

Milward, H. B., and K. Provan. 1998. "Measuring Network Structure." *Public Administration* 76 (Summer): 387-407.

Mintzberg, Henry. 1995. "Some Fresh Air for Management?" In *Mary Parker Follett, Prophet of Management: A Celebration of Writings from the 1920s,* edited by Pauline Graham, 199-204. Washington, D.C.: Beard Books.

Moore, James F. 1993. "Predators and Prey: A New Ecology of Competition." *Harvard Business Review* May-June: 75-86.

Morris, Randall C. 1991. *Process Philosophy and Political Ideology: The Social and Political Thought of Alfred North Whitehead and Charles Hartshorne.* Albany, NY: State University of New York Press.

Morse, Ricardo S. 2006. "Prophet of Participation: Mary Parker Follett and Public Participation in Public Administration." *Administrative Theory & Praxis* 28 (1): 1-32.

Morton, Noel O'R., and Stefanie A. Lindquist. 1997. "Revealing the Feminist in Mary Parker Follett." *Administration & Society* 29 (3): 348-71.

Nabatchi, Tina. 2010. "Addressing the Citizenship and Democratic Deficits: The Potential of Deliberative Democracy for Public Administration." *The American Review of Public Administration* 40 (4): 376-99. doi:10.1177/0275074009356467.

Nabatchi, Tina. 2012. "Putting the "Public" Back in Public Values Research: Designing Participation to Identify and Respond to Values." *Public Administration Review* 72 (5): 699-708. doi:10.1111/j.1540-6210.2012.02544.x.

NASPAA. 2009. NASPAA Accreditation Standards. Washington, D.C.: National Association of Schools of Public Affairs and Administration.

Neufeldt, Victoria, ed. 1996. *Webster's New World College Dictionary*. 3rd ed. New York: Macmillan.

Newcomer, Kathryn E., and Heather Allen. 2010. "Public Service Education: Adding Value in The Public Interest." *Journal of Public Affairs Education* 16 (2): 207-29.

Nickel, Patricia Mooney, and Angela M. Eikenberry. 2006. "Beyond Public vs. Private: The Transformative Potential of Democratic Feminist Management." *Administrative Theory & Praxis* 28 (3): 359-80.

Nietzsche, Friedrich. (1901) 1968. *Will to Power*. New York: Vintage Books.

Nohria, Nitin. 1995. "Mary Parker Follett's View on Power, the Giving of Orders, and Authority: An Altenrative to Hierarchy or a Utopian Ideology?" In *Mary Parker Follett, Prophet of Management: A Celebration of Writings from the 1920s*, edited by Pauline Graham, 154-62. Washington, D.C.: Beard Books.

North, Douglass C. 1990. *Institutions, Institutional Change and Economic Performance*. Cambridge: Cambridge University Press.

Novicevic, Milorad M., Michael G. Harvey, M. Ronald Buckley, Daniel Wren, and Leticia Pena. 2007. "Communities of Creative Practice: Follett's Seminal Conceptualization." *International Journal of Public Administration* 30 (4): 367-85.

O'Connor, Ellen S. 1996. "Lines of Authority: Readings of Foundational Texts on the Profession of Management." *Journal of Management History* 2 (3): 26-49.

O'Connor, Ellen S. 2000. "Integrating Follett: History, Philosophy and Management." *Journal of Management History* 6 (4): 167-90.

Ormaechea, Jose Maria. 2001. "Mondragon's Ten Basic Principles." *Social Policy* 32 (2): 4-9.

Osborn, Stephen G. , Avner Vengosh, Nathaniel R. Warner, and Robert B. Jackson. 2011. "Methane Contamination of Drinking Water Accompanying Gas-Well Drilling and Hydraulic Fracturing." *Proceedings of the National Academy of Sciences* 108: 8172-176.

Osborne, David, and Ted Gaebler. 1992. *Reinventing Government: How the Entrepreneurial Spirit is Transforming the Public Sector.* Reading, MA: Addison-Wesley.

Ostrom, Vincent. (1973) 1989. *The Intellectual Crisis in American Public Administration.* 2nd ed. Tuscaloosa, AL: University of Alabama Press.

Parker, Lee D. 1984. "Control in Organizational Life: The Contribution of Mary Parker Follett." *The Academy of Management Review* 9 (4): 736-45.

Parker, Sir Peter. 1995. "Most Quoted—Least Heeded: The Five Senses of Follett." In *Mary Parker Follett, Prophet of Management: A Celebration of Writings from the 1920s,* edited by Pauline Graham, 282-90. Washington, D.C.: Beard Books.

Parsons, Talcott. 1968. *The Structure of Social Action: A Study in Social Theory With Special Reference to a Group Of Recent European Writers.* New York: Free Press.

Patalon, Miroslaw. 2009. "Discursive Construction of the Subject and Inter-religious Dialogue from the Perspective of Process Theology." In *The Process Perspective: The Philosophical Basis of Inter-religious Dialogue,* edited by Miroslaw Patalon. Newcastle upon Tyne: Cambridge Scholars Publishing.

Peirce, Charles S. 1877. "The Fixation of Belief." *Popular Science Monthly* 12: 1-15.

Perry, James L., and Kenneth L. Kraemer. 1986. "Research Methodology in the Public Administration Review, 1975-1984." *Public Administration Review* 46: 215-26.

Pesch, Udo. 2008. "The Publicness of Public Administration." *Administration & Society* 40: 170-93.

Pfeffer, Jeffrey. 1997. *New Directions for Organization Theory: Problems and Prospects.* Oxford: Oxford University Press.

Phillips, John R. 2010. "Scholarship and Public Service: The Life and Work of Mary Parker Follett." *Public Voices* XI (2): 47-69.

Pittenger, Norman. 1989. *Becoming and Belonging: The Meaning of Human Existence and Community.* Wilton, CN: Morehouse Publishing.

Plein, L. Christopher, and Jeremy Morris. 2005. "Promoting Smart Growth Through Participation and Partnership: The Community Design Team in Rural West Virginia." In *Partnerships for Smart Growth: University-Community Collaboration for Better Public Places*, edited by Wim Wiewel and Gerrit-Jan Knaap, 165-80. Armonk, NY: M. E. Sharpe.

Posner, Paul L. 2009. "The Pracademic: An Agenda for Re-Engaging Practitioners and Academics." *Public Budgeting & Finance* 29 (1): 12-26.

Pratt, Scott L. 2011. "American Power: Mary Parker Follett and Michel Foucault." *Foucault Studies* (11): 76-91.

Provan, Keith G., and Patrick Kenis. 2008. "Modes of Network Governance: Structure, Management, and Effectiveness." *Journal of Public Administration Research and Theory* 18 (2): 229-52. doi:10.1093/jopart/mum015.

Prozorov, Sergei. 2014a. *Ontology and World Politics: Void Universalism I.* Edited by Edkins Jenny and Nick Vaughan-Williams. 2 vols. Vol. 1, *Interventions.* New York: Routledge.

Prozorov, Sergei. 2014b. *Theory of the Political Subject: Void Universalism II.* Edited by Edkins Jenny and Nick Vaughan-Williams. 2 vols. Vol. 1, *Interventions.* New York: Routledge.

Pruitt, Dean G., and Steven A. Lewis. 1975. "Development of Integrative Solutions in Bilateral Negotiation." *Journal of Personality and Social Psychology* 31 (4): 621-33.

Raadschelders, Jos C. N., and Kwang-hoon Lee. 2011. "Trends in the Study of Public Administration: Empirical and Qualitative Observations from the Public Administration Review, 2000-2009." *Public Administration Review* 71 (1): 19-33.

Ramos, Alberto Guerreiro. 1981. *The New Science of Organizations: A Reconceptualization of the Wealth of Nations.* Buffalo, NY: University of Toronto Press.

Randolph, John. 2012. "Creating the Climate Change Resilient Community." In *Collaborative Resilience: Moving Through Crisis to Opportunity*, edited by Bruce Evan Goldstein, 127-48. Cambridge: The MIT Press.

Reid, Margaret, and Will Miller. 1997. "Bridging Theory and Administrative Practice: The Role of a Capstone Course in a P. A. Program." *International Journal of Public Administration* 20 (10): 1769-789.

Risse, Thomas. 2004. "Global Governance and Communicative Action." *Government and Opposition* 39 (2): 288-313.

Rittel, Horst W. J., and Melvin Webber. 1973. "Dilemmas in a General Theory of Planning." *Policy Sciences* 4 (2): 155-69.

Roll, Stephen, and Nicole Thomas. 2014. "The Legacy of Mary Parker Follett in Contemporary Scholarship." In *Mastering Public Administration: From Max Weber to Dwight Waldo*, edited by Brian R. Fry and Jos C. N. Raadschelders, 172-80. Washington, D.C.: CQ Press.

Root, Vernon M. 1953. "Eternal Objects, Attributes, and Relations in Whitehead's Philosophy." *Philosophy and Phenomenological Research* 14 (2): 196-204.

Roy, Mathieu, and Harold Crooks. 2011. *Surviving Progress.* Canada: Big Picture Media Corporation.

Ryan, Lori V., and Matthew A. Rutherford. 2000. "Mary Parker Follett: Individualist or Collectivist? Or Both?" *Journal of Management History* 6 (5): 207-23.

Sabatier, Paul A. 1988. "An Advocacy Coalition Framework of Policy Change and the Role of Policy-Oriented Learning Therein." *Policy Sciences* 21 (2/3): 129-68.

Sabatier, Paul A., and Hank C. Jenkins-Smith. 1999. "The Advocacy Coalition Framework: An Assessment." In *Theories of the Policy Process: Theoretical Lenses on Public Policy*, edited by Paul A. Sabatier, 117-68. Boulder, CO: Westview Press.

Salamon, Lester M. 2005. "Training Professional Citizens: Getting Beyond the Right Answer to the Wrong Question in Public Administration." *Journal of Public Affairs Education* 11 (1): 7-20.

Salimath, Manjula S., and David J. Lemak. 2004. "Mary P. Follett: Translating philosophy into a Paradigm of Lifelong Learning." *Management Decision* 42 (10): 1284-296.

Sampson, Edward E. 1988. "The Debate on Individualism: Indigenous Psychologies of the Individual and Their Role in Personal and Societal Functioning." *American Psychologist* 43 (1).

Sandoval, Chela. 2000. *Methodology of the Oppressed.* Minneapolis: University of Minnesota.

Sarup, Madan. 1989. *An Introductory Guide to Post-Structuralism and Post-modernism.* Athens, GA: University of Georgia Press.

Sass, Mary. 2007. Integration is Not Collaboration: Implication for Win-Win Negotiations. In *International Association for Conflict Management,* edited by Donald E. Gibson. Budapest, Hungary: Fairfield University.

Savas, E. S. 2000. *Privatization and Public-Private Partnerships.* New York: Chatham House.

Schein, Edgar H. 2003. "On Dialogue, Culture, and Organizational Learning." *Reflections* 4 (4): 27-38.

Schilling, Melissa A. 2000. "Decades Ahead of Her Time: Advancing Stakeholder Theory Through the Ideas of Mary Parker Follett." *Journal of Management History* 6 (5): 224-42.

Schmidt, Mary R. 1993. "Grout: Alternative Forms of Knowledge and Why They Are Ignored." *Public Administration Review* 53 (6): 525-30.

Schön, Donald A. 1983. *The Reflective Practitioner: How Professionals Think in Action.* New York: Basic Books.

Schumpeter, Joseph A. 1943. *Capitalism, Socialism, and Democracy.* 6th ed. London: Routledge.

Seifter, Harvey, and Peter Economy. 2001. *Leadership Ensemble: Lessons in Collaborative Management from The World's Only Conductorless Orchestra.* New York: Henry Holt & Company.

Selber, Katherine, and David M. Austin. 1997. "Mary Parker Follett: Epilogue to or Return of a Social Work Management Pioneer?" *Administration in Social Work* 21 (1).

Selznick, Philip. 1949. *TVA and the Grass Roots.* Berkeley: University of California Press.

Senge, Peter. 1990. *The Fifth Discipline: The Art and Practice of the Learning Organization.* New York: Doubleday.

Senge, Peter M. 1994. "The Art and Practice of the Learning Organization." In *The New Paradigm in Business: Emerging Strategies for Leadership and Organizational Change,* edited by Michael L. Ray and Alan Rinzler, 126-38. New York: Jeremy P. Tarcher.

Shafritz, Jay M., Albert C. Hyde, and Sandra J. Parkes, eds. 2004. *Classics of Public Administration.* 5th ed. Belmont, CA: Wadsworth.

Shapiro, Daniel L. 2012. "Negotiation, Principled." In *Encyclopedia of Peace Psychology,* edited by Daniel J. Christie, 703. Malden, MA: Blackwell Publishing.

Shapiro, Matthew A. 2003. "Toward an Evolutionary Democracy: the Philosophy of Mary Parker Follett." *World Futures* 59: 585-90.

Shaviro, Steven. 2009. *Without Criteria: Kant, Whitehead, Deleuze, and Aesthetics.* Cambridge, MA: Massachusetts Institute of Technology Press.

Sherburne, Donald W. 1966. *A Key to Whitehead's Process and Reality.* Chicago: University of Chicago Press.

Sherburne, Donald W. 1967. "Whitehead without God." *The Christian Scholar* L (3).

Simon, Herbert A. (1945) 1997. *Administrative Behavior: A Study of Decision-Making Processes in Administrative Organizations.* Vol. 4th. New York: Free Press.

Smadja, Claude. 2000. Time to Learn from Seattle. *Newsweek*, January 17, 64.

Sogunro, Olesegun Agboola. 2004. "Efficacy of Role-playing Pedagogy in Training Leaders: Some Reflections." *The Journal of Management Development* 23 (3/4): 355-71.

Somasundaran, Ponisseril, Partha Patra, Raymond S. Farinato, and Kyriakos Papadopoulos. 2014. *Oil Spill Remediation: Colloid Chemistry-Based Principles and Solutions.* New York: John Wiley & Sons.

Sørensen, Eva, and Jacob Torfing. 2005a. "The Democratic Anchorage of Governance Networks." *Scandinavian Political Studies* 28 (3): 195-218.

Sørensen, Eva, and Jacob Torfing. 2005b. "Network Governance and Post-Liberal Democracy." *Administrative Theory & Praxis* 27 (2): 197-237.

Sørensen, Eva, and Jacob Torfing. 2009. "Making Network Governance Effective And Democratic through Metagovernance." *Public Administration* 87 (2): 234-58. doi:10.1111/j.1467-9299.2009.01753.x.

Sorokin, Pitirim. (1937) 1957. *Social and Cultural Dynamics: A Study of Change in Major Systems of Art, Truth, Ethics, Law and Social Relationships.* 5 vols. Vol. Revised and Abridged. Boston: Porter Sargent.

Speth, James Gustave. 2008. *The Bridge at the Edge of the World: Capitalism, the Environment, and Crossing from Crisis to Sustainability.* New Haven, CT: Yale University Press.

Stallings, Robert A. 1986. "Doctoral Programs in Public Administration: An Outsider's Perspective." *Public Administration Review* 46: 235-40.

Stallings, Robert A., and James M. Ferris. 1988. "Public Administration Research: Work in PAR, 1940-1984." *Public Administration Review* 48: 580-87.

Steinfeld, Henning, Pierre Gerber, Tom Wassenaar, Vincent Castel, Mauricio Rosales, and Cees De Haan. 2006. Livestock's Long Shadow. Rome: Food and Agriculture Organization of the United Nations.

Stever, James A. 1986. "Mary Parker Follett and the Quest for Pragmatic Administration." *Administration & Society* 18 (2): 159-77.

Stewart, Rosemary. 1996. "Why the Neglect?" *Organization* 3 (1): 175-79.

Stivers, Camilla. 1990. "Toward a Feminist Perspective in Public Administration Theory." *Women in Politics* 10 (4): 481-90.

Stivers, Camilla. 1994. "The Listening Bureaucrat: Responsiveness in Public Administration." *Public Administration Review* 54 (4): 364-69.

Stivers, Camilla. 1996. "Mary Parker Follett and the Question of Gender." *Organization* 3 (1): 161-66.

Stivers, Camilla. 2000. *Bureau Men, Settlement Women: Constructing Public Administration in the Progressive Era*. Lawrence, KS: University Press of Kansas.

Stivers, Camilla. 2002a. *Gender Images in Public Administration: Legitimacy and the Administrative State*. Second ed. Thousand Oaks, CA: Sage.

Stivers, Camilla. 2002b. "Toward Administrative Public Space: Hannah Arendt Meets the Municipal Housekeepers." *Administration & Society* 34: 98-102.

Stivers, Camilla. 2006. "Integrating Mary Parker Follett and Public Administration." *Public Administration Review* 66 (3): 473-76.

Stivers, Camilla. 2008. *Governance in Dark Times: Practical Philosophy for Public Service*. Washington, D.C.: Georgetown University Press.

Stout, Margaret. 2009a. "Enhancing Professional Socialization through the Metaphor of Tradition." *Journal of Public Affairs Education* 15 (3): 289-316.

Stout, Margaret. 2009b. "You Say You Want a Revolution?" *International Journal of Organization Theory and Behavior* 12 (2): 291-309.

Stout, Margaret. 2010a. "Back to the Future: Toward a Political Economy of Love and Abundance." *Administration & Society* 42 (1): 3-37.

Stout, Margaret. 2010b. "Climbing the Ladder of Participation: Establishing Local Policies for Participatory Practice." *Public Administration and Management* 15 (1): 46-97.

Stout, Margaret. 2010c. "Reclaiming the (Lost) Art of Ideal-Typing in Public Administration." *Administrative Theory & Praxis* 32 (4): 491-519.

Stout, Margaret. 2012a. "Competing Ontologies: A Primer for Public Administration." *Public Administration Review* 72 (3): 388-98.

Stout, Margaret. 2012b. "Toward a Relational Language of Process." *Administrative Theory & Praxis* 34 (3): 407-32.

Stout, Margaret. 2013a. "Delivering an MPA Emphasis in Local Governance and Community Development through Service Learning and Action Research." *Journal of Public Affairs Education* 19 (2): 217-38.

Stout, Margaret. 2013b. *Logics of Legitimacy: Three Traditions of Public Administration Praxis.* Boca Raton, FL: CRC Press.

Stout, Margaret. 2014. "The Many Faces of Unity." *Public Administration Quarterly* 38 (2): forthcoming.

Stout, Margaret, Koen P. R. Bartels, and Jeannine M. Love. 2014. Collaborative Governance: Why Dispositions, Styles of Relating, and Modes of Association Matter. In *Trans-Atlantic Dialogue.* Lugano, Switzerland.

Stout, Margaret, and Maja H. Holmes. 2013. "From Theory to Practice: Utilizing Integrative Seminars as Bookends to The Master of Public Administration Program of Study." *Teaching Public Administration* 31: 186-203.

Stout, Margaret, and Jeannine M. Love. 2013a. "Ethical Choice Making." *Public Administration Quarterly* 37 (2): 278-94.

Stout, Margaret, and Jeannine M. Love. 2013b. "Relational Process Ontology: A Grounding for Global Governance." *Administration & Society.* doi:10.1177/0095399713490692.

Stout, Margaret, and Jeannine M. Love. 2014. "The Unfortunate Misinterpretation of Miss Follett." *Public Voices* 13 (2): 11-32.

Stout, Margaret, and Jeannine M. Love. 2015a (forthcoming). Follett, Mary Parker. In *Encyclopedia of Public Administration and Public Policy,* edited by Melvin J. Dubnick and Domonic A. Bearfield. New York: Taylor and Francis Group.

Stout, Margaret, and Jeannine M. Love. 2015b. *Dystopic Utopias: Barriers to Governance in a Global Context.* Morgantown, WV: West Virginia University.

Stout, Margaret, and Joao Salm. 2011. "What Restorative Justice Might

Learn from Administrative Theory." *Contemporary Justice Review* 14 (2): 203-25.

Stout, Margaret, and Carrie Staton. 2011. "The Ontology of Process Philosophy in Follett's administrative Theory." *Administrative Theory & Praxis* 33 (2): 268-92.

Stroup, Jim. 2007. Book Review: Mary Parker Follett—Prophet of Management. In *Managing Leadership: The Strategic Role of the Senior Executive*. San Diego, CA.

Stueber, Karsten. 2008. Empathy. In *The Stanford Encyclopedia of Philosophy*, edited by Edward N. Zalta. Stanford, CA: Stanford University.

Susskind, Lawrence, Sarah McKearnan, and Jennifer Thomas-Larme, eds. 1999. *The Consensus Building Handbook*. Thousand Oaks, CA: Sage.

Swartz, David L. 2003. "From Critical Sociology to Public Intellectual: Pierre Bourdieu and Politics." *Theory and Society* 32 (5-6): 791-823.

Talisse, Robert B. 2003. "Can Democracy Be a Way of Life? Deweyan Democracy and the Problem of Pluralism." *Transactions of the Charles S. Peirce Society* XXXIX (1): 1-21.

Taylor, Frederick Winslow. 1911. *The Principles of Scientific Management*. New York: Harper & Brothers.

Thorne, Kym. 2010. "Narcissistic and Dangerous "Alphas": "Sovereign Individuals" and the Problem of Cultivating the "Civic" in Cyberspace." *International Journal of Critical Accounting* 2 (1): 96-109.

Tilman, David, Kenneth G. Cassman, Pamela A. Matson, Rosamond Naylor, and Stephen Polasky. 2002. "Agricultural Sustainability and Intensive Production Practices." *Nature* 418 (8 August): 671-77.

Tonn, Joan C. 1996. "Follett's Challenge for Us All." *Organization* 3 (1): 167-74.

Tonn, Joan C. 2003. *Mary P. Follett: Creating Democracy, Transforming Management*. New Haven, CT: Yale University Press.

Trist, Eric L., and K. W. Bamforth. 1951. "Some Social and Psychological Consequences of the Longwall Method of Coal Getting." *Human Relations* 4: 3-38.

Urwick, Lyndall, ed. 1949. *Freedom & Co-ordination: Lectures in Business Organisation by Mary Parker Follett*. London: Management Publications Trust, Ltd.

Urwick, Lyndall, ed. 2013. *Freedom & Co-ordination: Lectures in Business Organisation by Mary Parker Follett*. Abingdon: Routledge.

Ventriss, Curtis. 1991. "Reconstructing Government Ethics: A Public Philosophy of Civic Value." In *Ethical frontiers in public management: Seeking new strategies for resolving ethical dilemmas*, edited by James S. Bowman, 114-34. San Francisco: Jossey-Bass.

von Bertalanffy, Ludwig. 1975. *Perspectives on General System Theory: Scientific-Philosophical Studies*. New York: George Braziller Press.

Wachhaus, Aaron. 2014. "Governance beyond Government." *Administration & Society* 46 (5): 573-93.

Waldner, Leora S., and Debra Hunter. 2008. "Client-based Courses: Variations in Service Learning." *Journal of Public Affairs Education* 14 (2): 219-39.

Waldo, Dwight. 1952. "The Development of a Theory of Democratic Administration." *American Political Science Review* 46 (March):81-103.

Waldo, Dwight. (1948) 1984. *The Administrative State: A Study of the Political Theory of American Public Administration*. Second ed. New York: Holmes & Meier Publishers.

Waldo, Dwight. 1988. "The End of Public Administration?" *Public Administration Review* 48 (5): 929-32.

Walton, Richard E., and Robert B. McKersie. 1965. *A Behavioral Theory of Labor Relations: An Analysis of a Social Interaction System*. New York: McGraw Hill.

Wamsley, Gary L. 1996. "A Public Philosophy and Ontological Disclosure as the Basis for Normatively Grounded Theorizing in Public Administration." In *Refounding Democratic Public Administration: Modern Paradoxes and Postmodern Challenges*, edited by Gary L. Wamsley and James F. Wolf, 351-401. Thousand Oaks, CA: Sage.

Wang, Zhihe. 2012. *Process and Pluralism: Chinese Thought on the Harmony of Diversity*. Edited by Nicholas Rescher, Johanna Seibt and Michel Weber. Vol. 23, *Process Thought*. Frankfurt: Ontos Verlag.

Weber, Max. 1946. "Bureaucracy." In *From Max Weber: Essays in Sociology*, edited by Hans H. Gerth and C. Wright Mills, 196-244. New York: Oxford University Press.

Weber, Max. 1949. *The Methodology of the Social Sciences*. New York: The Free Press.

Weinberg, Lisa. 1996. "Seeing through Organization: Exploring the Constitutive Quality of Social Relations." *Administration & Society* 28 (2): 177-204.

Westley, Francis, and Henry Mintzberg. 1989. "Visionary Leadership and Strategic Management." *Strategic Management Journal* 10 (S1): 17-32.

Wettenhall, Roger. 2001. "Public or Private? Public Corporations, Companies and the Decline of the Middle Ground." *Public Organization Review: A Global Journal* 1: 17-40.

Wheatley, Margaret J. 2006. *Leadership and the New Science: Discovering Order in a Chaotic World.* Third ed. San Francisco: Berrett-Kohler Publishers Inc.

Wheelock, Leslie Delapena, and Jamie L. Callahan. 2006. "Mary Parker Follett: A Rediscovered Voice Informing the Field of Human Resource Development." *Human Resource Development Review* 5 (2): 258-73.

Whitaker, Gordon E., and Maureen Berner. 2004. "Learning Through Action: How MPA Public Service Team Projects Help Students Learn Research and Management Skills." *Journal of Public Affairs Education* 10 (4): 279-94.

White, Jay D. 1986. "Dissertations and Publications in Public Administration." *Public Administration Review* 46: 227-34.

White, Orion F. 1990. "Reframing the Authority/Participation Debate." In *Refounding Public Administration*, edited by Gary L. Wamsley, Robert N. Bacher, Charles T. Goodsell, Philip S. Kronenberg, John A. Rohr, Camilla Stivers, Orion F. White and James F. Wolf, 182-245. Newbury Park, CA: Sage Publications.

White, Stephen K. 2000. *Sustaining Affirmation: The Strengths of Weak Ontology in Political Theory.* Princeton, NJ: Princeton University Press.

Whitehead, Alfred North. 1948. *Science and the Modern World.* New York: The New American Library.

Whitehead, Alfred North. (1933) 1967. *Adventures of Ideas.* New York: Free Press.

Whitehead, Alfred North. (1929) 1978. *Process and Reality: An Essay in Cosmology.* Edited by David Ray Griffin and Donald W. Sherburne. Corrected edition. New York: Simon and Shuster.

Whitehead, Alfred North. (1925) 1997. *Science and the Modern World.* New York: Free Press.

Wieman, Henry Nelson. 1946. *The Source of Human Good.* Chicago: University of Chicago Press.

Wildavsky, Aaron. 1979. *Speaking Truth to Power: The Art and Craft of Policy Analysis*. Boston: Little, Brown.

Wilson, Priscilla H., Kathleen Harnish, and Joel Wright. 2003. *The Facilitative Way: Leadership That Makes the Difference*. Shawnee Mission, KS: TeamTech Inc.

Witt, Matthew T. 2007. Mary Parker Follett: Retrospect & Prospect. In *CMS5 2007*. Manchester, England.

Witt, Matthew T. 2010. "Pretending Not to See or Hear, Refusing to Signify: The Farce and Tragedy of Geocentric Public Affairs Scholarship." *American Behavioral Scientist* 53 (6): 921-39.

Wolin, Sheldon. 1981. "The New Public Philosophy." *Democracy: A Journal of Political Renewal and Radical Change* 1 (4): 23-36.

Wright, Bradley E., Lepora J. Manigault, and Tamika R. Black. 2004. "Quantitative Research Measurement in Public Administration: An Assessment of Journal Publications." *Administration & Society* 35 (6): 747-64.

Yoder, Diane, E., and Terry L. Cooper. 2005. "Public-Service Ethics in a Transnational World." In *Ethics in Public Management*, edited by H. George Frederickson and Richard K. Ghere. Armonk, NY: M.E. Sharpe, Inc.

Author Biographies

MARGARET STOUT is an assistant professor of Public Administration at West Virginia University. Her research explores the role of public and nonprofit practitioners in achieving democratic social and economic justice with specific interests in administrative theory, public service leadership and ethics, and sustainable community development. She has a particularly strong interest in the ontological underpinnings of these issues. Her published work can be found in *Logics of Legitimacy: Three Traditions of Public Administration Praxis* (CRC Press), as well as in numerous academic journals. She actively serves in leadership roles in the Public Administration Theory Network and the American Society for Public Administration. She serves on the editorial boards of *Administrative Theory & Praxis, Public Policy and Administration,* and *Teaching Public Administration* and provides peer review for a host of other academic journals. Dr. Stout's first career was in human resource development, with a focus on work/life balance programming. Leading directly out of related experiences in state-wide and regional community and economic development initiatives, her second career was in community and youth development, serving as an executive director, project manager, and consultant to a host of nonprofit and government agencies in Arizona. She enjoys bringing these varied practitioner experiences into her current career as a professor, particularly through service learning, outreach, and applied research.

JEANNINE M. LOVE is an assistant professor of Public Administration at Roosevelt University in Chicago, Illinois. Her research analyzes the rhetorics of individualism and freedom in political theory and practice, paying particular attention to issues of economic justice. She has been working in public administration since 2000, when she began working as a child support caseworker in Columbus, Ohio. The ethical and practical inconsistencies she witnessed as a "street level bureaucrat," particularly the problematic marginalization of the county's poorest residents, continues to motivate her research. She brings this practical perspective to both her teaching and researching in the field of Public Administration. Her work is published in a variety of academic journals.

MIROSLAW PATALON is a full professor and chair of the faculty of Sociology and Social Work at the Pomeranian University in Slupsk, Poland. He also works at the State Higher Vocational School in Elblag. Formerly he was a professor and executive dean of the Social Sciences Faculty at the University of Gdansk. From 1989 to 2003 he was a pastor of Baptist churches in Wroclaw and Gdansk. He is the author of books and articles on the philosophy and sociology of religion and the theory of education. Professor Patalon is a member of the Whitehead Metaphysical Society and the International Process Network and has presented at conferences in Poland, the U.S., China, Japan, India, Israel, and many European countries.

Index

A

actual entity. *See* process philosophy
actual occasion. *See* process philosophy
administration, *practice of* 13, 246, 251, 253, 281; *business* 13, 155, 167, 169.
   See also public administration
administrative theory 1, 5, 14, 16, 154, 197, 199, 211-12, 215, 235, 236, 283.
   See also integrative process
authority 26, 33, 97, 107, 113, 116, 119ff, 125, 129ff, 136, 138, 140, 152, 154,
   156ff, 179, 180ff, 200, 214, 219, 230, 251, 266, 269, 275, 289, 292; *emer-*
   gent 158, 164, 165, 169, 172ff, 182. *See also* leadership
autonomy 114, 143, 164, 170, 192

B

Barber, Benjamin 115, 242
biology 15, 30, 203, 219
Bohm, David 255, 262-63, 277-78
Braidotti, Rosi 290

C

Cabot, Richard 7, 12, 15, 36n1, 54, 92, 94, 186, 188, 238
capitalism 147-49, 150, 216, 257-62, 268
Catlaw, Thomas 283
circular behavior 50, 51, 54, 55, 162, 190, 233
circular response 15, 29ff, 34ff, 38ff, 45, 47ff, 50ff, 60, 63n1, 67, 69-70, 72, 74,
   89, 99, 102, 133, 139, 162, 189-90, 193-95, 198, 213, 220, 231, 232, 245,
   250-251
climate change. *See* environmental crisis
co-creation 23, 29-32, 35, 39, 44, 45, 51, 55, 58, 60, 61, 62, 66, 75, 77, 80, 82,
   84, 86n13, 88, 90, 92, 98, 99, 101, 104, 143, 149, 159, 171, 189, 194-95,
   197-99, 202, 203, 205, 206, 214, 220, 228, 232, 235, 239, 241, 272, 276,

E

environmental crisis 2, 254, 255-58, 265, 268, 273; *ecosystems* 256, 257, 271;
　　　sustainability 2, 258, 268
epistemology, dynamic relational 73-83, 170, 228. *See also* pragmatism
ethics 2, 10, 11, 13, 55, 88, 94-110, 128, 134, 152, 175, 224, 230, 233ff, 254,
　　　264, 290; *integrative* 94, 95, 97ff, 103-105, 109
evidence-based practice 251
evil 44, 90, 101, 126, 287
experts, role of 66ff, 71-73, 74, 75, 80ff, 86, 122, 123, 127, 158, 162, 170, 172,
　　　174, 179, 180, 182, 214, 224, 236, 251, 285, 268, 287

F

Fayol, Henri 157
federalism 15, 36, 138-39, 140, 141, 158, 163, 229, 236, 237, 239, 242, 276;
　　　inclusive 114, 138-39, 140, 142, 143, 232, 235, 237, 239, 249, 276,
feminism 1, 2, 225, 246, 250
freedom 116, 125, 129, 130, 131, 135, 143, 144n8, 164, 197, 212, 235, 259,
　　　263, 264, 291, 292
Freud, Sigmund 14, 40, 45, 47, 68, 102
functional unity 33, 55, 130, 153, 157ff, 166, 167, 172, 190, 216, 233, 236 251;
　　　functional unifying 157, 158, 166-68, 170, 171, 173ff, 179, 236

G

gerundial language 26, 34, 47
Gestalt 14, 25, 40, 45, 47-51, 54, 56, 61, 63, 139, 232
global financial crisis 258, 260
globalization 2, 18, 114, 219, 223, 241, 249, 254-265, 267, 271, 273, 274, 291
God 18, 88-90, 107, 119, 189, 192, 194-98, 208; *divinity* 90, 91, 92
governance 1, 3, 16ff, 18-19, 35, 114, 115, 123, 126, 129, 137, 142, 143, 154,
　　　179, 180, 186, 187, 206, 208, 219, 223, 224, 225, 226, 228, 229, 230,
　　　231, 235ff, 241-43, 245, 251, 253, 254-72, 273, 274, 275-92; *collabora-
　　　tive* 181, 182, 226, 230, 242, 269, 270, 272; *global* 224, 269, 276; *group*
　　　18, 114, 143, 231, 235, 236; *participatory* 272, 276. *See also* self-gover-
　　　nance; groups
Green, T. H. 86, 135, 144
groups 9, 10, 39, 40ff, 47-63, 75, 89, 94, 96, 99, 105ff, 119, 132, 133, 135ff,
　　　140, 141-42, 157, 159, 163, 164, 171, 174, 175, 199, 200, 203, 206,
　　　218ff, 230, 231, 233, 234, 237, 239, 247, 248, 263, 270, 271, 279, 284,
　　　288; *group process* 7, 9, 47,113, 132, 134, 148, 158, 171, 180, 190, 199,
　　　218, 219, 220, 221, 233, 237, 279. *See also* governance
Gulick, Luther 157

conflict; integration; integrative method; interweaving; synthesis
true individual 40ff, 45, 55, 56-58, 60ff, 90, 135, 136, 148, 150, 218, 232
typology 16, 17, 18, 154, 269

U

unifying state 27, 34, 92, 135, 139, 140, 152
Urwick, Lyndal 8, 12, 157, 212, 216

W

Weber, Max 13, 16, 156, 158
Whitehead, Alfred North *i-ii,* 7, 14, 15, 18, 145, 184, 186-209, 228
whole a-making 26, 29, 35, 39, 50, 54, 56, 57, 61, 62, 63, 75, 89, 90, 135, 167,
    195, 214, 219, 232, 246, 249. *See also* synthesis, total situation; harmo-
    nization; integration

Z

zero-sum game 96, 118, 238, 249, 250

www.ingramcontent.com/pod-product-compliance
Lightning Source LLC
Chambersburg PA
CBHW031116020426
42333CB00012B/106